Photographer's Guide to the Sony DSC-RX10

Photographer's Guide to the Sony DSC-RX10

Getting the Most from Sony's Advanced Digital Camera

Alexander S. White

White Knight Press
Henrico, Virginia

Published by
White Knight Press
9704 Old Club Trace
Henrico, Virginia 23238
www.whiteknightpress.com
contact@whiteknightpress.com

ISBN: 978-1-937986-22-3 (paperback)
978-1-937986-23-0 (e-book)

Printed in the United States of America

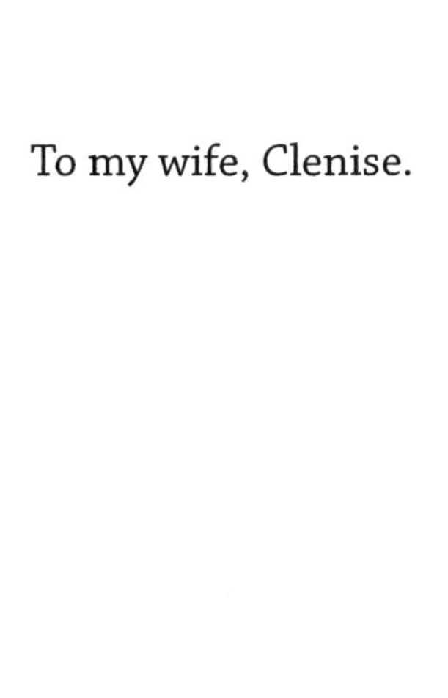

To my wife, Clenise.

Contents

CHAPTER 3:

CHAPTER 4:

Chapter 5:

Chapter 6:
Playback and Printing 251

Chapter 7:
The Custom and Setup Menus 273

CHAPTER 8:

Appendix B:

Appendix C:

Introduction

Over the past few years, Sony has produced a succession of camera models that have distinguished themselves from the competition. The Cyber-shot DSC-RX100 and its enhanced, Wi-Fi-enabled sibling, the DSC-RX100 II, have won wide acclaim for packing a tremendous range of features that produce superb image quality into an amazingly compact body. At the higher end of the price range, Sony offers the Cyber-shot DSC-RX1 and RX1R, which provide full-frame sensors in very compact sizes. More recently, Sony released the Alpha A7 and A7R, full-frame mirrorless models that take interchangeable lenses, again, with compact bodies.

There have been other noteworthy Sony models in the past year or so; I will not take the time and space to mention others here. My point is that I have found it impossible to ignore the wealth of cameras that Sony has been producing. I previously published guide books for the DSC-RX100 and RX100 II, and, when Sony released the Cyber-shot DSC-RX10, I could not resist writing a new guide book for this camera. The RX10 incorporates many of the great attributes of the RX100 and RX100 II, but adds new features, notably a more powerful telephoto lens with a constant aperture of f/2.8, enhanced video capabilities, and a great variety of customizable controls.

The RX10 is well equipped with advanced shooting features. You can set the camera to its Intelligent Auto shooting mode and get good results most of the time with no further settings. However, the camera also offers manual control of focus and exposure, continuous shooting, exposure bracketing, Raw format, excellent low-light performance, superior build quality, and many special features, including a variety of Creative Style and Picture Effect settings. The RX10, like many of its contemporaries, includes a built-in HDR (high dynamic range) shooting option. The RX10 also provides HD (high-definition) video shooting with the ability to control aperture and shutter speed while recording movies.

The camera includes a hot shoe that can accept an external flash, stereo microphone, external LCD display, or other items. The RX10 includes Wi-Fi (wireless) connectivity with the ability to connect to compatible smartphones and tablets using the very convenient near field communication (NFC) system, which lets you just touch two devices together to connect them wirelessly.

The RX10 is not the ideal tool for all situations, of course. For example, if you want to photograph wildlife or other subjects from a distance, you do not have much telephoto power with the moderate optical zoom range of this camera: 24mm to 200mm. The ability to control the camera remotely by Wi-Fi is limited, and the sensor, although larger than average, is not so large as to provide the blurred backgrounds that a full-frame sensor can. Overall, though, the camera is a remarkably versatile device for a photographer who wants to be well equipped for many still and video opportunities without packing a large array of equipment and lenses.

My goal is to provide a thorough guide to the camera's features, explaining how they work and when you might want to use them. The book is aimed largely at beginning and intermediate photographers who are not satisfied with the documentation that comes with the camera and who prefer a more complete explanation of the camera's controls and menus. For those seeking more advanced information, I discuss some topics that go beyond the basics, and I include in the appendices information about additional resources. I will provide updates at my website, whiteknightpress.com, as warranted.

One note on the scope of this guide: I live in the United States, and I bought my camera here. I am not very familiar with the variations for cameras sold in Europe or elsewhere, such as different chargers. The photographic functions are generally not different, so this guide should be useful to photographers in all locations. I should note that the frame rates for HD video are different in different areas: the version of the RX10 sold in the U.S. uses the 60 frames per second (fps) setting for NTSC video, whereas cameras sold in Europe use 50 fps for PAL video, although they can be set to use the NTSC system through a menu option. The video functions and operations are not different, just the frame rates. I have stated measurements of distance and weight in both the Imperial and metric systems, for the benefit of readers in various countries around the world.

Finally, I would like to acknowledge the excellent assistance provided by Jonathan Hurwitt and John Dancocks, who reviewed a draft and made many valuable suggestions. Most of all, though, as always, I relied most heavily on the wonderful support of every kind provided by my wife, Clenise.

Chapter 1: Preliminary Setup

Setting Up the Camera

When you purchase your Sony RX10, the box should contain the camera itself, battery, charger, shoulder strap, lens cap, lens hood, micro USB cable, and brief instruction pamphlet. Sony also lists as included items the protective cap that is inserted into the accessory shoe and the eyepiece cup that is attached to the viewfinder. There may also be a warranty card and some advertising flyers. There is no CD with software or a user's guide; the software programs supplied by Sony are accessible through the Internet.

To install PlayMemories Home, the software for viewing and working with images and videos on Windows-based computers, go to the following Internet address: http://www.sony.net/pm. If you have a Macintosh computer, you can download a more limited version of the PlayMemories Home software, which does not include some features such as uploading to social network sites. That version is available at http://www.sony.co.jp/imsoft/Mac/.

You also can install Sony's Image Data Converter software, which converts the camera's Raw images so you can edit them on a computer. That software is available for download for both Windows-based computers and Macs at the locations listed above.

You might want to attach the shoulder strap as soon as possible, so you can support the camera with the strap over your shoulder or around your neck.

Charging and Inserting the Battery

The Sony battery for the DSC-RX10 is the NP-FW50. With this camera, the standard procedure is to charge the battery while it's inside the camera. To do this, you use the supplied USB cable, which plugs into the camera and into the supplied Sony charger or a USB port on your computer. There are pluses and minuses to charging the battery while it is inside the camera. On the positive side, you don't need an external charger, and the camera can charge automatically when it's connected to your computer. You also can find many portable charging devices with USB ports; many newer automobiles have USB slots where you can plug in your RX10 to keep up its charge.

One drawback is that you cannot use the camera while the battery is being charged inside the camera. Also, the Sony charger cannot charge another battery outside of the camera. One solution to this situation is to purchase at least one extra battery and a device to charge your batteries externally. I'll discuss batteries, chargers, and other accessories in Appendix A.

For now, charge the battery by inserting it into the camera and connecting the charger. You first need to open the battery compartment door on the bottom of the camera and put in the battery. You can only insert it fully into the camera one way; the way I prefer to do this is to look for the rectangular set of connectors on the battery, and insert the battery so those connectors are positioned close to the front of the camera as the battery goes into the compartment, as shown in Figure 1-1 and Figure 1-2.

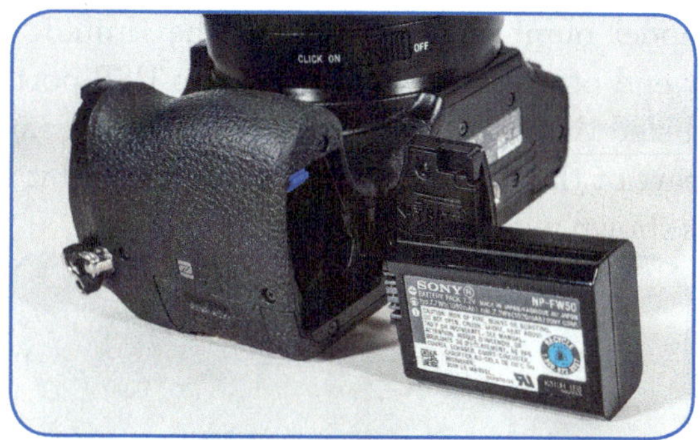

Figure 1-1. Battery Ready to Go into Camera

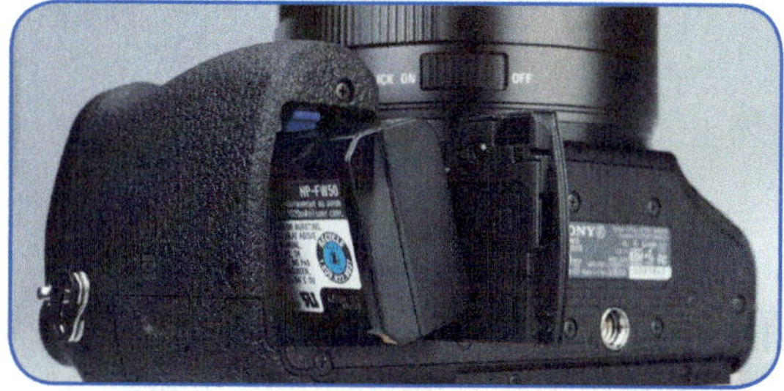

Figure 1-2. Battery Going into Camera

You may have to nudge aside the blue latch that holds the battery in place, which is seen in FIGURE 1-3.

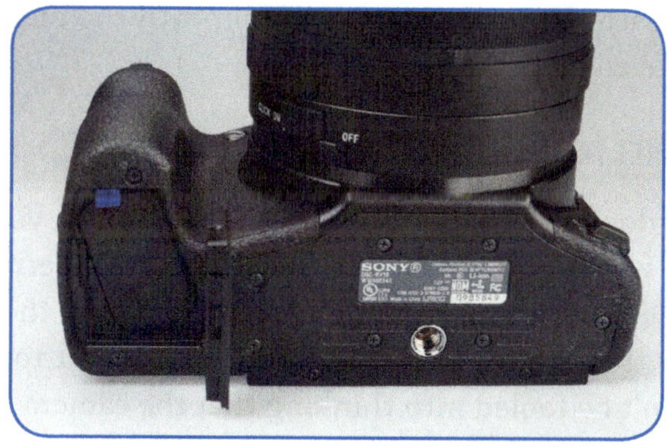

Figure 1-3. Battery Secured by Latch

With the battery inserted and secured by the latch, close the battery compartment door and slide the ridged latch on the door to the closed position. Then plug the larger, rectangular end of the USB cable into the corresponding slot on the provided AC charger, which is model number AC-UB10D in the United States. Plug the smaller end of the cable into the micro USB port. This port, which is labeled the Multi port, is located under a small door on the lower part of the camera's left side as you hold it in shooting position, as shown in FIGURE 1-4.

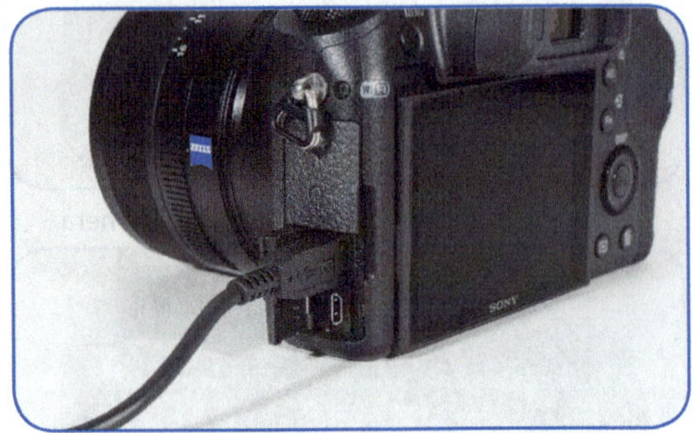

Figure 1-4. Charging Cable Plugged into Camera

Plug the charger's prongs into a standard electrical outlet. A small orange lamp to the right of the camera's Multi port will light up steadily while the battery is charging; when it goes out, the battery is fully charged. The full charging cycle should take about 310 minutes. (If the charging lamp flashes, that indicates a problem with the charger or a problem with the temperature of the camera's environment.)

Choosing and Inserting a Memory Card

The RX10 does not ship with a memory card. If you turn the camera on with no card inserted, you will see the error message "NO CARD" flashing in the upper-left corner of the screen. If you ignore this message and press the shutter button to take a picture, don't be fooled into thinking that the camera is storing it in internal memory, because that is not the case.

Actually, the camera will temporarily store the image and play it back if you press the Playback button, but the image will not be permanently stored. (I did manage to save a NO CARD image by using a video capture device to capture the image from the camera's HDMI port to my computer while it was still on the screen, but that is not a process you would want to do often.) Some other camera models have a small amount of built-in memory so you can take and store a few pictures even without a card, but the RX10 does not have any such safety net.

To avoid the frustration of having a great camera that can't save any images, you need to purchase and insert a memory card. The RX10 uses two basic types of memory storage. First, it can use all varieties of SD cards, which are quite small—about the size of a large postage stamp. These cards come in several varieties; some examples are shown in FIGURE 1-5.

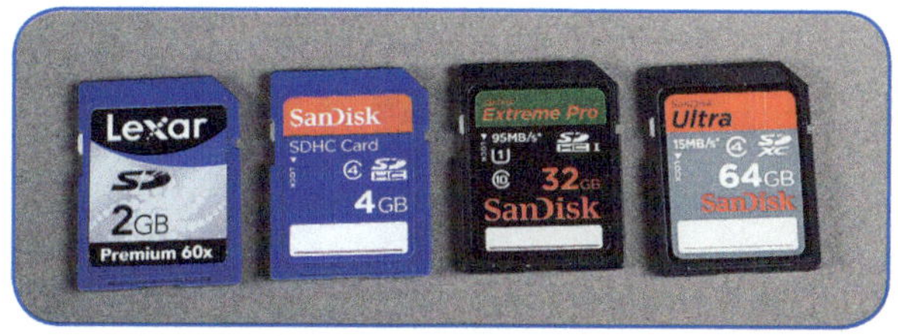

Figure 1-5. Card Types: SD 2GB, SDHC 4GB, SDHC 32GB, SDXC 64 GB

The standard card, called simply SD, comes in capacities from 8 MB (megabytes) to 2 GB (gigabytes). A higher-capacity card, SDHC, comes in sizes from 4 GB to 32 GB. The newest, and highest-capacity card, SDXC (for extended capacity) comes in sizes of 48 GB, 64 GB, 128 GB, and 256 GB; this version of the card can have a capacity up to 2 terabytes (TB), theoretically, and SDXC cards generally have faster transfer speeds than the smaller-capacity cards. There also is a special variety of SD card called an Eye-Fi card, which I will discuss a bit later in this chapter.

The RX10 also can use micro-SD cards, which are smaller cards, often used in smartphones and other small devices. These cards operate in the same way as SD cards, but you have to use an adapter that is the size of an SD card to insert this tiny card in the RX10 camera, as shown in FIGURE 1-6.

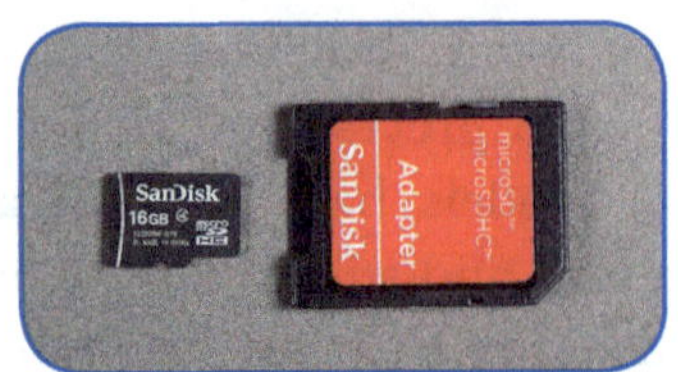

Figure 1-6. Micro-SD Card and Adapter

In addition to using the various types of SD cards, the RX10, being a Sony camera, also can use Sony's proprietary storage devices, known as Memory Stick cards. These cards are similar in size and capacity to SD cards, but with a slightly different shape, as shown in FIGURE 1-7.

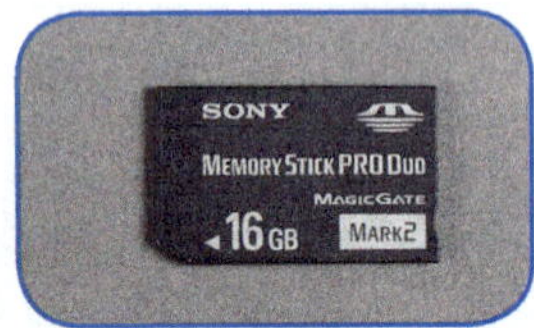

Figure 1-7. Memory Stick PRO Duo Memory Card

Memory Stick cards come in various types. The ones that can be used in the RX10 are the Memory Stick PRO Duo, Memory Stick PRO-HG Duo, Memory Stick XC-HG Duo, and Memory Stick Micro (M2). The Memory Stick Micro, like the micro-SD card, requires an adapter for use in the camera.

In my experience, the type of card you use does not matter. Any of the various types of SD or Memory Stick cards should work well. The factors that really matter are capacity and speed. The capacity to choose depends on your needs. If you're planning to record a good deal of HD video or a large number of Raw-format photos, you should get a large-capacity card, but don't get carried away—the largest cards have such huge capacities that you may be wasting money purchasing them.

There are several variables to take into account in computing how many images or videos you can store on a particular size of card, such as which aspect ratio you're using (16:9, 3:2, 4:3, or 1:1), picture size, and quality. Here are a few examples of what can be stored on an 8 GB SD card or Memory Stick card. If you're using the standard 3:2 aspect ratio, you can store about 355 Raw images (the highest quality), 520 of the highest-quality JPEG images (Large size and Extra Fine quality), or about 1,200 of the lower-quality Standard images (Large size).

You can fit about 35 minutes of the highest-quality HD video on an 8 GB card. That same card will hold about five hours of video at the lowest quality, 640 x 480 pixels, also known as VGA quality. The RX10 is limited to recording about 29 minutes of video in any format in any one sequence. The high-quality MP4 format can be recorded only for 15 minutes in one sequence, because of the 2 GB file size limit.

One other consideration is the speed of the card. A high rate of speed is important to get good results for recording images and video with this camera. You should try to find a card that writes data at a rate of 6 MB/second or faster to record HD video. If you go by the Class designation, a Class 4 card should be sufficient for shooting stills, and a Class 6 card should suffice for recording video, but I recommend using Class 10 cards. Newer cards, such as the Lexar Professional and SanDisk Extreme Pro, shown in FIGURE 1-8, come with the UHS designation, for ultra high speed; these cards have roughly the same speed as a Class 10 card.

If you choose one of these cards, you should have no problems with any level of video recording. A fast card also will help when you set the camera for continuous shooting of still images.

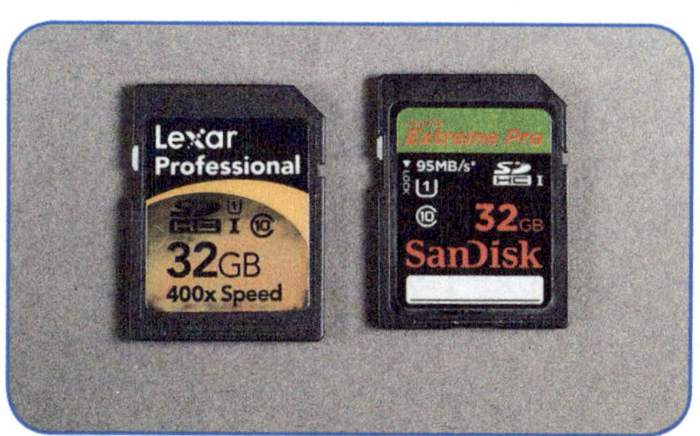

Figure 1-8. High-Speed SDHC Cards

If you have an old computer with a built-in card reader, or just an old external card reader, there is some chance it will not read the newer SDHC cards. In that case, you would have to either get a new reader that will accept SDHC cards or download images from the camera to your computer using the USB cable. Using the newest variety of card, SDXC, also can be problematic with older computers.

If your computer has a recent version of its operating system, it will be able to read SDXC cards if you use a compatible card reader.

As I write this, 64 GB SDXC cards cost about $30 and up, and prices are dropping. If you don't mind the risk of losing a great many images or videos if you lose the card, you might want to choose an SDXC card with a capacity of 64 GB, or even 128 GB. At this writing, 256 GB SDXC cards are selling for about $450. Those cards are extremely fast, but I question whether it is a good idea to risk $450 on your ability to keep track of a tiny item that can slip into a pocket and end up in the laundry without too much trouble.

You also may want to consider getting an Eye-Fi card. This special type of device looks much like an ordinary SDHC card, but it includes a tiny transmitter that lets it connect to a Wi-Fi network and send images to your computer as soon as the images have been recorded by the camera. You also may be able to use Direct Mode, which lets the Eye-Fi card send images directly to a computer, smartphone, tablet, or other device without needing a network, though Direct Mode can be tricky to set up.

I have tested both the 16 GB and 8 GB versions of the Pro X2 Eye-Fi card with the RX10, and they work well. Uploaded images are sent to the Pictures/Eye-Fi folder on my computer. The Pro X2 models, shown in Figure 1-9, can handle Raw files and video files as well as the smaller JPEG files.

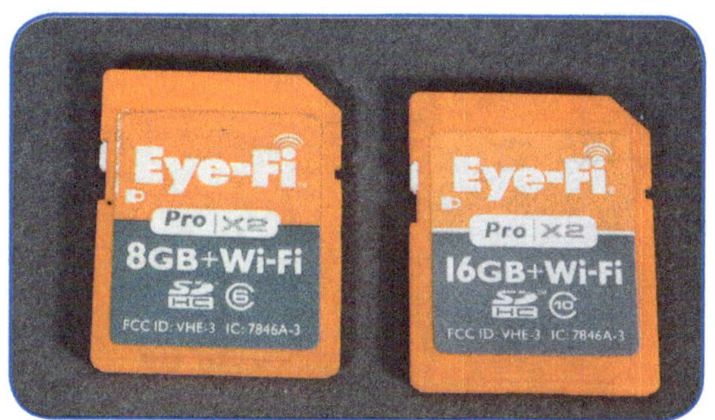

Figure 1-9. Eye-Fi Pro X2 SDHC Memory Cards

Another type of Eye-Fi card, the Mobi, is designed for transfer of images and videos (up to 2 GB per file) directly from the camera to a smartphone or tablet. There are similar cards available from other companies, such as the Toshiba FlashAir, the ez Share, and the Transcend Wi-Fi card.

Of course, the RX10 camera has built-in Wi-Fi capability, as discussed in Chapter 9, so you don't need to use an Eye-Fi card or the equivalent to transfer images. If you already have one or more wireless SD cards and are accustomed to that system, you should be able to use the cards in your RX10, but you now have other options for wireless transfer that may make more sense.

If you decide to use a Memory Stick card, be sure you have a card reader that can accept those cards, which, as noted above, are not the same shape as SD cards and require readers with compatible slots.

Once you have chosen a card, open the small door on the right side of the camera that covers the memory card compartment, and slide the card into the slot until it catches. You insert an SD card with its label pointing toward the back of the camera, as shown in Figure 1-10; insert a Memory Stick card with its label pointing toward the front of the camera.

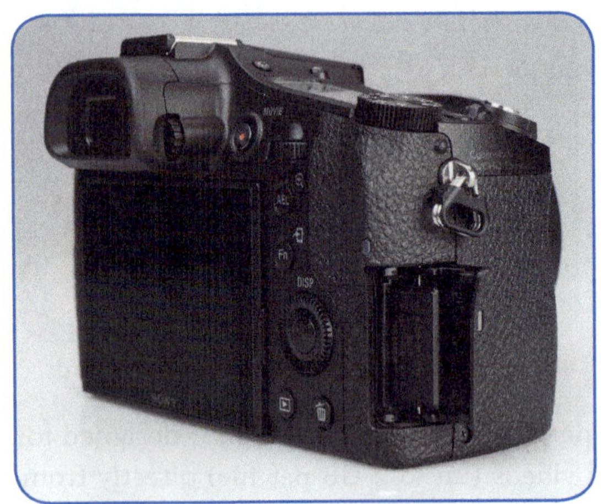

Figure 1-10. SD Card Going into Camera

Push the card down firmly until it catches and stays in place. To remove either type of card, push down on its edge until it releases and springs up, so you can grab it.

Once the card has been pushed down until it catches, close the compartment door and make sure it is firmly latched.

Although the card may work well when newly inserted in the camera, it's a good idea to format a card when first using it in the camera, so it will have the correct file structure and will have any bad areas blocked off from use. To do this, turn on the camera by pressing the power switch to the right, then press the Menu button at the upper left of the camera's back. Next, press the Right button (right edge of the Control wheel on the camera's back) multiple times until the small orange line near the top of the screen is positioned under the number 5, and the toolbox icon at the far right of the screen is highlighted, as shown in FIGURE 1-11.

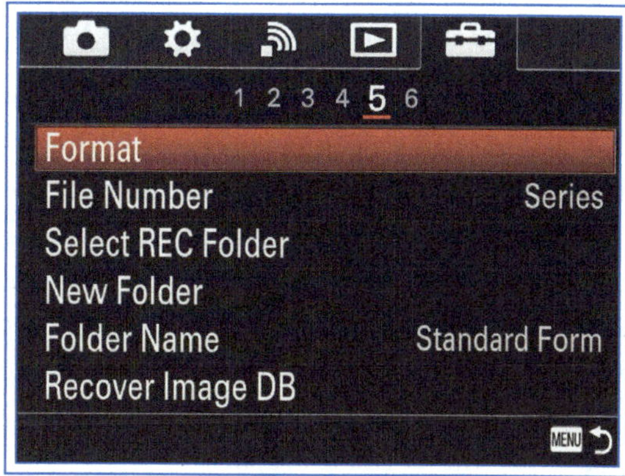

Figure 1-11. Format Menu Option

(I will refer to the other three edges of the Control wheel as the Left, Up, and Down buttons, and to the button in the middle of the wheel as the Center button.)

The toolbox icon indicates the Setup menu. The orange highlight bar should already be positioned on the top line of the menu, on the Format command; if not, press the Up or Down button, or turn the Control wheel, until the Format command is highlighted.

Press the Center button when the Format line is highlighted. On the next screen, seen in Figure 1-12, highlight Enter and press the Center button again to carry out the command.

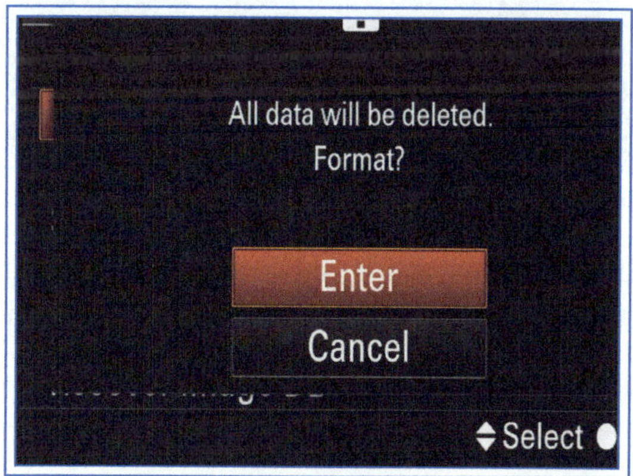

Figure 1-12. Format Confirmation Screen

Setting the Date, Time, and Language

You need to make sure the date and time are set correctly before you start taking pictures, because the camera records that information (sometimes known as "metadata," meaning data beyond the information in the picture itself) invisibly with each image and displays it later if you want. It is, of course, important to have the date (and the time of day) correctly recorded with your archives of digital images. The camera may prompt you to set these items the first time you turn it on. If not, or if you need to change the settings, follow these steps:

1. Turn the camera on, then press the Menu button. Press the Right button enough times to move the orange line underneath the number 4 while the Setup menu's toolbox icon is highlighted, as shown in Figure 1-13.

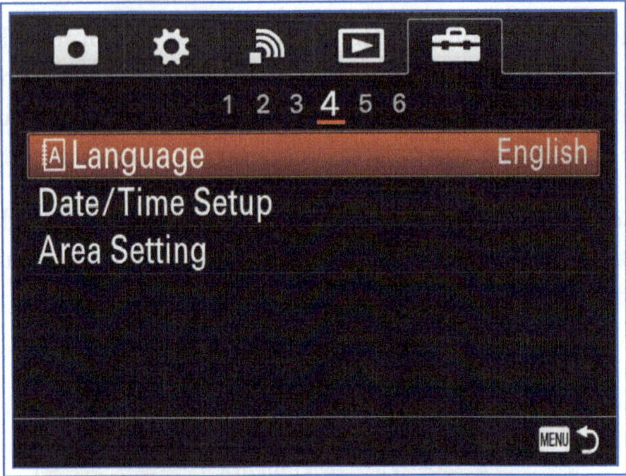

Figure 1-13. Screen 4 of Setup Menu

2. Press the Down button to move the orange highlight bar to the Date/Time Setup line on the menu screen, and press the Center button to move to the next screen, shown in Figure 1-14.

Figure 1-14. Date/Time Setup Screen

3. Highlight the Date/Time option, press the Center button, and then, by pressing the Left and Right buttons or by turning the Control wheel, move left and right through the month, day, year, and time settings, as shown in FIGURE 1-15.

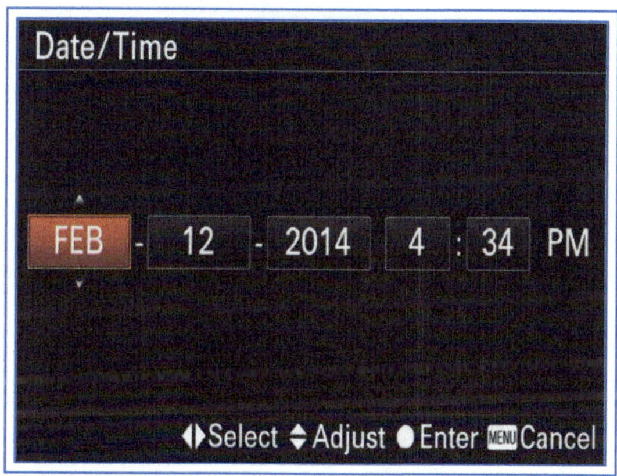

Figure 1-15. Date/Time Settings Screen

4. Change them by pressing the Up and Down buttons. When everything is set correctly, press the Center button to confirm. Then use a similar method to adjust the Daylight Savings (On or Off) and Date Format options, if necessary.

If you need to change the language that the camera uses for menus and other messages, press the Menu button and navigate to the Language item, which is one line above the Date/Time Setup item, as shown in Figure 1-13. Press the Center button to select it. You then can select from the available languages on the menu, as shown in Figure 1-16.

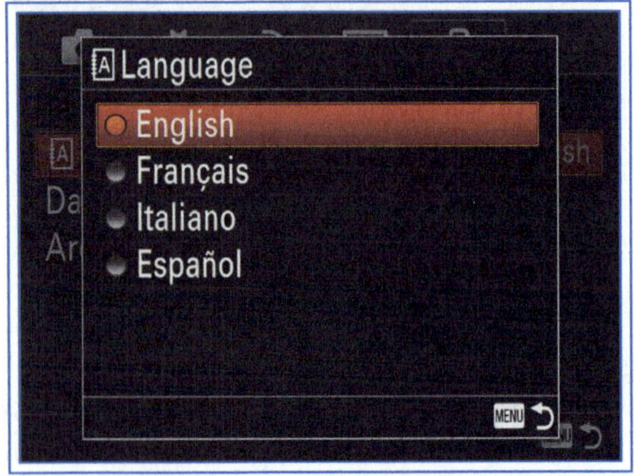

Figure 1-16. Language Selection Screen

Chapter 2: Basic Operations

Overview of Shooting Still Images

Now that the Sony RX10 has the correct time and date set and a charged battery inserted along with a memory card, I'll discuss the steps to get your camera into action and to capture a usable image to your memory card.

Introduction to Main Controls

Before I discuss settings, I will introduce the camera's main controls to give a better idea of which button or dial is which. I won't discuss the controls in detail here; there is more information in Chapter 5. For now, I will include images showing the physical buttons, switches, and dials of the RX10. You may want to refer back to these images for a reminder about each control as you go through this book.

Top of Camera

On top of the camera are some of the most important controls and dials, as shown in Figures 2-1 and 2-2.

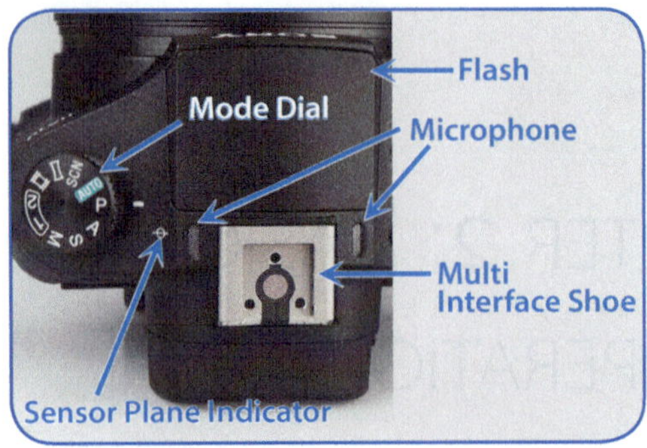

Figure 2-1. Top of Camera - Left Side

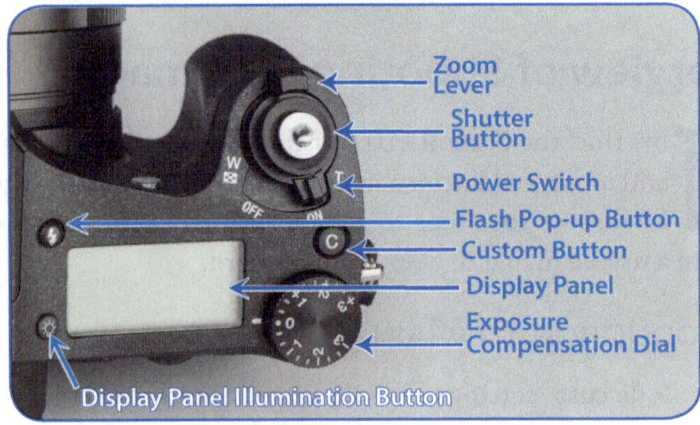

Figure 2-2. Top of Camera - Right Side

You use the mode dial to select a shooting mode for stills or video. For basic shooting without making many other settings, turn the dial so the green AUTO label is next to the white marker; this will set the camera to one of its most automatic modes. The round, silver-colored shutter button is used to take pictures. Press it halfway to evaluate focus and exposure; press it all the way to take a picture. The zoom lever, surrounding the shutter button, can be used to zoom the lens in and out between its telephoto and wide-angle settings. The lever also is used to change the views of images in playback mode. The power switch turns the camera on and off.

The flash is normally stored inside the top of the camera; it pops up when you press the flash pop-up button. The exposure compensation dial is used to increase or decrease the brightness of images; just turn the dial to a positive or negative value. The C button, or Custom button, can be programmed to perform any one of several camera operations, such as adjusting ISO or Drive Mode. The Multi Interface shoe is used for attaching a flash, microphone, or other accessory that can communicate with the camera. The openings for the built-in microphone also are on top of the camera.

The display panel on the right side of the camera's top shows information about current settings. You can press the panel illumination button, to the left of the panel, to light up the display. Finally, the sensor plane mark indicates the position of the image sensor, for use when you need to measure the precise distance from the sensor to your subject.

Back of Camera

FIGURE 2-3 shows the main controls on the camera's back.

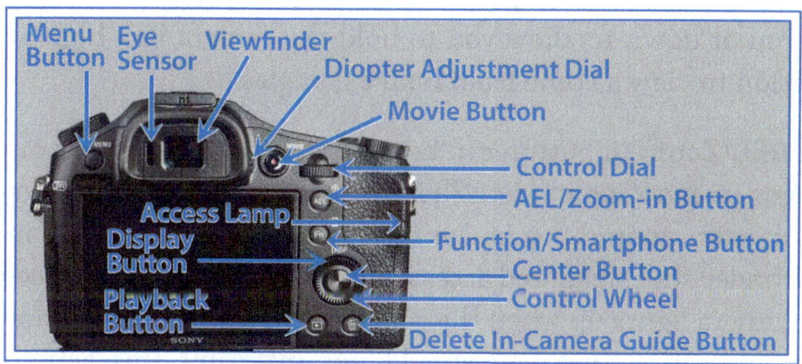

Figure 2-3. Controls on Back of Camera

The diopter adjustment dial is used to adjust the viewfinder for your vision. The red Movie button starts and stops the recording of a video sequence. The Menu button calls up the camera's system of menu screens with various settings for shooting and other values, such as control button functions, audio features, and others. In shooting mode, the Function (Fn) button calls up a menu of camera functions for easy access. In playback mode, pressing this button can send an image to a smartphone or tablet. The Playback button places the camera into playback mode, so you can view your recorded images. The Delete/In-Camera Guide (Help) button, marked by a trash can icon, acts as the Delete or Trash button in playback mode, for erasing images. In shooting mode, pressing this button calls up information that explains menu options.

The Control wheel is a rotary dial for navigating through menu screens and other screens with camera settings. In addition, each of the wheel's four edges acts as a direction button when you press it in, for navigating through menu screens and moving items such as the focus frame. The button in the center of the wheel (Center button) is used to confirm selections and for some miscellaneous operations. The top edge of the wheel (Up button) also serves as the Display button. You can press this button to choose the various display screens in either shooting or playback mode. The LCD screen—which displays the scene viewed by the camera along with the camera's settings and plays back your recorded images—tilts up or down to allow you to hold the camera in a high or low position to view a scene from unusual angles.

The AEL/Zoom-in button can be used to lock the exposure of your images in shooting mode. When the camera is in playback mode, this button zooms the image displayed on the screen or in the viewfinder. The small, red access lamp at the extreme right edge of the camera lights up when the camera is writing data to a memory card, indicating that you should not interrupt this activity by trying to use the camera or turn it off.

Front of Camera

There are several items to point out on the camera's front, including the lens and its components, as shown in Figures 2-4 and 2-5.

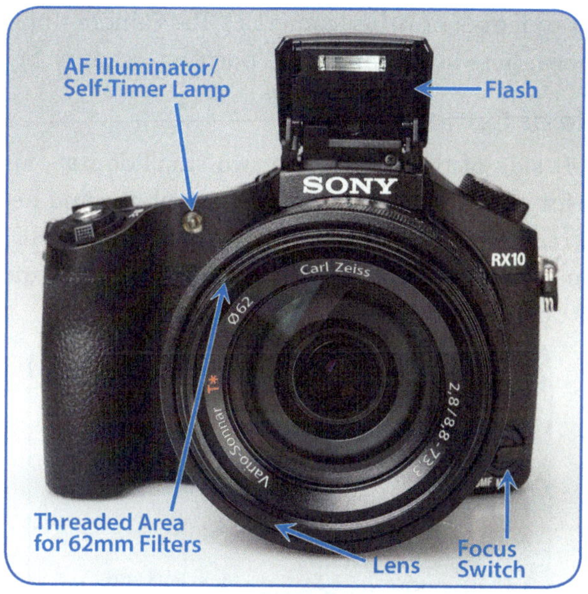

Figure 2-4. Items on Front of Camera

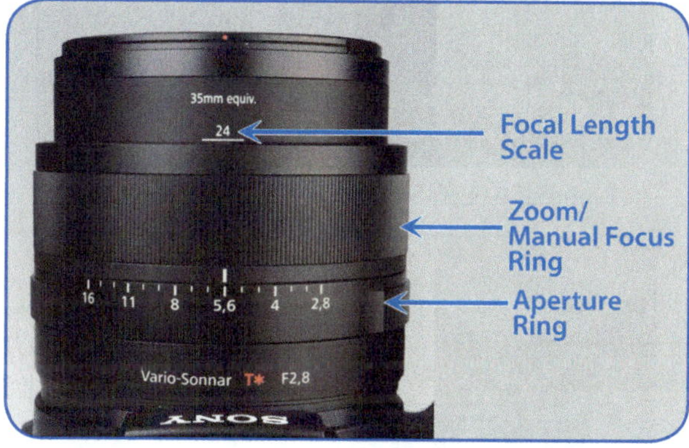

Figure 2-5. Lens Assembly

The AF Illuminator/Self-timer Lamp lights up to signal the operation of the self-timer and to provide illumination so the camera can use its autofocus system in dark areas. The lens itself has a 35mm equivalent focal length range of 24mm to 200mm and an aperture range of f/2.8 to f/16.0. (The actual focal length of the lens is 8.8mm to 73.3mm; the "35mm equivalent range" is commonly used to state the focal length in a way that can easily be compared to lenses of other cameras.) The camera's built-in flash unit is shown here in its popped-up position, ready to be fired.

Left Side of Camera

On the left side of the camera are two small doors, one covering the jacks for connecting an external microphone and headphones for video recording, and one covering the Multi and HDMI ports, as seen in FIGURE 2-6 with the doors closed and Figure 2-7 with the doors open, showing the ports.

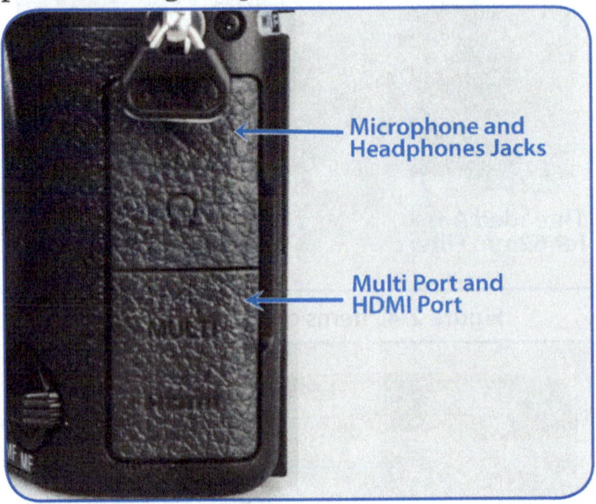

Figure 2-6. Left Side of Camera - Doors Closed

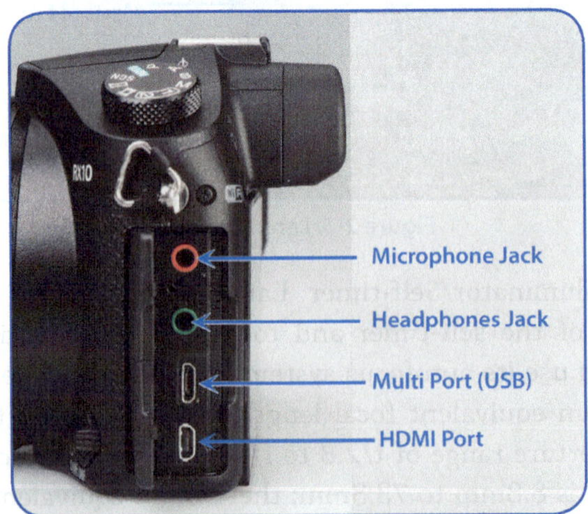

Figure 2-7. Left Side of Camera - Doors Opened

The microphone port accepts a standard 3.5mm stereo microphone that will record sound for your video recordings. The headphones port is where you can plug in headphones for monitoring the sound recording.

Under the lower door, the top port, called the Multi port, is where you connect the USB cable that is supplied with the camera to charge the battery, to connect the RX10 to a computer to upload images, or to connect to a printer to print images directly from the camera. The bottom port, the HDMI port, is for connecting the camera to an HDTV to view your images and videos.

Right Side of Camera

The right side of the camera, shown in Figure 2-8, houses the memory card slot, which is concealed under a small door with a notch in it. Grab the door by the notch and pull it open to expose the card slot.

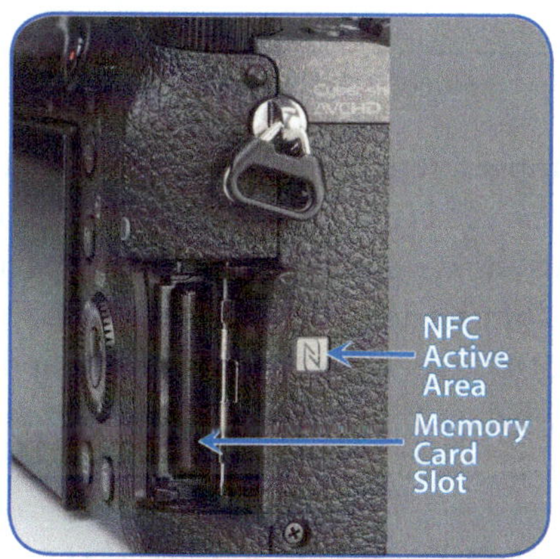

Figure 2-8. Right Side of Camera

The other item of note on this side of the camera is the NFC active area, designated by a fancy letter N. You can touch another device that uses near field communication, such as an Android smartphone or tablet, to that spot to activate a wireless connection, as discussed in Chapter 9.

Bottom of Camera

Finally, as shown in FIGURE 2-9, on the bottom of the camera are the tripod socket and the battery compartment.

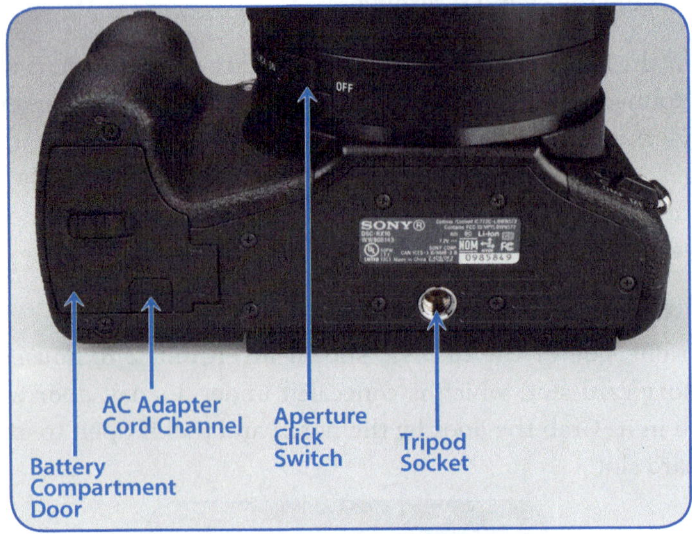

Figure 2-9. Bottom of Camera

The battery compartment door has a small flap that opens to make room for the cord to the AC adapter, if you use that optional accessory. In this view, you also can see the aperture click switch on the bottom of the lens. That switch lets you turn off the clicking sound of the aperture ring, so the sound is not recorded on videos. The label on the camera's bottom lets you know if your camera uses the 60i (NTSC) or 50i (PAL) video standard.

Fully Automatic: Intelligent Auto Mode

Now I'll discuss how to use these controls to start taking pictures and videos. Here's a set of steps if you want to let the camera make most decisions for you. This is a good approach for a quick shot without fiddling with too many settings.

1. Remove the lens cap and turn the camera with the lens facing toward you. Find the focus switch at the lower right and turn

the switch so the small black line points to the S indicator, for single autofocus, as shown in FIGURE 2-10.

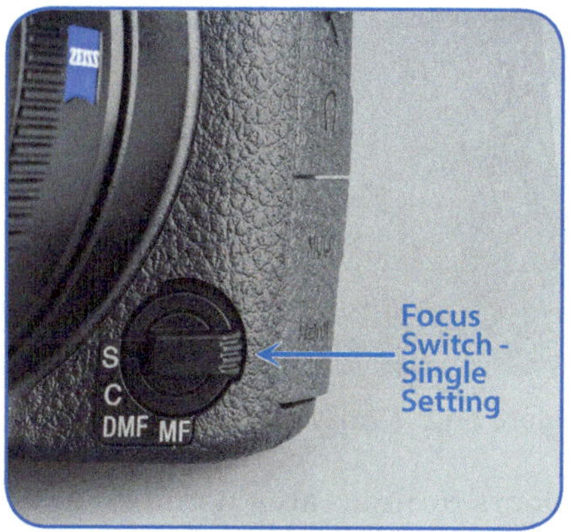

Figure 2-10. Focus Switch Set for Single Autofocus

2. Move the power switch on top of the camera to the On position. The LCD screen will illuminate to show that the camera has turned on. (If you see a message about creating an image database file, that means the memory card contains some images recorded by another camera. Select Enter to dismiss the message and then proceed.)
3. Find the mode dial on top of the camera at the left, and turn it so the green AUTO label is next to the white indicator line, as shown in FIGURE 2-11.

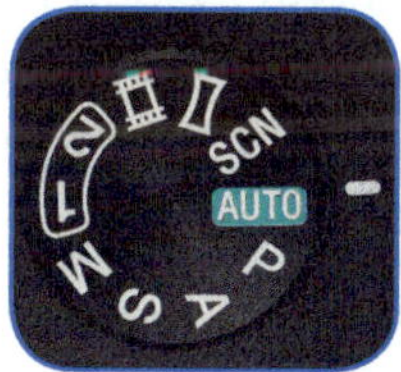

Figure 2-11. Mode Dial Set for Auto Mode

4. This sets the camera to the Intelligent Auto shooting mode. If you see the help screen that describes the mode (called the mode dial guide by Sony), shown in FIGURE 2-12, press the Center button to dismiss it. (I'll explain how to dispense with that help screen altogether in CHAPTER 7.)

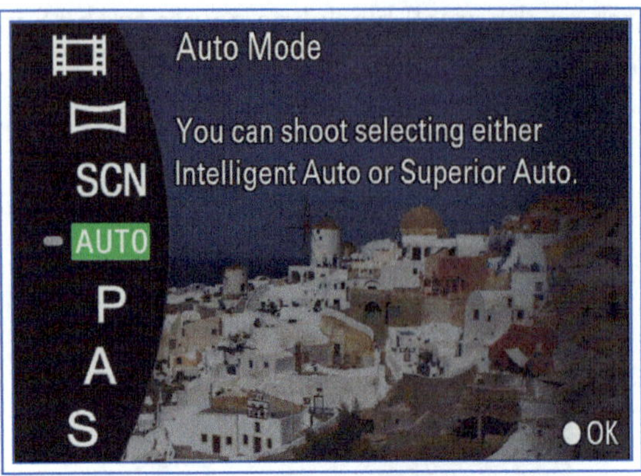

Figure 2-12. Mode Dial Guide for Auto Mode

5. If you're indoors or in an area with low light, press the flash pop-up button, located on top of the camera to the right of the built-in flash unit, to release the flash unit and cause it to pop up. If you don't do this, the flash cannot be fired.

6. Press the Menu button at the upper left of the camera's back to activate the menu system. As I discussed in Chapter 1, navigate through the menu screens by pressing the Right and Left buttons. The Shooting menu is headed by the camera icon; the Custom menu by the gear icon; the Wi-Fi menu by the Wi-Fi symbol; the Playback menu by the triangular Playback symbol; and the Setup menu by the toolbox icon. The currently active menu system has its symbol outlined by a gray line. You can tell which numbered screen of that menu system is active by looking at the small orange line (cursor) beneath the numbers.

7. When a given screen is selected, navigate up and down through the options on that screen by pressing the Up and Down buttons or by turning the Control wheel right or left. When the orange selection bar is on the option you want, press the Center button to select that item. Then press the Up and Down buttons or turn the Control wheel to highlight the value you want for that option, and press the Center button to confirm it. You can then continue making menu settings;

when you are finished with the menu system, press the Menu button to go back to the live view, so you can take pictures.

8. Using the procedure in Step 7, make the settings shown in Table 2-1 using the menu system. For menu options not listed here, any setting is acceptable for now.

Table 2-1. Suggested Settings for Intelligent Auto Mode

SHOOTING MENU	
Image Size	L: 20M
Aspect Ratio	3:2
Quality	Extra Fine
Drive Mode	Single Shooting
Flash Mode	Autoflash
AF Illuminator	Auto
Lock-on AF	Off
Smile/Face Detection	Off
Soft Skin Effect	Off
Auto Object Framing	Off
Auto Mode	Intelligent Auto
SteadyShot (Stills)	On
Color Space	sRGB
CUSTOM MENU	
Zebra	Off
MF Assist	On
Focus Magnification Time	No Limit
Grid Line	Off
Auto Review	2 Seconds
Peaking Level	Mid

Table 2-1. Suggested Settings for Intelligent Auto Mode

Peaking Color	Red
Exposure Settings Guide	Off
Pre-AF	Off
Zoom Setting	Optical Zoom Only
Finder/Monitor	Auto
AEL w/Shutter	Auto
Exposure Comp. Setting	Ambient & Flash
Write Date	Off
Zoom Func. on Ring	Standard
Movie Button	Always
Dial/Wheel Lock	Unlock

If you don't want to go through the steps to make all of these settings, don't worry; you are likely to get very usable images even if you don't adjust most of these settings at this point. I have not included here any recommendations for the Wi-Fi, Playback or Setup menus; the default settings should work well in Intelligent Auto mode. I will discuss all of the menu options later in the book.

9. Press the Menu button again to make the menu disappear, if it hasn't done so already.

10. Aim the camera to compose the picture. Locate the zoom lever on the ring that surrounds the shutter button on the top right of the camera. Push that lever to the left, toward the letter "W" on the camera body, to get a wider-angle shot (including more of the scene in the picture), or to the right, toward the letter "T," to get a telephoto, zoomed-in shot. Or, if you prefer, grasp the outermost ridged area of the lens and turn the lens barrel itself to zoom in and out.

11. Once the picture looks good on the display, gently press the shutter button halfway and pause in that position. You should hear a beep and see one or more sets of green focus brackets on the LCD screen indicating that the subject will be in focus, as shown in FIGURE 2-13.

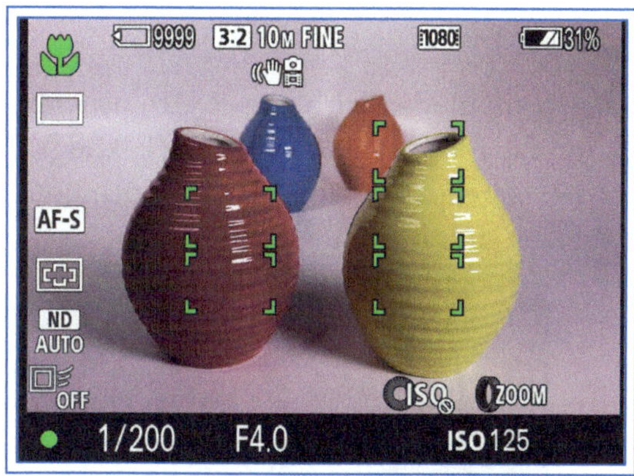

Figure 2-13. Autofocus Indicators on Screen

You also should see a green disc in the extreme lower-left corner of the screen. If that green disc lights up steadily, the image is in focus; if it flashes, the camera was unable to focus. In that case, you can re-aim and see if the autofocus system does better from a different distance or angle.

12. After you have made sure the focus is sharp, push the shutter button all the way to take the picture.

Variations from Fully Automatic

Although the RX10 takes care of the basic settings for you when it's set to Intelligent Auto mode, this camera, unlike some other compact models, still lets you make a number of adjustments to fine-tune the shooting process.

Focus

With some compact cameras, you have few or no options for focus settings in the most automatic shooting mode. With the RX10, you always can control the camera's focus method, because of the physical focus switch. No matter what shooting mode is in effect, you always can turn this switch to a different setting, depending on how you want to focus the lens. I will give a brief overview of focus options here, with further discussion in the chapters that discuss the various menu options and physical controls.

Focus Modes

There are four focus modes with the RX10, as indicated by the four settings for the focus switch (S, C, DMF, and MF), as shown in FIGURE 2-14: single-shot autofocus, continuous autofocus, direct manual focus, and manual focus.

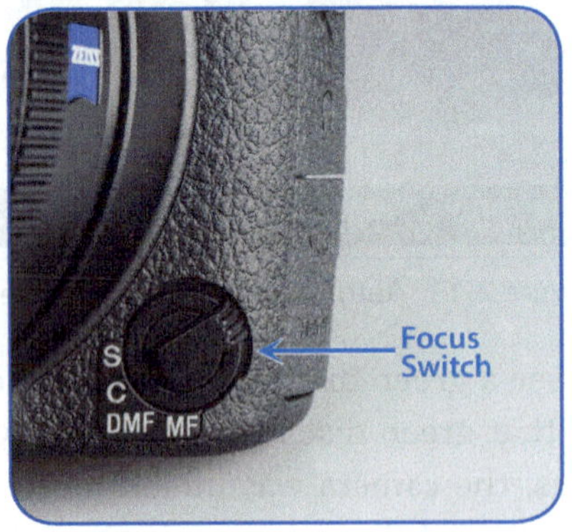

Figure 2-14. Focus Switch

For this discussion, I'm assuming you have the Pre-AF menu option set to Off, as indicated earlier in Table 2-1.

With the S setting, the camera starts to focus when you press the shutter button halfway down. At that point, it tries to achieve sharp focus on an object in the focus area. If it can focus sharply, it beeps and displays one or more green focus frames and a solid green disk. The focus stays locked at that distance as long as you hold the shutter button halfway down; you can then press the button the rest of the way down to take the picture.

With the C setting, when you press the shutter button halfway, the camera attempts to focus on an object in the focus area, but it then continues to adjust the focus as needed, if the camera or the subject moves. The camera does not lock the focus setting until you press the button all the way down to take the picture. The camera never displays a focus frame on the screen. The green disk appears in the lower left of the display when focus is achieved, but, as shown in FIGURE 2-15, it is surrounded by curving lines to indicate that the camera is continuing to adjust focus.

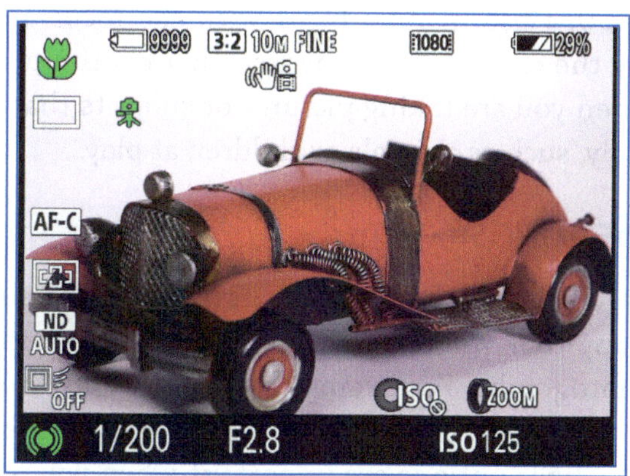

Figure 2-15. Indicator for Continuous Autofocus

With the DMF setting, the camera lets you use both the autofocus capability of single autofocus and the manual focusing capability. With this combination of two focus modes, you can press the shutter button halfway to let the camera use autofocus, and then continue to adjust focus by turning the focus ring manually. Or, you can start to adjust focus manually in order to let the camera know approximately where the focus should be centered, and then press the shutter button halfway to let the camera fine-tune the focus on that subject.

Finally, with the MF setting, the focusing is entirely up to you. You turn the focus ring to bring the image into sharp focus, thereby taking full control. You might use manual focus in a dark or reflective environment where the camera would have difficulty, or in a situation where the camera might not focus on the subject that is most important to you. Another use of manual focus is for extreme closeup shots, when you need to adjust the focus distance very precisely. As I will discuss in Chapter 4 and Chapter 7, you can set the camera to provide assistance with manual focusing through several menu options.

My preference is to use the S setting for single autofocus in most situations. In tricky focusing environments, such as taking pictures of the moon through a telescope, as discussed in Chapter 9, I use manual focus with the focus-assisting aids provided by the camera. You may find that continuous autofocus is useful when you are taking pictures of subjects that are moving unpredictably, such as animals or children at play.

Other Settings

There are several other items that can be adjusted in Auto mode, but not many that will have an immediate and noticeable effect on your photography. For example, you can adjust items such as the aspect ratio (shape) of your images as well as the image size and quality. Those options are important when you want to have more control over your images, but, for general picture-taking in Intelligent Auto mode, they are not critical. I have set forth recommended settings in Table 2-1, and I will discuss details of those options in Chapter 4.

However, there are a few menu options that you might want to take advantage of when you first use the RX10 in Intelligent Auto mode, and I will discuss those briefly now.

First, you might want to turn on face detection, so that, when the camera sees a human face, it will set its focus, exposure, and other settings to expose the face properly. To do this, navigate to screen 5 of the Shooting menu and select the Smile/Face Detection menu option. Press the Center button and, on the next screen, select the next-to-bottom icon, depicting a face with the word On, as shown in Figure 2-16.

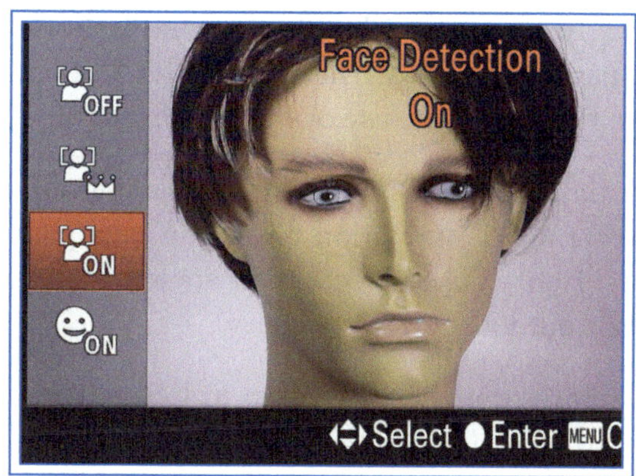

Figure 2-16. Menu Option for Face Detection Turned On

With that setting, the camera will try to detect faces. You also can register particular faces for the camera to detect and you can set the camera to be triggered by smiles; I will discuss face registration in CHAPTER 7 and smile detection in CHAPTER 4.

You also might want to use the Soft Skin Effect option, so the camera will use processing to soften the appearance of skin tones. That option is located on screen 5 of the Shooting menu.

Another setting you might want to try for basic shooting is the Auto Mode option, the first item on screen 6 of the Shooting menu. Normally, this option is set to Intelligent Auto. If you select the other available setting, Superior Auto, the camera will use the same settings and functions as with Intelligent Auto mode, but it will go one step further. In appropriate conditions, the camera will use its special multiple-shot options. That is, if the environment is dark or lighted from behind (backlit), the camera may take a rapid burst of shots using a high ISO setting, and combine those shots internally to produce a composite image of higher quality than otherwise would be possible. I will discuss that option in CHAPTER 3.

Flash

Now I will provide more details about using the RX10's built-in flash unit, because that is something you may want to use on a regular basis. In CHAPTER 4 I'll discuss the Flash Mode settings, Flash Compensation, and the prevention of "red-eye." In APPENDIX A, I'll discuss the use of external flash units.

The built-in flash on the RX10 is not especially powerful, but it can provide enough illumination to let you take pictures in dark areas and to brighten up subjects that would otherwise be lost in shadows, even outdoors on a sunny day.

There is one important point to keep in mind about the built-in flash unit on the RX10: The flash will never pop up by itself, even if the menu settings or the ambient lighting would require use of the flash. In order for the flash to be available for use, you have to release it using the flash pop-up button, located on top of the camera to the right of the flash. In a way, this is a good system, because you can always be certain the flash will not fire by just not popping it up, when you are in a museum or other area that does not permit the use of flash. If you think you may need the flash, though, be sure to release it with this button before it is needed.

To control how the flash is used once it is popped up, you have to use the Flash Mode menu option, located on screen 2 of the Shooting menu. (You could set one of the control buttons to call up this menu option, as discussed in CHAPTER 7, but you still would be using the menu option.)

When you call up the Flash Mode option, using either the menu system or a button assigned to that option, you will see a vertical menu at the left of the screen, as shown in FIGURE 2-17. That menu contains icons representing the six Flash Mode options—a lightning bolt with the universal "no" sign crossing it out, for Flash Off; a lightning bolt with the word "Auto," for Autoflash; a lightning bolt alone, for Fill-flash (meaning the flash will always fire); a lightning bolt with the word "Slow," for Slow Sync; a lightning bolt with the word "Rear," for Rear Sync; and a lightning bolt with the letters WL, for the Wireless setting.

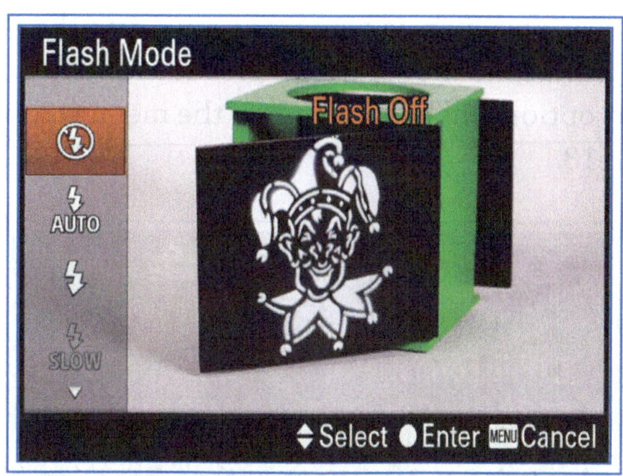

Figure 2-17. Flash Mode Menu Options

With the camera in Intelligent Auto mode, the last three choices will appear dimmed; if you highlight one of those and press the Center button to select it, the camera will display a message saying you cannot make that selection in this shooting mode.

I discussed earlier how to set the flash unit to the Autoflash mode. If, instead of Autoflash, you choose Fill-flash, you will see the lightning bolt icon on the screen at all times (if the flash is popped up and no other icon interferes), and the flash will fire regardless of whether the camera's exposure system believes flash is needed. You can use this setting when you are certain that you want the flash to fire, such as in a dimly lighted room. This setting also can be useful in some outdoor settings, even when the sun is shining, such as when you need to reduce the shadows on your subject's face. There is an illustration of the use of Fill-flash in Chapter 4.

When the camera is set for certain types of shooting, such as using the self-timer with multiple shots, the flash is forced off and cannot be turned on. With some other settings, such as continuous shooting, the flash will fire if you set it to do so, but the use of flash will limit the use of the other setting. In other words, instead of doing rapid continuous shooting, the camera will take multiple images but at a reduced rate, because the flash cannot recycle fast enough to fire repeatedly in rapid succession.

In some situations, such as when you are using the Anti Motion Blur setting of Scene mode, the Flash Mode menu will not even appear; that option will be dimmed on the menu screen, as shown in FIGURE 2-18.

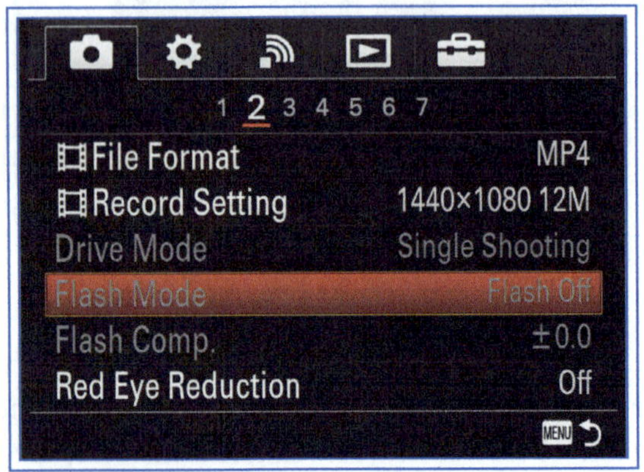

Figure 2-18. Flash Mode Option Dimmed on Shooting Menu

If you set the mode dial to P, for Program mode, and then use the menu system to select a flash mode, you will see the same six options for Flash Mode on the menu, but this time the Autoflash option will be dimmed because that selection is available only in the more automatic modes. In addition, the Flash Off option will be dimmed; that option is available only in Auto mode. Of course, if you don't want the flash to fire, you can just leave the flash unit retracted.

In summary, when using Intelligent Auto mode, if you don't want the flash to fire because you are in a museum or similar location, you can select the Flash Off mode. If you want to leave the decision whether to use flash up to the camera, you can select Autoflash mode. If you want to make sure that the flash will fire no matter what, you can select Fill-flash mode. In CHAPTER 4, I'll explain the other flash options—Slow Sync, Rear Sync, and Wireless—and I'll discuss other flash-related topics. For now, you have the information you need to select a flash mode when the camera is set to the Intelligent Auto shooting mode.

Drive Mode: Self-Timer and Continuous Shooting

The Drive Mode menu option provides more adjustments you may want to make when using Intelligent Auto mode. Select this menu item from screen 2 of the Shooting menu, and the camera will display a vertical menu for Drive Mode, as shown in Figure 2-19.

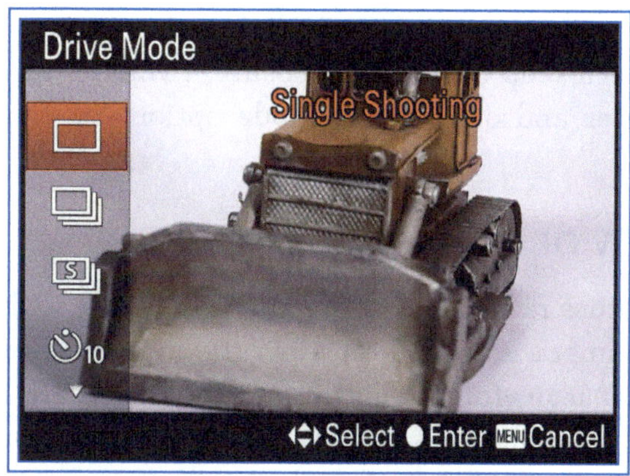

Figure 2-19. Drive Mode Menu Options

You navigate through the options on this menu by pressing the Up and Down buttons or by turning the Control wheel.

I will discuss the Drive Mode options more fully in Chapter 4. For now, you should be aware of a few of the options. (I will skip over some others.) If you select the top option, represented by a single rectangular frame, the camera is set for single shooting mode; when you press the shutter button, a single image is captured. With the second option, whose icon looks like a stack of images, the camera is set for continuous shooting, in which it takes a rapid burst of images while you hold down the shutter button.

If you choose the fourth option, whose icon is a dial with a number beside it, the camera uses the self-timer. Use the Left and Right buttons to choose either 2 or 10 seconds for the timer delay and press the Center button to confirm. Then, when you press the shutter button, the shutter will be triggered after the specified number of seconds.

The 10-second delay is useful when you need to place the camera on a tripod and join a group photo; the 2-second delay is useful when you want to make sure the camera is not jiggled by the action of pressing the shutter button. This option helps when you are taking a picture for which focusing is critical, such as an extreme closeup or a time exposure. I will discuss the use of the self-timer and other Drive Mode options in more detail in Chapter 4.

Overview of Movie Recording

Now I'll discuss recording a short movie sequence with the RX10. Once the camera is turned on, turn the mode dial to select the green AUTO icon, for Intelligent Auto mode. There is a special Movie mode setting marked by the movie film icon on the mode dial, but you don't have to use that mode for shooting movies; I'll discuss the use of that option and other details about movie-recording options in Chapter 8.

For now, press the Menu button to get access to the menu system, then navigate to screen 2 of the Shooting menu. On the top line of that screen, highlight the File Format option and press the Center button to go to the sub-menu with two choices for the format of movie recording. Be sure the top option, AVCHD (Advanced Video Coding High Definition), is highlighted; that format provides the highest quality for your videos.

For the rest of the settings, I will provide a table like the one included earlier in this chapter for shooting still images. The settings shown in Table 2-2 are standard ones for shooting high-quality movies.

Table 2-2. Suggested Shooting Menu Settings for Movies in Intelligent Auto Mode

File Format	AVCHD
Record Setting	60p 28M (PS)
SteadyShot (Movies)	Active
Auto Slow Shutter	On
Audio Recording	On
Audio Out Timing	Live
Wind Noise Reduction	Off

There are some other settings you can make for still images on the Shooting menu that will affect movie recording; I will discuss that topic in CHAPTER 8. For now, if you are going to be shooting a movie that shows people's faces, you may want to go to screen 5 of the Shooting menu and set the Face Detection item to On. You can leave the other items set as they were for shooting still images, as listed in TABLE 2-1.

Now you have made all of the necessary settings for recording a movie. Aim the camera at your subject, and when you are ready to start recording, press and release the red Movie button at the upper-right corner of the camera's back. (If you see an error message, go to screen 4 of the Custom menu, marked by a gear icon, and set the Movie Button option to Always.)

The screen will display a red REC icon in the lower-left corner of the display, next to a counter showing the elapsed time in the recording, as shown in FIGURE 2-20. The camera may also display two green recording-level indicators to show the volume of sound being recorded for channel 1 and channel 2, depending on other menu options.

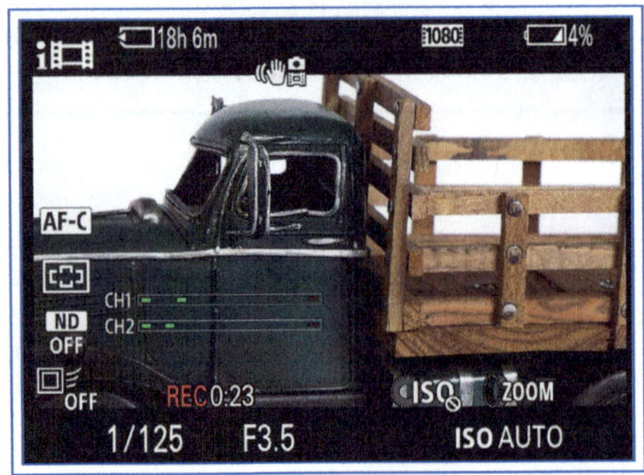

Figure 2-20. REC Indicator on Screen During Video Recording

Hold the camera as steady as possible (or use a tripod), and pan (move the camera side to side) smoothly if you need to.

The camera will keep shooting until it reaches a recording limit, or until you press the red Movie button again to stop the recording. (The maximum time for continuous recording of any one scene is about 29 minutes in most situations.)

The camera will automatically adjust exposure as lighting conditions change. You can zoom the lens in and out as needed, but you should do so sparingly if at all, to avoid distracting the audience and to avoid recording sounds of zooming the lens on the sound track. When you are finished, press the Movie button again, and the camera will save the footage.

Those are the basics for recording video clips with the RX10. I'll discuss movie options in more detail in Chapter 8.

Viewing Pictures

Before I cover more advanced settings for taking still pictures and movies, as well as other matters of interest, I will discuss the basics of viewing your images in the camera.

Review While in Shooting Mode

Each time you take a still picture, the image will show up on the LCD screen (or in the viewfinder) for a short time, if you have the Custom menu's Auto Review option set to turn on this function. I'll discuss the details of that setting in CHAPTER 7. By default, your image will stay on the screen for 2 seconds after you take a new picture. If you prefer, you can set that display to last for 5 or 10 seconds, or to be off altogether.

Reviewing Images in Playback Mode

To review images taken previously, you enter playback mode by pressing the Playback button—the one with the small triangle icon to the lower left of the Control wheel. To view all still images and movies for a particular date, go to screen 1 of the Playback menu and set the View Mode option to Date View. If you prefer, you can set View Mode to show only stills, only AVCHD movies, or only MP4 movies.

Once you choose a viewing option, you can scroll through recorded images and movies by pressing the Left and Right buttons or by turning the Control wheel or Control dial. Hold down the Left or Right button to move more quickly through the images. You can enlarge the view of any still image by moving the zoom lever on top of the camera toward the T position, and you can scroll around in the enlarged image using the four direction buttons.

If you press the zoom lever in the other direction, toward the wide-angle setting, the image will return to normal size. If you press the lever once more in that direction, you will see an index screen with a number of thumbnail images (either 9 or 25, depending on a Playback menu option), and a further press brings up a calendar screen for selecting images by date. You can select images from the index and date screens by pressing the Center button on a highlighted thumbnail image. I'll discuss other playback options in CHAPTER 6.

Playing Movies

To play movies, move through the files by the methods described above until you find the movie you want to play. You should see a triangular playback icon inside a circle, as shown in Figure 2-21.

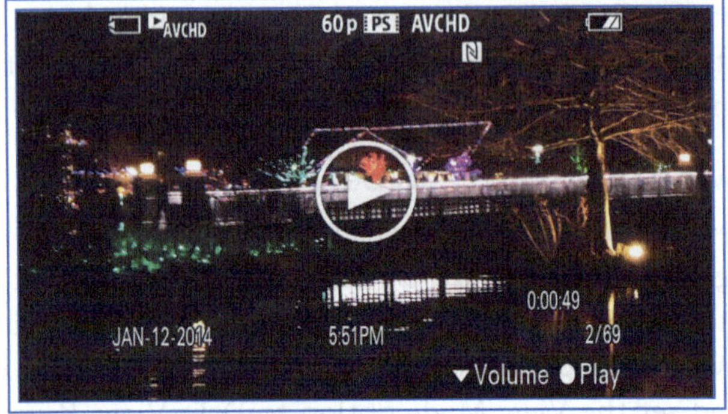

Figure 2-21. Movie Ready to Play

Press the Center button to start the movie playing. Then, as shown in Figure 2-22, you will see prompts at the bottom of the screen showing the controls you can use, including the Center button to pause and resume playback.

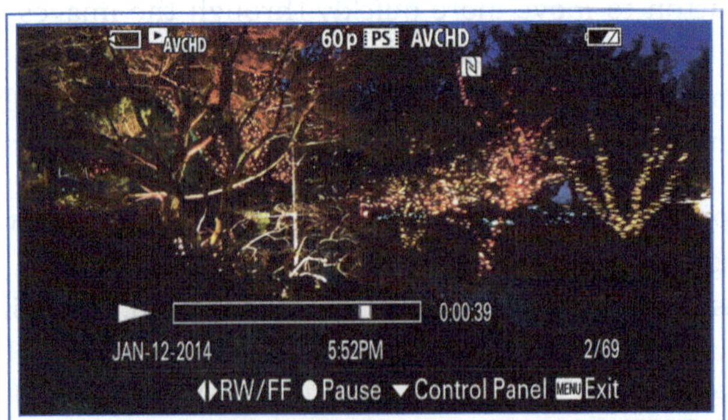

Figure 2-22. Movie Playback - Basic Controls

(If you don't see the controls, press the Display button until they appear.) You also can press the Down button to bring up a more detailed set of controls on the screen, as shown in Figure 2-23.

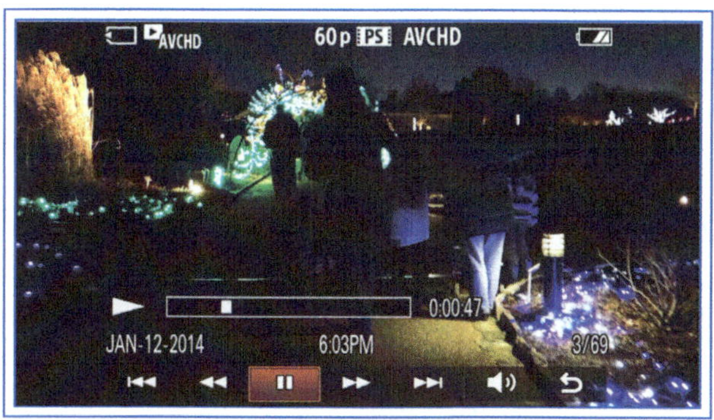

Figure 2-23. Movie Playback - Detailed Controls

To change the volume, pause the movie and press the Down button to bring up the detailed controls; then navigate to the speaker icon, next to last at the right of those controls. Press the Center button to select volume, then use the Control wheel or the Right and Left buttons to adjust the volume. You also can adjust the volume before a movie starts playing, by pressing the Down button to bring up the volume control. To exit from playing the movie, press the Playback button. (I'll discuss other movie playback options in Chapter 8.)

If you want to play the movies on a computer or edit them with video-editing software, you can use the PlayMemories Home software that is provided through the Sony web site. You also can use any other program that can deal with AVCHD and MP4 video files, such as Adobe Premiere Elements, Adobe Premiere Pro, Final Cut Express, Final Cut Pro, iMovie, or Windows Movie Maker, depending on what type of computer you are using.

CHAPTER 3: Shooting Modes

Until now, I have discussed the basics of setting up the camera for quick shots, using Intelligent Auto mode to take pictures with settings controlled mostly by the camera's automation. As with other advanced cameras, though, with the Sony RX10 there is a large range of other options available, particularly for still images. To explain this broad range of features, I need to discuss two subjects—shooting modes and the Shooting menu options. In this chapter, I'll discuss the shooting modes; in CHAPTER 4, I'll discuss the Shooting menu.

Whenever you set out to capture still images, you need to select one of the shooting modes available on the mode dial: Intelligent Auto, Program Auto, Aperture Priority, Shutter Priority, Manual exposure, Memory Recall 1 or 2, Sweep Panorama, or Scene Selection. (The only other mode available is for movies.) So far, I have discussed primarily the Intelligent Auto mode. Now I will discuss the others, after some review of the first one.

Intelligent Auto Mode

I've already discussed this shooting mode in some detail. This is a good choice if you need to take a quick shot and don't have much time to fuss with settings such as ISO, White Balance, aperture, shutter speed, or focus. It's also a good mode to select when you hand the camera to someone else to take a photo of you and your companions.

For example, when I spotted a deer in our back yard early one morning, I ran upstairs to grab my RX10 and quickly set it to Intelligent Auto mode. I fired off a few shots and managed to capture the view seen in FIGURE 3-1 before he disappeared into a neighbor's yard.

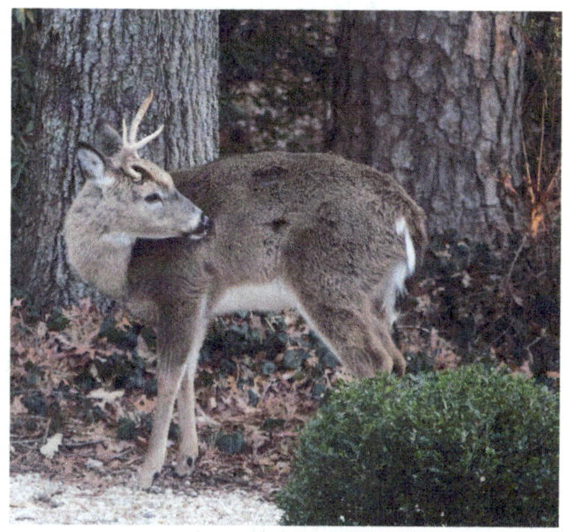

Figure 3-1. Intelligent Auto Mode Example Image 1

A week or so later, on a trip to the local botanical garden, I used Intelligent Auto for several images, including the view in FIGURE 3-2 of the garden's annual evening exhibition of holiday lights.

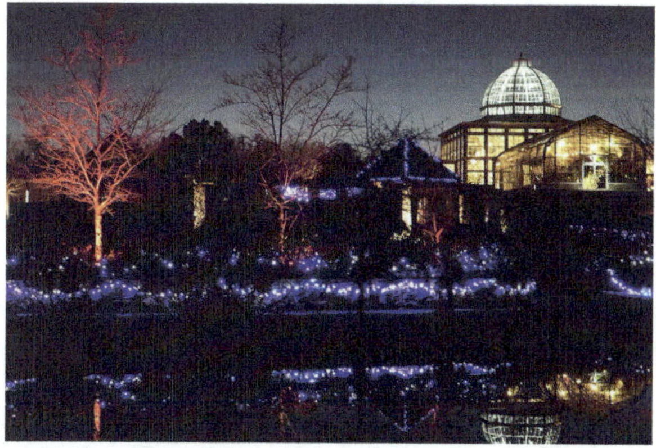

Figure 3-2. Intelligent Auto Mode Example Image 2

To set this mode, turn the mode dial to the green AUTO label, as shown in FIGURE 3-3.

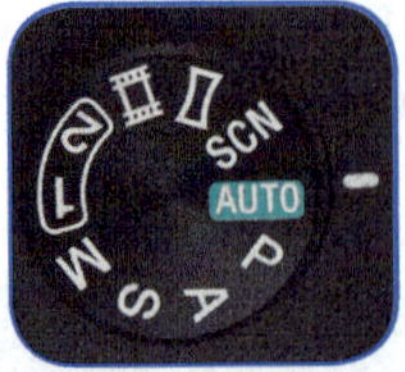

Figure 3-3. Mode Dial Set to Intelligent Auto Mode

When you select this mode, the camera makes several decisions for you and limits your options in some ways. The camera will select the shutter speed, aperture, and ISO setting, along with several other settings over which you will have no control. For example, you can't set White Balance to any value other than Auto, and you can't choose a metering method or use exposure bracketing. You can, however, use quite a few features, as discussed in CHAPTER 2, including Flash Mode, some settings of Drive Mode, Face Detection, and others. You also can use sophisticated options such as the Raw format, which I will discuss in CHAPTER 4 when I discuss other Shooting menu options.

One interesting aspect of this mode is that the camera tries to figure out what sort of subject or scene you are shooting. Some of the subjects the camera will attempt to detect are Baby, Portrait, Night Portrait, Night Scene, Landscape, Backlight, Low Brightness, and Macro. It also will try to detect certain conditions, such as whether a tripod is in use or whether the subject is walking, and it will display appropriate icons for those situations. So, if you see different icons when you aim at various subjects in this shooting mode, that means the camera is evaluating the scene for factors such as brightness, backlighting, the presence of human subjects, and the like, so it can use the best possible settings for the situation.

For FIGURE 3-4, the camera evaluated a scene with a human face and appropriately used its Portrait setting. The Portrait icon is seen in the upper-left corner of the screen.

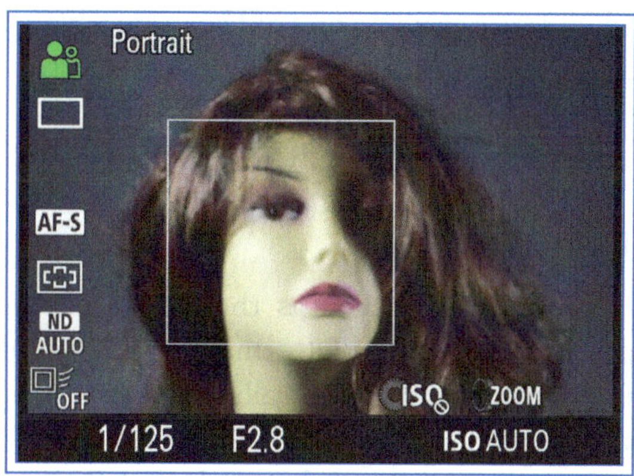

Figure 3-4. Portrait Scene Detected in Auto Mode

Figure 3-5 shows the use of automatic scene recognition for a subject closer to the lens. The camera interpreted the scene as a macro, or closeup shot, and switched automatically into Macro mode, indicated by the flower icon.

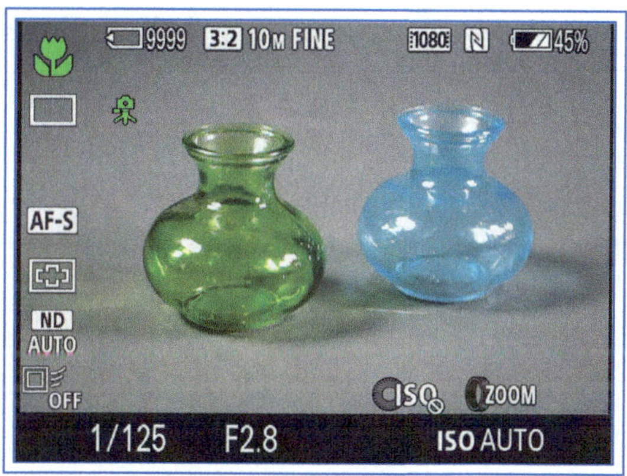

Figure 3-5. Macro Scene Detected in Auto Mode

In addition, the camera correctly detected that it was attached to a tripod, as indicated by the tripod icon to the lower right of the macro symbol.

Of course, scene recognition depends on the camera's programming, which may not interpret every scene the same way that you would. If that becomes a problem, you may want to make individual settings using one of the more advanced shooting modes, such as Program, Aperture Priority, Shutter Priority, or Manual. Or, you can use the SCN setting on the mode dial and select a scene setting that better fits the current situation.

Superior Auto Mode

With some Sony cameras, such as the RX100 II, there are two Auto settings on the mode dial—one for Intelligent Auto and one for a slightly different mode called Superior Auto. With the RX10, Sony has included this second automatic mode, but has not given it a separate position on the mode dial. Instead, you have to go to screen 6 of the Shooting menu and select the Auto Mode menu option. When you select that item, you will see a screen for choosing Intelligent Auto or Superior Auto. If you select the lower icon for Superior Auto, the camera will be set to that mode, as shown in Figure 3-6.

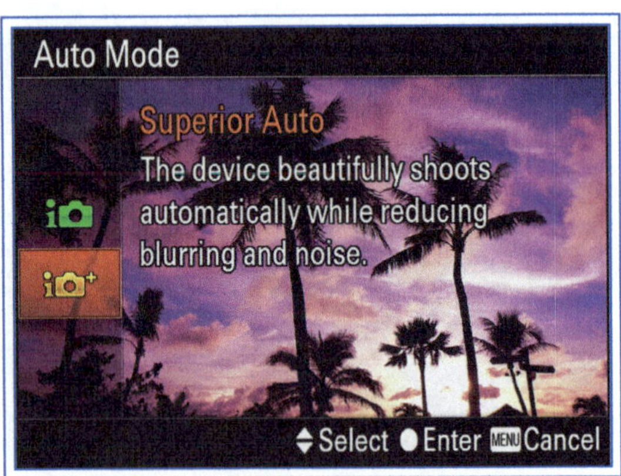

Figure 3-6. Superior Auto Mode Selection Screen

Superior Auto mode includes all features and functions of Intelligent Auto mode, but adds extra features. In Superior Auto mode, as with Intelligent Auto, the camera uses its scene detection capability to try to determine what subject matter or conditions are present, such as a portrait, a dimly lit scene, and the like.

For many of these scenes, the camera will function just as it does in Intelligent Auto mode. However, in a few specific situations, the camera will take a different approach: It will take a rapid burst of shots and combine them internally into a single composite image of higher quality than would be possible with a single shot. The higher quality can be achieved because the camera generally has to raise the ISO setting to a fairly high level, which introduces visual "noise" into the image. By taking multiple shots and then combining them, the camera can average out and cancel some of the noise, thereby increasing the quality of the resulting image.

One problem with this system is that you have no control over when the camera decides to use this burst shooting technique. There are three situations in which the camera will do this: when it detects the need for settings called Anti Motion Blur, Hand-held Twilight, or Backlight Correction HDR. When the camera believes this special feature is needed, it fires a burst of shots; you will hear the rapid firing. Then, it will take longer than usual for the camera to process the multiple shots into a single composite image; you will likely see a message saying "Processing" on the screen for several seconds. When the camera is using this feature, which Sony calls "Overlay," you will see a small white icon in the upper-left corner of the display that looks like a stack of frames with a plus sign at its upper-right corner, as shown in Figure 3-7.

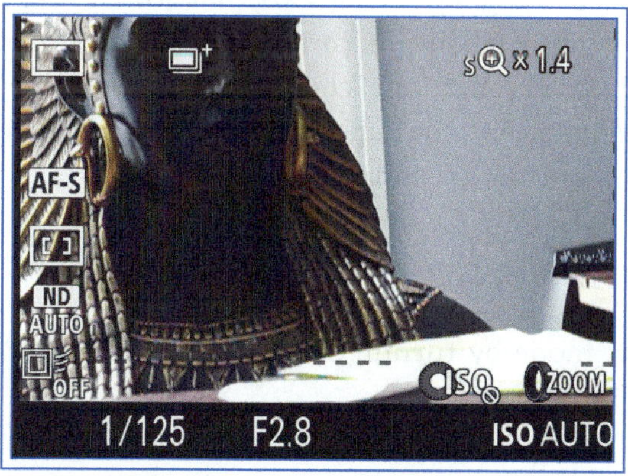

Figure 3-7. Overlay Icon on Screen in Superior Auto Mode

Two of the settings the camera may use in Superior Auto mode—Anti Motion Blur and Hand-held Twilight—are available also as selections in Scene mode, discussed later in this chapter. The third—Backlight Correction HDR—is available only in Superior Auto mode, and only when the camera decides to use it. None of the multiple-shot settings will function when Quality is set to Raw or Raw & JPEG.

I have not found much advantage in using the Superior Auto setting. However, there may be cases when the burst-shooting feature will improve image quality, so it is not a bad idea to use Superior Auto mode when shooting in low light or backlit conditions. As a general rule, though, I prefer to use a mode such as Program, discussed below, and set my own values for items such as DRO, HDR, ISO, and Metering Mode.

If you want to use Superior Auto mode, there is an easier way to get access to it than selecting Auto Mode from screen 6 of the Shooting menu. Instead, use the Function Menu Settings option on screen 4 of the Custom menu, and set one of the 12 settings for the Function button to Shoot Mode. Then, whenever you turn the mode dial to the AUTO setting, you can just press the Function button, and you will see the icon for the current setting for Auto Mode, either Intelligent Auto or Superior Auto. At this point, move the highlight block to that icon using the Left or Right button, and, when the icon is highlighted, turn the Control wheel to cycle through the choices. When your new selection (either Intelligent Auto or Superior Auto) is highlighted, just press the Function button to exit to shooting mode.

Program Mode

Choose this mode by turning the mode dial to the P setting, as shown in Figure 3-8.

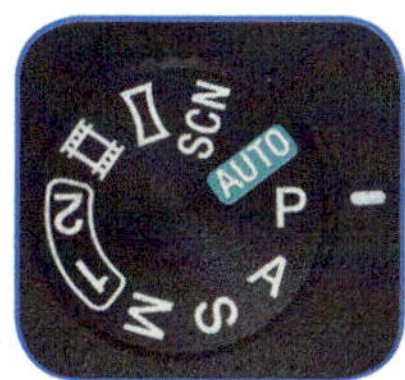

Figure 3-8. Mode Dial Set to Program Mode

Program mode (sometimes called Program Auto mode) lets you control many of the settings available with the RX10, apart from shutter speed and aperture, which the camera chooses on its own. You still can adjust the camera's automatic exposure to a fair extent by using exposure compensation, as discussed in Chapter 5, as well as exposure bracketing, discussed in Chapter 4, and Program Shift, discussed later in this chapter. You don't have to make a lot of decisions if you don't want to, because the camera will make reasonable choices for you as defaults.

You should note that, even though shutter speeds as long as 30 seconds are available in the Shutter Priority and Manual exposure modes, the camera will never choose a shutter speed longer than one second in Program mode. In addition, the camera will do its best to avoid selecting the most narrow apertures, f/11, and f/16, because those narrow apertures can cause distortion in your images arising from the diffraction effect, which reduces sharpness.

The Program Shift function is available only in Program mode; it works as follows. Once you have aimed the camera at your subject, the camera displays its chosen settings for shutter speed and aperture in the lower-left corner of the screen. At that point, you can turn the Control dial at the upper right of the camera's back, and the values for shutter speed and aperture will change, if possible under current conditions, to select different values for both settings while keeping the same overall exposure of the scene.

With this option, the camera "shifts" the original exposure to your choice of any of the matched pairs that appear as you turn the Control wheel. For example, if the original exposure was f/2.8 at 1/30 second, you may see equivalent pairs of f/3.2 at 1/25, f/3.5 at 1/20, and f/4.0 at 1/15, among others. When Program Shift is in effect, the P icon in the upper-left corner of the screen will have an asterisk to its right, as shown in FIGURE 3-9.

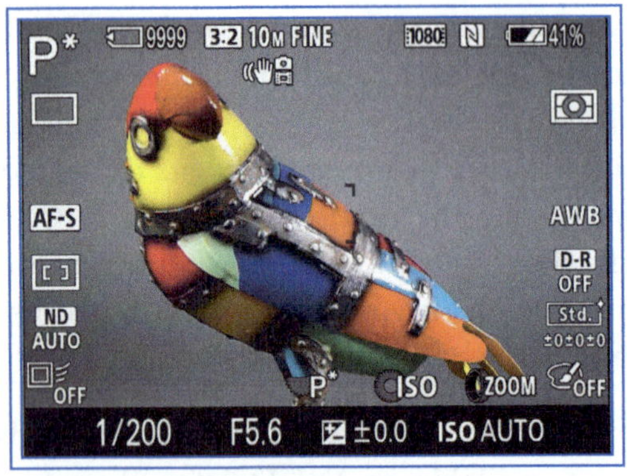

Figure 3-9. Program Shift Indicator on Screen

To cancel Program Shift, turn the Control dial until the original settings are back in effect or move the mode dial to another mode and then back to Program. You also can cancel it by pressing the flash pop-up button to pop up the flash unit; Program Shift cannot function when the flash is in use.

When would you use the Program Shift feature? You might want a slightly faster shutter speed to stop action better or a wider aperture to blur the background more, or you might have some other creative reason. This option lets the camera quickly evaluate the exposure, but gives you the option to tweak the shutter speed and aperture to suit your current needs.

It also is worth noting that, even though the camera will try to avoid setting an aperture of f/16 in Program mode on its own, you can still cause the camera to use f/16 using the Program Shift feature. That setting is not advisable because of the diffraction effect, which limits image sharpness at that narrow aperture, but the choice is available if you want to make it.

Of course, if you need to use a specific shutter speed or aperture, you probably are better off using Aperture Priority, Shutter Priority, or Manual exposure mode. However, having Program Shift available is useful when you're taking pictures quickly using Program mode, and you want a fast way to tweak the settings somewhat.

Another important aspect of Program mode is that it greatly expands the choices available through the Shooting menu, which controls many of the camera's settings. You will be able to make choices involving ISO sensitivity, Metering Mode, DRO/HDR, White Balance, Creative Style, Picture Effect, and others that are not available in the Auto modes. I won't discuss those settings here; if you want to explore that topic, see the discussion of the Shooting menu in Chapter 4 for information about all of the different selections that are available.

Aperture Priority Mode

You set the camera to the Aperture Priority shooting mode by turning the mode dial to the A setting, as shown in Figure 3-10.

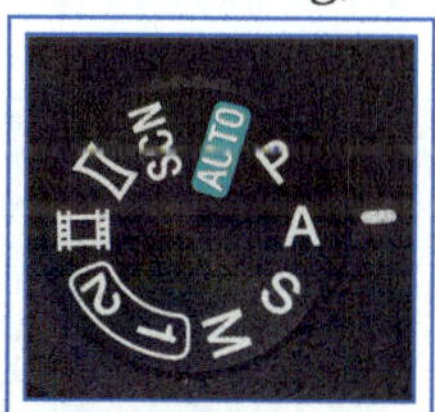

Figure 3-10. Mode Dial Set to Aperture Priority Mode

In this mode, you select the aperture and the camera chooses a shutter speed for proper exposure. With this mode, you can exercise control over depth of field of your shots. When you select a narrow aperture, such as f/16.0, the depth of field will be broad, with the result that more items will appear to be in sharp focus at varying distances from the lens. On the other hand, with a wide aperture, such as f/2.8, the depth of field will be relatively shallow, and you may be able to keep only one subject in sharp focus.

In FIGURES 3-11 and 3-12, the settings were the same except for aperture values. I focused on the pig figure in each case. For FIGURE 3-11, I set the aperture of the RX10 to f/2.8, the widest possible. With this setting, because the depth of field at this aperture was quite shallow, the model tractor in the background is quite blurry. I took FIGURE 3-12 with the camera's aperture set to f/16.0, the narrowest possible setting, resulting in a broader depth of field, making the tractor appear considerably sharper.

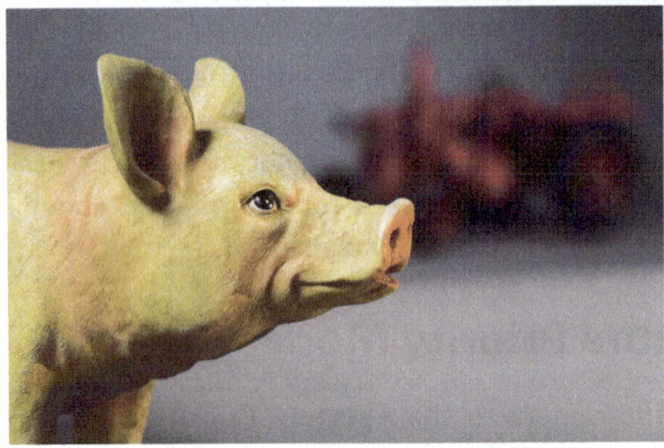

Figure 3-11. Aperture Set to f/2.8

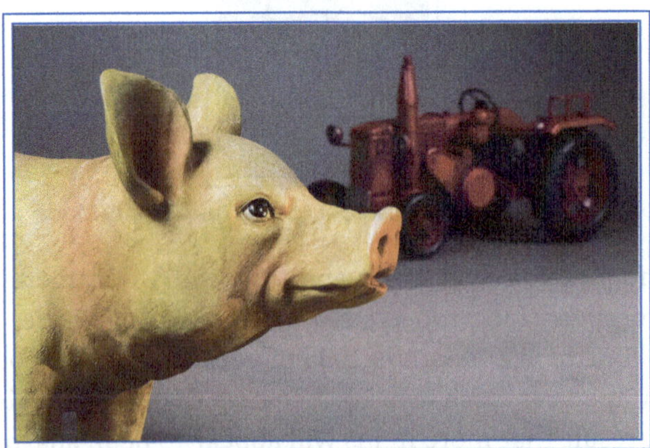

Figure 3-12. Aperture Set to f/16.0

These two photos illustrate the effects of varying your aperture by setting it wide (low numbers) when you want to blur the background and narrow (high numbers) when you want to enjoy a broad depth of field and keep subjects at varying distances in sharp focus. A need for a shallow depth of field arises often in the case of outdoor portraits and other images. If you can achieve a shallow depth of field by using a wide aperture, you can keep your subject in sharp focus but leave the background blurry. This effect is sometimes called "bokeh," a Japanese term for a pleasing blurriness of the background. In this situation, the fuzzy background can be a great asset, minimizing distraction from unwanted objects and highlighting the sharply focused portrait of your subject.

In FIGURE 3-13, I took a closeup shot of a rose in a rather cluttered room, blurring the background of scattered objects by setting the aperture as wide as possible to emphasize the focus on the flower.

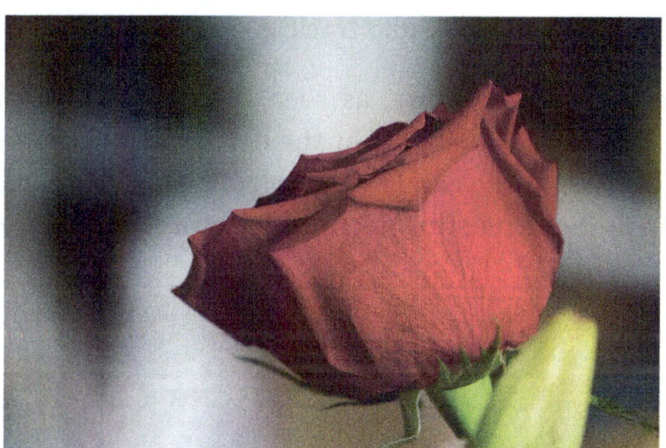

Figure 3-13. Bokeh Example

Here is the procedure for using this shooting mode. With the mode dial at the A setting, use the aperture ring to select the aperture value. The major settings are f/2.8, f/4, f/5.6, f/8, f/11, and f/16, but you can also make intermediate settings by turning the ring to one of the white lines between the numbered values. For example, between f/2.8 and f/4, you can select f/3.2 or f/3.5.

When you are shooting stills in either Aperture Priority or Manual exposure mode, I recommend setting the aperture click switch to its Click On position, as shown in FIGURE 3-14.

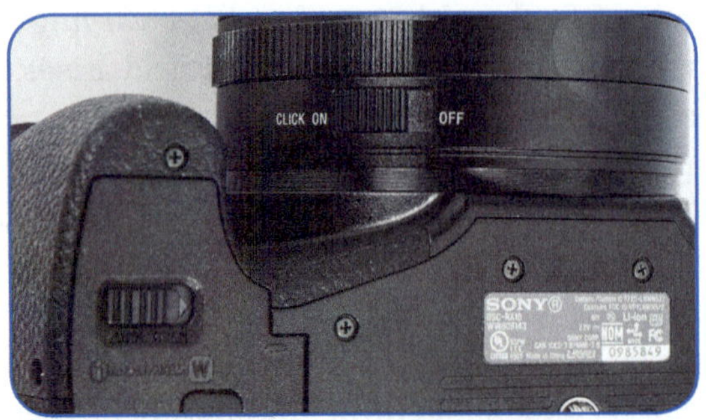

Figure 3-14. Aperture Click Switch at On Position

With that setting, the aperture ring clicks firmly into place for each available aperture setting, so you get definite feedback when the setting is made. The only reason to turn the click setting off is when you are shooting videos, because the sounds of the clicks are likely to be heard on the audio track.

When you set the aperture, as seen in FIGURE 3-15, the f-stop (f/2.8 in this case) will appear at the bottom of the screen next to the shutter speed. The camera will select a shutter speed that will result in a proper exposure given the aperture you have set.

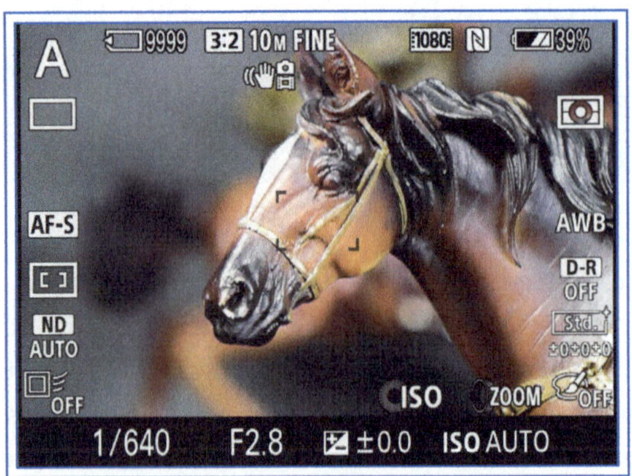

Figure 3-15. Aperture Setting on Screen

Although in most cases the camera will be able to select a corresponding shutter speed that results in a normal exposure, there may be times when this is not possible. For example, if you are in a very bright location with the aperture set to f/2.8, the camera may not be able to set a shutter speed fast enough to yield a proper exposure. In that case, the numbers for the fastest possible shutter speed (1/1600, in this case) will flash on the camera's display to show that the exposure cannot be set using that aperture. The camera will still let you take the exposure, but it may be too bright to be usable. Similarly, if conditions are too dark for a good exposure at the aperture you have selected, the slowest shutter speed (8", meaning 8 seconds) will flash.

Here is one very positive note about the aperture settings on the RX10. With many compact cameras, the widest aperture setting varies as the lens is zoomed in to longer focal lengths. For example, even though a camera's widest aperture is f/1.8 at the wide-angle setting of the lens, the widest aperture may shrink to, say, f/5.6 when the lens is zoomed all the way in. With the RX10, Sony has provided a "constant-aperture" zoom lens, whose maximum aperture of f/2.8 is available throughout the zoom range. Therefore, even when you have zoomed the lens all the way in for a telephoto shot, you can set the aperture to f/2.8 to blur the background or to expose the scene properly in dim lighting.

In Aperture Priority mode, as with Program mode, the full range of the camera's shutter speeds is not available. In this mode, the RX10 can set shutter speeds from 1/3200 second to 8 seconds, depending on the aperture setting. (At the widest apertures, such as f/2.8, the fastest shutter speed available is 1/1600 second; at the narrowest apertures, such as f/16.0, the fastest speed available is 1/3200 second.)

It's also important to note here that, as discussed earlier for Program mode, when you set an aperture as narrow as f/11 or f/16 with this camera, lens diffraction comes into play and limits the sharpness of your images. So, unless you have a fairly strong reason to use f/16, such as a need to maximize depth of field in a brightly lighted area, you should try to use apertures no more narrow than f/8.0 if possible.

Shutter Priority Mode

In Shutter Priority mode, you choose the shutter speed you want and the camera will set the corresponding aperture to achieve a proper exposure of the image.

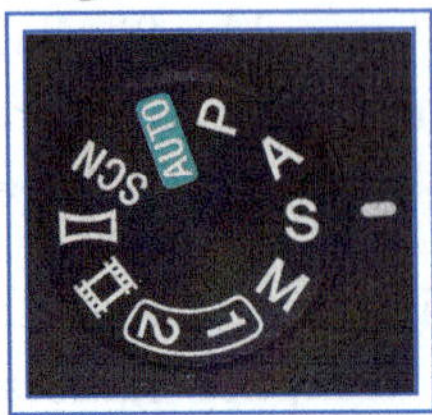

Figure 3-16. Mode Dial Set to Shutter Priority Mode

In this mode, designated by the S position on the mode dial, as shown in Figure 3-16, you can set the shutter to be open for a time ranging from 30 seconds to 1/3200 of a second. If you are photographing fast action, such as a baseball swing or a hurdles event at a track meet, and you want to stop the motion with a minimum of blur, you should select a fast shutter speed, such as 1/1000 of a second. For Figure 3-17 and Figure 3-18, I dropped a group of colorful plastic balls in front of the camera, using different shutter speeds to achieve different effects.

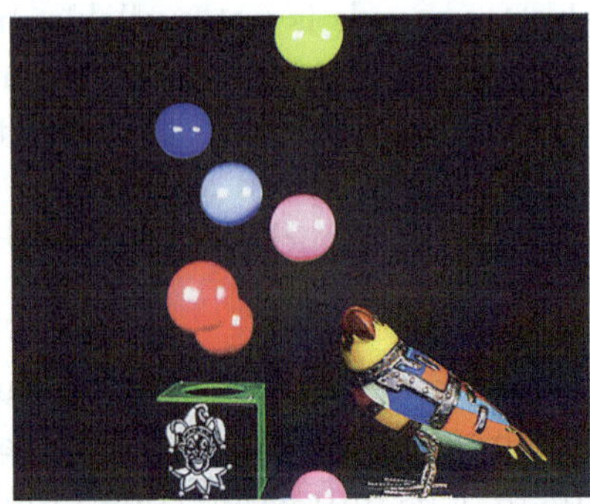

Figure 3-17. Shutter Speed Set to 1/500 Second

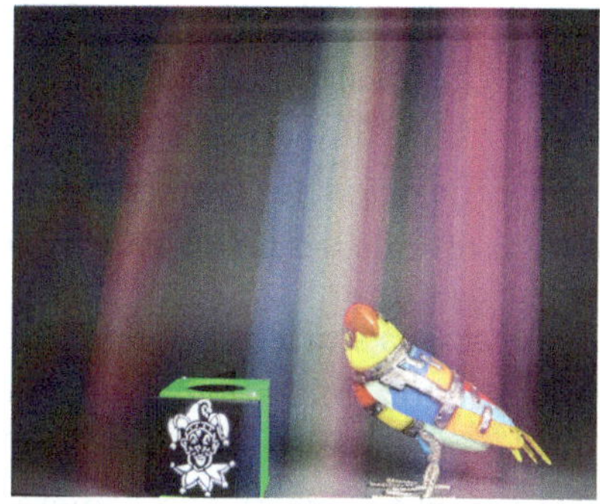

Figure 3-18. Shutter Speed Set to ½ Second

In FIGURE 3-17, with the shutter speed set at 1/500 second, the balls are frozen in mid-air. In FIGURE 3-18, with the shutter speed set to 1/2 second, the balls blend together into continuous streams of color. In this case, by varying the shutter speed you can dramatically change the nature of the image.

You select this mode by turning the mode dial to the S indicator, as shown in FIGURE 3-16. Then you select the shutter speed by turning the Control dial, at the upper right of the camera's back.

If you turn on the Exposure Settings Guide option on screen 2 of the Custom menu, you will see a circular display of the shutter speeds as you turn the Control dial, as shown in FIGURE 3-19.

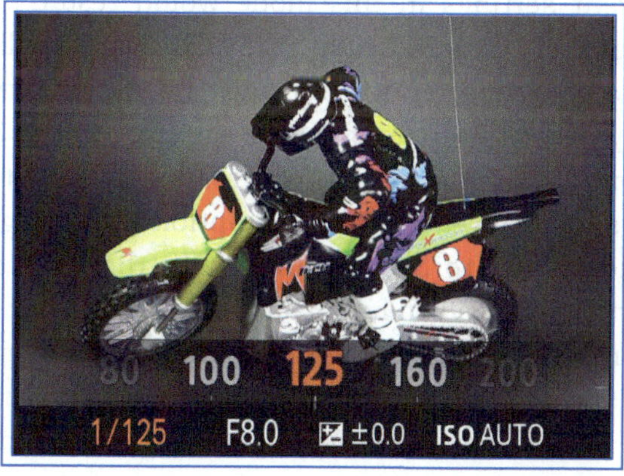

Figure 3-19. Circular Shutter Speed Display on Screen

Although the RX10 uses the letter "S" to stand for Shutter Priority on the mode dial and to designate this mode on the live view screen, it uses the notation "Tv" on the Shooting mode display in Shutter Priority mode, next to the Control dial icon. Tv stands for time value, a synonym often used for shutter speed.

As you cycle through various shutter speeds, the camera will select the appropriate aperture to achieve a normal exposure, if possible. As I discussed in connection with Aperture Priority mode, if you select a shutter speed for which the camera cannot select an aperture that will yield a good exposure, the aperture reading at the bottom of the display will flash. The flashing aperture means that proper exposure at the selected shutter speed is not possible at any available aperture, according to the camera's calculations.

For example, if you set the shutter speed to 1/320 second in a fairly dark indoor environment, the aperture number (which will be f/2.8, the widest setting) may flash, indicating that proper exposure is not possible. As I discussed for Aperture Priority mode, you can still take the picture if you want to, though it may not be usable. A similar situation may take place if you select a slow shutter speed (such as 4 seconds) in a relatively bright location.

If the current settings in this mode would result in an image that is excessively dark or bright, the LCD display will grow dark or bright to show that effect, but only if a menu option is set a certain way. If you want to see how the final image would look while viewing it on the display, go to screen 2 of the Custom menu and set the Live View Display option to Setting Effect On. If the option is set to Setting Effect Off, then the display will show a normal image even in unusually bright or dark conditions. That option is discussed further in Chapter 7. (This situation is unlikely to happen in Aperture Priority mode, because of the wide range of shutter speeds the camera can use to achieve a good exposure.)

Note that Sony has programmed the RX10 not to use apertures more narrow than f/11 in this shooting mode; if you aim the camera at a bright subject in Shutter Priority mode, you may see the f/11 aperture setting blink, indicating that the exposure cannot be made properly under current conditions. This is apparently because Sony has determined that an aperture of f/16 is too likely to cause lens diffraction that has a negative impact on image sharpness. If you want to use an aperture setting of f/16, you will have to use Aperture Priority Mode, Manual exposure mode, or Program mode, possibly using Program Shift.

Manual Exposure Mode

One of the many features of the RX10 that distinguish it from more ordinary compact cameras is that it has a fully manual exposure mode, a useful tool for photographers who want to exert full creative control over exposure decisions.

The technique for using this mode is not too different from what I discussed for the Aperture Priority and Shutter Priority modes. To control exposure manually, set the mode dial to the M indicator, as shown in Figure 3-20.

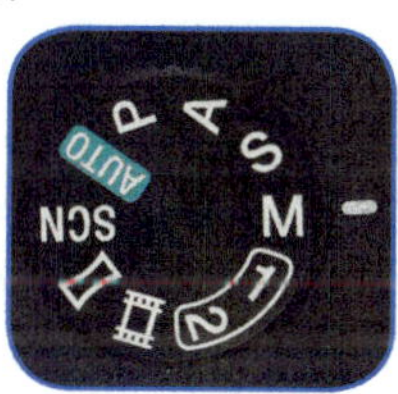

Figure 3-20. Mode Dial Set to Manual Exposure Mode

You now have to control both shutter speed and aperture by setting them yourself. To set the aperture, turn the aperture ring; to set the shutter speed, turn the Control dial at the upper right of the back of the camera. The values you set will appear at the bottom of the display, as shown in Figure 3-21.

As you adjust shutter speed and aperture, a third value, to the right of the aperture value, will also change. That value is shown by a positive, negative, or zero number next to a box with the letters "M.M." (for "metered manual").

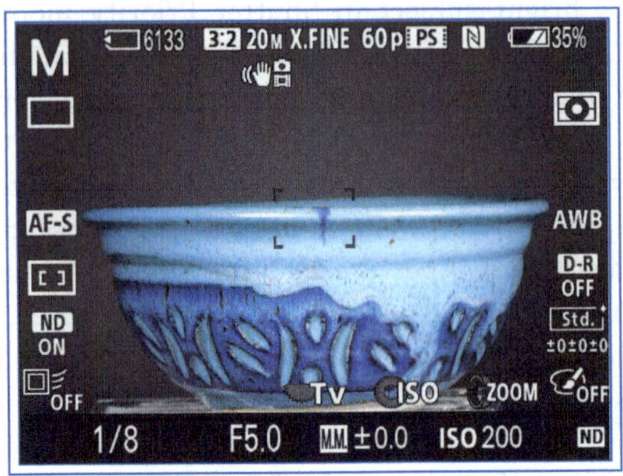

Figure 3-21. Settings on Screen in Manual Exposure Mode

That figure represents any deviation from what the camera's metering system considers to be a normal exposure. So, even though you are setting the exposure manually, the camera will still let you know whether the selected aperture and shutter speed will produce a standard exposure.

If the settings you chose will result in a dark exposure, the M.M. value will be negative; for a bright exposure, it will be positive. The value can go up or down only to +2.0 or -2.0 EV (exposure value) units; after that point, the value will flash, indicating that the camera considers the exposure excessively abnormal. The ISO indicator will also blink if Auto ISO is in effect. In that case, the M.M. indicator will be replaced by an exposure compensation icon, because exposure compensation is available in Manual mode when Auto ISO is in effect.

You can then change the shutter speed, aperture, and/or ISO setting to stop the blinking, or you can just leave the settings as they are; you may want to have the overall exposure unusually dark or light for creative purposes.

Of course, you can ignore the M.M. indicator; it is there only to give you an idea of how the camera would meter the scene. You very well may want part or all of the scene to be darker or lighter than the metering would indicate to be "correct."

As with Shutter Priority mode, depending on the setting for the Live View Display menu option, the camera's display may reflect the effect of the current settings on the brightness of the exposure. If you want the camera to show how dark or light the image would be with the current settings in Manual exposure mode, you need to go to screen 2 of the Custom menu and set the Live View Display item to the Setting Effect On option. If you set this menu item to Setting Effect Off, then the display screen or viewfinder will show a normally exposed view, even if an image taken with the current settings would be unusually dark or bright.

With Manual exposure mode, the settings for aperture and shutter speed are independent of each other. When you change one, the other one stays unchanged until you adjust it manually. The camera is leaving the creative decisions about exposure entirely up to you, even if the resulting photograph would be washed out by excessive exposure or underexposed to the point of near-blackness.

The range of apertures you can set in this mode is the same as for Aperture Priority: f/2.8 to f/16. As noted earlier, in Manual mode you can set the aperture to f/16, even though the camera will not choose that setting in Shutter Priority mode.

The overall range of shutter speeds in this mode is the same as for Shutter Priority mode—1/3200 second to 30 seconds. However, as with Aperture Priority and Shutter Priority modes, you can set the speed to 1/2000 second only when the aperture is set to f/4.0 or higher, and you can set speeds of 1/2500 and 1/3200 only when the aperture is f/8.0 or higher.

With Manual exposure mode there is one important addition to the available range of shutter speeds: In Manual mode, you can set the shutter speed to the BULB setting, just beyond the 30-second mark, as shown in FIGURE 3-22.

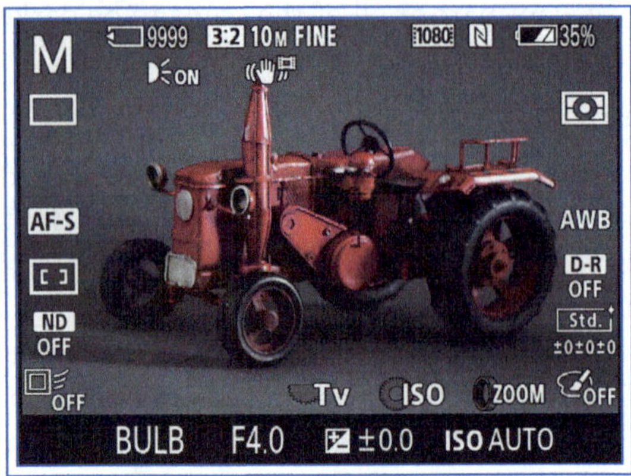

Figure 3-22. BULB Setting on Screen

With this setting, you have to press and hold the shutter button; as long as it is held down, the shutter will stay open. You can use BULB to take photos in almost-complete darkness by holding the shutter open for a minute or longer. One problem with doing so is that it is very difficult to avoid jiggling the camera and thereby causing blur to the image. As discussed in APPENDIX A, you can use Sony's wired remote control, model RM-VPR1, to trigger the camera without touching it. In addition, Sony has provided the RX10 with a threaded shutter button, so you can screw in a standard, mechanical cable release, and trigger the shutter by pressing the plunger on that device.

Another excellent feature of Manual mode on the RX10 is that you can set ISO to Auto. With many other cameras, when the camera is set to Manual mode you have to set ISO to a numerical value, such as 200. (I'll discuss ISO, a measure of the camera's sensitivity to light, in CHAPTER 4.) With the RX10, you can set ISO to Auto and let the camera adjust the ISO value to achieve a good exposure using your chosen shutter speed and aperture, if possible.

This feature can be very useful. For example, suppose you are photographing a craftsman at work on a project on his workbench.

You may want to use a fairly fast shutter speed to stop the action, and a narrow aperture to achieve a broad depth of field to keep as much of the scene in focus as possible. You can make the settings, such as 1/250 second and f/11, and then let the camera adjust the ISO level as necessary in order to expose the image normally.

Another feature available in this mode is Manual Shift, which is similar to Program Shift, discussed earlier. To use Manual Shift, after making your settings rotate the aperture ring while pressing the AEL button. When you do this, as the aperture changes, the camera will reset the shutter speed to a value that maintains the original exposure value. For example, if the original settings were f/5.6 at 1/125 second, when you select Manual Shift and rotate the aperture ring to the f/8.0 position, the camera will set the shutter speed to 1/60 second, maintaining the original exposure. In this way, you can tweak your settings to favor a particular shutter speed or aperture without affecting the overall exposure. An asterisk will appear in the lower right corner of the display while you hold down the AEL button, as shown in Figure 3-23.

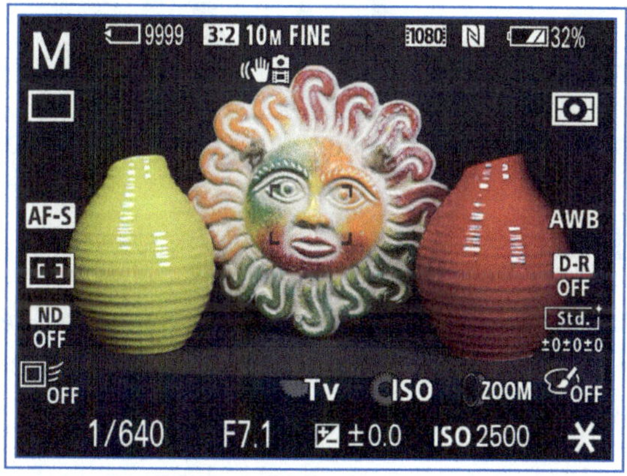

Figure 3-23. Manual Shift Indicator on Screen

I use Manual exposure mode often, for various purposes. One use is for taking a series of images at different exposures to be combined with software into a composite HDR (high dynamic range) image. I will discuss that technique in Chapter 4. I also use Manual mode when using a third-party external flash unit with the RX10, as discussed in Appendix A. In that situation, the flash does not interact with the camera's autoexposure system, so it's necessary to set the exposure manually.

Manual mode also is useful for special applications, such as making silhouettes, when you underexpose the subject heavily in order to emphasize its shape, as shown in Figure 3-24. For this shot, I placed a knight figure in front of a flash with a softbox, and set the RX10 to Manual mode, using f/8.0 for 1/50 second at ISO 200.

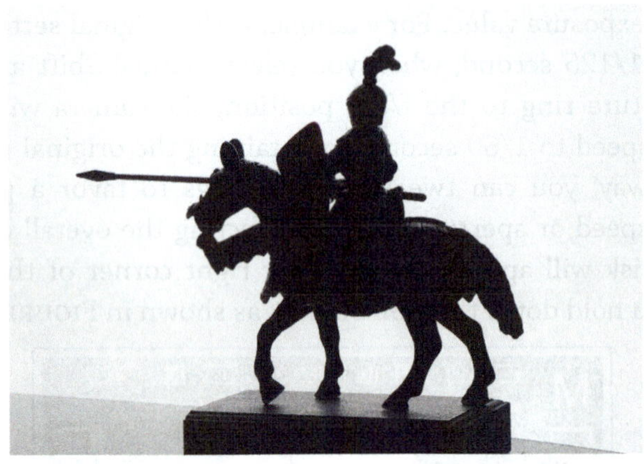

Figure 3-24. Manual Mode, f/8.0, 1/50 Second, ISO 200

Scene Mode

Scene mode, represented by the SCN setting on the mode dial, as shown in Figure 3-25, is quite different from the other shooting modes I have discussed.

This mode does not have a single defining feature, such as permitting control over one or more aspects of exposure. Instead, when you select Scene mode and then choose a particular scene type within that mode, you are telling the camera what sort of environment the picture is being taken in and what type of image you are looking for, and you are letting the camera make the decision as to what settings to use to produce that result.

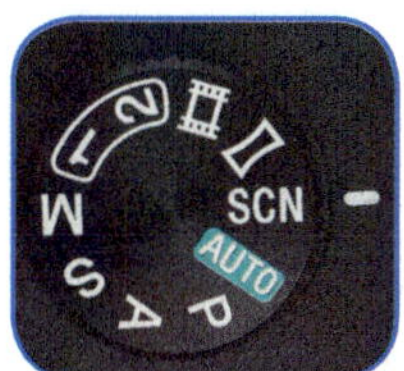

Figure 3-25. Mode Dial Set to Scene Mode

One aspect of using Scene mode is that with most of its settings, you cannot select many of the options that are available in Program, Aperture Priority, Shutter Priority, and Manual Exposure mode, such as Creative Style, Picture Effect, Metering Mode, White Balance, Focus Area, and ISO. There also are some menu settings and control options that are available with certain scene settings but not others, as discussed later in this chapter.

Although some photographers may not like Scene mode because it seems to take creative decisions away from you, I find it useful in various situations. Remember that you don't have to use these scene types only for their labeled purposes; you may find that some of them offer a group of settings that is well suited for shooting scenarios that you regularly encounter. I'll discuss how Scene mode works, and you can decide for yourself whether you might take advantage of it on occasion.

Enter Scene mode by turning the mode dial to the SCN indicator, as in Figure 3-25. Now, unless you want to use the setting that is already in place, you need to select from the list of 9 scene settings. There are several ways to do this, depending on current settings.

If the Mode Dial Guide option is turned on through screen 2 of the Setup menu, then, whenever you turn the mode dial to the SCN setting and press OK, the Scene Selection menu, shown in Figure 3-26, will appear.

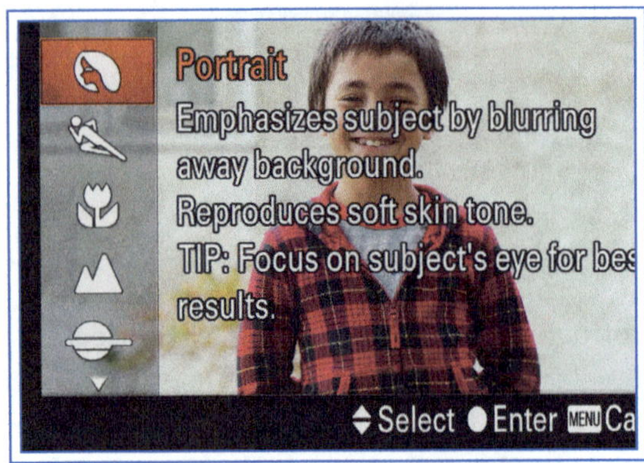

Figure 3-26. Scene Selection Menu Options

If the mode dial guide is not turned on, or if the camera is already set to Scene mode, then you can go to screen 6 of the Shooting menu and call up the Scene Selection item, which produces the same menu as shown in Figure 3-26.

Once the Scene Selection menu is on the display, scroll through the 9 selections on that menu using the Up and Down buttons, the Control wheel, or the Control dial. Press the Center button to select a setting and return to the shooting screen. You will then see an icon for that setting in the upper-left corner of the LCD display. (You may need to press the Display button to see a screen that includes the scene setting icon.) For example, Figure 3-27 shows the display when the Anti Motion Blur setting is selected.

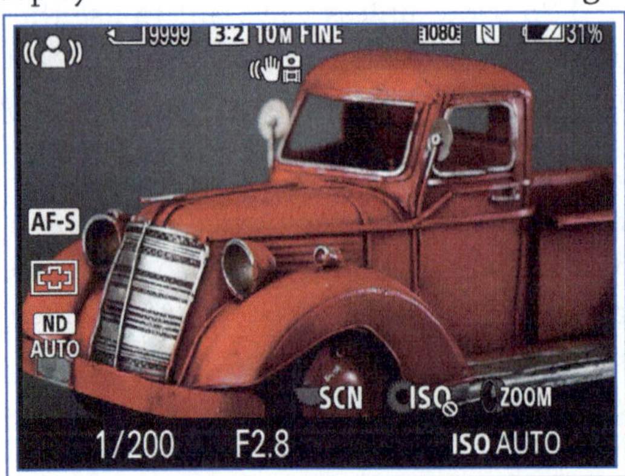

Figure 3-27. Anti Motion Blur Icon on Screen

One helpful point about the Scene mode menu system is that each scene type has a main screen with a brief description of the setting's uses as you move the selector over it, as shown in FIGURE 3-28, so you are not left trying to puzzle out what each icon represents.

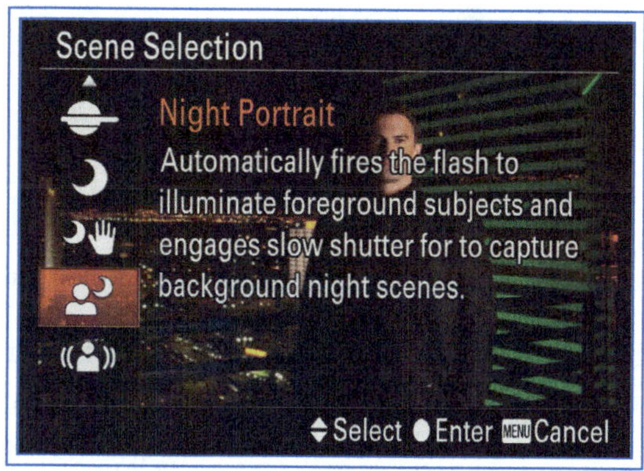

Figure 3-28. Descriptive Text for Scene Mode Setting

As you keep pushing the Up or Down button or using the Control wheel or Control dial to move the selector over the scene type icons, when you reach the bottom or top edge of the screen, the selector wraps around to the first or last icon and continues going.

As I discussed earlier in connection with Intelligent Auto mode, there is an easier way to select the sub-modes, such as Portrait, Landscape, and the like. Go to screen 4 of the Custom menu, choose the Function Menu Settings option, and assign the Shoot Mode option to the Function button. Then, whenever the mode dial is set to Scene, you can press the Function button to bring up the Function menu with the icon for the current Scene mode setting displayed, as shown in FIGURE 3-29.

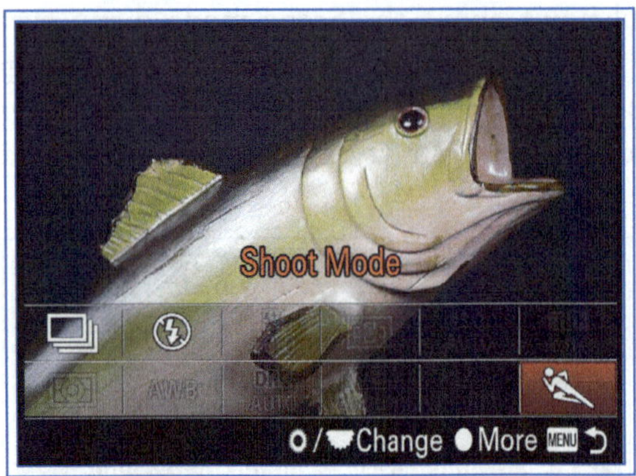

Figure 3-29. Function Menu Showing Shoot Mode Option

Highlight that icon using the Left or Right button and turn the Control wheel to scroll through the available settings (Portrait, Landscape, Sunset, etc.). When your choice is highlighted, press the Function button to exit back to shooting mode.

There is one more, even easier way to switch among the various scene types: Turn the Control dial while the shooting screen is displayed, and the camera will cycle through the scene selections. The scene-type icon will change, in the upper left of the display.

Those are the methods for selecting a scene type. But you need to know something about each option to decide whether it's one you would want to use. In general, each scene setting carries with it a variety of values, including things like focus mode, range of shutter speeds, sensitivity to various colors, and others.

It's helpful to note that some settings are designed for certain types of shooting rather than particular subjects such as sunsets or portraits. For example, the Anti Motion Blur and Hand-held Twilight settings are designed for difficult shooting environments, such as dimly lighted areas.

With that introduction, I will discuss the main features of each of the 9 choices, with a sample image for each of the settings.

Portrait

The Portrait setting is designed to produce flesh tones with a softening effect, as shown in Figure 3-30.

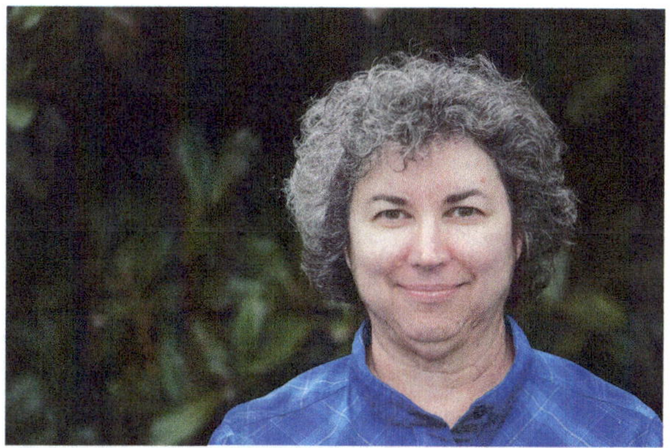

Figure 3-30. Portrait Example

You should stand fairly close to the subject and set the zoom to some degree of telephoto, such as 80mm or higher, so as to blur the background if possible; the camera will try to use a wide aperture to assist in this blurring. You may want to pop up the flash and use the Fill-flash setting to reduce shadows. If you want to improve the lighting, consider using off-camera flash with a softbox, as discussed in Appendix A.

If you are shooting a portrait in front of a busy background, such as a house, try to position the subject's head in front of a plain area, such as a light-colored wall, so the head will be seen clearly.

You can use the self-timer, but you cannot use bracketing or continuous shooting.

Sports Action

The Sports Action setting is for use when lighting is bright and you need to freeze the action of your subjects, such as athletes, children at play, pets, or other objects in motion. Depending on conditions, the camera may set a high ISO value so it can use a fast shutter speed to stop action. The camera sets itself for continuous shooting, so you can hold down the shutter button and capture a burst of images. In that way, you increase your chances of capturing the action at a perfect moment. You can switch to the fastest level of continuous shooting if you want, but you cannot set Drive Mode to single shooting and you cannot use the self-timer or any form of bracketing.

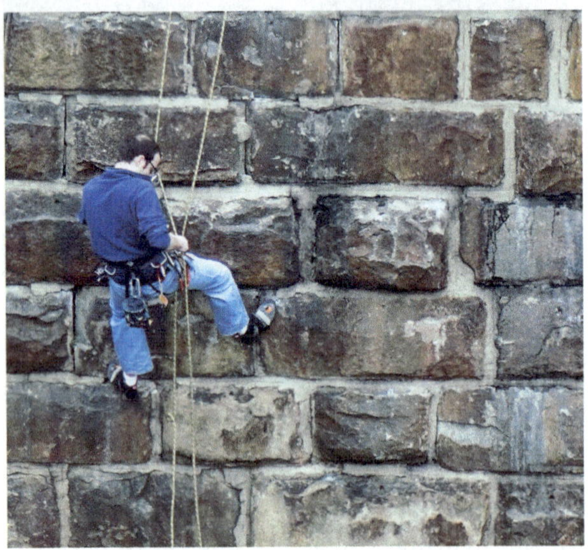

Figure 3-31. Sports Action Example

For the shot of a rope climber in Figure 3-31, the camera set itself to f/2.8 with an ISO setting of 800, which allowed it to use a shutter speed of 1/1250 second to freeze the action. Using the standard continuous shooting setting, I took a burst of several shots to catch this one of the climber descending a stone wall.

Macro

With the Macro setting, the RX10 sets itself up to take closeups. Although you can focus at close range in other shooting modes, it is convenient to use this setting to call up a group of options that are well suited for taking extreme closeups of flowers, insects, or other small objects.

When you select the Macro option, the camera will let you use the self-timer, but you cannot turn on continuous shooting.

With the RX10, there is no special setting for macro focus; in any focus mode, the camera can focus as close as about 1.2 inches (3 cm) when the lens is zoomed out to its wide-angle setting. When the lens is zoomed in all the way to its telephoto setting, it can focus as close as about 12 inches (30 cm).

Even when the camera is set to the Macro setting in Scene mode, you can use the manual focus option. This can be an excellent approach when using Macro because you can fine-tune the focus, which becomes critical and hard to measure precisely when you are photographing insects or other objects in extreme closeups. To use manual focus, just turn the focus switch on the front of the camera, below the lens, to the MF position. Then, use the focus ring on the lens to adjust the focus. You also can use the direct manual focus option; I will discuss focus options further in CHAPTER 4.

In FIGURE 3-32, I used the Macro setting to take a picture of weathered connectors on a fence in a local park. I focused as close to the subject as I could, using the single-autofocus mode. I will discuss other aspects of macro shooting in CHAPTER 9.

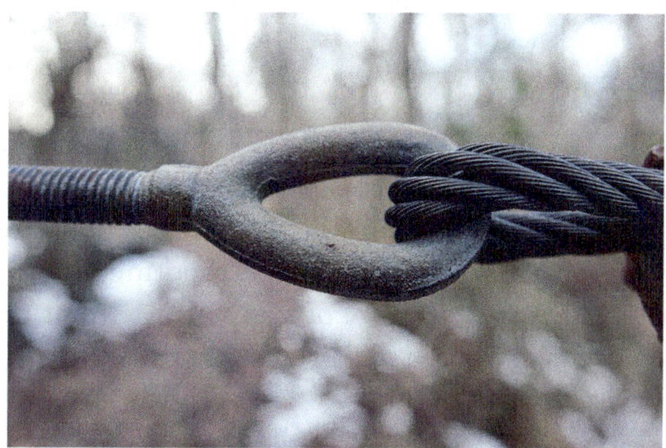

Figure 3-32. Macro Example

Landscape

Landscape is one Scene mode setting that I use often. It is very convenient to turn the mode dial to the SCN position and pull up the Landscape setting when I'm taking pictures at a scenic location. The camera will let you use Fill-flash in case you want to shoot an image of a person close to the camera in front of a building or other attraction, and it boosts the brightness and intensity of colors somewhat. You cannot use continuous shooting, but you can use the self-timer. Figure 3-33 is an example taken using this setting to capture a view of the area under a bridge near the James River.

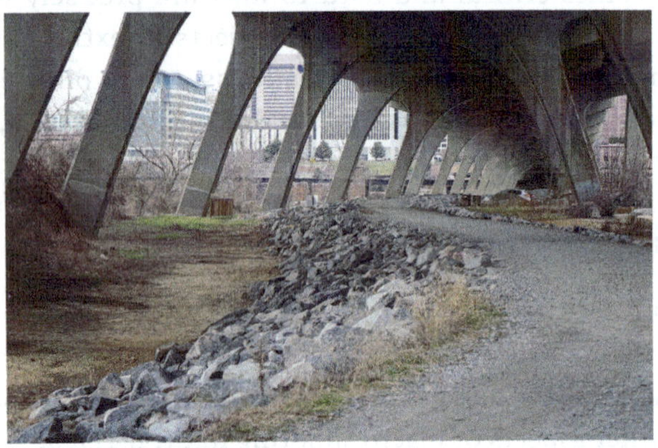

Figure 3-33. Landscape Example

Sunset

This setting is designed to capture the reddish hues of the sky as the sun rises or sets. You can use Fill-flash if you want to, so you can take a portrait of a person with the sunset or sunrise in the background. You cannot use continuous shooting, but you can use the self-timer. The main feature of this setting is that the camera boosts the intensity of the reddish colors in the scene.

Of course, as I noted earlier, you don't have to limit the use of this, or any Scene mode setting, to the subject its name implies. For example, if you are photographing red and orange leaves of trees that are changing colors in autumn, you might want to try the Sunset option to create an enhanced view of the brightly colored foliage. In FIGURE 3-34, I used this setting for a scene at the botanical garden shortly before sunset, to emphasize the warm colors of the late afternoon sky and of the brick plaza.

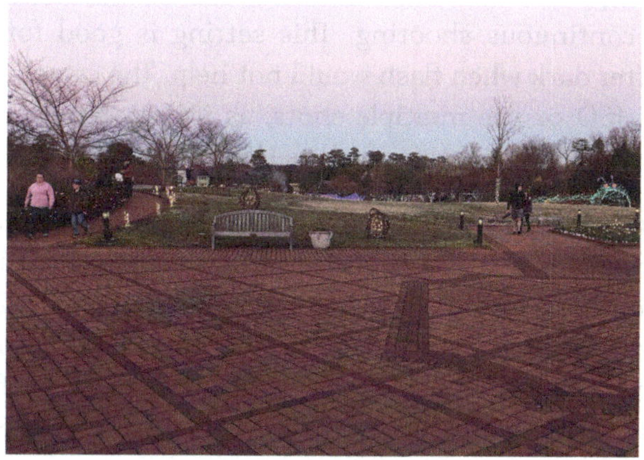

Figure 3-34. Sunset Example

In FIGURE 3-35, I set up an indoor shot using a candle with a colorful sun plaque and two small vases. With the Sunset setting, the image took on a much warmer look than normal, with an appearance somewhat like firelight.

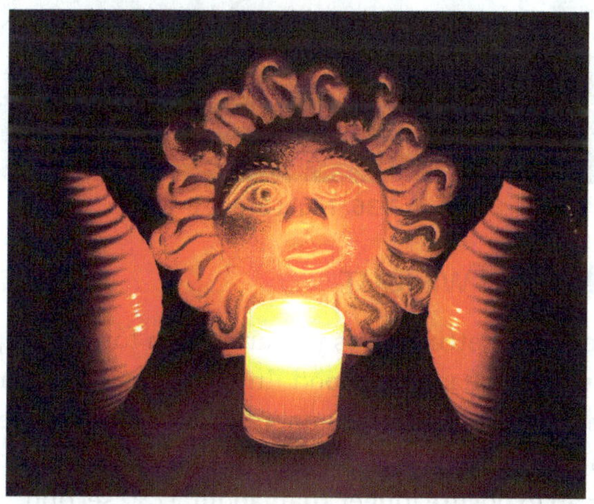

Figure 3-35. Sunset Scene Setting Used for Indoor Shot

Night Scene

The Night Scene setting is designed to preserve the natural look of a nocturnal setting. The camera disables the flash; if the scene is quite dark, you should use a tripod to avoid camera motion during the long exposure that may be needed. You can use the self-timer, but not continuous shooting. This setting is good for outdoor scenes after dark when flash would not help. The camera does not raise the ISO or use multiple shots, as it does with some other modes used in dim lighting, such as Hand-held Twilight.

In Figure 3-36, I used the Night Scene setting to photograph the lighted conservatory at the local botanical garden. I had the camera on a tripod and used the self-timer with its 2-second setting to avoid camera shake. The camera used a relatively long shutter speed of 0.3 second with an aperture of f/2.8 and preserved image quality by using a low ISO setting of 125.

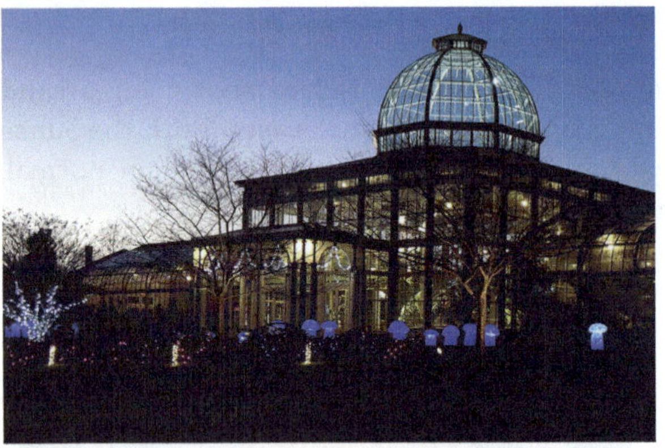

Figure 3-36. Night Scene Example

Hand-Held Twilight

This Scene mode setting gives you an option for taking pictures in low light without flash or tripod. In dim lighting, blurring of the image can happen when the camera uses a slow shutter speed to expose the image properly, because it is hard to hold the camera steady for an exposure longer than about 1/30 second.

To counter the effects of blurring, with Hand-held Twilight the camera raises the ISO to a higher-than-normal level so it can use a fast shutter speed and still admit enough light to expose the image properly. Because higher ISO settings result in increased noise, the RX10 takes a burst of shots and combines them through internal processing into a single composite image with reduced noise.

Hand-held Twilight is useful for a landscape or other static subject at night when you cannot use a tripod or flash. If you can use a tripod, you might be better off using the Night Scene setting, discussed above. Or, if you don't mind using flash, you could just use Intelligent Auto, Program, or one of the more ordinary shooting modes. Hand-held Twilight is a very useful option when it's needed, but it will not yield the same overall quality as a shot at a lower ISO with the camera on a steady support.

With Hand-held Twilight, you cannot use any Drive Mode or Flash Mode settings. The flash is forced off, and the camera is set for single shooting only; you cannot use the self-timer. If Quality is set to Raw, the camera will change it to Fine temporarily.

In FIGURE 3-37, I used this setting at the botanical garden for a hand-held shot of the conservatory building and a lighted fountain.

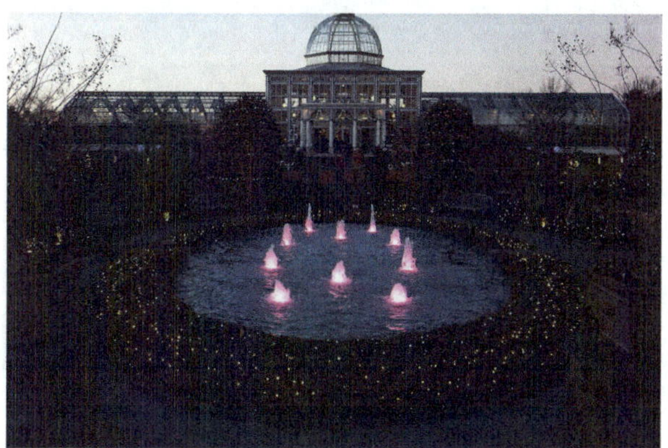

Figure 3-37. Hand-held Twilight Example

The camera shot this image at f/2.8 and set the ISO to 200, with a shutter speed of 1/40 second, fast enough to hand-hold the camera without noticeable motion blur. As I noted above, this setting is excellent for hand-held shots of motionless subjects in dim light. If there is motion involved, you may do better with the Anti Motion Blur setting, discussed later in this section.

Night Portrait

This night-oriented setting is for taking a portrait when you are willing to use flash. With Night Portrait, the camera takes only one shot and it activates the flash in Slow Sync mode. I will discuss the Slow Sync setting and provide an example in Chapter 4. Basically, with this Flash Mode setting, the camera uses a slow shutter speed, so that as the flash illuminates the portrait subject in the foreground, there is enough time for the natural light to illuminate the background also. You cannot use the Flash Off setting for Flash Mode, though you can leave the flash unit retracted, and the camera will still let you take the picture.

You can use the self-timer, but not continuous shooting. Because of the slow shutter speed, you should use a tripod if possible to avoid motion blur.

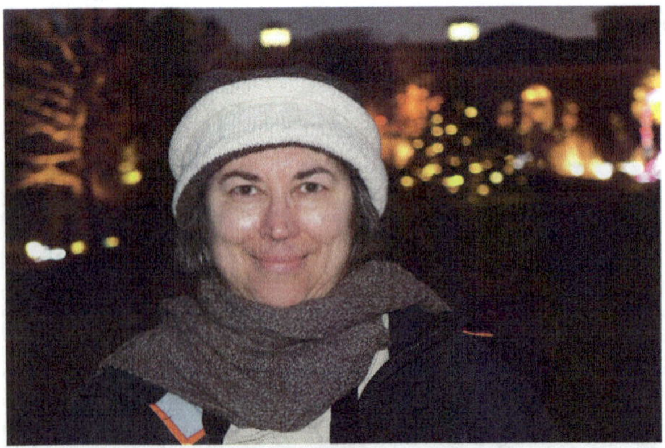

Figure 3-38. Night Portrait Example

In FIGURE 3-38, the lights in the background show up fairly clearly because the camera used a slow shutter speed of 1/4 second. I used a tripod, which eliminated camera shake, but you also should advise the subject not to move during the long exposure.

Anti Motion Blur

Like other night-oriented options, this Scene mode setting is not meant for a particular subject, but for dim lighting, using a technique similar to that used by the Hand-held Twilight setting, discussed above. Just as with Hand-held Twilight, with Anti Motion Blur the camera raises the ISO to a higher-than-normal level, takes a burst of shots, and combines them into a single composite image with reduced noise. What is remarkable about this setting, though, is that the camera also counteracts blur from motion of the subject to a fair extent, by analyzing the shots and rejecting those with motion blur as much as possible.

The Anti Motion Blur setting is likely to use a higher ISO setting than Hand-held Twilight to maximize the camera's ability to capture the scene in dim light. Anti Motion Blur is useful as the light is fading if you don't want to use flash, as shown in FIGURE 3-39. For this image, taken shortly after sunset, the camera used a high ISO setting along with its multiple-shot processing.

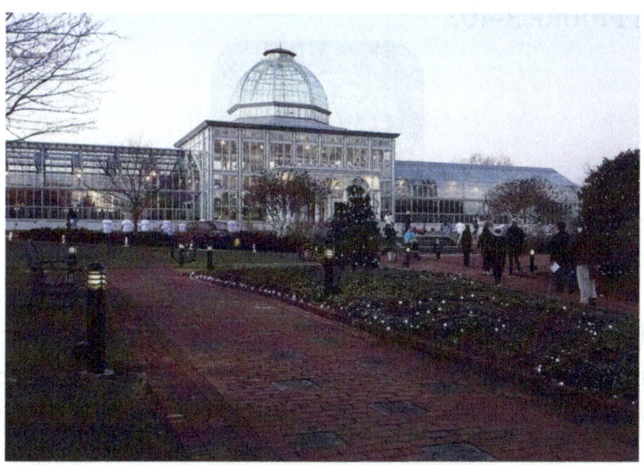

Figure 3-39. Anti Motion Blur Example

You should not expect good results if you use this setting with fast-moving subjects, because the camera will not be able to eliminate the motion blur. With slower-moving subjects, though, like the people in FIGURE 3-39, the RX10 can do a good job of minimizing blur. With this setting, you cannot set the Drive Mode or the Flash Mode. As with Hand-held Twilight, if Quality is set to Raw, the camera will change it to Fine while this setting is in use.

Sweep Panorama Mode

The next setting on the mode dial is designed for a specific purpose—the shooting of panoramic images. The RX10, like many other Sony cameras, has an excellent ability to automate the capture of panoramas. If you follow the fairly simple steps involved, the camera will stitch together a series of images internally and produce a high-quality final result with a dramatic, wide (or tall) view of a scenic vista or other subject that lends itself to panoramic depiction.

It is significant that Sony has given this shooting mode its own spot on the mode dial, indicating the importance of this type of photography nowadays. Because of this placement on the dial, you can quickly set the camera to take panoramas. Just turn the mode dial to select the icon that looks like a long, squeezed rectangle, as shown in FIGURE 3-40.

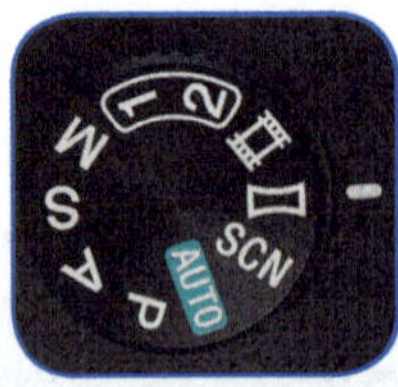

Figure 3-40. Mode Dial Set to Sweep Panorama Mode

You will immediately see a message telling you to press the shutter button and move the camera in the direction of the arrow that appears on the screen, as shown, in FIGURE 3-41.

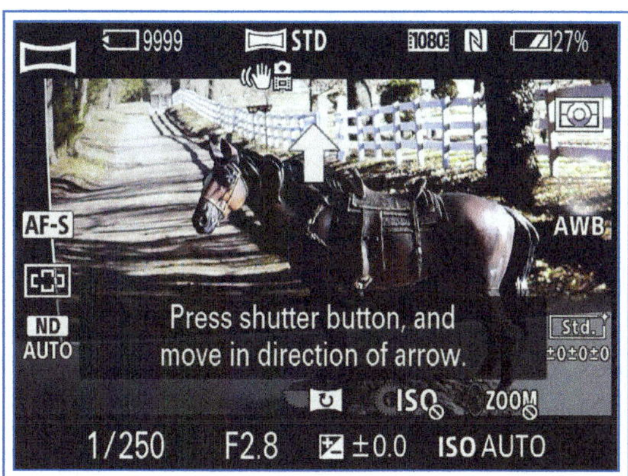

Figure 3-41. Prompt Message for Panorama Shot

At that point, you can follow the directions and likely get excellent results. However, the camera allows you to make a number of choices for your panoramic images using the Shooting menu. Just press the Menu button, and you will go to the menu screen that is currently being displayed.

Navigate to the Shooting menu, which limits you to fewer choices than in most other shooting modes because several options are not appropriate for panoramas. For example, the Image Size, Aspect Ratio, and Quality settings are dimmed and unavailable. Also, options such as Drive Mode, Flash Mode, and Focus Area are of no use in this situation and cannot be selected. In addition, you will not be able to zoom the lens in; it will be fixed at its wide-angle position. (If the lens was zoomed in previously, it will zoom back out automatically when you switch the mode dial to the Sweep Panorama selection.)

You will, however, see two options on screen 1 of the Shooting menu that are not available for selection in any other shooting mode: Panorama Size and Panorama Direction, as shown in Figure 3-42.

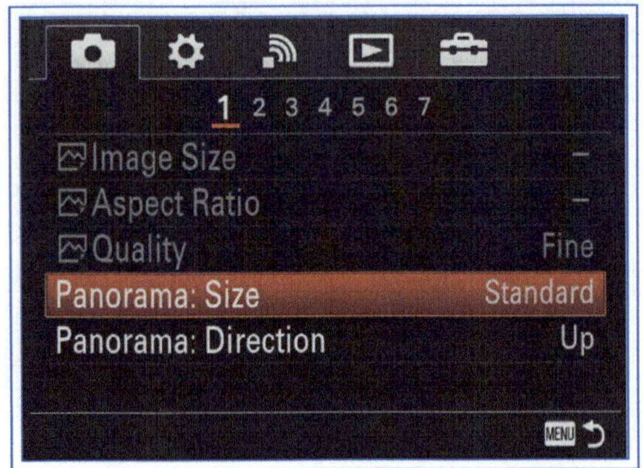

Figure 3-42. Panorama Size and Direction Menu Options

If you select Panorama Size, you will see two options, Standard and Wide.

With Standard, a horizontal panorama will have a size of 8192 by 1856 pixels, which is a resolution of about 15 megapixels (MP). If you choose Wide, a horizontal panorama will have a size of 12416 by 1856 pixels, resulting in a resolution of about 23 MP. (This figure is larger than the camera's maximum resolution of 20 MP because with the panorama settings, the camera is taking multiple images and stitching them together.)

A vertical panorama at the Standard setting is 3872 by 2160 pixels, or about 8.3 MP; a vertical panorama at the Wide setting is 5536 by 2160 pixels, or about 12 MP.

The Panorama Direction option lets you choose Right, Left, Up, or Down for the direction in which you will sweep the camera to create the panorama.

There is a very convenient shortcut for choosing the direction for your panorama. Just turn the Control dial while the panorama shooting screen is displayed, and the direction arrow will change to a different position. You can cycle through all four positions with quick turns of this dial.

Also, you can use the Direction setting with different orientations of the camera to get different results than usual. For example, if you set the direction to Up and then hold the camera sideways while you sweep it to the right, you will create a horizontal panorama that has 2160 pixels in its vertical dimension rather than the standard 1856.

Those are the main settings for panoramas. There are a few other options you can select for panoramas on the Shooting menu, including Metering Mode, White Balance, Creative Style, and SteadyShot. I will discuss all of these menu options in CHAPTER 4. You also can set the focus mode using the focus mode switch. In my opinion, the best options for these settings for shooting panoramas are the ones shown in TABLE 3-1, at least as a starting point.

Table 3-1. Suggested Settings for Panoramas

Focus Mode	Single-shot AF
Metering Mode	Multi
White Balance	Auto White Balance
Creative Style	Standard
SteadyShot	On, or use tripod

One other setting you can make when shooting panoramas is exposure compensation, using the exposure compensation dial. I will discuss that function in CHAPTER 5. In the context of shooting panoramas, this feature can be quite useful because the camera will not change the exposure if the camera is pointed at areas with varying brightness. So, for example, if you start sweeping from a dark area on the left, the camera will set the exposure for that area. If you then sweep the camera to the right over a bright area, that part of the panorama will be overexposed and possibly washed out in excessive brightness. To correct for this effect, you can reduce the exposure using exposure compensation. In this way, the initial dark area will be underexposed, but the brighter area should be properly exposed. Of course, you have to decide what part of the panorama is the one you most want to have the proper exposure.

Another way to deal with this issue is to point the camera at the bright area before starting the shot and press the shutter button halfway to lock the exposure, then go back to the dark area at the left and start sweeping the camera. In that way, the exposure will be locked at the proper level for the bright area.

Once you have made all of the settings you want for your panorama, follow the directions on the screen. Press and release the shutter button and start moving the camera at a steady rate in the direction you have chosen. I tend to shoot my panoramas moving the camera from left to right, but you may have a different preference. You will hear a steady clicking as the camera takes multiple shots during the sweep of the panorama. A white box and arrow will move across the screen; your task is to finish the camera's sweep at the same moment that the box and arrow finish their travel across the scene. If you move the camera too quickly or too slowly, the panorama will not succeed; if that happens, just try again.

Generally speaking, panoramas work best when the scene does not contain moving objects such as cars or pedestrians because when items are in motion, the multiple shots are likely to capture images of the same object more than once in different positions.

It is advisable to use a tripod if possible, so you can keep the camera steady in a single plane as it moves. If you don't have a tripod available, you might try using the electronic level that Sony provides with the RX10. You have to activate the level using the Display Button option on screen 2 of the Custom menu, as discussed in Chapter 7. Then press the Display button until the screen with the electronic level appears. Make sure the outer tips of the level stay green as much as possible, and the resulting panorama should benefit from the level shooting.

In addition to exposure, as discussed above, focus and White Balance are fixed as soon as the first image is taken for the panorama.

When a panoramic shot is played back in the camera, it is initially displayed at a small size so the whole image can fit on the display screen. You can then press the Center button to make the panorama scroll across the display at a larger size, using the full height of the screen.

FIGURE 3-43 and FIGURE 3-44 are sample panoramas, both shot from left to right using the Standard setting, hand-held.

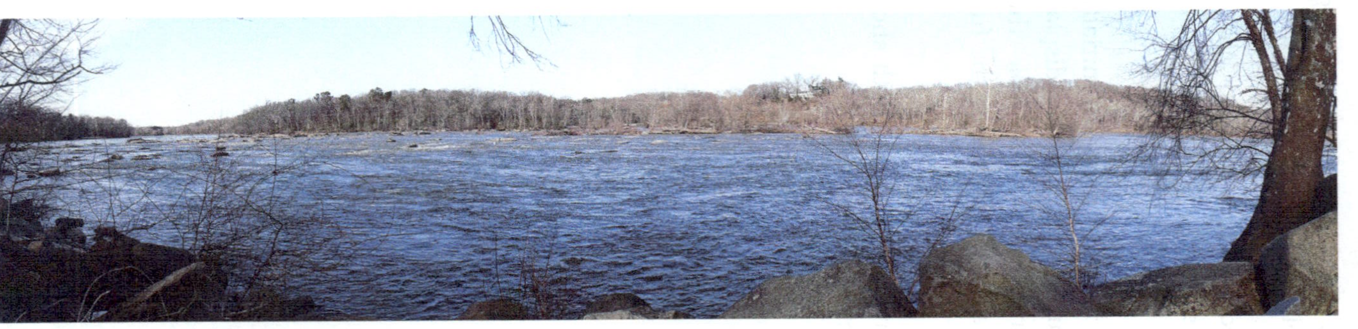

Figure 3-43. Panorama: James River Viewed from Pony Pasture Rapids, Richmond, Virginia

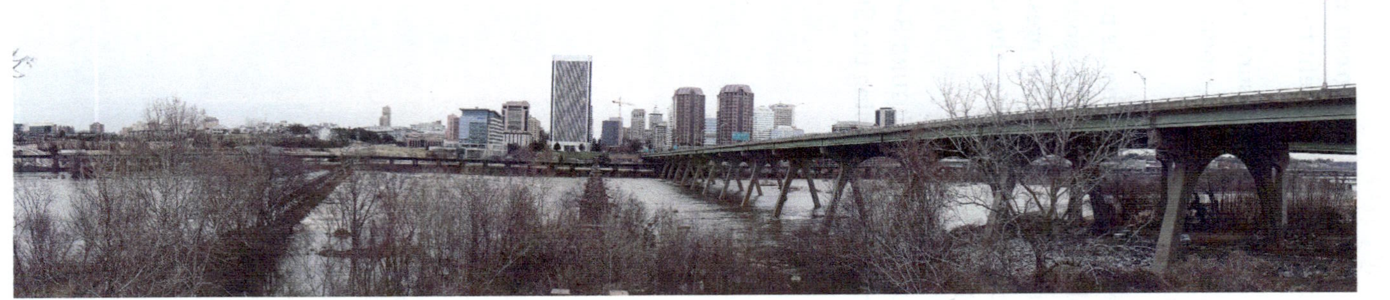

Figure 3-44. Panorama: Skyline of Richmond, Virginia

Memory Recall Mode

There is one more shooting mode left to discuss, apart from Movie mode, which I will discuss in CHAPTER 8. This last mode, called Memory Recall, is a powerful tool that gives you expanded options for your photography.

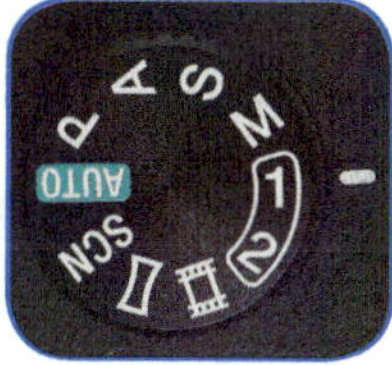

Figure 3-45. Mode Dial at Memory Recall Position 1

When you turn the mode dial to one of the two numbered positions, 1 or 2 (as shown in FIGURE 3-45), you are, in effect, selecting a custom-made shooting mode that you create with your own favorite settings. You can set up the camera just as you want it—with stored values for items such as shooting mode, shutter speed, aperture, zoom amount, White Balance, ISO, and other menu settings—and then recall all of those values instantly just by turning the mode dial to either position 1 or position 2, depending on which one you used to store those settings. With the RX10, unlike some other camera models, you can store settings for any shooting mode, including the Intelligent Auto and Scene modes.

Here is how this works. First, set up the camera with all of the settings you want to recall. For example, suppose you are going to do street photography. You may want to use a fast shutter speed, say 1/250 second, in black and white, at ISO 800, using continuous shooting with autofocus, Large and Extra Fine JPEG images, and shooting in the 4:3 aspect ratio.

The first step is to make all of these settings. Set the mode dial to Shutter Priority and use the Control dial to set a shutter speed of 1/250 second. Then press the Menu button to call up the Shooting menu and, on screen 1, select L for the image size, 4:3 for Aspect

Ratio, and Extra Fine for Quality. Then move to screen 2 and choose continuous shooting for Drive Mode. On screen 3, set ISO to 800, then on screen 4 set White Balance to Daylight. Next, scroll down two positions to the Creative Style option and select the B/W setting, for black and white. You also may want to push the zoom lever all the way to the left for wide-angle shooting. You can set any other available Shooting menu options as you wish, but the ones listed above are the ones I will consider for now.

Once these settings are made, press the Menu button (if the menu isn't still on the screen) to call up the Shooting menu, and navigate to the Memory item, shown in FIGURE 3-46, which is the final item on the last screen of the menu.

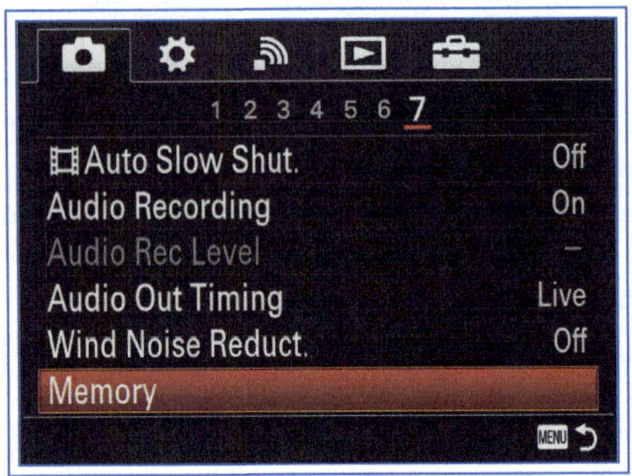

Figure 3-46. Memory Menu Option

After you press the Center button, you will see a screen like the one in FIGURE 3-47, showing icons and values for all of the settings currently in effect and the numbers 1 and 2 at the upper-right corner of the display. The message "Select Register" appears at the upper left of the screen, indicating that you can now assign all of the settings shown on the display to register number 1 or 2 of the Memory Recall mode. In the example shown here, the number 1 is highlighted. Now press the Center button, and you will have selected register 1 to store all of the settings you just made.

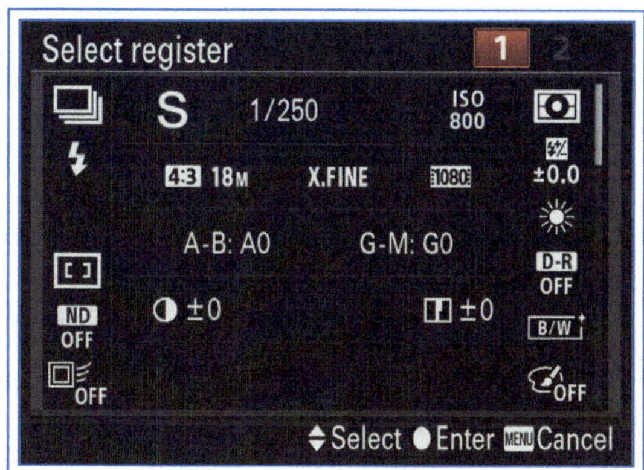

Figure 3-47. Memory Settings Screen

Note the short gray bar at the right side of the Memory screen shown in Figure 3-47. That bar indicates that you can scroll down through other screens to see additional settings that are in effect, such as ISO Auto Maximum and Minimum, AF Illuminator, SteadyShot, and several others. Use the Up and Down buttons to scroll through those screens.

Next, to check how this worked, try making some very different settings, such as setting the camera for Manual exposure with a shutter speed of 1 second, Creative Style set to Vivid, continuous shooting turned off, the zoom lever moved all the way to the right for telephoto, and Quality set to Raw. Then turn the mode dial back to the number 1 MR position. You will see that all of the custom settings you made have instantly returned, including the zoom position, shutter speed, and everything else. You can then press the Center button to exit back to the shooting screen and continue shooting with those settings.

This is a wonderful feature, and it is more powerful than similar options on some other cameras, which can save menu settings but not values such as shutter speed and zoom position, or can save settings only for the less-automatic shooting modes, but not the Scene and Auto modes. What is also quite amazing is that if you now switch back to Manual exposure mode, the camera will restore the settings that you had in that mode before you turned to the MR mode. (The position of the zoom lens will not revert to where it was, though.)

This mode is very versatile, because you can store many settings for any shooting mode, including Program, Aperture Priority, Shutter Priority, Manual Exposure, and even the Scene, Auto, Sweep Panorama, and Movie modes. You can store settings from the Shooting menu, as well as the shutter speed and optical zoom settings. So, for example, you could set up one of the two memory registers to recall Scene mode using the Macro setting, with the lens zoomed back to its wide-angle position. In that way, you could be ready for closeup shooting on a moment's notice.

There are some important settings you cannot save to a Memory Recall slot: focus mode, aperture, and exposure compensation, all of which are controlled by physical dials or controls. Presumably, Sony decided it would be confusing to let you store these settings, which could mean the actual setting could be in conflict with the position of the control that adjusts it. So, if you call up a group of settings using a numbered slot on the mode dial, you need to remember to make any other settings that require the use of a physical control. In the example discussed above, you would need to turn the focus switch to the C position for continuous autofocus, in order to have the camera adjust its focus between shots.

Overall, though, this feature is powerful and useful. With one twist of the mode dial, you can call up a complete group of settings tailored for a particular type of shooting. It is worth your while to experiment with this feature and develop two groups of settings that work well for your shooting needs.

Chapter 4: The Shooting Menu

The Shooting menu, symbolized by the camera icon, is the most important of the RX10's menu systems. On its 7 screens, it provides settings for many critical adjustments, including Image Size, Quality, Drive Mode, Flash Mode, Focus Area, ISO, Metering Mode, White Balance, and numerous others. There are some items that are adjusted outside the menu system, such as focus mode and exposure compensation, but, unless you are content to use the default settings provided by Intelligent Auto mode or a Scene mode setting, you will be using the options on the Shooting menu heavily.

The available menu options vary depending on the setting of the mode dial on top of the camera. For example, if the camera is set to Intelligent Auto mode, the menu options are fairly limited because that mode is designed for a user who doesn't want to make many settings. In Sweep Panorama mode, the options also are limited because of the specialized nature of that mode. For the following discussion, I'm assuming you have the camera set to Program mode, because with that mode you have access to most of the options on the Shooting menu.

Turn the mode dial to P, which represents Program mode, as shown in Figure 4-1.

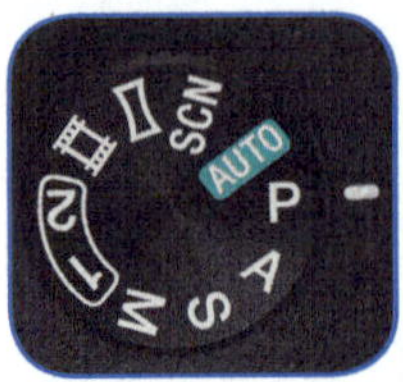

Figure 4-1. Mode Dial Set to Program Mode

For the following discussion, I'm assuming you have not turned on the Tile Menu option on screen 2 of the Setup menu; that option displays a different, "tiled" menu screen before you get to the main menu screen, as discussed in CHAPTER 7.

Enter the menu system by pressing the Menu button and look at the top line, with 5 icons that represent the five menu systems. From left to right, they are: Shooting (camera icon); Custom (gear); Wi-Fi (Wi-Fi icon); Playback (triangle); and Setup (toolbox). The last menu that you used will be highlighted by a black area with thin gray lines around it. For example FIGURE 4-2 shows the display when the Custom menu is active.

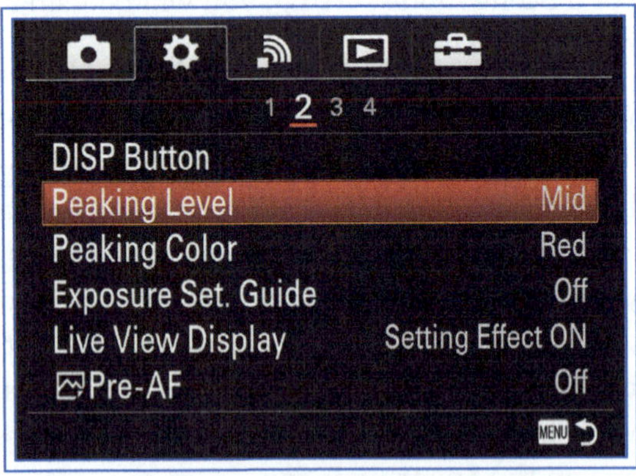

Figure 4-2. Gear Icon for Custom Menu Highlighted on Menu Screen

To move quickly through the icons for the 5 menus, press the Up button to place the orange highlight in the line of icons. Then press the Left or Right button or turn the Control dial to move the highlight to the icon for the menu you want to use. If you start from the screen in FIGURE 4-2, press the Up button twice to highlight the gear, then press the Left button to move to the camera icon for the Shooting menu, as shown in FIGURE 4-3.

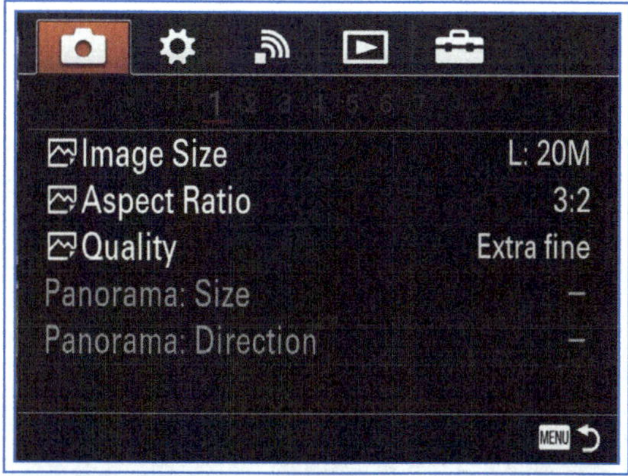

Figure 4-3. Camera Icon for Shooting Menu Highlighted

Then, press the Down button, and the orange highlight will move to the first item on screen 1 of the Shooting menu, Image Size, as shown later, in FIGURE 4-5. The number 1 near the top of the screen will have an orange line beneath it to show that the first screen of this menu is currently displayed. You can move through the 7 numbered screens of the menu using the Right button or the Control dial to reach the screen you want. Or, if you want to move through the items on screen 1, use the Down button or turn the Control wheel to scroll through these items.

In this chapter, I will discuss only the Shooting menu; I will discuss the other menu systems in CHAPTER 6 (Playback), CHAPTER 7 (Custom and Setup), and CHAPTER 9 (Wi-Fi).

The Shooting menu contains numerous options divided among the 7 numbered screens. In most cases, each option (such as Image Size) occupies one line, with its name on the left and its current setting (such as L: 20M) on the right. In other cases (such as Auto Mode, Scene Selection, and Movie), there may be only a small dash on the right side of the screen, meaning you have to press the Center button (middle of the Control wheel) to get access to further options, or that the selection is not currently applicable. For example, if the camera is set to Program mode, the Scene Selection item on screen 6 of the Shooting menu will be followed by a dash, because no scene type can be selected when the camera is set to Program mode.

You also will see that some items on the menu screens are dimmed, as the Auto Mode, Scene Selection, and Movie options are in FIGURE 4-4, for example.

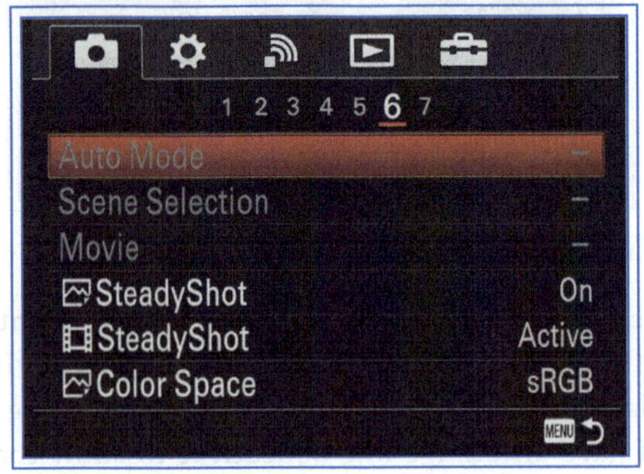

Figure 4-4. Several Options Dimmed on Shooting Menu

This means that those options are not available for selection in the current context. In this case, the camera was set to Program mode; the Auto Mode option is available only when the mode dial is set to AUTO, the Scene Selection option is available only when the mode dial is set to Scene mode, and the Movie option is available only when the mode dial is set to Movie mode.

To follow the discussion below of the options on the Shooting menu, leave the shooting mode set to Program, which gives you access to all but a few options on the Shooting menu. (I'll also discuss the options that are available in other modes as I come to them.) I'll start at the top of screen 1 and discuss each option on the way down the list for each of the 7 screens.

The first screen of this menu is shown in FIGURE 4-5.

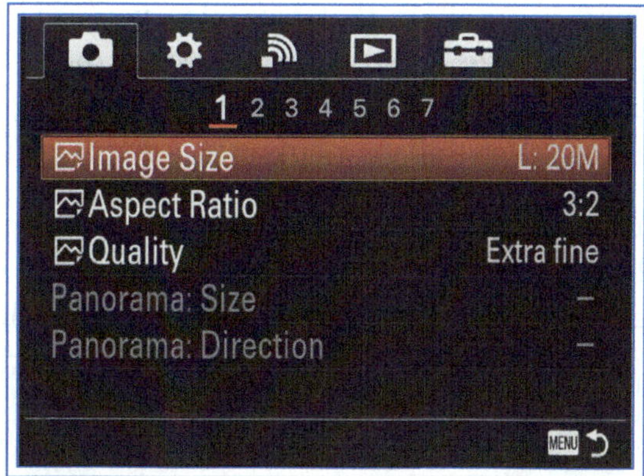

Figure 4-5. Screen 1 of Shooting Menu

Image Size

This first option lets you select the resolution, or pixel count, of still images. The Image Size setting is related to the next two entries on the menu, Aspect Ratio and Quality, to control the overall appearance and "quality" of your images, in a broad sense.

The Image Size setting itself controls only the size in pixels of the image that is recorded by the camera. The Sony RX10 has an unusually large digital sensor for a camera of its type, and that sensor has a high maximum resolution. The sensor is capable of recording a still image with 5472 pixels, or individual points of light, in the horizontal direction and 3648 pixels vertically. When you multiply those two numbers together, the result is about 20 million pixels, often referred to as megapixels, MP, or M.

The resolution of still images is important mainly for printing your images. If you need to produce large prints (say, 8 by 10 inches or 20 by 25 cm), you should select a high-resolution setting for Image Size. You also should choose the largest setting if you believe you may need to crop out a small portion of the image and enlarge it for closer viewing. For example, if you are shooting photos of wildlife and the animal or bird you are interested in is in the distance, you may need to enlarge the image digitally to see that subject in detail. In that case, also, you need the highest setting for Image Size. Even when you don't need to print or enlarge your images, though, I recommend choosing the largest size in order to preserve all your options, as discussed later.

Available settings for Image Size with are L, M, S, and VGA, for Large, Medium, Small, and VGA, as shown in Figure 4-6. Not all of these are available in all situations, as I'll discuss below.

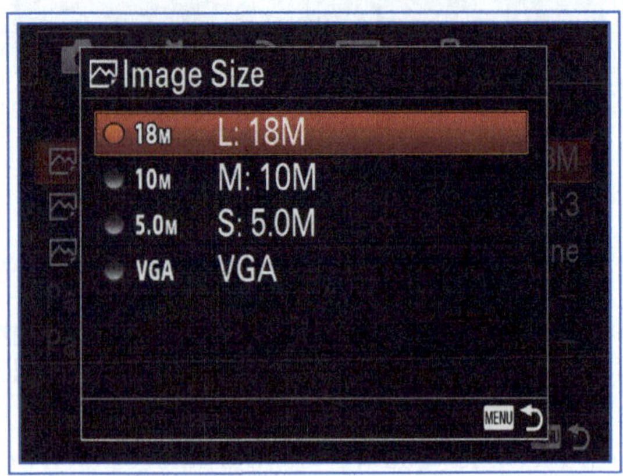

Figure 4-6. Image Size Menu Options Screen

When you select one of the first three of these options from the Shooting menu, the camera will display a setting such as L: 18M, meaning Large: 18 megapixels. The number of megapixels will change depending on the setting for Aspect Ratio, discussed below. This change occurs because when the shape of the image changes, the number of horizontal pixels or the number of vertical pixels changes also to form the new shape. For example, if the Aspect Ratio setting is 3:2, the maximum number of pixels is used because 3:2 is the aspect ratio of the camera's sensor. However, if you set Aspect Ratio to 16:9, the number of horizontal pixels (5472) stays the same, but the number of vertical pixels is reduced from 3648 to 3080 to form the 16:9 ratio of horizontal to vertical pixels. When you multiply those two numbers (5472 and 3080) together, the result is about 17 million pixels, which the camera states as 17M, as shown in Figure 4-7.

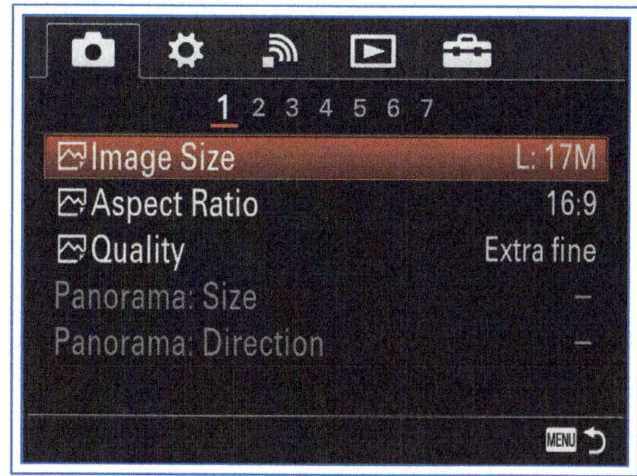

Figure 4-7. Menu Screen When Aspect Ratio Set to 16:9

VGA, the smallest setting, is available only if Aspect Ratio is set to 4:3. Otherwise, this option does not appear on the menu. VGA stands for video graphics array, a term used for older computer screens, which have a 4:3 aspect ratio. The pixel count for this setting is low—640 by 480 pixels, a resolution of 0.3 M, less than one megapixel. This small size is good if you need to send images by e-mail or need to store a great many images on a memory card.

One of the few reasons to choose an Image Size smaller than L would be if you were running out of space on your memory card and had to keep taking pictures in an important situation. Table 4-1 shows approximately how many images can be stored on an 8 GB memory card for various settings.

Table 4-1. Images That Fit on 8 GB Card with Aspect Ratio at 3:2

	Large	Medium	Small
Raw & JPEG	235	290	315
Raw	355	—	—
Extra Fine	520	865	1300
Fine	700	1295	1995
Standard	1200	2020	2870

As you can see, if you use an 8 GB SD card, which is a fairly reasonable size nowadays, you can fit about 235 images on the card even at the maximum settings of 3:2 for Aspect Ratio, Large for Image Size, and Raw & JPEG for Quality. If you limit image quality to Extra Fine, with no Raw images, you can fit about 520 images on the card. If you reduce Image Size to Small, you can store roughly 1,200 images. I am unlikely ever to need more than about 300 images in any one session. And, of course, I can use a larger memory card or multiple memory cards.

If space on your memory card is not a consideration, I recommend you use the L setting at all times. You never know when you might need the larger-sized image, so you might as well use the L setting and be safe. Your situation might be different, of course. If you take photos for a purpose such as making identification cards, you might use the Small setting to store the maximum number of images on a memory card and reduce expense. For general photography, though, I rarely use any setting other than L for Image Size. (One exception is when I want to increase the range of the optical zoom lens without losing image quality; see the discussion of Clear Image Zoom and related topics later in this chapter.)

One more note: when Quality, discussed later in this chapter, is set to Raw, the Image Size option is dimmed and unavailable for selection because you cannot select an image size for Raw images; they are always at the maximum size, as shown in Table 4-1. With the Raw & JPEG setting, though, you can still select a value for Image Size; that value will apply to the JPEG file that is created along with the Raw file.

Aspect Ratio

This second option on the Shooting menu lets you choose the shape of your still images. The choices are the default of 3:2, as well as 16:9, 4:3, and 1:1, as shown in Figure 4-8.

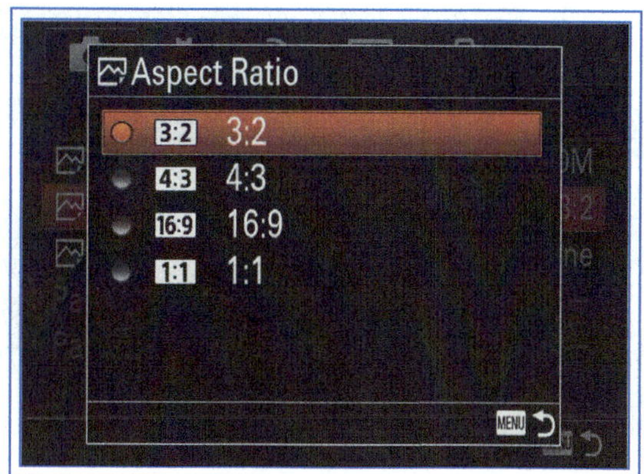

Figure 4-8. Aspect Ratio Menu Options Screen

As I discussed under Image Size, above, these numbers represent the ratio of the width to the height. For example, with the 16:9 setting, the image is 16 units wide for every 9 units of height. The aspect ratio that uses all pixels on the image sensor is 3:2. With any other aspect ratio, some of the pixels are cropped out.

If you want to record every possible pixel, you should use the 3:2 setting. If you shoot using that setting, you can always alter the aspect ratio of the image later with editing software such as Photoshop by cropping away parts of the image. However, if you want to have your final images in a certain shape, such as 16:9 for viewing on an HDTV, and don't plan to do post-processing on a computer, the aspect ratio settings of this menu item may be just what you want. It also can be helpful to set the aspect ratio if you want to compose your image in the camera using the appropriate shape on the camera's display screen.

The RX10 provides more options in this area than many other cameras do. After each of the aspect ratios discussed below, I am including an image I took of a scene I set up to illustrate the areas that are included or cropped out for the various settings.

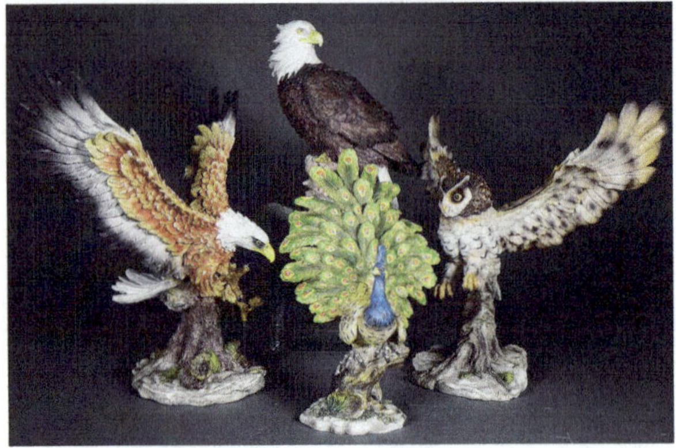

Figure 4-9. Aspect Ratio 3:2

The default 3:2 setting, seen in FIGURE 4-9, has the maximum number of pixels and is the ratio used by traditional 35mm film. This aspect ratio can be used without cropping to make prints in the common U.S. size of 6 inches by 4 inches (15 cm by 10 cm).

The 4:3 setting, shown in FIGURE 4-10, is in the shape of a traditional (non-widescreen) computer screen, so if you want to view your images on that sort of display, this may be your preferred aspect ratio.

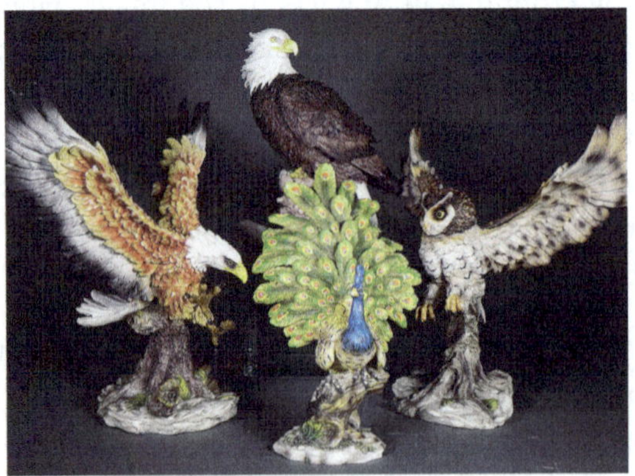

Figure 4-10. Aspect Ratio 4:3

Also, as was discussed earlier in connection with Image Size, if you want to use the VGA setting for Image Size, the camera must be set to the 4:3 aspect ratio. With this setting, some pixels are lost at the left and right sides of the image.

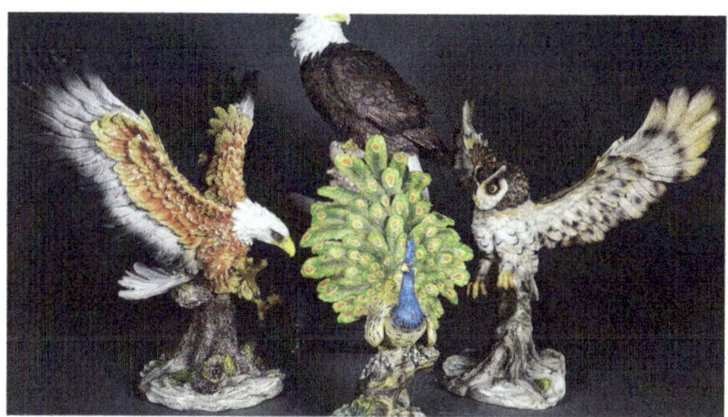

Figure 4-11. Aspect Ratio 16:9

The 16:9 setting, illustrated in FIGURE 4-11, is a "widescreen" one, with a shape like that of HD television sets. You might use 16:9 to show images on an HDTV set or for a composition with subject matter stretched out in a horizontal arrangement. As you can see in the sample image, with this setting some pixels are cropped out at the top and bottom, though none are lost at the left or right.

The 1:1 ratio, shown in FIGURE 4-12, represents a square, which some photographers like because of its symmetry and because its neutrality leaves open many possibilities for composing images. With the 1:1 setting, the camera crops pixels from the left and right sides of the image to achieve the final shape.

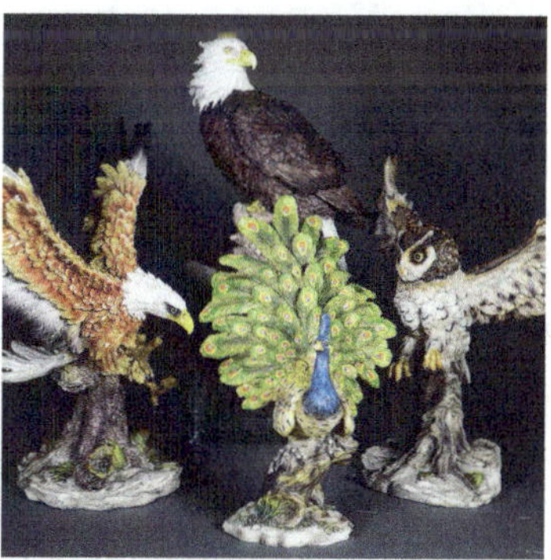

Figure 4-12. Aspect Ratio 1:1

The Aspect Ratio setting is available in all shooting modes except Sweep Panorama. Although you can set Aspect Ratio when the camera is in Movie mode (mode dial at movie-film icon), the setting will have no effect until you switch to a mode such as Program, in which the setting can be made. This is because you cannot take still images with the mode dial at the Movie position.

Quality

The Quality setting, below Aspect Ratio, is one of the most important Shooting menu options. The choices are Raw, Raw & JPEG, Extra Fine, Fine, and Standard, as shown in Figure 4-13.

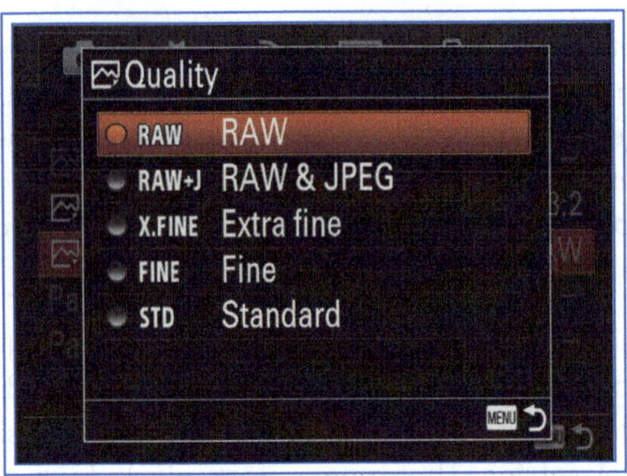

Figure 4-13. Quality Menu Options Screen

The term "quality" in this context concerns the way the images are processed. JPEG (non-Raw) images are digitally "compressed" to reduce their size without losing too much information. The more an image is compressed, the greater the loss of detail in the image. Raw files are the least compressed and have the highest quality, though they come with some complications, as discussed below. All other (non-Raw) formats used by the RX10 (as with most similar cameras) are classified as JPEG, which is an acronym for Joint Photographic Experts Group, an industry group that created the JPEG standard. JPEG files come in three varieties on the RX10: Extra Fine, Fine, and Standard. The Extra Fine setting provides the least compression; images captured with the Fine or Standard setting undergo increasing amounts of compression, resulting in smaller files with somewhat reduced quality.

Here are some guidelines for these settings. First, you need to choose between Raw and JPEG. Raw files are larger than JPEG files, so they take up more space on your memory card and on your computer than JPEGs. But Raw files offer advantages over JPEG files. When you shoot in the Raw format, the camera records as much information as it can and preserves that information in the file it saves. When you open a Raw file on your computer, you can extract that information in various ways. For example, you can change the exposure or white balance of the image when you edit it on the computer, just as if you had changed your settings while shooting. The Raw format gives you what almost amounts to a chance to travel back in time to improve some of the settings that you didn't get quite right when you pressed the shutter button.

Raw is not a cure-all; you cannot fix bad focusing or excessive underexposure or overexposure. But you can improve exposure-related issues such as brightness and white balance with your Raw-processing software. You can use the Image Data Converter software that comes with the RX10 to view or edit Raw files, and you can use other programs, such as Adobe Camera Raw, that have been updated to handle Raw files from this camera.

Using Raw can have disadvantages, depending on your needs. The files are quite large; Raw images taken with the RX10 are about 20 MB in size, while Large JPEG images I have taken have been from about 2 to 10 MB, depending on the settings used. Some composite JPEG images, such as those taken with the Hand-held Twilight setting, have been about 15 MB in size.

Also, you can't immediately send Raw files by e-mail or print them out; you first have to use Raw-processing software to convert them to JPEG or another standard format. If you are pressed for time, you may not want to take that extra step. Finally, some features of the RX10 are not available when you are using the Raw format, such as the Auto HDR, Digital Zoom, and Picture Effect settings on the Shooting menu.

If you're undecided as to whether to use Raw or JPEG, you can choose Raw & JPEG, the second option for the Quality menu item. With that setting, the camera records both a Raw and a JPEG image when you press the shutter button. The advantage with that approach is that you have a Raw image with the highest quality and with the ability to do extensive post-processing manipulation, and you also have a JPEG image that you can use more quickly for viewing, e-mailing, or printing. The disadvantages are that this setting consumes more storage space than saving images in just Raw or JPEG format, and it can take the camera longer to store the images, so there may be a delay before you can take your next shot or a slowdown in burst shooting, if you are using that option.

When you select Raw & JPEG, you can still select an Image Size setting that will apply only to the JPEG image; the Raw image, as noted earlier, is always of the maximum size. You cannot select a Quality setting for the JPEG image with the Raw & JPEG selection; the JPEG image will always be fixed at the Fine setting for Quality (not Extra Fine).

The best way to preserve the quality of your images and your options for post-processing and fixing exposure mistakes later is to choose Raw files. However, if you want to use features such as Sweep Panorama mode, some Scene mode types such as Anti Motion Blur, the Picture Effect menu option, and others, which are not available with Raw files, then choose JPEG. If you do choose JPEG, I strongly recommend that you choose the Large size and Extra Fine quality, unless you have an urgent need to conserve storage space on your memory card or on your computer. If you want Raw quality and are not concerned about storage space or speed of shooting, choose Raw & JPEG. However, you will still not be able to use Picture Effect and some other options.

Panorama Size and Panorama Direction

These next two commands on the Shooting menu are available only when the mode dial is set to Sweep Panorama mode. I discussed these settings in CHAPTER 3, in connection with the discussion of that shooting mode.

The second screen of the Shooting menu begins with the File Format option, as seen in FIGURE 4-14.

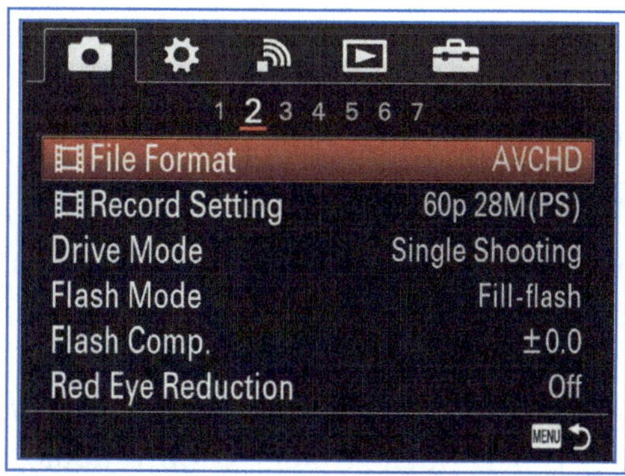

Figure 4-14. Screen 2 of Shooting Menu

File Format

The File Format command applies only for recording movies. If you want your movies to be recorded at the highest quality, choose AVCHD. If you prefer to record them in a format that is easier to edit and manipulate on a computer or other device, choose MP4. I will discuss this menu item in more detail in CHAPTER 8, where I discuss video recording.

Record Setting

This menu option, like File Format, applies only to video recording. The available options are different depending on whether you select AVCHD or MP4 for the File Format option. If you choose AVCHD and want the highest quality, choose 60p

28M(PS). If you choose MP4 and want high quality, choose 1440 x 1080 12M. (Don't choose VGA unless you are pressed for storage space and can settle for much lower quality.) I will discuss this option in more detail in CHAPTER 8.

Drive Mode

This option gives you access to the continuous-shooting features of the RX10. These features give you powerful capabilities for shooting a burst of images with one extended press of the shutter button; taking a "bracket" of several exposures with slightly different values for settings of exposure, White Balance, or dynamic range (DRO); and using the self-timer.

When you highlight this menu option and press the Center button, a menu appears at the left of the screen as shown in FIGURE 4-15, with nine choices represented by icons: Single Shooting, Continuous Shooting, Speed Priority Continuous Shooting, Self-timer, Self-timer (Continuous), Continuous Exposure Bracketing, Single Exposure Bracketing, White Balance Bracketing, and DRO Bracketing. (You have to scroll down to see the last five choices.)

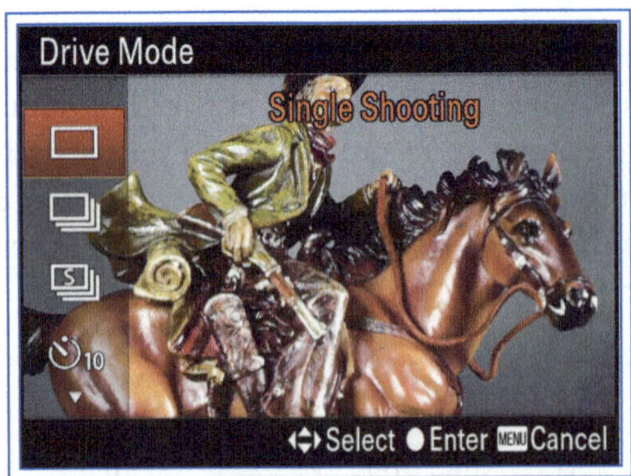

Figure 4-15. Drive Mode Menu Options Screen

Details for each of these Drive Mode settings are discussed below.

Single Shooting

This is the normal mode for shooting still images. Select this option, the top choice on the Drive Mode menu, when you want to turn off all continuous shooting. In some cases, having one of the continuous-shooting options selected will make it impossible to make other settings, such as Soft Skin Effect or Long Exposure Noise Reduction. If you find you cannot make a certain setting, it can be helpful to select single shooting to see if that removes the conflict and fixes the problem.

As noted earlier, this option is not available with the Sports Action setting of Scene mode.

Continuous Shooting

This second option on the Drive Mode menu, highlighted in Figure 4-16, gives the RX10 the ability to shoot a continuous series of still images as you hold down the shutter button.

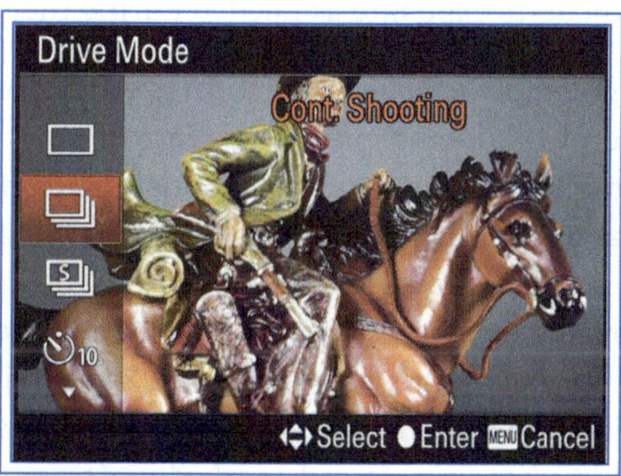

Figure 4-16. Continuous Shooting Menu Option

This capability is useful in many contexts, from shooting an action sequence at a sporting event to taking a series of shots of a portrait subject to capture changing facial expressions. I often use this setting for street photography to increase my chance of catching an interesting scene.

The Continuous Shooting option is the first of two types of burst shooting available with the RX10. When you select this choice, the camera will shoot continuously when you hold down the shutter button. If you have the focus switch on the front of the camera set to the AF-S position for single autofocus, the camera will not adjust its focus during the burst of shots. But, if you set the focus mode to AF-C for continuous autofocus, the camera will adjust focus for each shot. As you can imagine, this focusing may not be exact because of motion by the subject, the camera, or both, but the camera will try to re-focus while the burst continues.

If you want the camera to adjust its exposure during the series of continuous shots, you need to go to screen 3 of the Custom menu and check the setting of the AEL w/Shutter menu item. If that item is set to On, the camera will lock exposure when you press the shutter button, and exposure will be locked throughout the burst as it was set for the first image, even if lighting changes dramatically. However, if you set AEL w/Shutter to Off, then the camera will adjust its exposure as needed during the burst of shots.

Depending on conditions such as lighting, other camera settings, and the speed of the memory card, the rate of burst shooting can vary considerably. With optimal conditions, the camera can shoot at about 2 frames per second (fps) using this setting. I tested this option using a Lexar Professional 128 GB SDXC card, one of the faster cards available. With Quality set to Fine, the camera fired a long series of shots at a rate between 1 and 2 fps. With Quality set to Raw & JPEG, the camera started shooting its burst at a slightly slower pace but shooting slowed markedly after about 16 shots. With slower memory cards, the camera shot at slower speeds.

Although you can turn on the flash when the Continuous Shooting option is selected, and the camera will actually take a series of shots as you hold down the shutter button, the time between shots may be several seconds because the flash cannot recycle quickly enough to take a rapid series of shots. The Image Size setting does not appear to affect the shooting rate.

The speed of this first continuous-shooting mode is not very great compared to that of the Speed Priority option, discussed below. However, being able to take a stream of shots with focus adjusted for each one can be worth the reduction in speed when your subject is moving or when you need to focus on moving subjects or subjects at varying distances.

Speed Priority Continuous Shooting

If you need to shoot a series of images at the fastest rate possible, then the Speed Priority Continuous Shooting option, highlighted in Figure 4-17, is the one to choose.

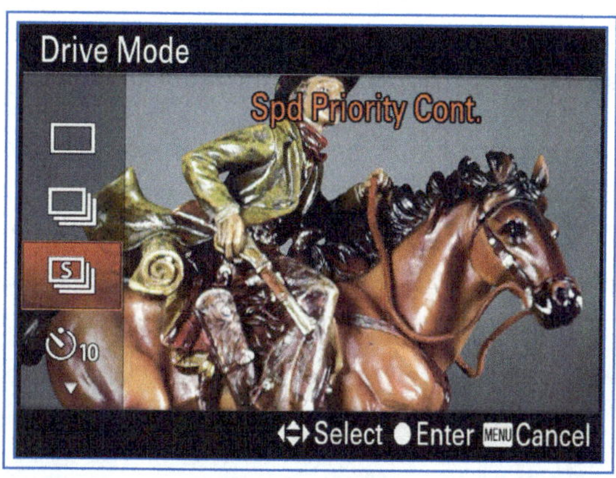

Figure 4-17. Speed Priority Continuous Menu Option

With this selection, the camera captures images at a rate up to about 10 fps. The trade-off for speed is that the camera will not adjust focus between shots, even if you set the focus switch for continuous autofocus. As with the standard Continuous Shooting setting, with Speed Priority the camera will adjust exposure for each shot if the AEL w/Shutter menu option is set to Off; if that menu option is set to On, the camera will lock the exposure with the first shot and will not adjust it for the remaining shots.

Also, the Quality setting affects the efficiency of the Speed Priority setting. When I used my fastest memory card and set the camera to take either Raw & JPEG or just Raw shots, the continuous shooting came to a complete stop after the first rapid burst of about 10 shots and then slowed to a pace of less than 1 fps. With Quality set to Fine, the camera took one rapid burst of about 25 shots and then eased off to a slower pace of about 2 shots per second. As with the standard Continuous Shooting option, using the flash slows down the shooting drastically. Also, using slower memory cards has a noticeable impact on the speed of continuous shooting.

Once you have finished taking a burst of shots, it can take the camera a while to record them all to the memory card; the red access lamp at the right edge of the camera's back will flash while the camera writes the images to the card. You can't take more shots or play back existing ones until that lamp turns off.

Figure 4-18 is a composite that includes a series of images I took using continuous shooting, to illustrate how rapidly the camera can fire its shutter with the burst settings. The camera captured several clear images of the climber as he descended the rock wall.

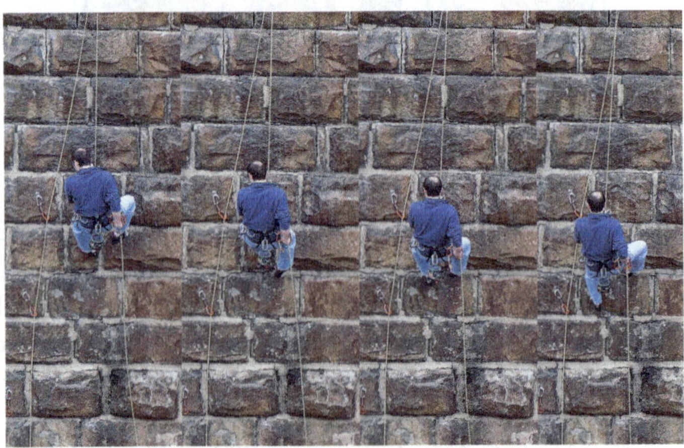

Figure 4-18. Continuous Shooting Example

Neither of the burst-shooting options is available when the mode dial is set to the Movie or Sweep Panorama position. Also, burst shooting is not available with any of the Scene mode settings except Sports Action. (With that setting, single shooting is not available.)

Self-Timer

The next icon down on the menu of Drive Mode options represents the self-timer, as shown in Figure 4-19.

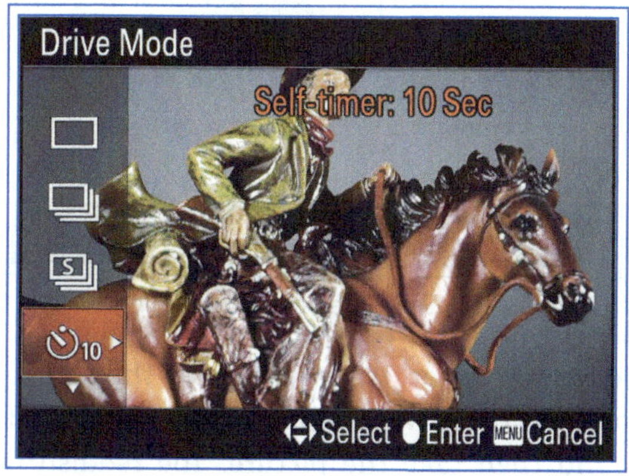

Figure 4-19. Self-Timer Menu Options Screen

The self-timer is useful when you need to be the photographer and also appear in a group photograph. You can place the RX10 on a tripod, set the timer for 10 seconds, and join the group before the shutter clicks. The self-timer also is helpful when you don't want to ruin the image by jiggling the camera as you press the shutter button. For example, when you're taking a macro shot very close to the subject, focusing is critical and any bump to the camera could cause motion blur. Using the self-timer lets the camera settle down after the shutter button is pressed, before the image is recorded.

Once you select the self-timer option, you are presented with two choices: 10 seconds and 2 seconds. When the self-timer option is highlighted, press the Left or Right button on the Control wheel or turn the Control dial to choose between these options. Once you have made this selection, the self-timer icon will appear in the upper-left corner of the display with the chosen number of seconds (10 or 2) displayed next to the icon, as shown in Figure

4-20. (If you don't see the icon, press the Display button until the screen with the various shooting icons appears.)

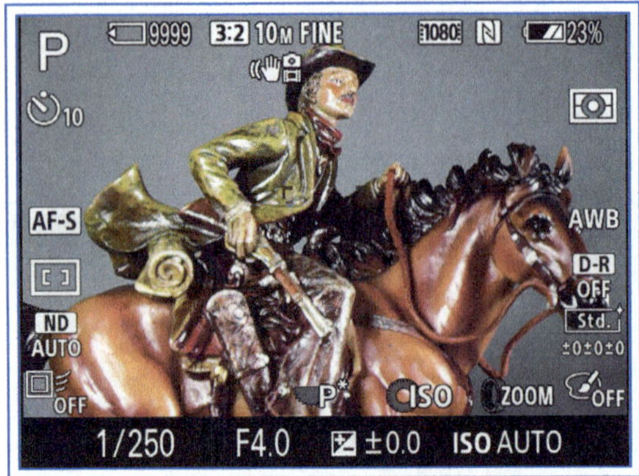

Figure 4-20. Self-Timer Icon on Shooting Screen

Once the self-timer is set, when you press the shutter button to take a picture, the timer will count down for the specified number of seconds and then take the picture. The reddish lamp on the front of the camera will blink, and the camera will beep during the countdown.

You cannot use the Continuous AF setting for the focus mode with either of the self-timer options. If you turn the focus switch to that position, the camera will reset the focus mode to single autofocus while any self-timer setting is in effect.

If you want to take multiple shots using the self-timer, you can use another option on the Drive Mode menu, discussed below.

Self-Timer (Continuous)

The next item down on the Drive Mode menu, shown in Figure 4-21, gives you another variation on the self-timer.

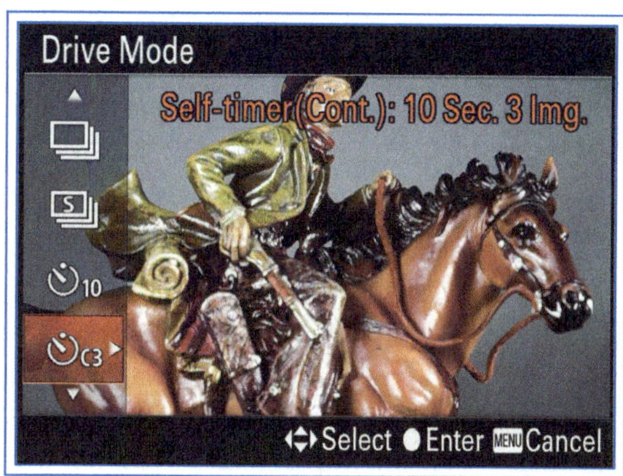

Figure 4-21. Self-Timer Continuous Menu Option

In this case, the menu option lets you set the camera to take multiple shots after the timer counts down. The delay for this timer is set at 10 seconds and cannot be changed. Using the Left and Right buttons or the Control dial, you can set the camera to take either three or five shots after the delay. This option can be useful when you are taking a group photo. When a series of shots is taken, you increase the chance of getting at least one shot in which no one's eyes are closed and everyone is looking at the camera and smiling. You can choose any settings you want to for Image Size and Quality, including Raw & JPEG, and you will still get three rapidly fired shots, though the speed of the shooting will decrease slightly at the highest Quality settings. As noted above, you cannot use the Continuous AF setting with the self-timer.

Exposure Bracketing–Continuous

This next option on the Drive Mode menu, shown in Figure 4-22, lets you set up the camera to take three images continuously with one press of the shutter button but with a different exposure level for each image, thereby giving you a greater chance of having one image that is properly exposed.

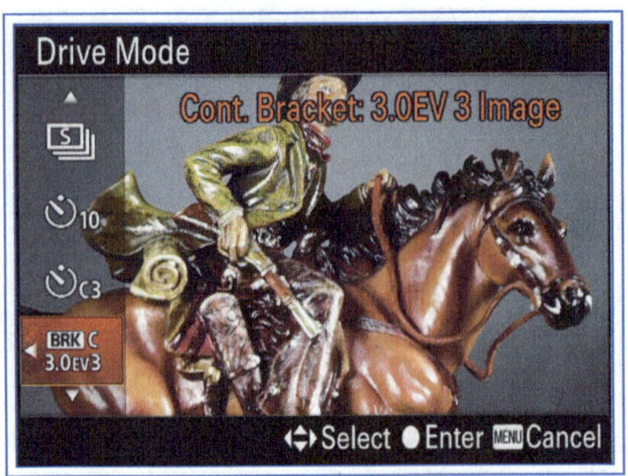

Figure 4-22. Exposure Bracket Continuous Menu Option

This feature can be of use when you are faced with a scene that has both dark and bright areas and you are not sure what overall exposure will be best. It also can be used for taking three exposures at different values that you can later combine in editing software to create a composite HDR image.

When you highlight this option, you will see a horizontal triangle indicating that, using the Left and Right buttons or the Control dial, you can select one of seven combinations of the difference in exposure value and the number of images in the bracket. These choices include exposure value intervals (EV) of 0.3, 0.7, 1.0, 2.0, or 3.0 EV with a bracket of 3 exposures, or EV interval of 0.3 or 0.7 with 5 exposures. The decimal numbers represent the difference in EV among the multiple (3 or 5) exposures that the camera will take.

For example, if you select 0.7 EV as the interval for 3 exposures, the camera will take three shots—one at the metered exposure level; one at a level 0.7 EV (or stop) below that, resulting in a darker image; and one at a level 0.7 EV above that, resulting in a brighter image. If you want the maximum exposure difference among the shots, select 3.0 EV as the interval for 3 shots.

Once you have set this option as you want it and composed your shot, press and hold the shutter button and the camera will take the 3 or 5 shots in rapid succession while you hold down the button.

If you set this option for 3 exposures, the first one will be at the metered value, the second one underexposed by the selected interval, and the third one overexposed to the same extent. If you set it for 5 exposures, the first 3 shots will have the values noted above, the fourth will have the most negative EV, and the fifth will have the most positive EV. (You can change this order using the Bracket Order menu option, discussed in Chapter 7.)

If you pop up the flash and set it to fire, using the Fill-flash setting for example, the flash will fire for each of the bracketed shots and the exposure will be varied, but you have to press the shutter button for each shot, after the flash has recycled. (The orange dot to the right of the flash icon on the screen shows when the flash is ready to fire gain.)

You can use exposure compensation, in which case the camera will use the image with exposure compensation as the base level, and then take exposures that deviate under and over the exposure of the image with exposure compensation.

When ISO is set to Auto, the camera adjusts the ISO setting to achieve the different exposure levels for the multiple images. If ISO is set to a specific value, the camera varies the shutter speeds for the multiple shots.

Exposure Bracketing–Single

The next option is similar to the previous one, except that, with this selection, you have to press the shutter button for each shot; the camera will not take multiple shots while you hold down the shutter button. You have the same 7 choices for combinations of EV intervals and numbers of exposures. You might want to choose this option when you need to pause between shots for some reason, such as if you are using a model who needs to have some costume or makeup adjustments for each exposure.

Apart from requiring individual shutter presses, this option works the same as continuous exposure bracketing. For example, you can use flash and you can change the order of the exposures using the Bracket Order menu option.

None of the bracketing options—exposure, White Balance, or DRO—is available in the Intelligent Auto, Scene, Sweep Panorama, or Movie shooting mode.

White Balance Bracket

The next option at the bottom of the Drive Mode menu, White Balance Bracket, seen in Figure 4-23, works the same way as Exposure Bracketing, except that the value that is varied for the three shots is White Balance rather than exposure.

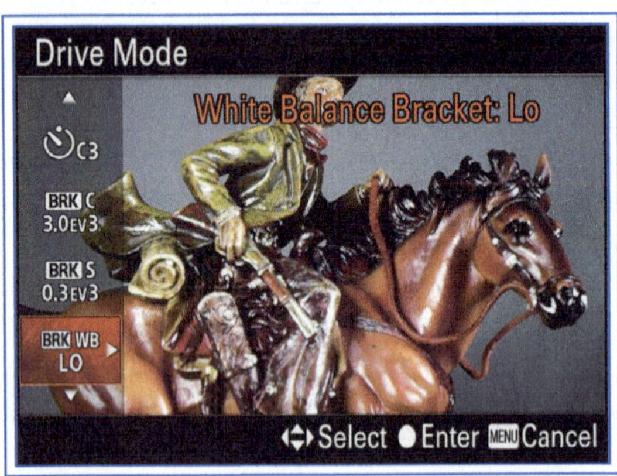

Figure 4-23. White Balance Bracket Menu Option

Using the Left and Right buttons, you first select either Lo or Hi for the amount of deviation from the normal White Balance setting. Then, when you press the shutter button (you don't have to hold it down), the camera will take a series of three shots—one at the normal setting; the next one setting a lower color temperature, resulting in a "cooler," more-bluish image; and the last one setting a higher color temperature, resulting in a "warmer," more-reddish image. See the discussion of the White Balance setting later in this chapter for more information about color temperature. When you use this form of bracketing, unlike exposure bracketing, you will hear only one shutter sound because the camera takes just one image, with one quick shutter press, and then electronically creates the other two exposures with the different White Balance values.

You can change the order of the exposures using the Bracket Order option on screen 3 of the Custom menu.

DRO Bracket

This final option on the Drive Mode menu lets you set the RX10 to take a series of three shots at different settings of the DRO (dynamic range optimizer) option. I'll discuss DRO later in this chapter. Essentially, DRO alters the RX10's image processing to even out the contrast between shadowed and bright areas. It can be difficult to decide how much DRO processing to use, and this option gives you a way to experiment with several different settings before you decide on the amount of DRO for your final image.

As with White Balance Bracket, you can select between Hi and Lo for the DRO interval. Also, as with White Balance Bracket, you only need to press the shutter button once, briefly; the camera will record the 3 different exposures electronically. The order of these exposures is not affected by the Bracket Order menu option.

Flash Mode

In Chapter 2, I discussed the use of the RX10's built-in flash, which is controlled with the Flash Mode menu option. As I discussed earlier, that is the fourth option on screen 2 of the Shooting menu.

There are six options on the Flash Mode menu—Flash Off, Autoflash, Fill-flash, Slow Sync, Rear Sync, and Wireless—the first four of which are shown in Figure 4-24.

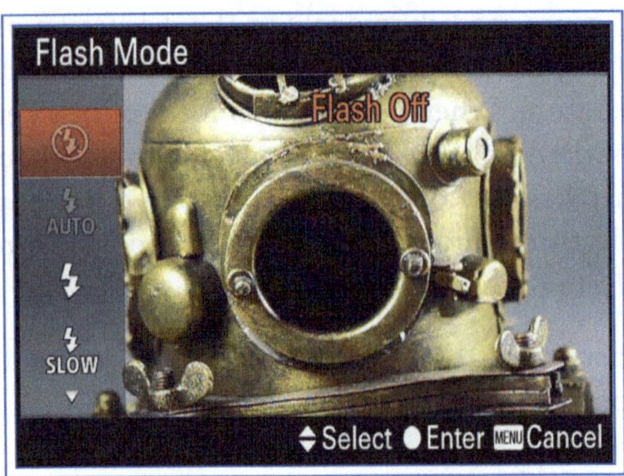

Figure 4-24. Flash Mode Menu Options Screen

There is no shooting mode in which all six options are available. Here are brief summaries of the settings I discussed in Chapter 2, followed by details about the options I did not discuss there.

Flash Off

With the RX10, this setting is not available in any shooting modes except Intelligent Auto and Scene. In Scene mode, Flash Off is available with the Portrait, Sports Action, Macro, Landscape, and Sunset settings. Flash Off is automatically selected for the Night Scene, Hand-held Twilight, and Anti Motion Blur settings. The Night Portrait setting uses Slow Sync.

Of course, in any shooting mode, you can just leave the flash unit stored inside the camera. If you do that, the flash cannot pop up and cannot fire. So, if you are in a museum or other area where you don't want the flash to fire, just leave the flash tucked inside the camera, and you won't have to worry.

Autoflash

When you select Autoflash, you are leaving it up to the camera's programming to decide whether or not to fire the flash. The camera will analyze the lighting and other aspects of the scene and decide whether to use the flash without any further input from you. This selection is available only with the Intelligent Auto mode and with the Portrait and Macro settings of Scene mode. When Autoflash is turned on, the camera will display a lightning bolt symbol in the upper left corner of the display if it has decided to fire the flash, as shown in Figure 4-25. If no lightning bolt appears in that position, then the flash will not fire for the next shot.

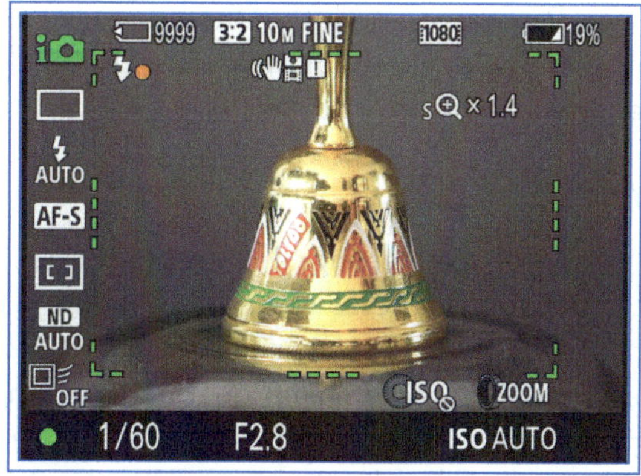

Figure 4-25. Lightning Bolt Icon Showing Flash Will Fire

Fill-Flash

With Fill-flash, you are making a definite decision to use flash. No matter what the lighting conditions are, if you choose this option, the flash will fire. This is the setting to use to soften shadows on a subject's face, or to correct the lighting when a subject is backlit.

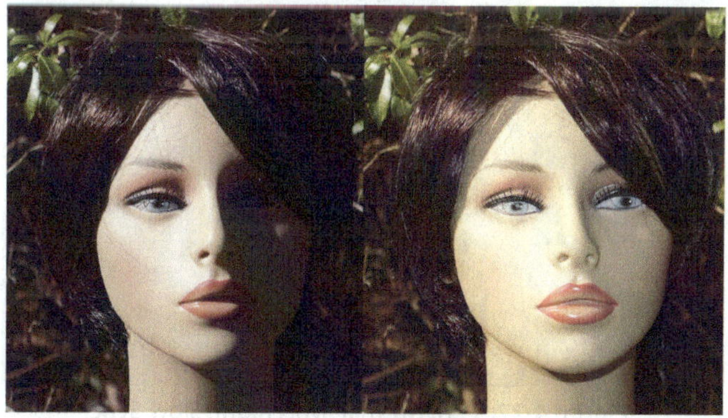

Figure 4-26. Left: No Flash, Right: Fill-Flash

For example, for FIGURE 4-26, I took two shots of a mannequin outdoors: one with flash off (left image) and one with Fill-flash (right image). The left image is heavily shadowed on the right side, while the right image is more evenly lighted and has additional highlights on the hair and lips.

Fill-flash is available for selection in all shooting modes except Movie, Sweep Panorama, and the Scene mode settings that don't permit you to change the flash setting (Night Scene, Night Portrait, Hand-held Twilight, and Anti Motion Blur).

Slow Sync

Slow Sync is one of the settings I did not discuss in detail in CHAPTER 2. This option is useful when you are taking a photograph of a subject at night. With this setting, the camera uses a relatively slow shutter speed so the ambient (natural) lighting will have time to register on the image. In other words, if you're in a fairly dark environment and fire the flash normally, the flash will light the main subject, but because the exposure time is short, the surrounding scene may be black. If you use Slow Sync, the slower shutter speed allows the surrounding scene to be visible also.

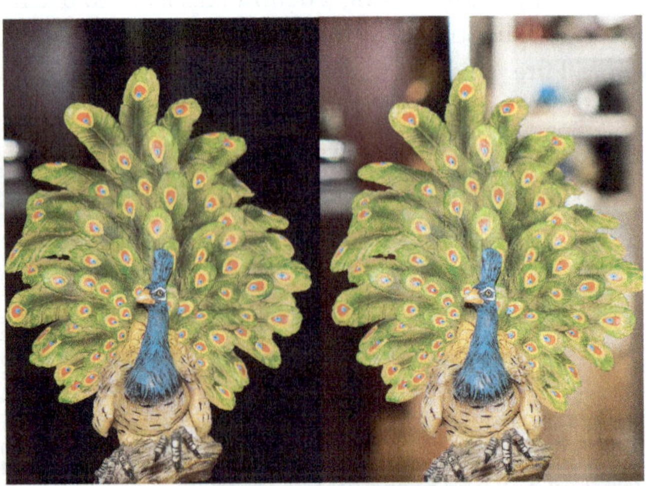

Figure 4-27. Left: Normal Sync, Right: Slow Sync

I took the two images in FIGURE 4-27 with identical room lighting and settings, except that I took the left image with Fill-flash and exposure set to f/2.8 at 1/60 second, and I took the right image with Slow Sync, resulting in an exposure at f/2.8 for one second. In the left image, the flash illuminated the figurine in the foreground, but the background is dark. In the right image, the contents of the room behind the figurine are illuminated by ambient light because of the much slower shutter speed.

When you use Slow Sync, you should plan to use a tripod because, in many cases, the camera will choose a very slow shutter speed, in the range of three seconds or even longer. Also, note that you can choose Slow Sync even when the camera is set to Shutter Priority mode. If you do so, you should select a slow shutter speed, because the whole point of this setting is to use a slow shutter speed to light the background with ambient light. If you set the camera to Shutter Priority mode, you can decide precisely which shutter speed to use, but it would not make sense to select a relatively fast speed, such as, say, 1/30 second. The same considerations apply for Manual exposure mode; the camera also will let you select Slow Sync for the Flash Mode setting in that shooting mode. You cannot select Slow Sync in Intelligent Auto mode or Scene mode.

Rear Sync

The next setting on the Flash Mode menu is Rear Sync. You should not need this option unless you encounter the particular situation it is designed for. If you don't activate this setting (that is, if you select any other flash mode in which the flash fires), the camera uses the unnamed default setting, which could be called "Front Sync." In that case, the flash fires very soon after the shutter opens to expose the image. If you choose the Rear Sync setting instead, the flash fires later, just before the shutter closes.

The reason for using Rear Sync is to help you avoid a strange-looking result in some situations. This issue arises, for example, with a relatively long exposure, say one-half second, of a subject with lights, such as a car or motorcycle at night, moving across your field of view. With normal (Front) sync, the flash will fire early in the process, freezing the vehicle in a clear image. However, as the shutter remains open while the vehicle keeps going, the camera will capture the moving lights in a stream extending in front of or on top of the vehicle. If, instead, you use Rear Sync, the initial part of the exposure will capture the lights in a trail that appears behind the vehicle, while the vehicle itself is not frozen by the flash until later in the exposure. With Rear Sync in this particular situation, if the lights in question are taillights that look more natural behind the vehicle, the final image is likely to look more natural than with the Front Sync (default) setting.

FIGURE 4-28 illustrates this concept using a remote-controlled model truck with a taillight. I took both pictures using the RX10's flash, using an exposure of 1/4 second in Shutter Priority mode.

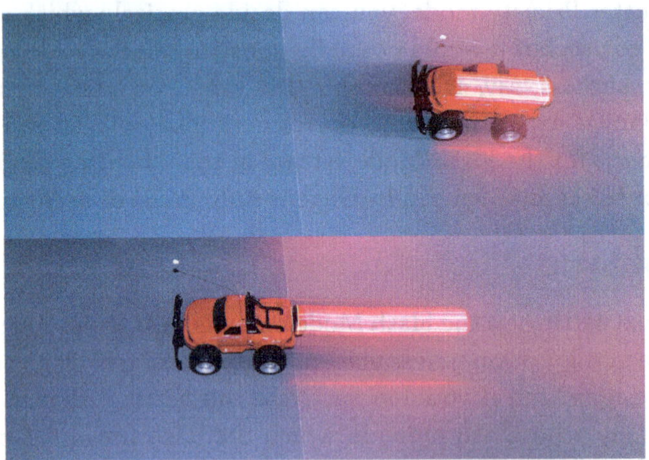

Figure 4-28. Top: Normal Sync, Bottom: Rear Sync

In the top image, with Fill-flash, the flash fired quickly and the light beams continued on to make the streaks of light appear on top of the truck. In the bottom image, using Rear Sync, the flash did not fire until the truck had traveled to the left, overtaking the place where the lights had made their streaks. For conveying a sense of natural motion, the Rear Sync setting, as seen here, is likely to give you better results than the default setting.

A good general rule is to use Rear Sync only when you have a definite need for it. Using this option makes it harder to compose and set up the shot because you have to anticipate where the main subject will be when the flash finally fires late in the exposure process. But, in the relatively rare situations when it is useful, Rear Sync can make a dramatic difference. Rear Sync is available only in the more advanced shooting modes: Program, Aperture Priority, Shutter Priority, and Manual exposure.

Wireless

The last setting on the Flash Mode menu, Wireless, gives you a powerful tool for controlling an off-camera flash unit using Sony's special wireless protocol. In order to take advantage of this setting, you need to have at least two flash units that are compatible with the Sony wireless system—one attached to the camera's accessory shoe and another one (or multiple units) positioned off the camera.

The flash on the camera acts as the controller. The built-in flash on the RX10 camera cannot act as a wireless controller using this protocol, so you need to use an external unit. The best option I know of for this purpose is the Sony HVL-F20M, a small and relatively inexpensive unit. I discuss it in Appendix A. One negative point about this unit is that it cannot act as a remote unit using the Sony wireless protocol, only as the controller. That is not much of a problem, though; you can just dedicate this unit as your controller and use other, larger units as the remote flash units.

The remote unit I have used is the Sony HVL-F43M, also discussed in Appendix A. This full-sized flash has features such as a rotating head and a built-in video light. For wireless purposes, it can serve as either the controller or the remote unit for the Sony protocol.

I will describe how to use these flash units for a shot using Aperture Priority mode; the procedure will be similar for other units.

1. Attach the HVL-F43M to the RX10, turn the camera and flash on, and set the camera to Aperture Priority mode. On the Shooting menu, set the Flash Mode to Wireless and press the shutter button halfway. Make sure the flash's display shows that it is now set to Wireless mode, on Channel 1. The red AF Illuminator light on the flash unit should now be flashing.
2. Remove the HVL-F43M flash from the camera and set it up aiming at your subject, on a light stand, on its own plastic stand, or handheld by the subject or other person, if you want.
3. Attach the HVL-F20M to the RX10 and turn the flash on by pulling it up into a vertical position.
4. On the RX10, set up your shot using Aperture Priority mode, which is one of the modes that permits the use of Wireless for Flash Mode.
5. On the RX10, select Flash Mode from the Shooting menu and set the mode to Wireless (WL). Make sure the camera is aimed at the subject, and that the flash from the HVL-F20M can be seen by the remote flash. (The line of sight can be indirect, from bouncing off of a wall or ceiling.)
6. Test the flash setup by pressing the AEL button on the RX10. You should see two flashes from the remote flash in quick succession.
7. Press the shutter button to take the picture.

The small flash on the camera sends a coded signal to the remote flash telling it to fire a pre-flash. The camera then evaluates that pre-flash and sets the remote flash to fire the flash at the proper intensity for the actual exposure. You will see the pre-flash, followed fairly quickly by the actual flash for the exposure.

Figure 4-29 shows a simple setup using this system, with the remote flash aimed to bounce off of the wall and ceiling near the subject and the controller flash on the camera.

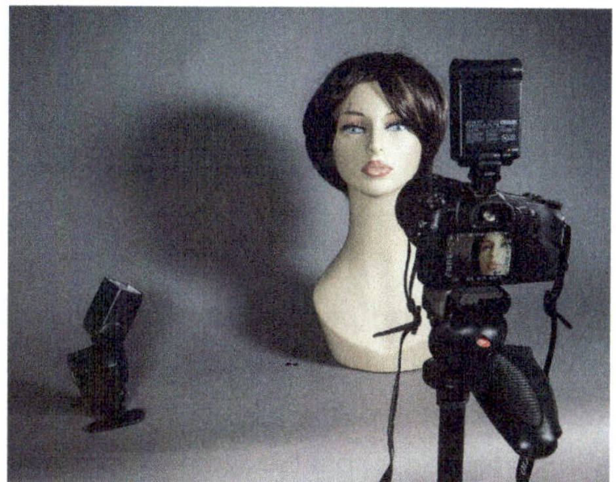

Figure 4-29. Setup for Shot Using Wireless Flash

FIGURE 4-30 shows an image taken with a setup similar to this one, using bounce flash from the HVL-F43M.

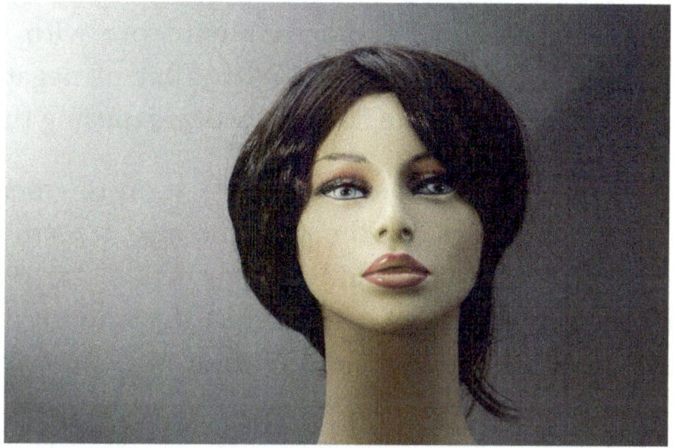

Figure 4-30. Image Taken with Wireless Flash Setup

This image was taken with the single remote flash shown here, and no other light sources. I used Aperture Priority mode, and the camera exposed the image for 1/60 second at f/2.8 using ISO 200.

There are other Sony flash units that work with the wireless flash protocol, including the HVL-F60M. You can use multiple external flash units if you want.

Flash Compensation

The Flash Compensation option controls the output of the built-in flash unit, or of an external unit if a compatible one is attached to the flash shoe. This function works the same way as exposure compensation, discussed in CHAPTER 5. The difference between the two options is that Flash Compensation varies only the intensity of the flash, but exposure compensation can vary the overall exposure of a given shot, whether or not flash is used. (You can control whether the exposure compensation dial adjusts flash output as well as exposure settings by using the Custom menu's Exposure Compensation Setting option, as discussed in CHAPTER 7.)

Flash Compensation is a good option when you don't want the subject to be overwhelmed by light from the flash. I often use this setting when I shoot a portrait outdoors with Fill-flash, to reduce shadows on the subject. With a bit of negative Flash Compensation, I can keep the flash from overexposing the image.

This menu item is simple to use: Highlight it on the menu screen and press the Center button, then, on the next screen, shown in FIGURE 4-31, press the Left and Right buttons or turn either the Control wheel or the Control dial to select the amount of positive or negative compensation you want. You can choose an amount from zero to plus or minus 3.0 EV.

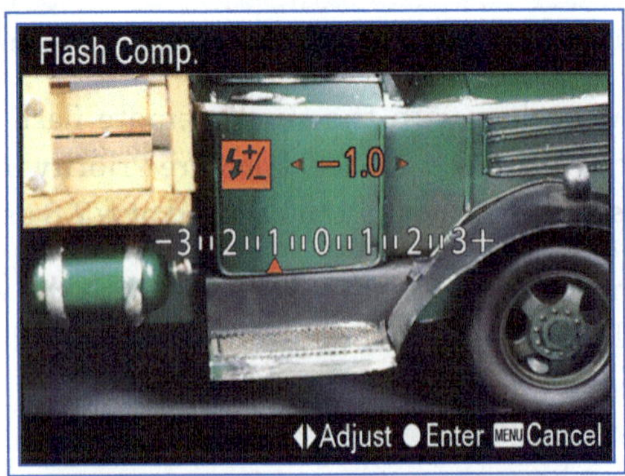

Figure 4-31. Flash Compensation Menu Option Setting Screen

Be sure to set the value to zero when you are done, because any setting you make will stay in place even after the camera has been powered off and on again. Flash Compensation is not available with the Intelligent Auto, Scene, or Sweep Panorama modes.

Red Eye Reduction

The last option on screen 2 of the Shooting menu lets you combat "red-eye"—the eerie glow in human eyes that results when on-camera flash lights up blood vessels on the retinas. If this option is turned on, then, whenever the flash is used, it fires some pre-flashes before the actual flash for the exposure. The pre-flashes are intended to cause the subject's pupils to narrow, reducing the chance that the later, full flash will enter the eyes, bounce off the retinas, and produce the unwanted red glow in the eyes.

I prefer to leave this option off and deal with red-eye with editing software, if necessary. However, if you will be taking flash photos at a party, you may want to use this menu option to minimize the occurrence of red-eye effects in the first place.

The next items to be discussed are found on screen 3 of the Shooting menu, shown in Figure 4-32.

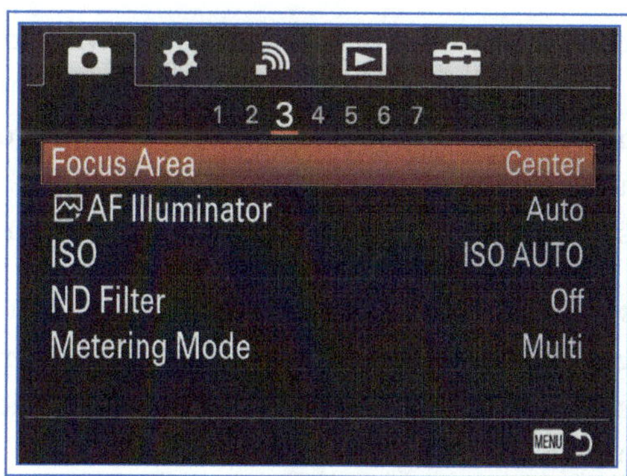

Figure 4-32. Screen 3 of Shooting Menu

Focus Area

The first option on this screen, Focus Area, lets you choose what area the camera focuses on when using autofocus. The two autofocus modes are single and continuous, selected with the focus switch. In addition, direct manual focus, or DMF, is a mode that lets you use both manual focus and autofocus. The Focus Area menu option sets the focus area for all three of those focus modes.

The choices for Focus Area, as shown in FIGURE 4-33, are, from top to bottom, Wide, Center, and Flexible Spot.

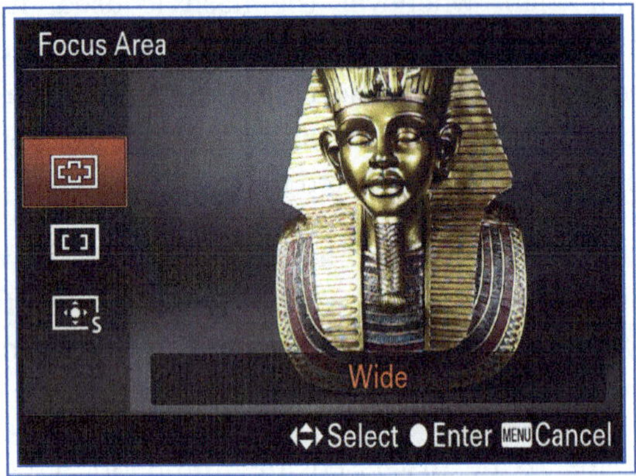

Figure 4-33. Focus Area Menu Options

The ways these selections operate vary somewhat depending on whether you select single autofocus or continuous autofocus with the focus mode switch. If you select direct manual focus, you can use autofocus with the same system as for single autofocus, so that choice is the same as single autofocus for this purpose.

I will discuss the following options assuming at first that you are using single autofocus or direct manual focus as your focus mode. I also will assume that you have the Lock-on AF option turned off on screen 5 of the Shooting menu.

Wide

With Wide, the RX10 uses 25 focus zones and tries to detect one or more items within the scene to focus on based on their locations. When it has achieved sharp focus on one or more of those items, the camera displays a green frame indicating the focus point. You may see one or several green frames on the screen, depending on how many objects are at the same distance. An example with multiple objects is shown in Figure 4-34.

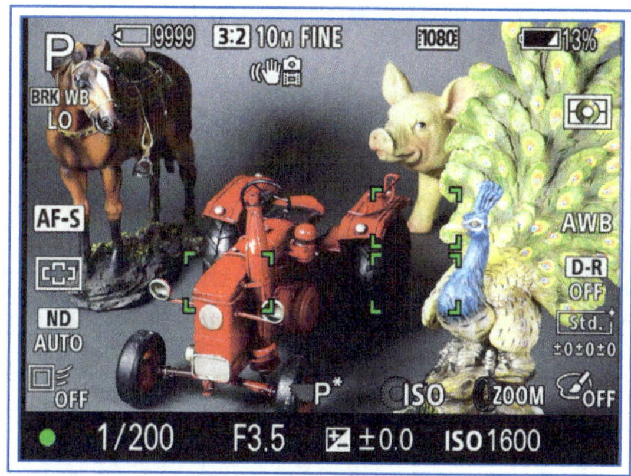

Figure 4-34. Green Focus Frames for Wide Focus Area Setting

When you are using single autofocus, the Wide option is excellent for general shots of landscapes, buildings, and the like. The camera displays green frames to show where it has set the focus.

In continuous autofocus mode, the RX10 does not display any focus frame with the Wide setting. The camera tries to keep focus on the subjects that appear to be the main ones. I don't recommend using Wide for Focus Area with continuous autofocus unless you are focusing on a single, clearly defined subject, so the camera will be able to maintain focus on the proper area.

Center

If you select Center for the Focus Area setting, the camera places a black focus frame in the center of the display, as shown in Figure 4-35, and focuses on whatever it finds within that frame.

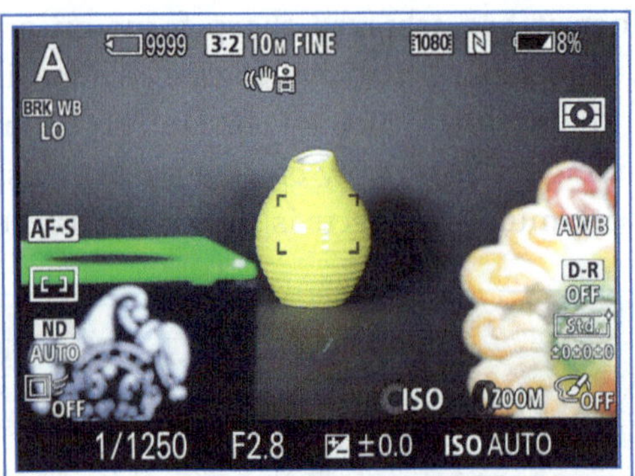

Figure 4-35. Center Focus Area Frame - Before Focusing

When you press the shutter halfway, if the camera can focus it will beep and the frame will turn green, as shown in Figure 4-36.

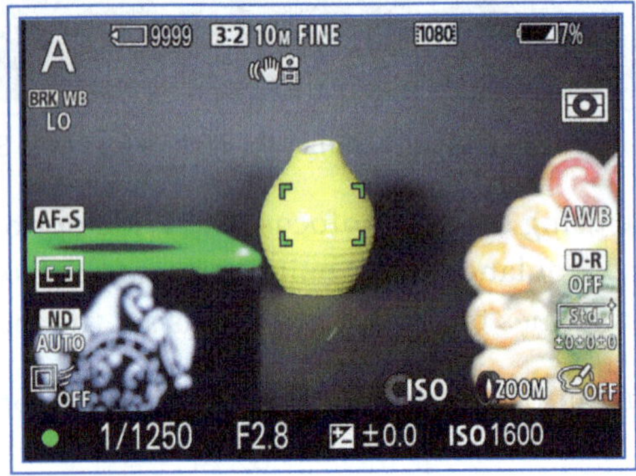

Figure 4-36. Center Focus Area Frame - After Focusing

This option is useful for an object in the center of the scene. Even if you need to focus on an off-center object, though, you can use this setting. For example, to focus on an object at the right, aim the camera with that object inside the focus frame and press the shutter button halfway to lock focus. Keeping the button pressed halfway, move the camera back so that object is on the right side, and press the shutter button all the way to take the picture.

If you turn on continuous autofocus using the focus mode switch, the camera still will display a black frame in the center of the screen. Then, when you press the shutter button halfway to focus, the frame will turn green when the camera achieves focus on an object inside that frame. As the camera or the subject moves, the camera will continue to re-focus on any object in the frame as you hold down the shutter button halfway. You can use this technique if you want to carry out your own focus-tracking, by moving the camera to keep the center frame targeted on a moving subject.

Flexible Spot

The third and final Focus Area option, Flexible Spot, gives you the most control over where the camera directs its autofocus operation, using a focus frame that you can move around the screen. You also can choose the size of the frame.

When you highlight this option on the Shooting menu, the camera displays the screen shown in Figure 4-37.

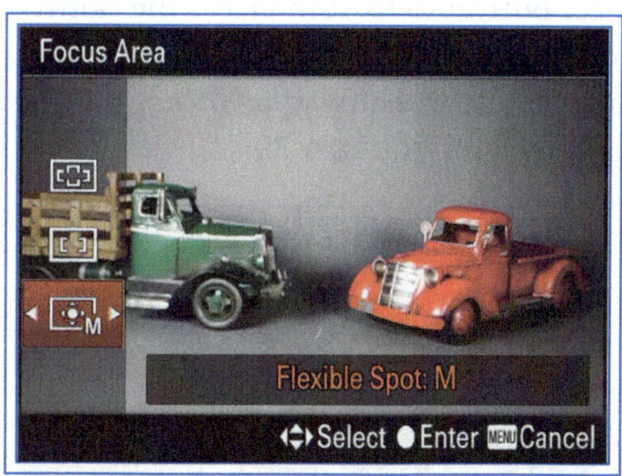

Figure 4-37. Flexible Spot Menu Option

On this screen, you can press the Right or Left button or turn the Control dial to select from the three options for the size of the Flexible Spot focus frame: L, M, or S, for Large, Medium, or Small. When you have selected the size, press the Center button, and you will see the screen shown in Figure 4-38, displaying an orange focus frame of that size with white arrows pointing to the four edges of the display.

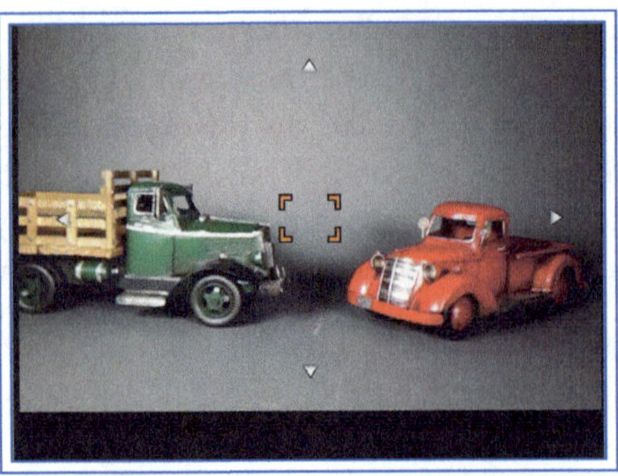

Figure 4-38. Flexible Spot Focus Frame - Ready to Be Moved

At this point, you can use the Control dial, the Control wheel, or all four direction buttons to move the frame around the display to any position. When you have the frame located where you want it, press the Center button to fix it in place. The camera will display a black frame of the chosen size in the chosen location. When you press the shutter button halfway to focus, the focus frame will turn green, as shown in Figure 4-39.

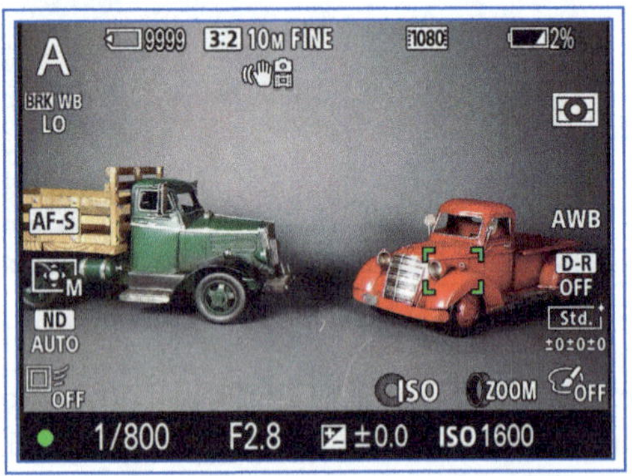

Figure 4-39. Flexible Spot Focus Frame After Focusing

This frame operates the same way as the frame for the Center option, except for the location and size (if the location and size were changed).

To return the frame quickly to the center of the screen, press the Delete (Trash) button while the frame is activated for moving, and it will move back to the exact center of the display.

This option is useful for focusing on a particular point, such as an object at the far right, without having to move the camera to place a focus frame over that object. This might be the situation if you are using a tripod, for example, and need to set up the shot with precision, focusing on an off-center subject. If the subject is small, using the smallest focus frame can make the process even easier.

If you use continuous autofocus, the Flexible Spot option works the same way as for the Center option, discussed above, except for the ability to change the size and location of the frame.

One problem with the Flexible Spot menu option is that it can be cumbersome to move the frame again once you have fixed it in place. The normal way to do this is to select the Focus Area menu option and repeat all of the steps discussed above. There are a couple of quicker ways to move the frame, though.

The easiest way to do this is to go to screen 4 of the Custom menu and select the Custom Key Settings option. On the next screen, select Center Button, and assign the Standard setting to that button. Then, whenever Flexible Spot is in effect, just press the Center button on the shooting screen, and the screen for moving the focus frame will appear. You can quickly use the direction buttons, Control dial, or Control wheel to move the frame where you want it, or you can press the Trash button to center it.

If you want to use the Center button for some other operation, you can assign Focus Area to one of the other control buttons, such as the Custom, AEL, Left, or Right button, using the Custom Key Settings menu option. Then, when you press the assigned button, the camera will immediately display the screen for choosing the size of the Flexible Spot frame. Or, you can assign Focus Area to the Function menu, which is called up by pressing the Function button. I will discuss that menu in Chapter 7.

My preference is to assign the Standard setting to the Center button. Then, to move the focus frame, I just press that button and it is an easy matter to adjust the frame's location. However, if you need to adjust the frame's size, you will need to use the Focus Area menu option, either by selecting it from the menu or by assigning that option to a control button. I will discuss the Custom Key Settings options further in CHAPTER 7.

AF Illuminator

The AF Illuminator menu item lets you disable the use of the reddish lamp on the front of the camera for autofocusing. By default, this option is set to Auto, which means that when you are shooting in a dim area, the camera will turn on the lamp briefly if needed to light up the subject and assist the autofocus mechanism in gauging the distance to the subject. If you would rather make sure the light never comes on for that purpose—to avoid causing distractions in a museum or other sensitive area, or to avoid alerting a subject of candid photography—you can set this option to Off. In that case, the lamp will never light up for focusing assistance, though it will still illuminate if the self-timer is activated.

ISO

ISO is a standard for gauging the light sensitivity of photographic film or digital sensors. The higher the ISO rating, the more sensitive the sensor is to light. Therefore, if you shoot an image or video using a high ISO value, you will not need as much light to achieve a normal exposure as you would with a lower ISO value. One result is that you can use a faster shutter speed, narrower aperture, or possibly both, than with a lower ISO.

The trade-off is that, with higher ISO values, the sensor is likely to produce visual "noise" that affects the image with an appearance of graininess. Camera makers have made considerable strides in creating sensors that can use high ISO values without too much noise, but there still is some drop-off in quality as ISO increases, particularly at the highest values.

Generally speaking, you should shoot your images with the camera set to the lowest ISO that will allow the image to be exposed properly. (One exception to this rule is if you want, for creative purposes, the grainy look that comes from shooting at a high ISO value.) For example, if you are shooting indoors in low light, you may need to set the ISO to a high value (say, ISO 1000), so you can expose the image with a reasonably fast shutter speed. Otherwise, if the camera uses a slow shutter speed, the resulting image would likely be blurry and possibly unusable.

Of course, high ISO settings are not a cure-all for poor lighting conditions. It is true that the RX10, with its backside-illuminated sensor, provides better low-light image quality than many cameras in its class. However, using the higher ISO settings is going to reduce image quality to a certain degree; the higher the ISO, the more such deterioration will be evident.

For example, FIGURE 4-40 includes two images of a colorful metallic bird taken with different ISO settings.

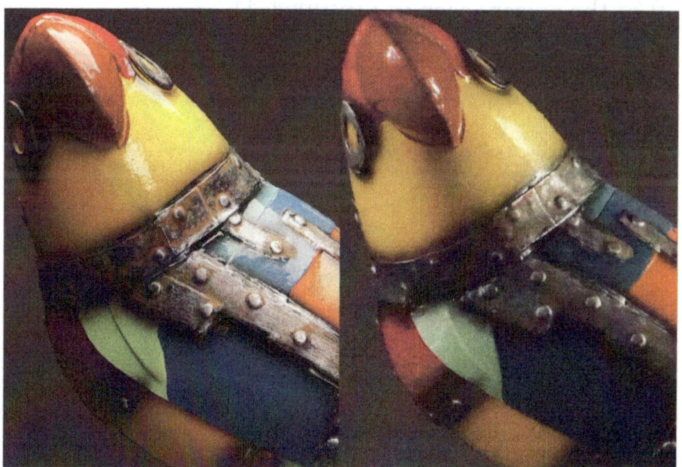

Figure 4-40. Left: ISO 125, Right: ISO 12800

I took the left shot with the RX10 set to ISO 125, and the right shot with ISO set to ISO 12800. I enlarged the views shown here to emphasize the effects of the ISO settings. As you can see, the image shot with the low ISO value is considerably less grainy than the high-ISO version.

To summarize: Shoot with low ISO settings (around 100 or 125) when possible; shoot with high ISO settings (1000 or higher) when necessary to allow a fast shutter speed to stop action and avoid blurriness, to allow a narrow aperture to achieve greater depth of field, or when desired to achieve a creative effect with graininess.

With that background, here is how to set ISO on this camera. As is discussed in detail in CHAPTER 7, one good feature of the RX10 is that you can get quick access to certain important settings, such as ISO, using the Function menu, or, if you want, by assigning the option to one of the camera's control buttons or the Control wheel. However, you can also set ISO from the Shooting menu.

ISO is the third item on screen 3 of this menu. After you highlight it, press the Center button to bring up the vertical ISO menu at the left of the screen, seen in FIGURE 4-41.

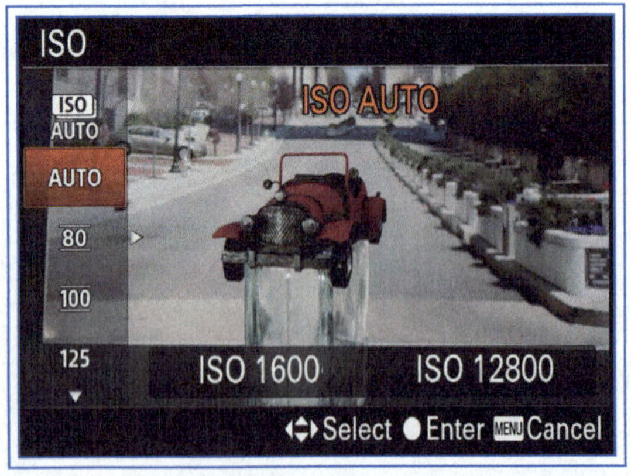

Figure 4-41. ISO Menu Options Screen

Scroll through the options by turning the Control wheel or Control dial or by pressing the Up and Down buttons to select a setting ranging from one of the top two options—Multi Frame Noise Reduction and Auto ISO—through 80, 100, 125, 160, 200, and other specific values, to a maximum of 12800 at the bottom of the scale. (If you want to use an ISO value higher than 12800, you need to use the Multi Frame Noise Reduction feature, discussed below.)

If you choose Auto ISO (the second option on the menu), the camera will select a numerical value automatically depending on the lighting conditions. However, one excellent feature of the RX10 is that you can select both the minimum and maximum levels for Auto ISO. In other words, you can set the camera to choose the ISO value automatically within a defined range such as, say, ISO 200 to ISO 1600. In that way, you can be assured that the camera will not select a value outside that range, but you will still leave some flexibility for the setting.

To set minimum and maximum values, while the orange highlight is on the Auto ISO option, press the Right button to move the highlight to the right side of the screen, where there are two rectangles that are labeled, when highlighted, ISO Auto Minimum and ISO Auto Maximum, as shown in Figure 4-42.

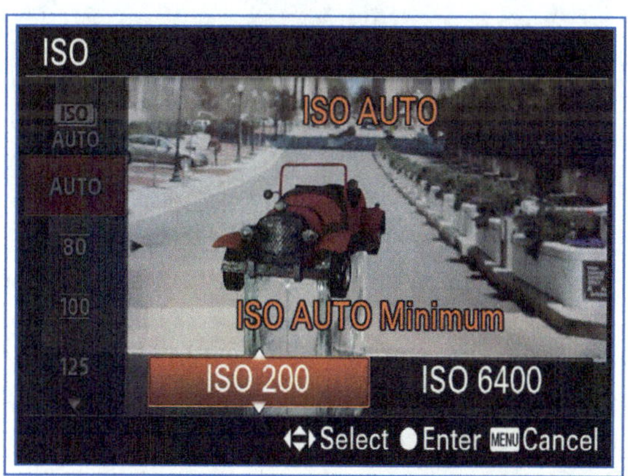

Figure 4-42. Screen for Setting ISO Auto Minimum and Maximum

Move the highlight to each of these blocks in turn using the Right button, and change the value as you wish, using the Up and Down buttons or turning the Control wheel or Control dial. You can set both the minimum and the maximum to values from 125 to 12800. When both values have been set, press the Center button to go back to the shooting screen.

Once those values are set, whenever you select Auto ISO, the camera will keep the ISO level within the range you have specified. Of course, you can always set a specific ISO value at any other level by selecting it from the ISO menu—the minimum and maximum values apply only when Auto ISO is selected.

Multi Frame Noise Reduction

Finally, I will discuss the top item on the ISO menu, whose icon includes the ISO label and a stack of frames. If you highlight that icon with the orange selection block, you will see the name of this option—Multi Frame Noise Reduction, as shown in Figure 4-43.

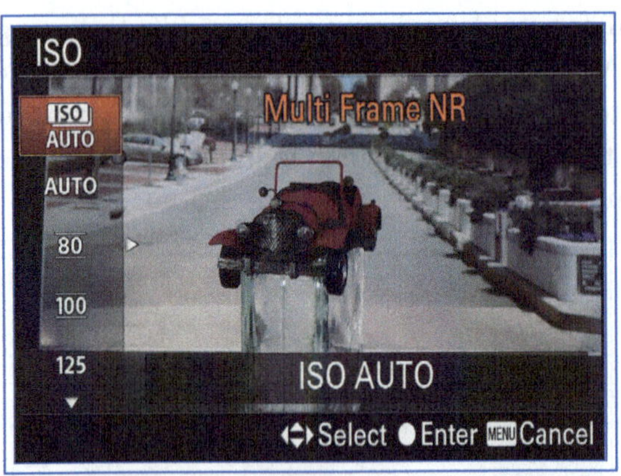

Figure 4-43. ISO Multi Frame Noise Reduction Setting

This special setting lets you select an ISO value as high as 25600, twice as high as the maximum value that you can set from the standard ISO menu. This value is an "expanded" setting, derived electronically from the camera's programming. When you press the shutter button using the Multi Frame Noise Reduction

(MFNR) option, the camera will take multiple shots in a rapid burst and combine them internally into a composite image with reduced noise. This processing counteracts the effects of using very high ISO values, which introduce noise into the image. The camera also attempts to select frames with minimal motion blur.

After you have selected MFNR, use the Right button to move the selection highlight to the right side of the screen. The highlight will then be on the selection block for the ISO setting to be used, as shown in FIGURE 4-44.

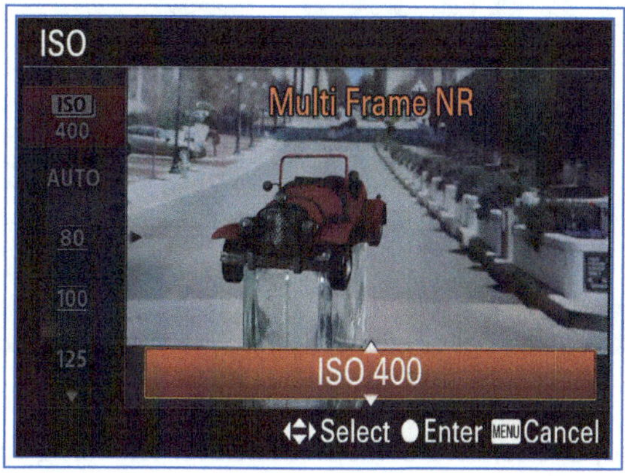

Figure 4-44. Screen for Setting Limit for ISO Multi Frame Noise Reduction

Use the Up and Down buttons or turn the Control wheel or Control dial to select a value, which can be set to Auto or to a specific value from 200 all the way up to 25600. If you choose Auto for this setting, then the camera will select an ISO value according to the lighting conditions, and it will take multiple shots using that value. It will also take into account the settings for Auto ISO Minimum and Maximum. You cannot use the flash when MFNR is in effect. Also, you cannot use some options, such as Raw (or Raw & JPEG) quality, Auto HDR, flash, continuous shooting, or Picture Effect with this setting.

Using MFNR is the only way to set the RX10 to ISO 25600. If you are faced with the prospect of taking pictures in an unusually dark environment, consider using this specialized setting, which really is more akin to a shooting mode than to an ISO setting.

In FIGURE 4-45, I used this setting to capture a hand-held view of an exhibit in a dimly lighted area of a garden display. The camera took the shot with MFNR at ISO 6400.

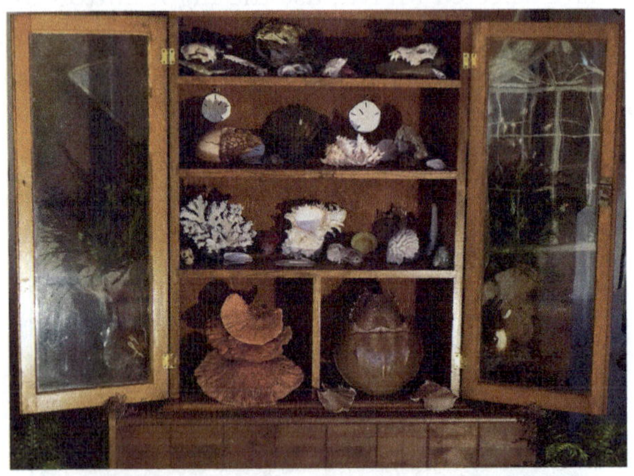

Figure 4-45. Example Using MFNR 6400

In the Auto, Scene, and Sweep Panorama shooting modes, Auto ISO is automatically set, and you cannot adjust the ISO setting.

Note that the settings for ISO 80 and 100 are surrounded by lines on the menu, as seen in FIGURE 4-44. The lines indicates that those settings are not native to the RX10's sensor, whose base ISO is 125. So, although using either of those settings reduces the sensor's sensitivity to light and reduces exposure, it does not improve dynamic range or reduce noise significantly.

ND Filter

The next item on screen 3 of the Shooting menu is the ND Filter setting. With this option, the RX10 gives you a way to reduce the amount of light entering the lens so you will have more flexibility in setting shutter speed and aperture.

The main use for this feature is when the lighting is bright and you need to use a slow shutter speed or a wide aperture. For example, you may need a slow shutter speed to blur the appearance of a waterfall. Or, you may need a wide aperture to blur the background for a portrait. If conditions are bright, it may not be possible to make the setting you need.

For example, I took FIGURE 4-46 on a bright day when I needed to use a slow shutter speed to blur the jets of water from a fountain.

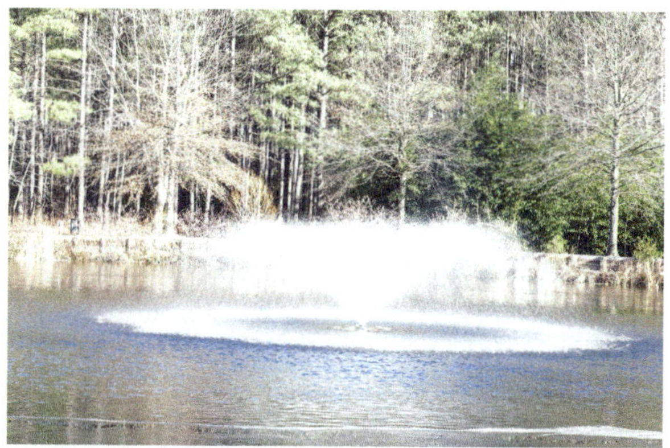

Figure 4-46. ND Filter Off

For this image, I set the camera to Shutter Priority mode and set the shutter speed to 1/10 second to smooth out the water streams. In this mode, as I discussed in CHAPTER 3, the RX10 will not use an aperture more narrow than f/11.0. I had set the ISO to its lowest native value, 125. As you can see, the image was horribly overexposed and unusable.

For FIGURE 4-47, I turned on the ND Filter option, which reduced the exposure setting by 3 EV. With this option enabled, I was able to use the shutter speed of 1/10 second and even was able to open up the aperture a bit, to f/9.0, still using ISO 125. With these settings, the image was exposed normally, and the water in the fountain was smoothed out to produce the desired effect.

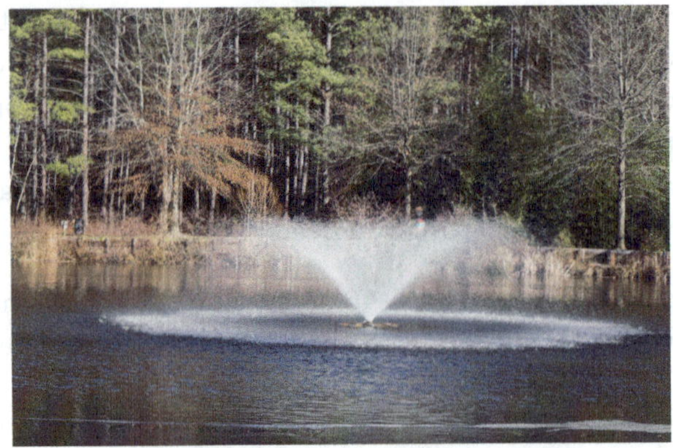

Figure 4-47. ND Filter in Use

This menu option has three possible settings, as shown in Figure 4-48: Auto, On, and Off.

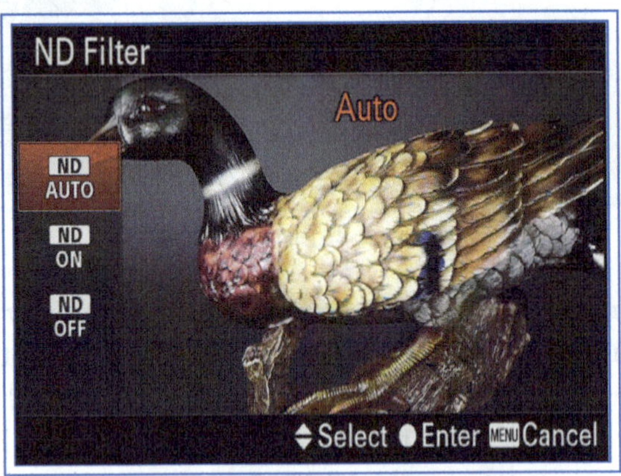

Figure 4-48. ND Filter Menu Options Screen

The second two are self-explanatory: The ND Filter is either used or not used. With Auto, the camera will activate the ND Filter if it detects a need to reduce the light. I prefer not to use that setting, because I like to make my own decisions about how to set the camera. In the Auto, Scene, and Sweep Panorama modes, you can't adjust this setting; the camera automatically uses the Auto option.

If you're using one of the PASM modes and taking casual shots, you might want to set ND Filter to Auto to give you more leeway in the settings you use for aperture and shutter speed without having to dig through the menu to turn on that feature. However, it might be a better idea to assign ND Filter to one of the camera's control buttons, as discussed in CHAPTER 7; if you do that, then it's an easy matter to press that button to call up the ND Filter menu screen and turn the filter on or off whenever you need to.

Metering Mode

This option lets you choose among the three patterns of exposure metering offered by the RX10—Multi, Center, and Spot—as shown in FIGURE 4-49.

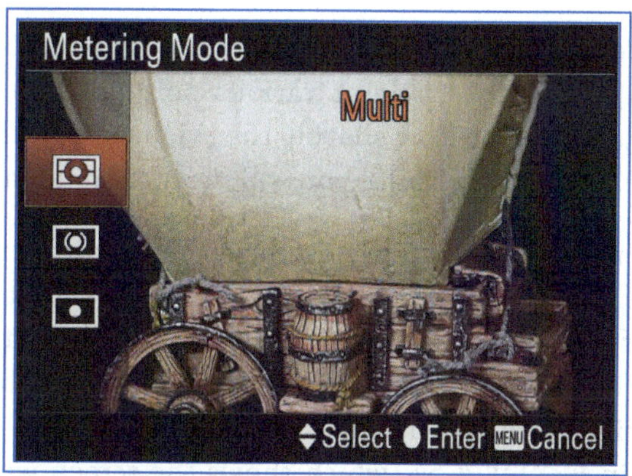

Figure 4-49. Metering Mode Menu Option Screen

This choice tells the camera's automatic exposure system what part of the scene to consider when setting the exposure. With Multi, the camera uses the entire scene that is visible on the camera's display. With Center, the camera measures all of the light from the scene, but it gives additional weight to the center portion of the image on the theory that your main subject is in or near the center. Finally, with Spot, the camera evaluates only the light that is found within the spot metering zone.

In Spot mode, the camera places a small circle in the center of the screen indicating the metered area, as seen in FIGURE 4-50.

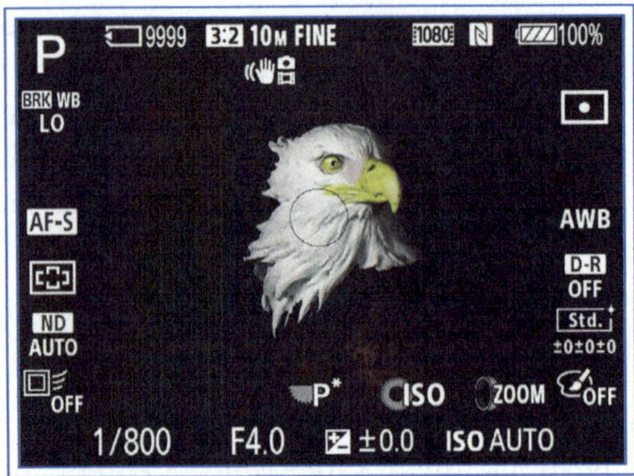

Figure 4-50. Spot Meter Circle on Display

You can see the effects of the Spot setting by selecting Program mode and aiming the circle at various points, some bright and some dark, and seeing how sharply the brightness of the scene on the LCD changes. With Multi, you will see more gradual changes.

With Spot metering, the circle on the screen is different from the frames the camera uses for the Center or Flexible Spot Focus Area settings. If you make either of those Focus Area settings at the same time as the Spot metering setting, you will see both a spot-metering circle and an autofocus frame in the center of the LCD screen, as in FIGURE 4-51, which shows the screen with the Spot metering and Center Focus Area settings in effect.

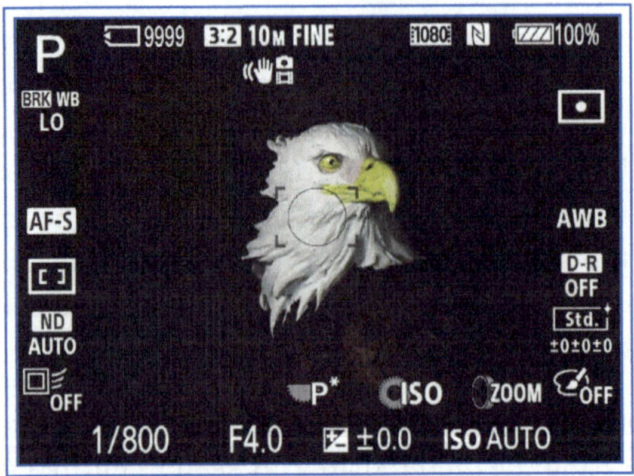

Figure 4-51. Spot Meter Circle and Center Focus Area Frame

Be aware of which of these settings is in effect, if either a circle or a frame is visible in the center of the screen. The circle is for spot metering, and the frame is for Center or Flexible Spot autofocus. (The Center frame is slightly larger than the Medium Flexible Spot frame and slightly smaller than the Large size of that frame.)

In Intelligent Auto and Scene modes, only Multi metering is available. Multi is the only setting available when you are using Digital Zoom or Clear Image Zoom, which are discussed in Chapter 7. You can still turn on either of those options with the Zoom Setting item on the Custom menu; the metering method will not be limited to Multi until you zoom the lens past the optical limit and into the Clear Image or Digital Zoom range.

The Multi setting is best used for scenes with relatively even contrast, such as landscapes, and for action shots, in which the location of the main subjects may move through different parts of the frame. Center is good for sunset scenes, and for other situations in which there is a large, central subject that contrasts with the rest of the scene. Spot is good for portraits, closeups, and other images with a small part of the scene whose exposure is critical. Spot is useful for bright lighting, as when a performer is lit by a spotlight.

The next Shooting menu settings are on screen 4 of the menu, as shown in Figure 4-52, starting with the White Balance option.

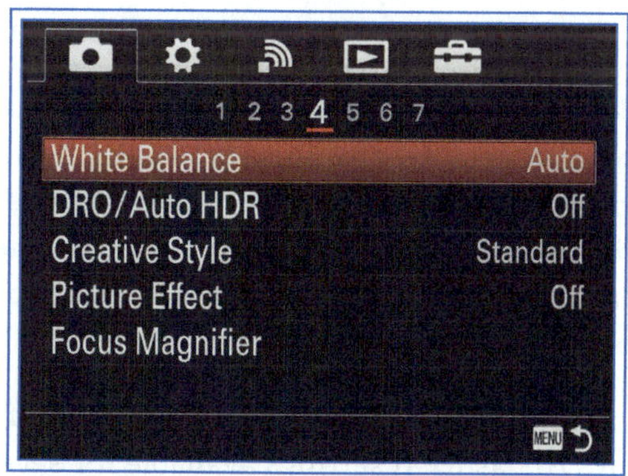

Figure 4-52. Screen 4 of Shooting Menu

White Balance

The RX10's sensor reacts differently to colors than the human eye does. When you or I see a scene in daylight or under artificial lighting, we generally do not notice a difference in the hues of the things we see depending on the light source. The camera, though, "sees" colors differently depending on the "color temperature" of the lighting for the scene. Color temperature is a numerical value expressed in Kelvin (K) units. A light source with a lower Kelvin rating produces a "warmer," or more reddish, light. A light with a higher Kelvin rating produces a "cooler," or more bluish, light. For example, candlelight is rated at about 1,800 K, indoor tungsten light (ordinary light bulb) is rated at about 3,000 K, outdoor sunlight and electronic flash are rated at about 5,500 K, and outdoor shade is rated at about 7,000 K.

With a film camera, you may need a colored filter in front of the lens or light fixture to "correct" for the color temperature of the light source. Any given color film is rated to expose colors correctly at a particular color temperature (or, to put it another way, with a particular light source). So, if you are using color film rated for daylight use, you can use it outdoors without a filter. But if you happen to be using that film indoors, you will need a color filter to correct the color temperature; otherwise, the resulting picture will look excessively reddish because of the imbalance between the film and the color temperature of the light source.

The RX10, like most current digital cameras, has a setting for Auto White Balance, which lets the camera choose the proper color correction to account for any given light source. The Auto White Balance setting works well, and it probably will do the job for you in many situations, especially if you are taking snapshots whose colors are not critical.

If you need more precision in the white balance of your shots, though, the RX10 has fixed settings available for several common light sources, as well as options for setting the white balance by color temperature and for setting a Custom White Balance by evaluating the current light source.

After highlighting this option, press the Center button to bring up the vertical menu at the left of the screen, shown in Figure 4-53.

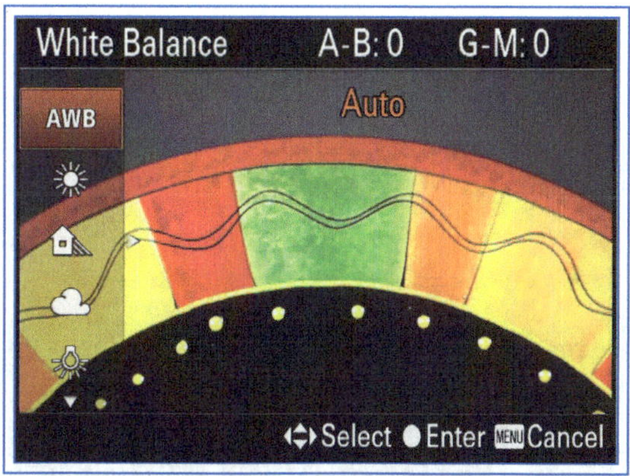

Figure 4-53. White Balance Menu Options Screen 1

Using the Up and Down buttons or turning the Control wheel or Control dial, scroll through the icons on that menu, which take up more than a full screen. The choices on the first screen are Auto White Balance (AWB), Daylight (sun icon), Shade (house icon), Cloudy (cloud icon), and Incandescent (round light bulb icon).

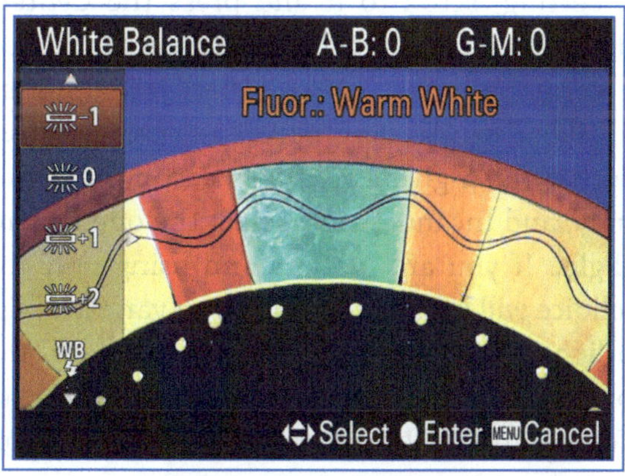

Figure 4-54. White Balance Menu Options Screen 2

The choices on the second screen, shown in Figure 4-54, are Fluorescent Warm White (fluorescent bulb icon with -1), Fluorescent Cool White (same, with 0), Fluorescent Day White (same, with +1), Fluorescent Daylight (same, with +2), and Flash (WB with lightning bolt icon).

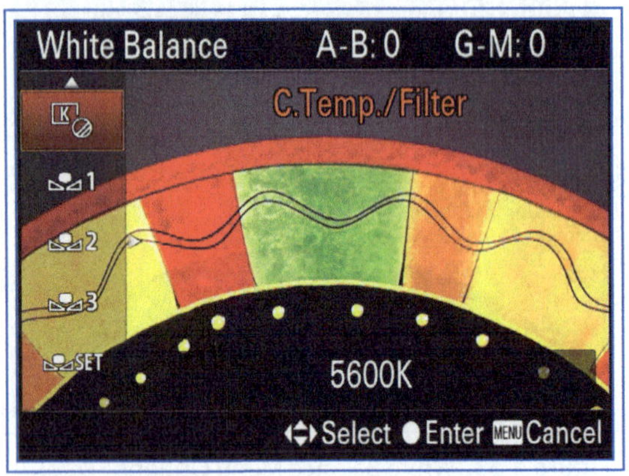

Figure 4-55. White Balance Menu Options Screen 3

The last choices, shown in Figure 4-55, are Color Temperature/ Filter (K and filter icon) and 3 Custom settings (special icon with 1, 2, or 3). Below the Custom icons is an icon with the word "SET," which represents the option for setting the Custom value.

To select a setting, scroll to it and press the Center button to select it. The settings are largely self-explanatory, because most describe a common light source. There are four settings for fluorescent bulbs, so you may need to experiment a bit to find the best setting for a given bulb. For settings such as Daylight, Shade, Cloudy, and Incandescent, select the one that matches the dominant light. If you are indoors and using only incandescent lights, the choice will be easy. If you have a variety of lights turned on and sunlight coming in through the windows, the situation may be more uncertain. In that case, you may want to use either the Color Temperature/Filter setting or the Custom option.

The Color Temperature/Filter option lets you set the color temperature of the light source. One way to do this is with a color temperature meter like the Sekonic Prodigi Color meter shown in Figure 4-56.

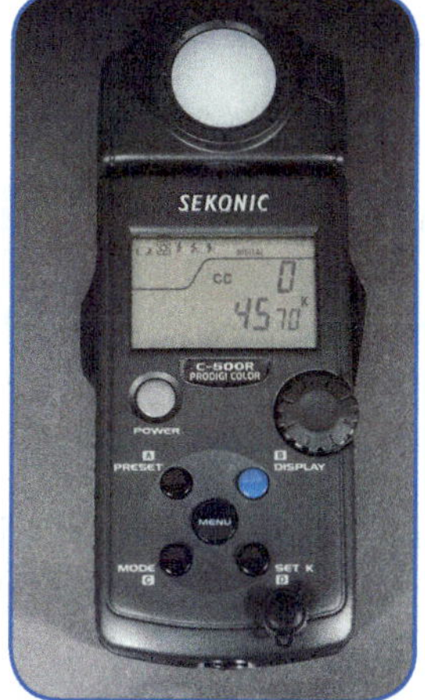

Figure 4-56. Prodigi Color Meter

That meter works well when I need extra accuracy in my settings. It is expensive, though, and you may not want to use that option. In that case, you can still use the Color Temperature/Filter option, but you will have to use guesswork or your sense of color. For example, if you are shooting under lighting from incandescent bulbs, you can use 3,000 K as a starting point, because that is an approximate value for that light source. Then you can change the value and watch the camera's display to see how natural the colors look. As you lower the color temperature setting, the image will become more "cool," or bluish; as you raise it, the image will appear more "warm," or reddish. Once you find the best setting, leave it in place and take your shots.

To make this setting, after you highlight the icon for Color Temperature/Filter, press the Right button to move the orange highlight to the right side of the camera's screen, so that it highlights the color temperature value, as shown in Figure 4-57.

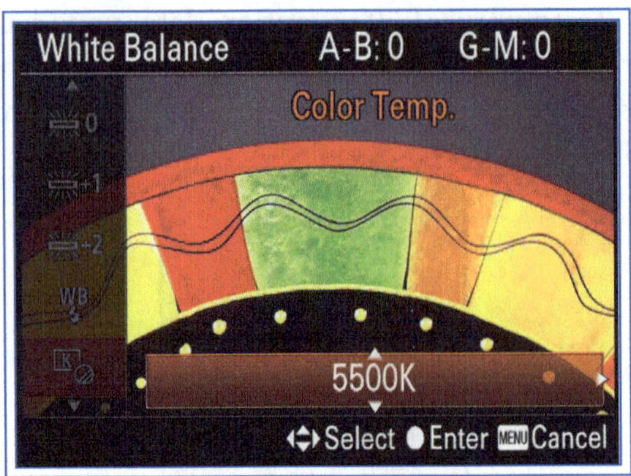

Figure 4-57. Color Temperature Setting Screen

Then raise or lower that number using the Up and Down buttons or by turning the Control wheel or Control dial.

If you don't want to work with color temperatures, you can set a Custom White Balance. This process can be confusing, because the Custom setting has several icons on the White Balance menu. The first three Custom icons, located just below the Color Temperature/Filter icon, are the ones to select when you want to set the camera to use one of three currently stored Custom White Balance settings. The fourth icon, with the word "SET" included, is the one to select when you want to obtain a new reading for one of the Custom White Balance settings by using the camera's special procedure for setting that value. Before you can use any of the three upper Custom icons, you need to make sure that you have used the lowest Custom icon to set the Custom White Balance value as you want it.

Here is the procedure for setting the Custom White Balance. First, highlight the Custom SET icon at the bottom of the White Balance menu. Press the Center button to select this option, and the camera will display a message saying "Press the [Center] button to capture data of central area of screen." (as shown in FIGURE 4-58).

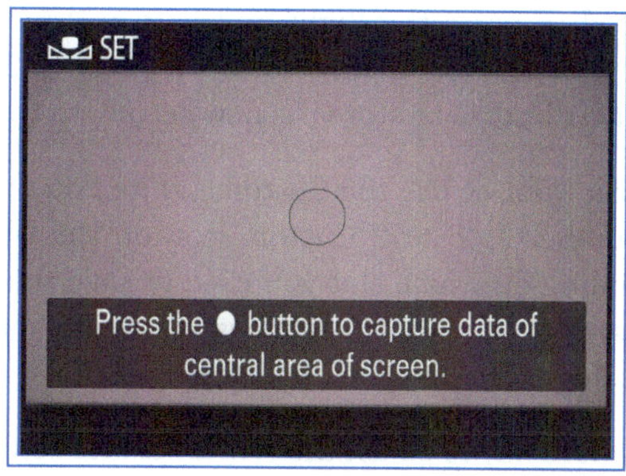

Figure 4-58. Prompt Message for Setting Custom White Balance

Aim the camera so the circle on the screen is filled with a solid white or gray color from a sheet of paper or other surface, with that surface illuminated by the light source you will be using.

Then press the Center button, and the camera will set the white balance. The display will show the color temperature along with variations along two color axes. You will see a number next to the letters "A-B" for the amber-blue axis and "G-M" for green-magenta.

If there is no variation along either of the axes, you will see a 0 next to the pair of letters. If there is some variation, you will see an indication such as G-M: G1, meaning 1 unit of variation toward green along the green-magenta axis, as shown in Figure 4-59.

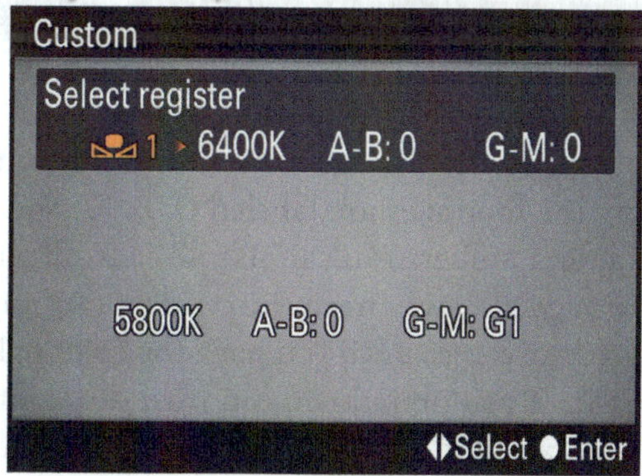

Figure 4-59. Results Screen for Custom White Balance

You then need to press the Right and Left buttons or turn the Control wheel or Control dial to select Register 1, 2, or 3. Then press the Center button to store the new setting to that register.

Whenever you want to use the Custom White Balance you saved, select the number 1, 2, or 3 Custom icon on the White Balance menu, depending on which slot you used to save the setting. You can change any of the custom settings whenever you want to, if you are shooting under different lighting conditions.

There is one more way to adjust the White Balance setting by taking advantage of the two color axes discussed above. If you really want to tweak the White Balance setting to the nth degree, when you have highlighted your desired setting (whether a preset or the Custom setting), press the Right button, and you will be presented with a screen for fine adjustments, as shown in FIGURE 4-60.

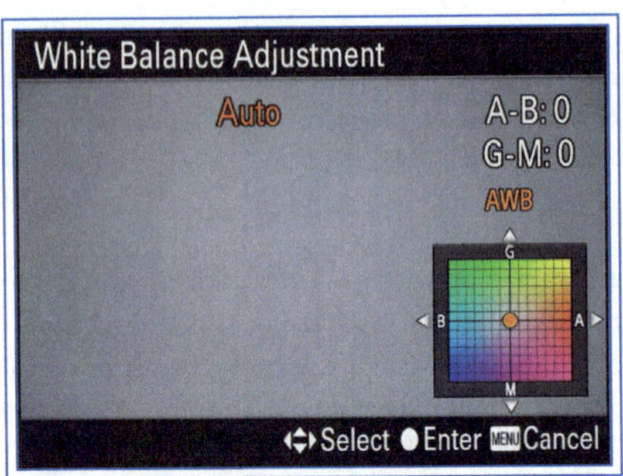

Figure 4-60. White Balance Adjustment Axes

You will see a pair of axes that intersect at a zero point, marked by an orange dot. The four axes are labeled G, B, M, and A for green, blue, magenta, and amber. You can use all four direction buttons to move the orange dot away from the center along any of the axes to adjust these four values until you have the color balance exactly how you want it. If you prefer, you can turn the Control wheel to adjust the G-M axis, and the Control dial to adjust the B-A axis. Be careful to undo any adjustments using these axes when they are no longer needed; otherwise, the adjustments will alter the colors of all images that are shot using this White Balance setting in a shooting mode for which White Balance can be adjusted, even after the camera has been powered off and then back on.

Two more notes: First, if you use Raw quality, you can always correct the White Balance setting after the fact in your Raw software. So, if you are using Raw, you don't have to worry so much about what setting you are using for White Balance. Still, it's a good idea always to check the setting before shooting to avoid getting caught with incorrect white balance when you are not using the Raw format.

Second, before you decide to use the "correct" White Balance setting in every situation, consider whether that is the best course of action to get the results you ultimately want. For example, I know of one photographer who generally keeps his camera set for Daylight White Balance even when shooting indoors because he likes the "warmer" appearance that comes from using that setting. I don't necessarily recommend that approach, but it's not a bad idea to give some thought to straying from a strict approach to white balance, at least on occasion.

White Balance cannot be adjusted for Intelligent Auto or Scene mode; the camera will use Auto White Balance in those modes.

Before I leave this topic, I am including a chart in Figure 4-61 that shows how the different White Balance settings affect images taken by the RX10. The images in the chart were taken under artificial light balanced for daylight, with the camera set for each available White Balance setting, as indicated on the chart. In my opinion, several of the results are acceptable. The only settings that are clearly off the mark for this light source are Incandescent, Fluorescent Warm White, and Fluorescent Cool White. The Auto White Balance setting did a good job of adjusting the camera for the lighting.

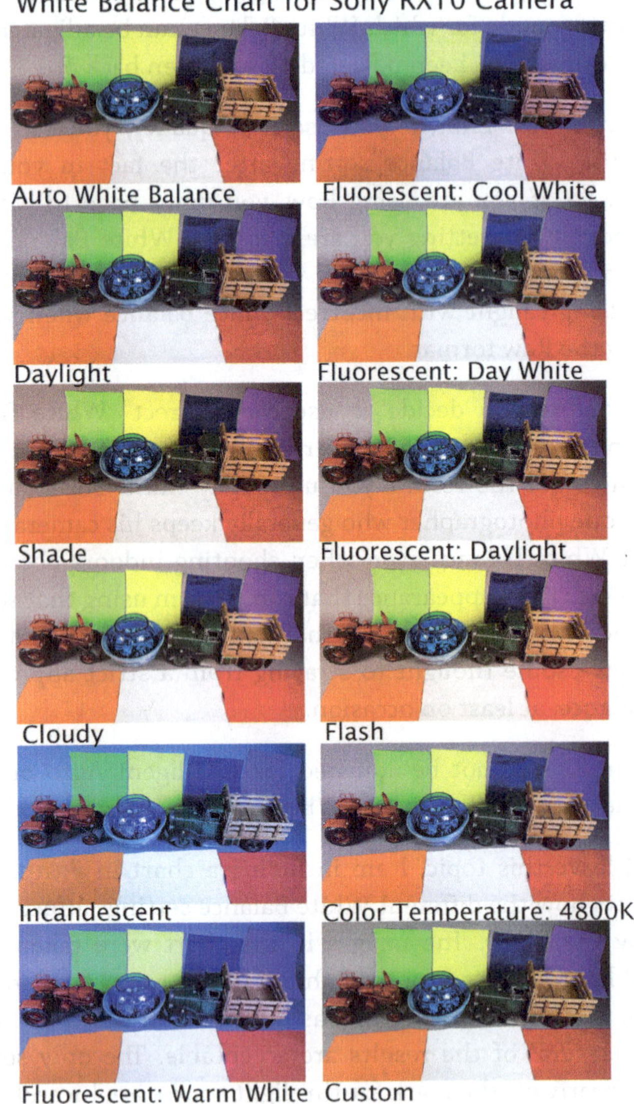

Figure 4-61. White Balance Settings Comparison Chart

DRO/Auto HDR

The next option on the Shooting menu helps you control the dynamic range of your shots and use the in-camera HDR processing of the RX10. With these settings, you can avoid problems with excessive contrast in your images. Such issues arise because digital cameras cannot easily process a wide range of dark and light areas in the same image—that is, their "dynamic range" is limited. So, if you are taking a picture in an area that is partly in bright sunlight and partly in deep shade, the resulting image is likely to have some areas in which the details are lost in the shadows, or some areas in which the highlights, or bright areas, are excessively bright, or "blown out," so, again, the details of the image are lost.

One way to deal with this situation is to use high dynamic range, or HDR techniques, in which multiple photographs of the same scene with different exposures are combined into one composite image that is more evenly exposed throughout the entire scene. The RX10 can take HDR shots on its own, or you can take separate exposures yourself and combine them in software on your computer into a composite HDR image. I will discuss the details of these HDR techniques a bit later in this chapter.

The RX10's DRO (Dynamic Range Optimizer) setting gives you another way to deal with uneven lighting, using special processing in the camera that can boost details in dark areas and reduce overexposure in bright areas at the same time, resulting in a single image with better-balanced exposure than would be possible otherwise.

To use the DRO feature, press the Menu button and highlight this option, then press the Center button to bring the DRO/Auto HDR menu up on the camera's display, as shown in FIGURE 4-62.

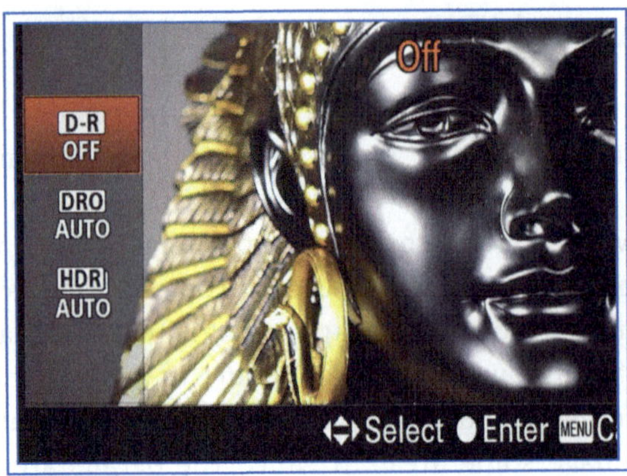

Figure 4-62. DRO/Auto HDR Menu Options Screen

Scroll through the options on that menu using the Up and Down buttons or turning the Control wheel.

With the first option, D-R Off, no special processing is used. If you select the second choice, you can then press the Right and Left buttons or turn the Control dial to move through the six choices for the DRO setting: Auto, or Level 1 through Level 5. With the Auto setting, the camera will analyze the scene and attempt to use an appropriate amount of DR processing. Otherwise, you can pick the level; the higher the number, the greater the degree of processing to even out the contrast between the light and dark parts of the image.

In Figure 4-63 through Figure 4-65, there are examples of the use of the various levels of DRO processing, ranging from Off to Level 5. For these images, I photographed two colorful items in an area that was in deep shade on the left and bright sunlight on the right, to see how well the DRO feature could even out the lighting and pull details out of the shadows.

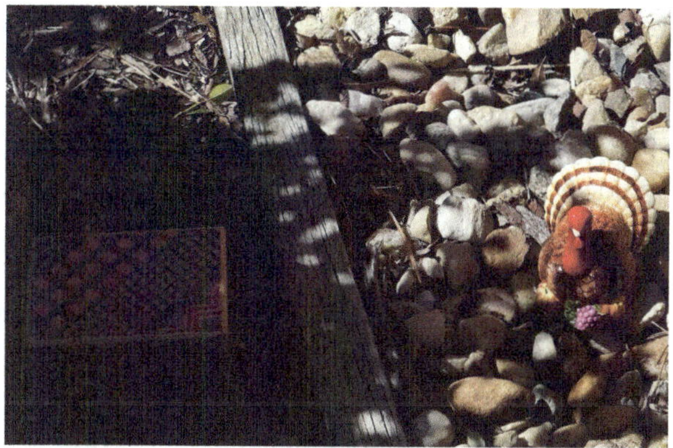

Figure 4-63. DRO Off

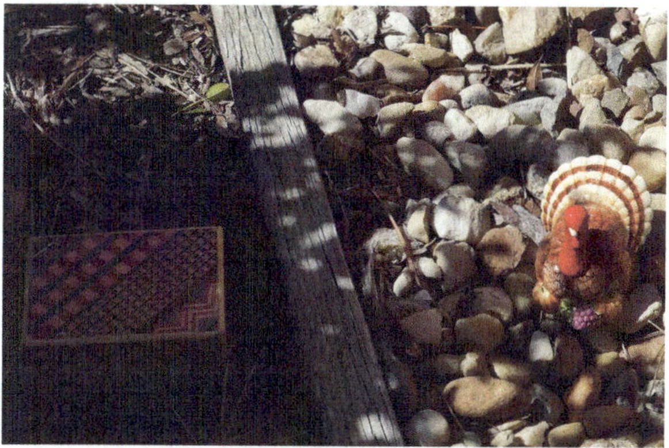

Figure 4-64. DRO Set to Level 3

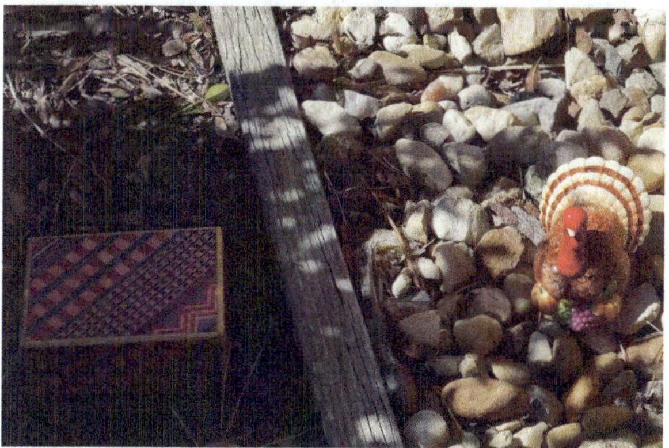

Figure 4-65. DRO Set to Level 5

The greater the level of DRO used, the more evenly the RX10 processed the lighting, by selectively enhancing details in the shadowy areas and reducing overall contrast. There is some risk of increasing noise in the dark areas with this sort of processing, but the RX10 does not seem to do badly in this respect; I have not seen increased noise levels in images processed with the DRO feature.

The final option for this item, HDR, involves in-camera HDR processing. With traditional HDR processing, the photographer takes several shots of a scene with a wide dynamic range, some underexposed and some overexposed, and merges them using Photoshop or other software to blend differently exposed portions from all of the images. The end result is a composite HDR image that can exhibit clear details throughout all parts of the image.

Because of the popularity of HDR, many makers have incorporated some degree of DR processing in their cameras to even out areas of excessive brightness and darkness so as to preserve details. With the RX10, as with many modern cameras, Sony has provided an automatic method for taking multiple shots that the camera combines internally to achieve one HDR composite image.

To use this feature, highlight the bottom option on the DRO/Auto HDR menu, as shown in Figure 4-66.

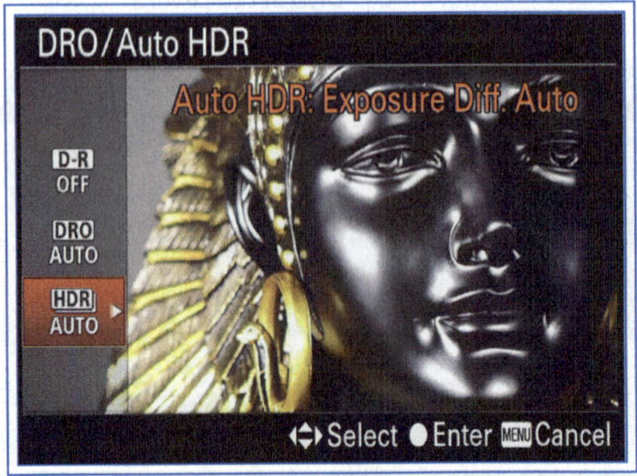

Figure 4-66. HDR Menu Option Highlighted on Menu Screen

Press the Right and Left buttons or turn the Control dial to scroll through the options for the HDR setting until you have highlighted the one you want, then press the Center button to select that option and return to the shooting screen. The seven available options are Auto HDR and HDR with EV settings from 1.0 through 6.0.

If you select Auto HDR, the camera will analyze the scene and the lighting conditions and select a level of exposure difference on its own. If you select a specific level from 1.0 to 6.0, the camera will use that level as the overall difference among the three shots it takes.

For example, if you select 1.0 EV for the exposure difference, the camera will take three shots in a rapid burst, each 1/2 of an EV level (f-stop) different in exposure from the next—one shot at the metered EV level, one shot at 1/2 EV lower, and one shot at 1/2 EV higher. If you choose the maximum exposure difference of 6.0 EV, then the shots will be 3.0 EV apart in their brightness levels.

When you press the shutter button, the camera will take three shots in a quick burst; you should either use a tripod or hold the camera very steady. When it has finished processing the shots, the camera will save the composite image as well as the single image that was taken at the metered exposure.

For Figure 4-67 through Figure 4-70, I set the RX10 on a tripod and took a series of images of a duck figure in front of a bright window. I took the first three shots with varied HDR settings on the RX10, and I created the final image by taking several shots using Manual exposure mode and combining them with HDR software.

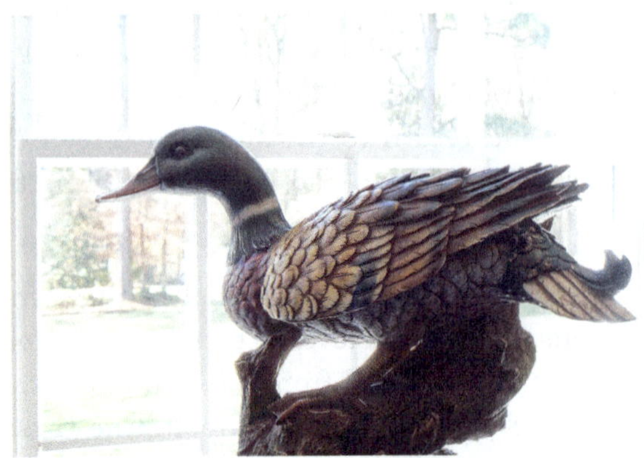

Figure 4-67. HDR Auto

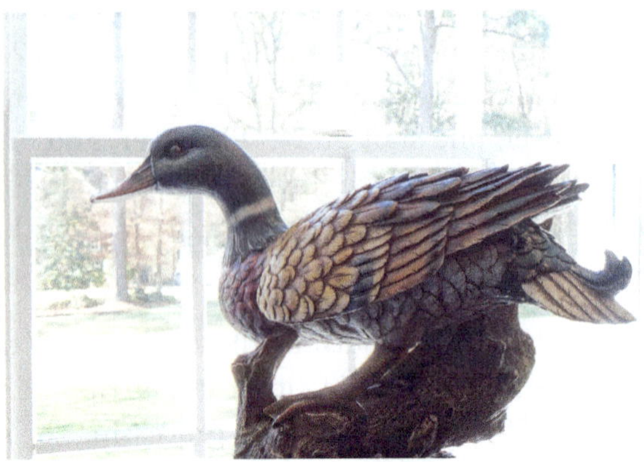

Figure 4-68. HDR Set to 3.0 EV

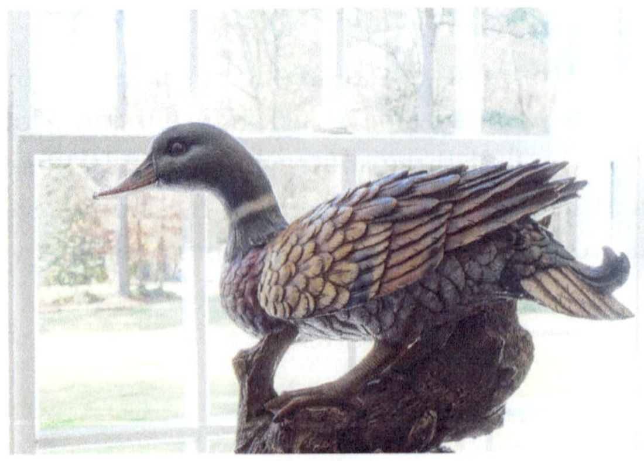

Figure 4-69. HDR Set to 6.0 EV

For FIGURE 4-67, HDR was set to Auto; for FIGURE 4-68, it was set to Level 3; and for FIGURE 4-69, it was set to its highest value, Level 6. The differences are not as dramatic as I might have expected, though some additional details are visible in the outdoor part of the scene in the shots with HDR turned on, and there are some more details in the shadowed areas of the duck. However, none of the three shots with the RX10's HDR turned on produced an image with evenly balanced brightness.

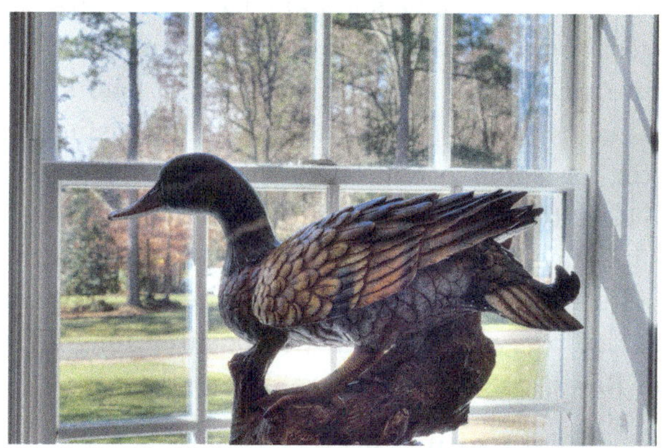

Figure 4-70. HDR Composite Image from Photomatix Pro Software

For comparison, I took several shots of the same scene using a range of exposure levels by varying the shutter speeds in Manual exposure mode. I merged those images together in Photomatix Pro software and tweaked the result until I got what seemed to be the optimal appearance of the duck and the outdoor scene. In my opinion, the HDR image done in software, shown in FIGURE 4-70, provides a more evenly illuminated view of the subject than either of the in-camera HDR shots taken by the RX10.

However, these images were taken under fairly extreme conditions. The in-camera HDR option is an excellent tool to use when you need to take pictures of scenes that are partly shaded and partly in bright sunlight, and you don't have the time or the inclination to take multiple pictures and combine them later with HDR software into a composite image.

My recommendation is to leave the DRO Auto setting turned on when you are taking general shots on a trip or for pleasure, especially if you don't plan to do any post-processing of the images using software. If the contrast in lighting for a given scene is extreme, then try at least some shots using the Auto HDR feature.

If you plan to do post-processing, then you may want to shoot using the Raw quality setting, so you can work with the shots later using post-processing software to achieve evenly exposed final images. You also might want to use Manual exposure mode or exposure bracketing to take a series of shots at different exposures, so you can blend them together using Photoshop, Photomatix, or some other HDR software. One great feature of the RX10 is that it provides unusually high levels of dynamic range in its Raw files, particularly if you shoot with low ISO settings. Therefore, you very well may be able to bring details out of the shadows and reduce overexposure in highlighted areas using your Raw processing software.

Note that the Auto HDR setting cannot be set if you are using Raw quality for your images. The DRO settings do work with Raw images, but they will have no effect on the Raw images unless you process them with Sony's Image Data Converter software.

In addition, the DRO and Auto HDR settings are unavailable in the Intelligent Auto, Scene, or Sweep Panorama modes. You can use the flash with these settings, but it will fire only for the first HDR shot, and it defeats the purpose of the settings to use flash, so you probably should not do so.

Creative Style

The Creative Style setting gives you a way to alter your images with in-camera adjustments to contrast, saturation (color intensity), and sharpness. Using the variety of settings available with this option, you can add or subtract intensity of color or make subtle changes to the look of your images, as well as shooting in monochrome.

Of course, if you plan to edit your images on a computer using software such as Image Data Converter, Photoshop, or Lightroom, you can duplicate these effects at that stage. But if you don't want to spend time processing your images that way, having the ability to alter the appearance of your shots using this menu option can add a good deal to the enjoyment of your photos.

To use this feature, highlight Creative Style, the third item on screen 4 of the Shooting menu, and press the Center button to move to the next screen, as shown in Figure 4-71.

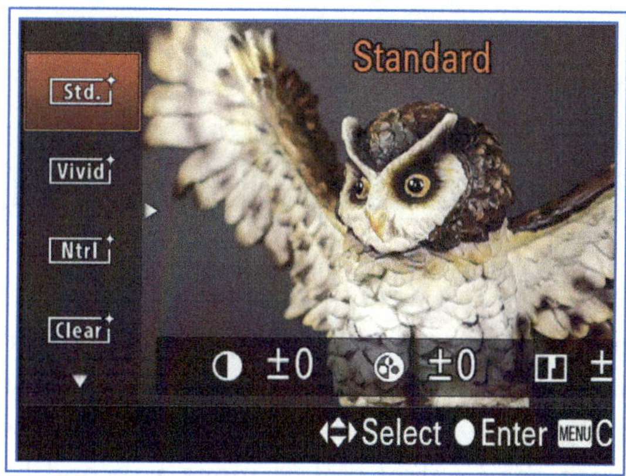

Figure 4-71. Creative Style Menu Options Screen

Using the Up and Down buttons or turning the Control wheel, scroll through the 13 main settings: Standard, Vivid, Neutral, Clear, Deep, Light, Portrait, Landscape, Sunset, Night Scene, Autumn Leaves, Black and White, and Sepia. If you want to choose one of these settings with no further adjustment, just press the Center button when your chosen option is highlighted.

If you select an option other than Standard, you may see a change reflected on the camera's display in shooting mode. For example, if you choose Sepia or Black and White, the screen will show the scene with that coloration. This effect will be visible, though, only if the Live View Display option on screen 2 of the Custom menu is set to Setting Effect On. If it is set to Setting Effect Off, the display will not show any change from the Creative Style setting.

You will still see an icon showing which setting is in effect, in the lower right of the screen. For example, FIGURE 4-72 shows the display when the Sepia setting is active but Setting Effect is off.

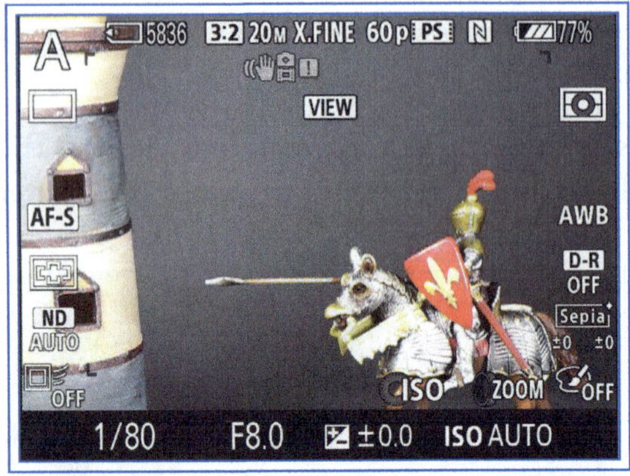

Figure 4-72. Sepia Setting with Setting Effect Off

To fine-tune the contrast, saturation, and sharpness for one of the Creative Style settings, move the orange highlight bar to the desired setting, such as Vivid or Portrait, and press the Right button or turn the Control dial to move a second highlight bar into the right side of the screen.

You will see a label above a line of three icons accompanied by numbers at the bottom of the screen, as shown in FIGURE 4-73.

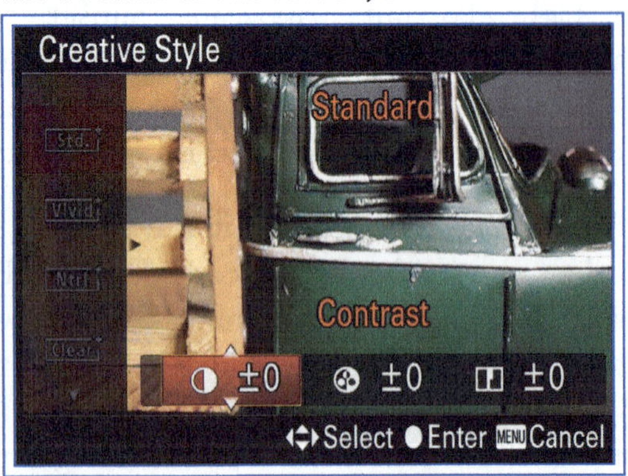

Figure 4-73. Creative Style Adjustment Screen

As you move the orange highlight left and right through those icons, the label will change to show which value is currently active and ready to be adjusted. When the chosen value (contrast, saturation, or sharpness) is highlighted, use the Up and Down buttons or turn the Control wheel to adjust the value upward or downward by up to 3 units. When the Black and White or Sepia setting is active, there are only two adjustments available—contrast and sharpness. Saturation is not available because it adjusts the intensity of colors and there are no colors to adjust.

By varying the amounts of these three parameters, you can achieve a considerable range of different appearances for your images. For example, by increasing saturation, you can add punch and make colors stand out. By adding contrast and/or sharpness, you can impose a "harder" appearance on your images, making them look grittier and more realistic. FIGURE 4-74 is a composite image in which the left shot was taken with the Standard setting with all three parameters adjusted to their minimums, and the right shot was taken with the same setting, but with the contrast, sharpness, and saturation all adjusted to their maximum levels of +3 units.

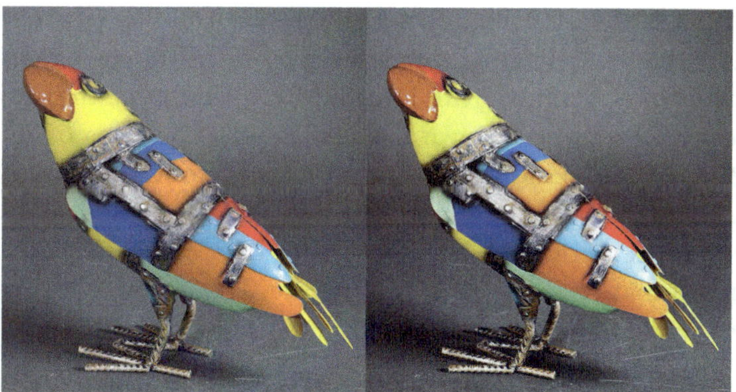

Figure 4-74. Left: Minimum Adjustments, Right: Maximum Adjustments

As you can see, the right image is noticeably darker, with a grittier look than the left one.

If you want to save your adjusted settings for future use, you can create and save six different custom versions, using any of the 13 basic settings with whatever adjustments you want. To do this, scroll down on the Creative Style menu to the numbered items, starting just below the Sepia item, as shown in Figure 4-75.

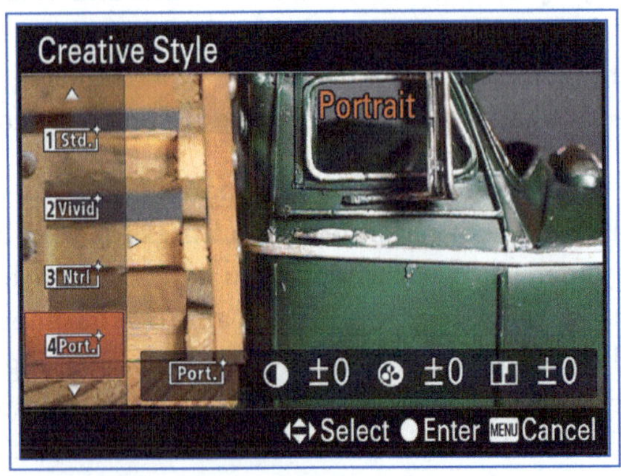

Figure 4-75. Numbered Settings for Creative Style

There are six of these numbered slots, of which four are visible on this screen. They all work in the same way. First, highlight one of the six numbered slots. Then, using the Control dial or the Right button, move the highlight to the right side of the screen, on the name of the setting (Vivid, Neutral, Deep, etc.). Use the Control wheel or the Up and Down buttons to select any one of the 13 settings. Then, scroll to the right and adjust contrast, saturation, and sharpness as you want it. When all the adjustments are made, press the Center button to accept them. Then, whenever you want to recall that setting for use, call up the Creative Style menu and scroll to the numbered slot for the style you adjusted.

The Creative Style option works with all shooting modes except Intelligent Auto mode and Scene mode. You can use it with the Raw format, but the results will vary depending on the Raw-conversion software you use. For example, I just shot a Raw image in Program mode using the Black and White setting. The image showed up in black and white on the camera's screen.

However, when I opened the image in Adobe Camera Raw and then in Photoshop, the image was in color; the Adobe software ignored the information in the image's data about the Creative Style setting. When I opened the image using Sony's Image Data Converter software, though, the image appeared in black and white because Sony's software recognized the Creative Style information. So, if you want to use this menu option with Raw files, you need to be aware that not all software will use that information when processing the images. Creative Style cannot be used when Picture Effect is being used.

FIGURES 4-76 and 4-77 include comparison photos showing each setting as applied to the same scene under the same lighting conditions to illustrate the different effects you can achieve with each variation. General descriptions of these effects are provided after the comparison charts.

Creative Styles Chart - Part 1

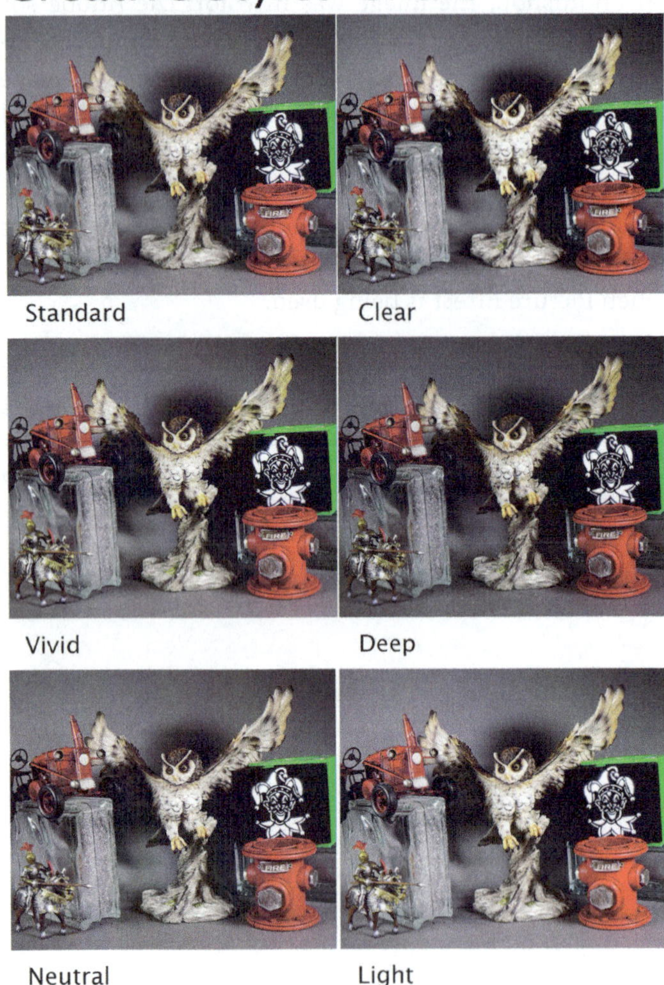

Figure 4-76. Creative Style Settings Comparison Chart - Part 1

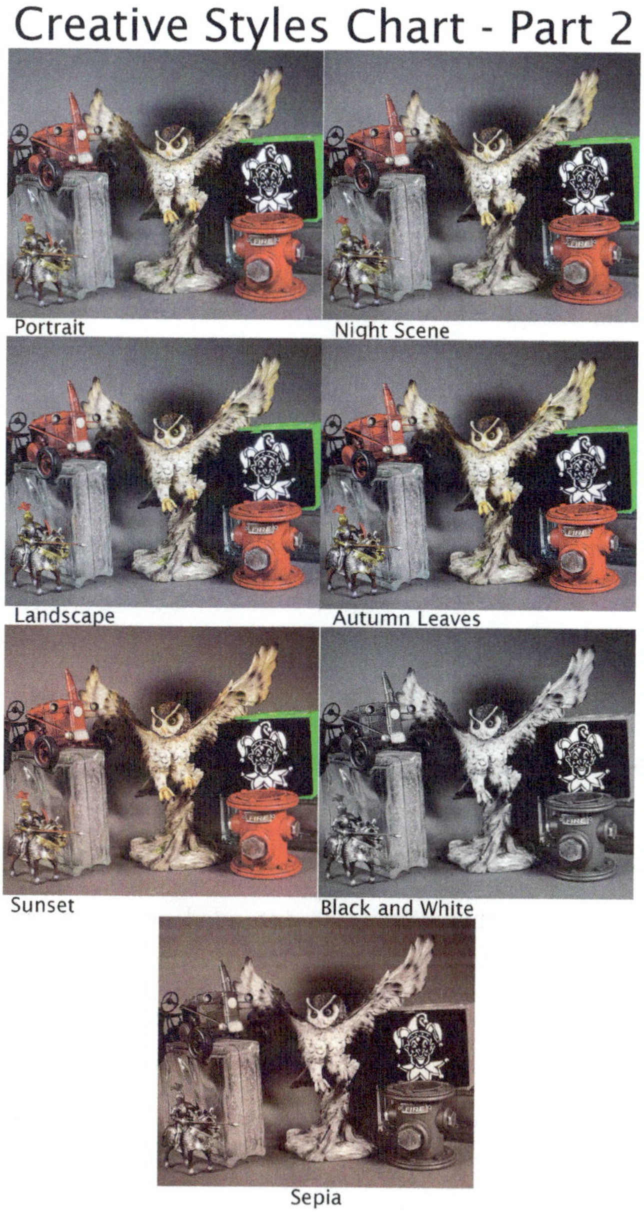

Creative Styles Chart - Part 2

Portrait

Night Scene

Landscape

Autumn Leaves

Sunset

Black and White

Sepia

Figure 4-77. Creative Style Settings Comparison Chart - Part 2

Standard

The Standard setting is equivalent to having this feature turned off; no special processing is applied to your images.

Vivid

The Vivid setting increases the saturation, or intensity, of all colors in the image. As you can see from the samples, it calls attention to the scene, though it does not produce very dramatic effects. The Vivid setting might work well if you want to emphasize the colors in images taken at a birthday party or at a carnival.

Neutral

With the Neutral setting, the RX10 leaves images with reduced saturation and sharpness, so you can process them to your own taste using software.

Clear

Clear, according to Sony, emphasizes the highlighted areas in the image, giving them added intensity. Some users feel this setting yields images with more intensity than the Vivid setting.

Deep

Sony says that this setting is intended to show the "solid presence" of the subject. In effect, it emphasizes the shadow tones and lowers the overall brightness of the image.

Light

This setting is the opposite of Deep; it emphasizes the highlight tones and results in a brighter, lighter appearance.

Portrait

The main feature of the Portrait setting is a reduction in the saturation and sharpness of colors to soften the appearance of skin tones. You might want to use this setting to take portraits that are flattering rather than harsh and realistic. Because this setting provides midrange values for the colors and contrast, some photographers find this to be their favored Creative Style setting for general photography.

Landscape

With the Landscape setting, the RX10 increases all three values—contrast, saturation, and sharpness—to make the features of a landscape, such as trees and mountains, stand out with clear, sharp outlines. It is similar to Portrait in its processing of colors, but the sharper outlines and contrast might be too strong for portraits.

Sunset

With the Sunset option, the camera increases the saturation to emphasize the red hues of the sunset. In my opinion, this setting produces more changes in color images than any of the others.

Night Scene

Night Scene lowers contrast in an attempt to soften the harsh effect that may result from shots taken in dark surroundings, without affecting the saturation or hues of the colors.

Autumn Leaves

This setting, designed for enhancing shots of fall foliage, increases the intensity of existing red and yellow tones in the image, but does not alter the color balance or introduce new reddish shades, as the Sunset setting does.

B/W

This setting removes all color, converting the scene to black and white. Some photographers use this setting to achieve a realistic look for their street photography.

Sepia

This second monochrome setting also removes the color from the image, but adds a sepia tone that gives an old-fashioned appearance to the shot.

The RX10 also has settings for Portrait, Landscape, and Sunset in Scene mode, discussed in Chapter 3. However, the similar settings of the Creative Style option are available in the more advanced shooting modes, including Program, Aperture Priority, Shutter Priority, and Manual Exposure, so you have access to other settings, such as ISO, Metering Mode, and others. And, as noted above, you can tweak Creative Style settings by fine-tuning contrast, saturation, and sharpness.

I don't often use the Creative Style settings, because I prefer to shoot with the Raw format and process my images in software such as Photoshop. I do occasionally use the Sunset setting to enhance an evening view. I believe the Creative Style settings would be of most value to a photographer who needs to take numerous photographs with a certain type of appearance and process them quickly. For example, a wedding photographer or sports photographer may not have time to process images in software; he or she may need to capture hundreds of images in a particular visual style and have them ready for a client or a publication without delay. For this type of application, the Creative Style settings are invaluable.

Picture Effect

The Picture Effect menu option includes a rich array of in-camera special effects. The Sony RX10 gives you a terrific variety of ways in which to add creative touches to your shots, and the Picture Effect settings are probably my favorites. Of course, there is a lot of competition in the arena of special-effects photography nowadays from photo apps that are available for smartphones (such as Instagram, Hipstamatic, and others), and there also is competition from the trend for using cameras like the Holga—film-based models whose images are purposely degraded to look old-fashioned, with low resolution, grain, and other attributes of images taken by cheap, plastic cameras. The Picture Effect option lets you delve into this area and other types of creative photo-making with considerable flexibility.

Picture Effect settings do not work with Raw images. If you set a Picture Effect option and then select Raw quality, the Picture Effect setting will be canceled. However, unlike the situation with Scene mode settings, you still have control over many of the important settings on the camera, including Image Size, White Balance, ISO, and, in most cases, Drive Mode. The Picture Effect menu option is not available with the Auto, Scene, or Sweep Panorama shooting mode. It is available for video recording to some extent, as I'll discuss later.

To use any of these effects, select the Picture Effect menu option as shown in FIGURE 4-78, and, as with other menu screens, scroll through the choices at the left of the screen.

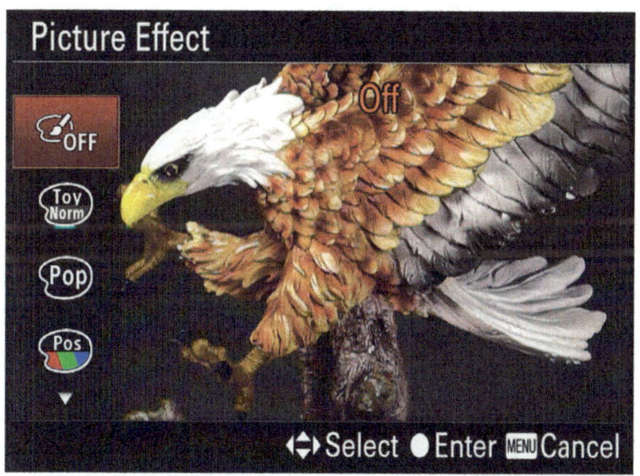

Figure 4-78. Picture Effect Menu Options Screen

Some selections have no further options, and some have additional settings that you can make by pressing the Left and Right buttons or by turning the Control dial.

I will discuss each option in turn. In FIGURE 4-79 and FIGURE 4-80, I provide two charts with one example image taken with each effect, all taken of the same scene—a lineup of objects with a variety of colors and textures. This sample scene does not fit well with all of the Picture Effect settings because some settings are more suited for subjects like flowers and plants, some for buildings, and some, like the Miniature Effect feature, for specialized situations. However, I believe it is useful to see how the various settings affect the same scene, so that is how the charts are set up. After the charts, I will discuss each of the settings and provide larger illustrations for some of them.

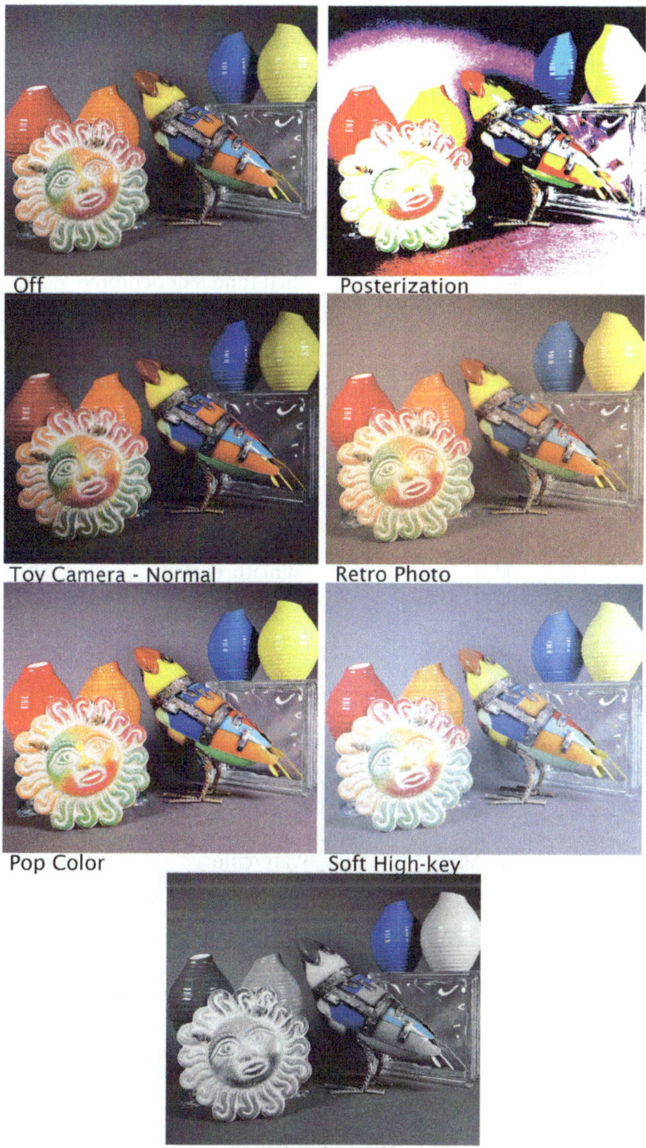

Figure 4-79. Picture Effect Settings Comparison Chart - Part 1

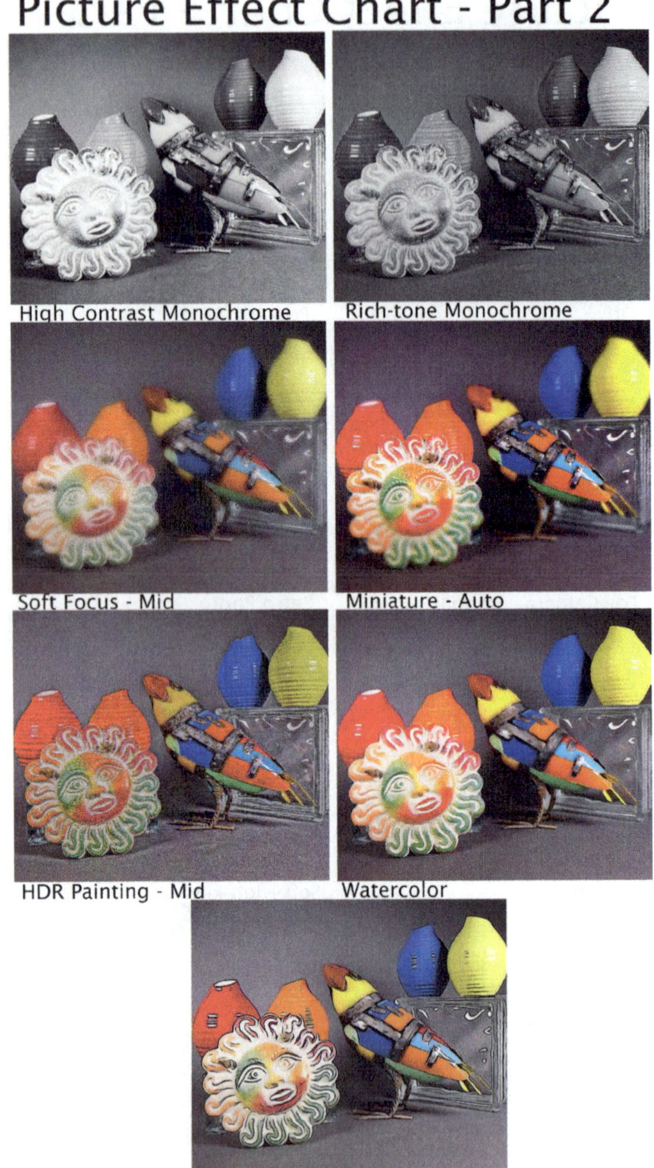

Figure 4-80. Picture Effect Settings Comparison Chart - Part 2

Following are details about each of the settings.

Off

This first option is used to cancel all Picture Effect settings. When you are engaged in ordinary picture-taking, you should make sure the Off setting is selected so that no unwanted special effects interfere with your images or conflict with your other settings.

Toy Camera

The Toy Camera option gives you an alternative to using a "toy" film camera such as the Holga, Diana, or Lomo, which are popular with artists for taking photos with grainy, low-resolution appearances. With all of the Toy Camera settings, the RX10 processes the image so it looks as if it were taken by a camera with a cheap lens: The image is dark at the corners and somewhat blurry.

The several sub-settings for Toy Camera, reached by pressing the Right and Left buttons or turning the Control dial, act as follows:

- Normal: No additional processing.
- Cool: Adjusts color to the "cool" side, resulting in a bluish tint.
- Warm: Uses a "warm" white balance, giving a reddish hue.
- Green: Adds a green tint, similar to dialing in an adjustment on the green axis for white balance.
- Magenta: Similar to the Green setting, but adjustment is along the magenta axis.

Figure 4-81 is an image of a green water fountain in a wooded area taken with the Toy Camera feature using its Green setting.

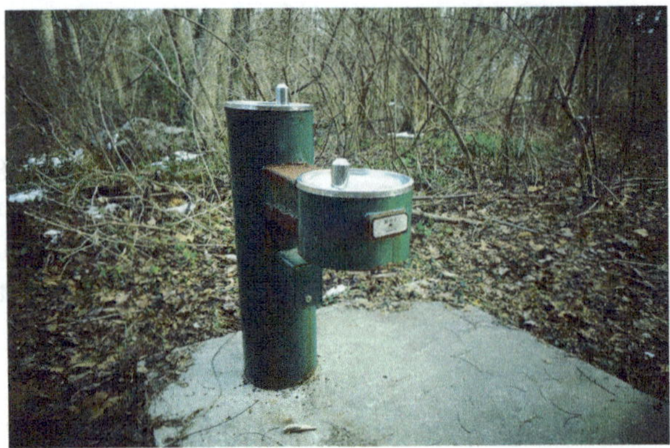

Figure 4-81. Toy Camera - Green Example

Pop Color

This next setting, according to Sony, is intended to give a "pop art" feel to your images through emphasis on bright colors. As you can see in Figure 4-82, which shows some colorful plastic mushrooms in a garden store, what you get with this setting is another way to add "punch" and intensity, along with added brightness, to your color images. You can try this setting as an alternative to the Vivid setting of the Creative Style option.

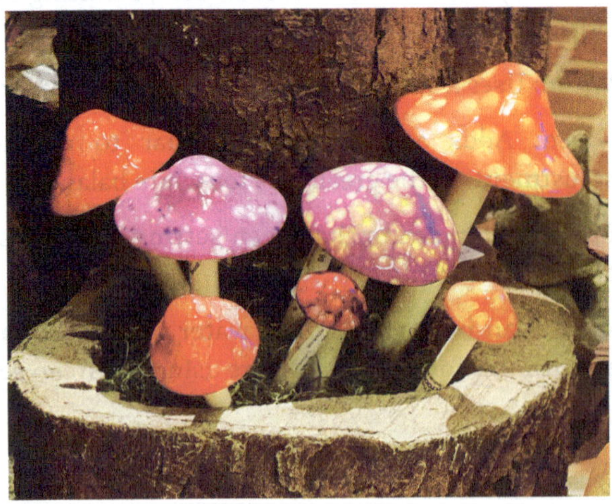

Figure 4-82. Pop Color Example

Posterization

The Posterization setting adds a fairly dramatic effect to your images.

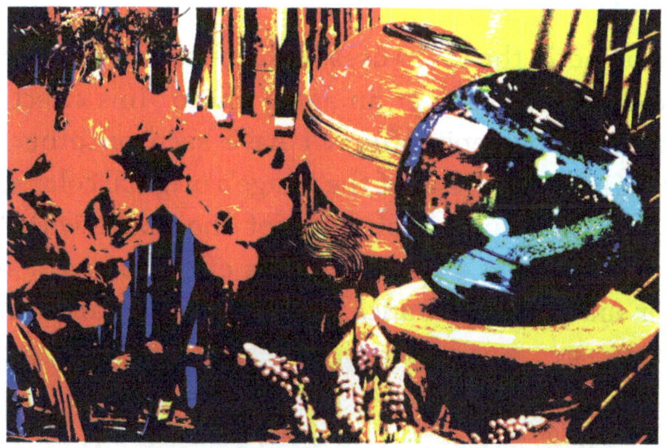

Figure 4-83. Posterization Example

Using the Right and Left buttons or the Control dial, you can choose to apply this effect in color or in black and white. In either case, with this effect the camera applies a distinctive form of processing that results in heightened emphasis on colors (or dark and light areas if you select black and white) and imbues the image with a high-contrast, pastel-like look. It is somewhat like one of the more exotic types of HDR processing. The number of different colors (or shades of gray) used in the image is decreased to make it look as if the image were created from just a few poster paints; the result has an unrealistic but dramatic effect, as you can see in the sample image in Figure 4-83.

It's a good idea to remember that with all of the Picture Effect settings, you can still make additional settings, including White Balance, exposure compensation, and others. With Posterization, you might try using some positive or negative exposure compensation, which can change the appearance of this effect dramatically. I have often found the results with this setting are improved by using negative exposure compensation to reduce the excessive brightness of the effect. In general, I recommend using the Posterization setting only when you want to achieve a striking artistic effect, perhaps to create a distinctive-looking poster or greeting card.

Retro Photo

With Retro Photo, the RX10 uses sepia tones and reduced contrast to mimic the appearance of an aging photo. This effect is not as pronounced as the sepia effects I have seen on other cameras; with the RX10, a good deal of the image's original color still shows up, but there is a subtle softening of the image with the sepia coloration. In Figure 4-84, I used this effect to give a somewhat antique or subdued appearance to objects in the garden store.

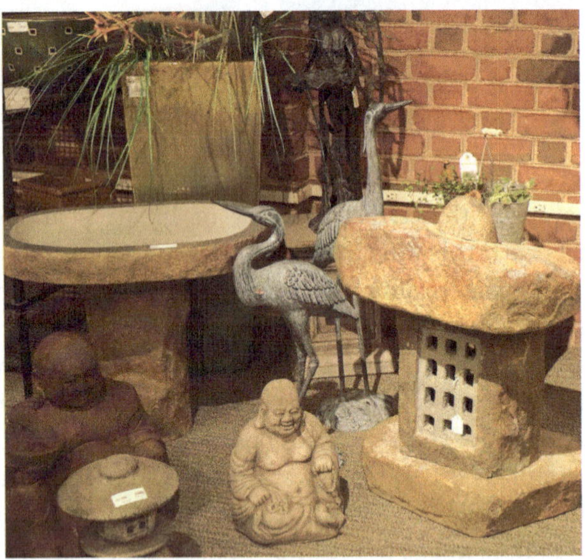

Figure 4-84. Retro Photo Example

Soft High-Key

"High key" is a technique in which a photographer uses bright lighting throughout the scene, striving for a bright overall look with light colors and few shadows. This technique often is used in fashion and advertising photography. With the RX10, Sony has added softness to give the image a bright, light appearance without the harshness that might otherwise result from the overexposed appearance. I enjoy the pleasant, relaxing look of images taken with this effect.

Partial Color

The Partial Color effect lets you choose a single color to retain in an image; the camera then reduces the saturation of all other colors to monochrome, so that only objects of the selected color remain in color in the image. I really enjoy this setting, which can be used to isolate a particular object with great dramatic effect.

In Figure 4-85, I used the Green setting to highlight a few objects in the garden store.

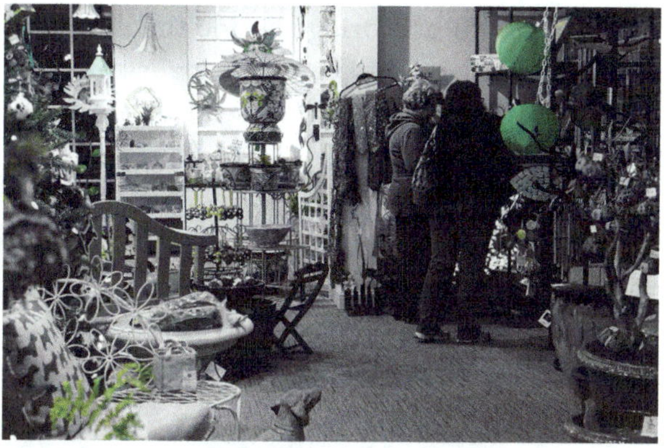

Figure 4-85. Partial Color - Green Example

The choices for the color to be retained are red, green, blue, and yellow; use the Left and Right buttons or the Control dial to select one of those colors. Then aim the camera at your subject; you will see on the LCD display what objects will show up in color. There is no direct way to adjust the color tolerance of this setting, so you cannot, for example, set the camera to accept a broad range of reds to be retained in the image. However, if you change the White Balance setting, the camera will perceive colors differently. So, if there is a particular object that you want to depict in color, but the camera does not "see" it as red, green, blue, or yellow, you can try selecting a different White Balance setting and see if the color will be retained. You also can fine-tune the White Balance setting using the color axes to add or subtract these hues if you want to bring a particular object within the range of the color that will be retained. Finally, by choosing a color that does not appear in the scene at all, you can take a straight monochrome photograph.

High Contrast Monochrome

This next setting is well explained by its label; it provides you with an easy way to take black-and-white photographs with a stark, contrasty appearance. You might consider this setting for street photography or any situation in which you are not looking for a soft or flattering appearance. I used this setting for Figure 4-86, in which I took a photo of a bridge beside the river. It seemed to me that the size and shape of the bridge structure, as well as the dark shadows, lent themselves to the use of this setting.

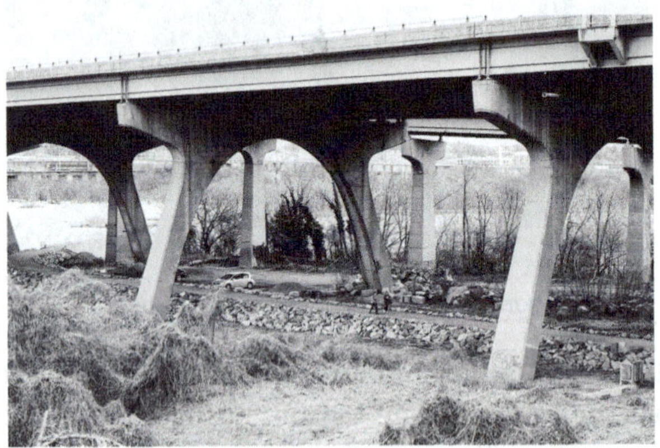

Figure 4-86. High Contrast Monochrome Example

Soft Focus

The Soft Focus effect is another setting that is variable; you can select either Low, Mid (as shown in the chart), or High by pressing the Right and Left buttons or turning the Control dial to scroll through those options. This effect is quite straightforward; the camera blurs the focus to achieve a dreamlike aura. Note that this is the first of several Picture Effect settings that cannot be previewed on the screen, even if the Setting Effect On option is chosen for Live View Display; you have to take the picture and then play it back to see the results of the Soft Focus setting. As I will discuss in CHAPTER 5, you also have the option of selecting manual focus and de-focusing the image to your own taste to achieve a similar effect.

For FIGURE 4-87, I used this effect for an image of a man walking down a path leading through the woods, with the idea that the Soft Focus setting would add an air of mystery.

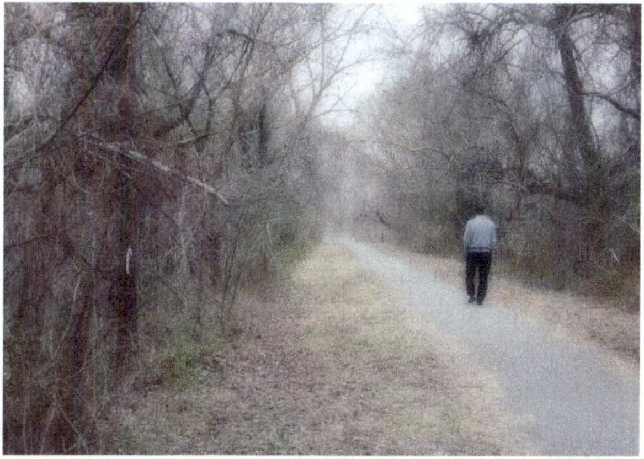

Figure 4-87. Soft Focus Mid Example

HDR Painting

The HDR Painting setting is similar to the HDR setting of the DRO/Auto HDR menu option. With this option, the camera takes a burst of three shots at different exposure settings and combines them internally into a single image to even out the dark and bright areas. Unlike the more standard HDR setting, this one does not let you select the exposure interval for the three shots, but it lets you choose Low, Mid (as shown in the chart), or High for the intensity of the effect. Also, it adds stylized processing to give the final image a painterly appearance. I like this setting quite a bit; you can achieve some very clear, dramatic images with this option. For example, in FIGURE 4-88, I shot a picture of colorful items in the garden store. I felt that this use of the High setting for the effect added clarity and definition to the picture.

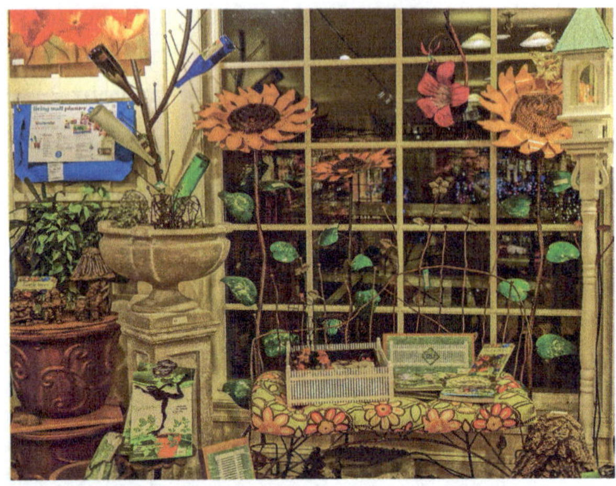

Figure 4-88. HDR Painting - High Example

In FIGURE 4-89, I took a different approach with this effect, using the Low setting for a shot of the area under the bridge near the river.

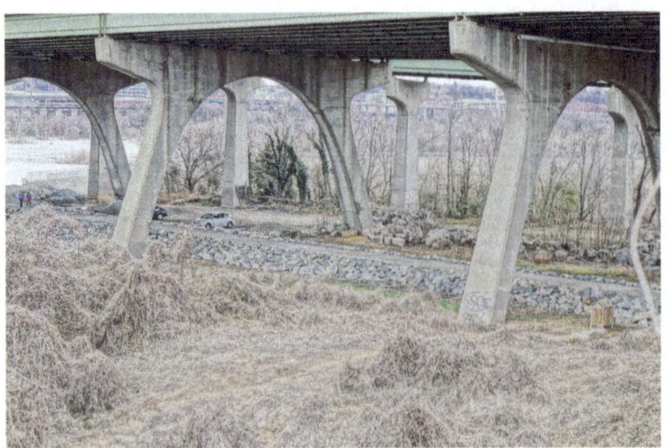

Figure 4-89. HDR Painting - Low Example

I felt that the Low setting was sufficient to make the various colors and textures in the scene stand out without becoming overwhelming. The HDR Painting setting can produce some ugly effects if it's used for the wrong subject, but in the right situations I have found it to be a great addition to the camera's set of creative tools.

Because the camera takes multiple images with this effect, you can't preview the results on the screen before taking the picture. In addition, it's advisable to use a tripod to avoid blur from camera motion while the three shots are being taken.

Rich-Tone Monochrome

The Rich-tone Monochrome setting can be considered as a black and white version of the HDR Painting setting. With this option, like that one, the RX10 takes a burst of three shots at different exposures and combines them digitally into a single composite photo with a broader dynamic range than would otherwise be possible. Unlike the color setting, though, this one does not let you select the intensity of the effect.

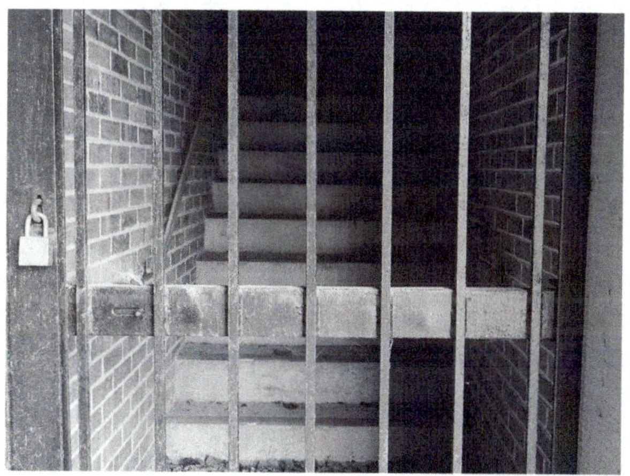

Figure 4-90. Rich-Tone Monochrome Example

I used it in Figure 4-90 for a photograph through an iron gate into a dark stairway. I like the deep, rich grayscale tones, reminiscent of images from high-quality black-and-white film.

Miniature

The next Picture Effect setting is called the Miniature effect. When you use this option, the camera adds blurring at one or more sides of an image or at the image's top or bottom to simulate the appearance of a photograph of a tabletop model or miniature. Such images often appear hazy in one or more areas, either because of the narrow depth of field of closeup photos, or because of the use of a tilt-and-shift lens, which causes blurring at the edges.

For this feature to work well, you need an appropriate subject. I have found that this effect works well when applied to something like a street scene or a train, which might actually be reproduced in a tabletop model. For example, if you are able to get a high vantage point above a road intersection or a railroad, you may be able to use this effect to make it look as if you had photographed a high-quality tabletop display.

After highlighting this option on the menu, press the Right and Left buttons to choose either Top, Middle (Horizontal), Bottom, Right, Middle (Vertical), Left, or Auto for the configuration of the effect. If you choose a specific area, that area will remain sharp. For example, if you choose Top, then, after you take the picture, the top area (roughly one-third) will remain sharp, and the rest of the image below that area will appear blurred. If you choose Auto, then the camera will select the area to remain sharp based on the area that was focused on by the autofocus system and by the camera's sensing how you are holding the camera.

You will not see how the effect will alter your image while viewing the scene, although the camera will place gray areas on the parts of the image that will ultimately be blurred, to give you a general idea of how the final product will look. I used the RX10 for an image of this sort in Figure 4-91, with the Miniature effect set to its Middle (Horizontal) orientation, leaving only the train cars in clear focus.

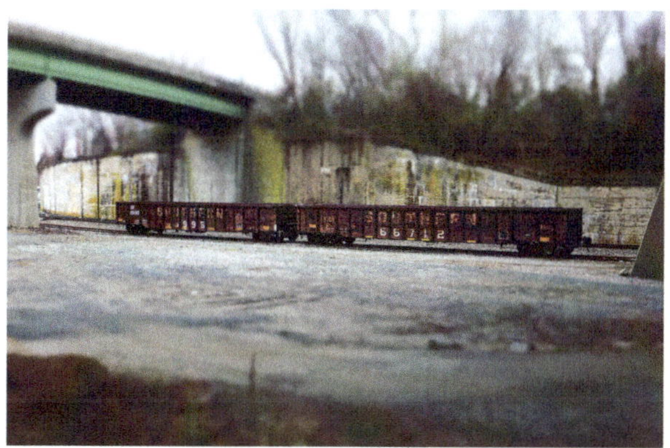

Figure 4-91. Miniature Effect Example

This effect can be a lot of fun if you are willing to experiment; it can take some work to find the right subject and the best arrangement of sharp and blurry areas to achieve a satisfying result.

One disappointing note is that this effect, like some other Picture Effect settings, cannot be used for movies with the RX10. I was surprised to find this, because miniature effects are often used for making movies with subjects that look like speeded-up models of trains, cars, and the like. But not with the RX10, for some reason.

Watercolor

The Watercolor effect is designed to blur the colors of an image somewhat and make it look as if it were painted with watercolors that are bleeding together. You need to choose a subject that lends itself to this sort of distortion. For example, I have found that the faces of dolls and other figures can be pleasantly altered to have an impressionistic appearance; larger objects may not be affected significantly by this somewhat subtle effect. I have also had some pleasing results with plants and trees. In Figure 4-92, I thought this effect worked well for a shot of train cars of different colors.

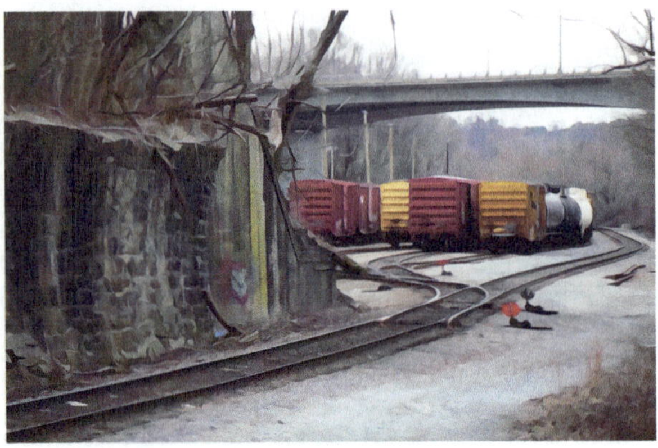

Figure 4-92. Watercolor Example

Illustration

The final Picture Effect setting, Illustration, is one of my favorites. This effect finds edges of objects and adds contrast, giving the appearance of a pen-and-ink illustration that has been colored in. You can set the intensity to Low, Mid (as shown in the chart), or High using the Right and Left buttons. If you choose a subject with a fair number of edges that can be outlined and a repeating pattern, you can achieve a pleasing appearance. This is another effect whose result you cannot see while viewing the live scene; you need to see the recorded image to check the final effect.

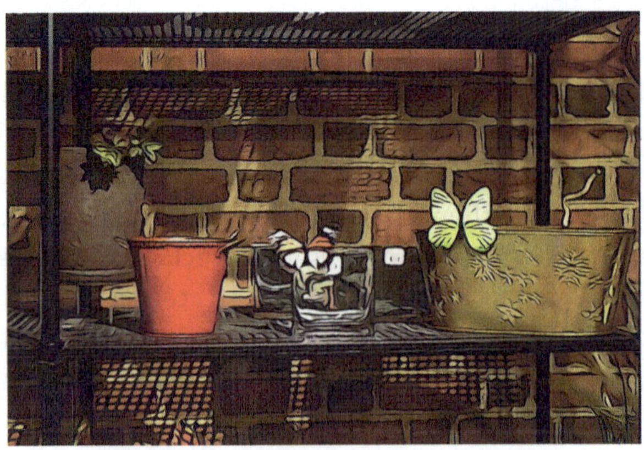

Figure 4-93. Illustration - High Example

As you can see in FIGURE 4-93, which was shot with Illustration at the High level, this effect can transform an ordinary view into a stylized image that is still recognizable. The images it produces may be more suited as decorative items than as depictions of actual subjects, but their appearance can be striking and unusual.

Here are some more notes about the Picture Effect settings. First, as with the Miniature effect, several options are not available when you are shooting movies or using any setting on the Drive Mode menu. Besides Miniature, these are Soft Focus, HDR Painting, Rich-tone Monochrome, Watercolor, and Illustration. If one of these effects is turned on when you press the Movie button, the camera will turn it off while the movie is being recorded and turn it back on after the recording ends. You cannot use some other options, including DRO/HDR and Creative Style, with any of the Picture Effect settings. And, as noted earlier, the Raw setting for Quality is not available for images taken with Picture Effect turned on.

Focus Magnifier

The Focus Magnifier menu option is available only when the focus mode switch is set to manual focus or direct manual focus. This option gives you a way to enlarge a small portion of the display so you can check the focus of that area as you turn the focus ring.

When you select this menu option, the camera will display an orange frame on the display, as seen in FIGURE 4-94.

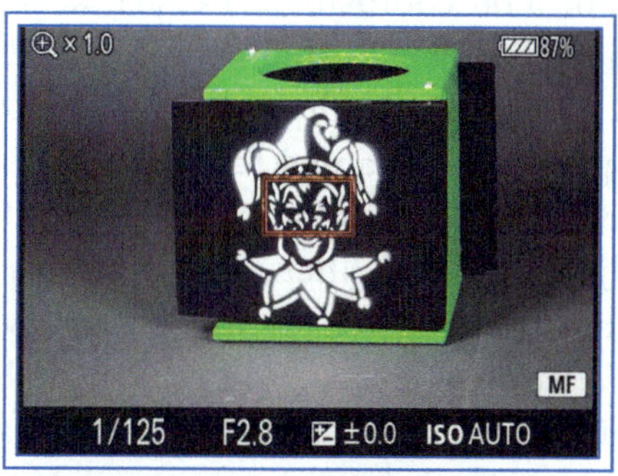

Figure 4-94. Focus Magnifier Frame on Display

You can move that frame to any position on the display, using the direction buttons, the Control wheel, or the Control dial. When the frame is located over the area where you want to check focus, press the Center button. The camera will then enlarge the area within the frame to 8.6 times normal, as shown in FIGURE 4-95.

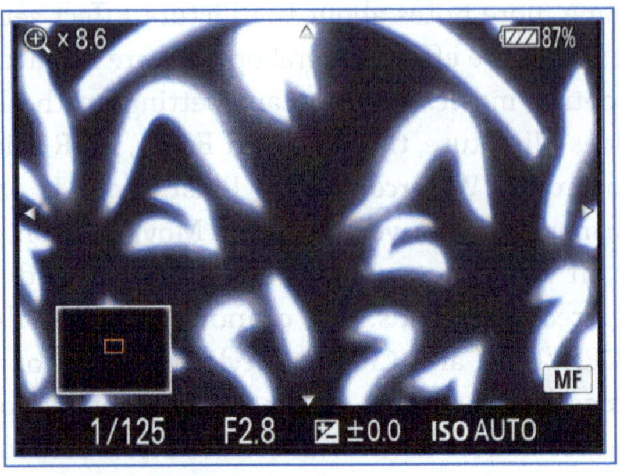

Figure 4-95. Display Enlarged to 8.6x

An inset square will show the position of the Focus Magnifier frame. You can still move the frame around the display while the display is enlarged. Press the Center button again, and the focus area will be magnified to 17.1 times normal. A final press will restore the display to normal size. Once you press the shutter button halfway, the magnifier frame will disappear. You can then call it up again using this menu option if you want to.

This option can be a bit confusing because it acts in a similar way to another option that is activated from screen 1 of the Custom menu, called MF Assist. As I will discuss in CHAPTER 7, when you turn on that option with manual focus in effect, the focus area is enlarged to 8.6 times normal as soon as you start turning the focus ring to adjust the focus. Then, once the focus area is enlarged with that option, pressing the Center button will magnify the focus area to 17.1 times normal. You can toggle between the 8.6 and 17.1 magnifications using the Center button, and exit to the shooting screen by half-pressing the shutter button.

In other words, if the MF Assist menu option is active, then the Center button always acts to magnify the focus area once you have started to adjust focus in manual focus mode. If you select the Focus Magnifier menu option, the difference is that pressing the Center button will magnify the display before you start focusing.

The advantage of using the Focus Magnifier menu option is that you can select the position of the enlarged focus area before you start adjusting focus. If you use the MF Assist option, the camera will enlarge the display as soon as you start turning the focus ring to adjust focus, and you will not be able to choose the location of the enlarged focus area until the display is already enlarged.

The MF Assist option works well for me, because it operates as soon as I start adjusting focus. However, if you prefer to be able to adjust the location of the frame for the enlarged focus area before starting to adjust focus, the Focus Magnifier option is useful.

The Focus Magnifier feature is easier to use if you assign it to one of the control buttons. For example, you can use the Custom Key Settings option on screen 4 of the Custom menu to assign Focus Magnifier to the Left button. Then, when you are using manual focus, you can press that button to bring the enlargement frame up on the display. You can then quickly adjust the position of the frame, press the Center button once or twice to enlarge that area, and then adjust the focus and take the picture.

The next menu options, starting with Long Exposure Noise Reduction, are found on screen 5 of the Shooting menu, which is shown in FIGURE 4-96.

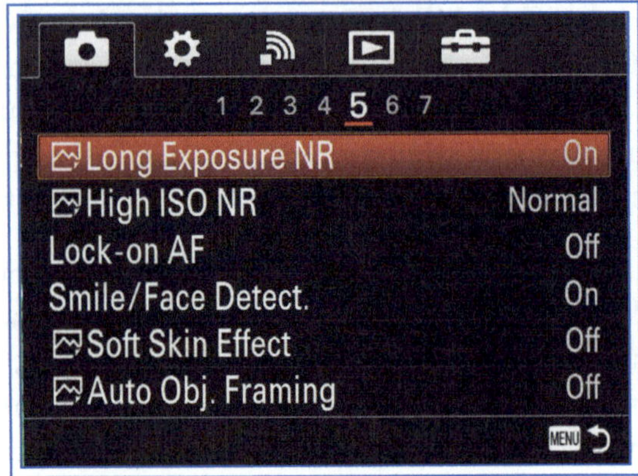

Figure 4-96. Screen 5 of Shooting Menu

Long Exposure Noise Reduction

This option uses processing to reduce the "noise" that affects images during exposures of 1/3 second or longer. This option is turned on by default. When it is turned on, the camera processes your shot for a time equal to the time of the exposure. So, if your exposure is for 2 seconds, the camera will process the shot for an additional 2 seconds, creating a delay before you can shoot again.

In some cases, this processing may remove details from your image. In addition, in certain situations you may prefer to leave the noise in the image because the graininess can be pleasing in some cases. Or, you may prefer to remove the noise using post-processing software. If you want to turn off this option, use this menu item to do so. This option is not available for adjustment when the camera is set for continuous shooting, exposure bracketing, panorama shooting, or when using Scene mode settings. The camera will select a setting for Long Exposure Noise Reduction in those cases. For example, the camera will turn this option off with the Sports Action and Hand-held Twilight Scene mode settings.

I recommend you make this setting based on the type of shooting you are doing. If you're taking casual shots or don't want to do post-processing, I suggest you leave this option turned on. But, if you are shooting with Raw quality or want to do processing with software, I recommend turning it off.

High ISO Noise Reduction

This next menu entry has three settings: Normal, Low, or Off; the default is Normal. This option, like the previous one, removes noise generated by a high ISO level. One problem with this sort of noise reduction is that it takes time to process your images after they are captured. You may want to set this option to Low or Off to minimize the delay before you can take another picture. If Quality is set to Raw, this option will be unavailable on the menu screen because this processing is not available for Raw images.

Lock-on AF

The Lock-on AF option is the RX10's mechanism for focus tracking, by which the camera can lock its focus frame on a moving object and automatically keep that object in focus as it moves. You have to take several steps to get this system to work, but once you have it operating, it is quite convenient.

The Lock-on AF option works differently depending on whether the camera is set for single autofocus or continuous autofocus using the focus switch. First, I will discuss the process using single autofocus, with the switch at the S position.

First, you need to go to the Custom Key Settings menu option on screen 4 of the Custom menu, and make sure the Center Button is assigned to the Standard function, so that button will activate tracking on your chosen subject.

Next, go to screen 5 of the Shooting menu and set Lock-on AF to On. The third option, On (Start w/Shutter), will be dimmed and unavailable at this point, because the focus mode is single autofocus. (That option is available only with continuous autofocus.)

The shooting screen should now show the message seen in Figure 4-97, saying the camera will track the subject nearest the center of the screen when you press the Center button.

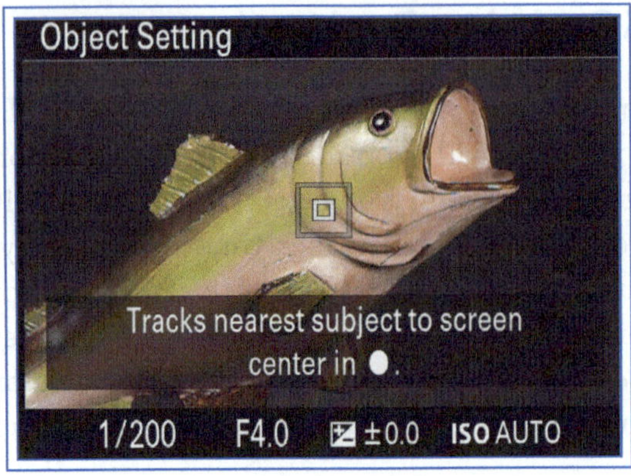

Figure 4-97. Lock-on AF Initial Message Screen

At this point, aim at your subject, and get it centered in the display. Then, press the Center button, and the camera should place a double white frame over the chosen subject, as shown in Figure 4-98. That frame should stay centered over the subject, even if the camera or subject moves, as long as the motion is not too violent. When you are ready to take the picture, press the shutter button halfway, and the focus frame should turn green. At that point, focus will be locked and will not be adjusted or tracked any further. You can press the shutter button all the way to take the picture.

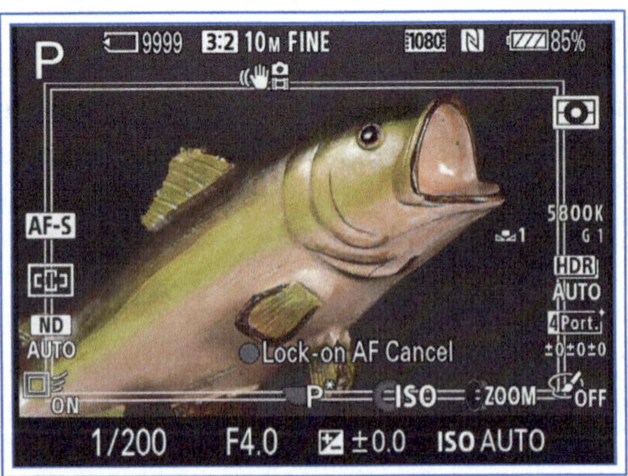

Figure 4-98. Lock-on AF Double White Frame

If you are using continuous autofocus, the process is somewhat different. You can use the same steps as for single autofocus and press the Center button to start tracking a subject, but you also have the option of using the shutter button to start the tracking.

To do that, select the third option on the Lock-on AF menu, On (Start w/Shutter). Then, when you have your subject centered on the screen, press the shutter button halfway and the camera will place a green double frame over the subject. Because continuous autofocus is in effect, the camera will keep adjusting focus even as you keep the shutter button halfway down. When you are ready, press the shutter button the rest of the way to take the picture.

Because this tracking function is designed for subjects that are in continuous motion, my preference is to set the focus switch to C for continuous autofocus, and then use the On (Start w/Shutter) option for Lock-on AF. If you prefer using the Center button to start tracking, though, you have that option available.

Smile/Face Detection

This option gives you access to two functions with different features. There are four separate entries on the vertical menu that pops up when this menu item is selected, shown in FIGURE 4-99.

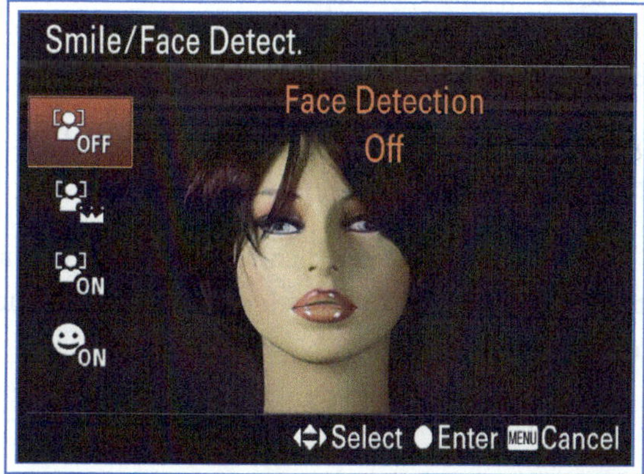

Figure 4-99. Smile/Face Detection Menu Options Screen

You can select the top setting to leave all options turned off, or you can select one of the other three, which operate as follows:

Face Detection On (Registered Faces)

This option is designated on the menu screen by an icon of a person's head and a crown. When you select this choice, the camera searches for faces that you have previously registered using the Face Registration option on the Custom menu, as discussed in Chapter 7. If it detects a registered face, it should consider that face to have priority, in which case it will place a green frame on the face and adjust the Focus Area, Flash Mode, and exposure values automatically to produce a good exposure for that particular face.

In daily shooting, I do not use this feature. It could be useful if you are taking pictures of children in a group setting and you want to make sure your own child is in focus and has his or her face properly exposed. I tried this feature out by registering one face and then aiming the camera at that face along with an unregistered face. In some cases, the camera picked the registered one as the priority face, but at other times it chose the unregistered one. Other users have reported good results with this feature, though, so, if it would be useful to you, by all means explore it further.

Face Detection On

This setting is similar to the previous one, except that it does not involve registered faces.

As shown in Figure 4-100, the camera will detect any human faces, up to eight in total, and select one as the main face to concentrate its settings on.

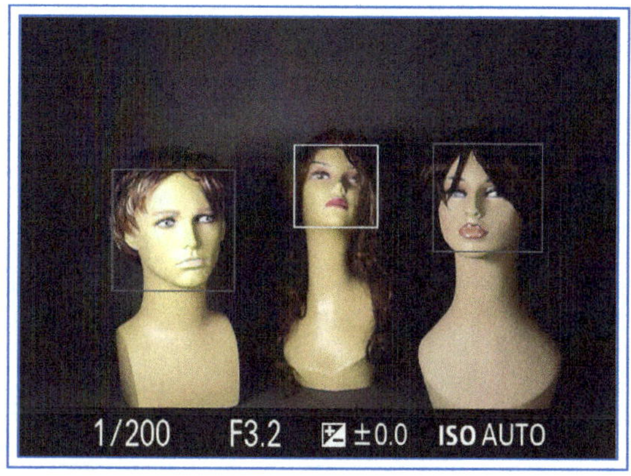

Figure 4-100. Multiple Faces Detected

Before you press the shutter button, the camera will display a white or gray frame around any face it finds. The white frame is used for the face the camera believes to be the main subject. When you press the shutter button halfway to lock focus and exposure, the frame over the face the camera has selected as the main face will turn green. The camera may place multiple green frames if there are multiple faces at the same distance from the camera.

Smile Shutter

The final option for this menu item is the Smile Shutter, which is a sort of self-timer that is activated when the subject smiles.

After highlighting this option, use the Left and Right buttons or the Control dial to choose the level of smile that is needed to trigger the camera—Slight Smile, Normal Smile, or Big Smile. Press the Center button to go back to the shooting screen, and aim the camera at the subject or subjects. (You can, of course, put the camera on a tripod and aim it at yourself, if you want.)

As shown in Figure 4-101, the camera will show a meter on the left of the screen with a pointer to indicate how large a smile is needed to trigger a shot.

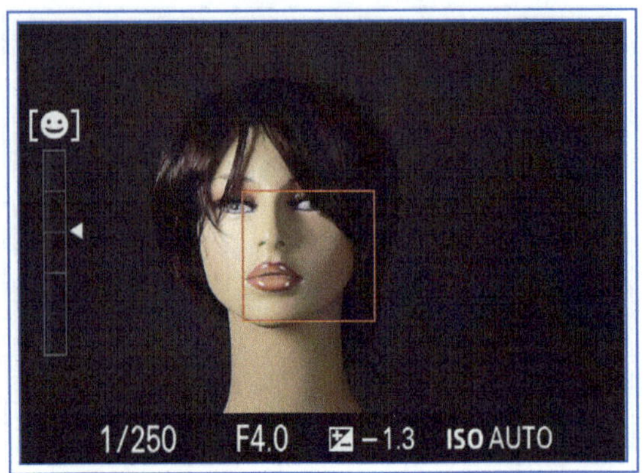

Figure 4-101. Smile Shutter Screen Showing Smile Meter

As soon as the camera detects a big enough smile from any person, the shutter will fire. If a person smiles again, the camera will be triggered again, with no limit on the number of shots that can be taken. In effect, this feature acts as a limited kind of remote control with one specific function. I consider this option to be something of a novelty, which can be entertaining but is not necessary for everyday photography. It might be useful if you want to encourage a child to smile for a portrait by telling him or her that the camera will only take the picture if the smile is big enough.

Soft Skin Effect

This menu option is designed to soften skin tones in the faces of your subjects. The option is dimmed and unavailable in some situations, such as when one of the Drive Mode options or the Raw setting for Quality is selected. Once you select it and turn it on, you can use the Right and Left buttons or the Control dial to set the level at Low, Mid, or High, as shown in FIGURE 4-102.

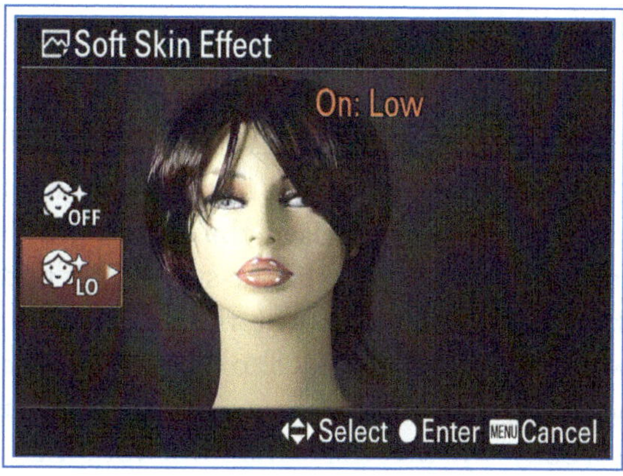

Figure 4-102. Soft Skin Effect Menu Options Screen

However, even if you are able to turn the soft skin option on, it will not have any effect unless you also have Face Detection turned on in the menu system, and the RX10 has detected a face.

When it works, this setting reduces the sharpness and contrast in areas that the camera perceives as skin tones. FIGURE 4-103 shows the results of a test I made using a mannequin. The image on the left was taken with the effect turned off; the image on the right had the setting at its High level. I found that the most noticeable area of softness is seen in the area of the mannequin's nose.

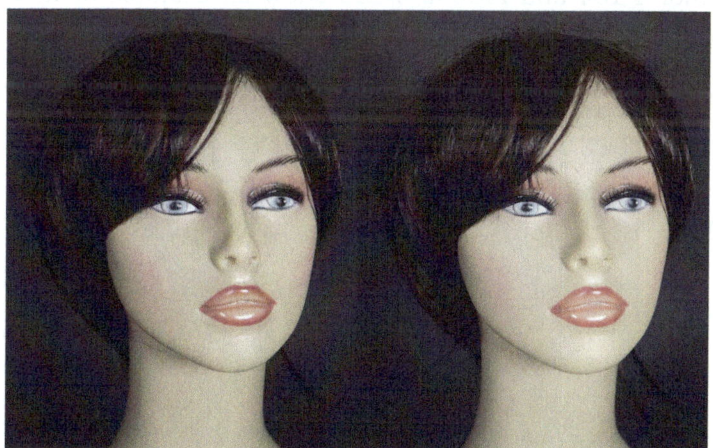

Figure 4-103. Soft Skin Effect Comparison Image

Auto Object Framing

This option provides a function that is somewhat unusual for any camera—it rearranges the composition of your shot based on its own electronic judgment. To activate it, set it to Auto on the menu. Then, when you compose your image, the camera will place a special frame around what it believes to be the subject if it finds the image can benefit by being cropped to fit the subject better. For this feature to work with faces, you need to have Face Detection turned on with the Smile/Face Detection menu option discussed above. Besides faces, Sony says that the feature will work with macro shots and objects tracked with Lock-on AF, if those subjects have been detected by the camera. In other words, the camera must have been set to the Macro setting of Scene mode or to Auto mode when it can detect Macro shots, or must have used Lock-on AF.

When you take a picture of the face or other subject, the camera may crop the image and produce a new version with the frame trimmed and resized to emphasize the subject in a more pleasing way. I found the camera would crop shots of faces fairly often, but I had difficulty getting the camera to crop a shot of any other subject, even when I used the Macro and Lock-on AF settings.

Figure 4-104 and Figure 4-105 show an example of how the camera cropped a shot of a mannequin's head.

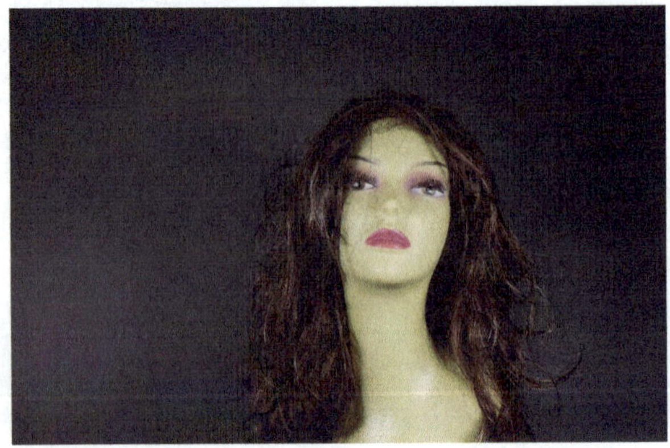

Figure 4-104. Auto Object Framing Example - Original

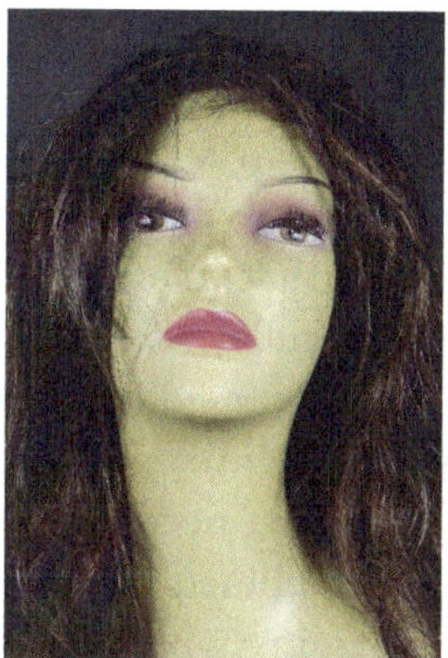

Figure 4-105. Auto Object Framing Example - Cropped by Camera

The camera's cropping looks appropriate, but I would rather do the cropping myself in Photoshop or just compose the image in this way to begin with. The camera saves both versions, so there is no harm in using this feature. It could be useful if you are pressed for time or are unable to get into position to take the shot you want.

This feature is available for selection only if the camera is set for autofocus with Focus Area set to Wide, and Quality set to Extra Fine, Fine, or Standard.

The next items to be discussed appear on screen 6 of the Shooting menu, seen in Figure 4-106.

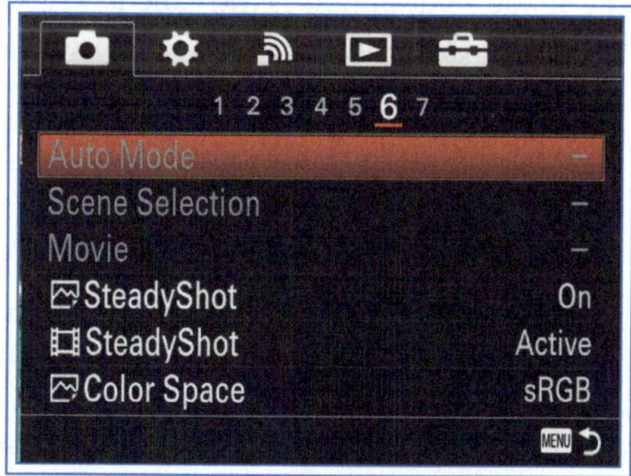

Figure 4-106. Screen 6 of Shooting Menu

Auto Mode

This option, the first choice on screen 6 of the Shooting menu, is available for selection only when the camera is set to Auto mode on the mode dial. In that mode, this menu option lets you choose either the default Intelligent Auto mode, or the enhanced Superior Auto mode. As I discussed in Chapter 3, Superior Auto mode is exactly the same as Intelligent Auto mode, except that the RX10 will, if it detects the need, shoot using its capabilities for multiple shots to be combined into a composite final image. This is likely to happen in dim lighting or backlighted situations, primarily. If you want to call up this option quickly, you can assign the Shoot Mode option to one of the slots on the Function button menu, as discussed in Chapter 7. (The Shoot mode option works in Auto Mode, Scene mode, and Movie mode, and lets you choose the sub-mode setting for whichever mode is currently in effect.)

Scene Selection

The second option on screen 6 is available for selection only when the RX10 is set to Scene mode using the mode dial. This option lets you select one of the 9 possible choices for the scene setting, as discussed in Chapter 3. As I noted in Chapter 3, there are two easier ways to change scene types than using this menu option. One is to assign the Shoot Mode option to the Function button menu, as discussed above. The other is just to turn the Control dial while the shooting screen is displayed; that action will scroll through all the available scene types when the camera is in Scene mode.

Movie

The Movie option is available for selection only when the mode dial is set to the Movie position, represented by a movie film icon. This option lets you set the exposure mode to be used by the camera when it is recording videos using Movie mode—Program, Aperture Priority, Shutter Priority, or Manual Exposure. Those modes operate somewhat differently in Movie mode than for shooting still images. I will discuss this option in detail in Chapter 8.

Here, again, you can assign the Shoot Mode option to one of the slots for the Function button menu, and that option will let you choose the exposure mode when the mode dial is set to the Movie position.

SteadyShot (Still Images)

SteadyShot is Sony's optical image stabilization system, which compensates for small movements of the camera to avoid motion blur, especially during exposures of longer than about 1/30 second. This setting is turned on by default, and I recommend leaving it on at all times, except when the camera is on a tripod. In that case, SteadyShot is not needed, and there is some chance it can "fool" the camera and result in an attempt to correct for motion that does not exist, resulting in image blur.

SteadyShot (Movies)

This next option is a different SteadyShot setting for movies; this menu has a movie film icon in front of its name, whereas the previous one, for still images, has a mountain-landscape icon in front of its name. I will discuss the video-oriented SteadyShot option in Chapter 8.

Color Space

With this option, you can choose to record your images using the sRGB "color space," the more common choice and the default, or the Adobe RGB color space. The sRGB color space has fewer colors than Adobe RGB; therefore, it is more suitable for producing images for the web and other forms of digital display than for printing. If your images are likely to be printed commercially in a book or magazine or it is critical that you be able to match a great many different color variations, you might want to consider using the Adobe RGB color space. I always leave the color space set to sRGB, and I recommend that you do so as well unless you have a specific need to use Adobe RGB, such as a requirement from a printing company that you are using to print your images.

If you are shooting your images with the Raw format, you don't need to worry so much about color space, because you can set it later using your Raw-processing software.

Screen 7, the final screen of options on the Shooting menu, is shown in FIGURE 4-107.

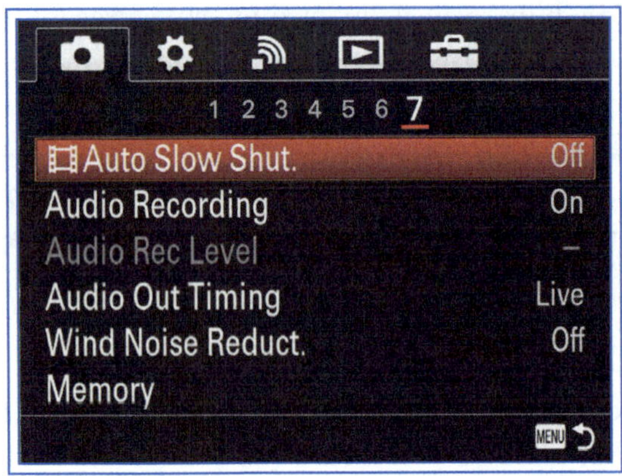

Figure 4-107. Screen 7 of Shooting Menu

Auto Slow Shutter

This first item on the final screen of the Shooting menu is preceded by a movie film icon, meaning it is used only when you are recording movies. This option lets the camera automatically set a slower shutter speed than normal when shooting a movie, in order to compensate for dim lighting. I will discuss this option in CHAPTER 8.

Audio Recording

The Audio Recording item on the Shooting menu can be set either on or off. If you are certain you won't need the sound recorded by the camera, then you can turn this option off. I never turn it off, because I can always turn down the volume of the recorded sound when playing the video. Or, if I am editing the video on a computer, I can delete the sound and replace it as needed—but there is no way to recapture the original audio after the fact if this option was turned off during the recording.

Audio Recording Level

This option is available for selection only when the camera is set to Movie mode using the mode dial. If you record movies by pressing the Movie button in any other shooting mode, the camera will set the level for recording sound, and you cannot control it. If the mode dial is set to Movie mode, then you can control the sound level using this menu option. I will discuss its use in Chapter 8.

Audio Out Timing

This is another option that applies only when recording movies. I will discuss it in Chapter 8.

Wind Noise Reduction

This option also is one that applies only to movies. I will discuss it in Chapter 8.

Memory

The final option on the Shooting menu, Memory, was discussed in Chapter 3 in connection with the Memory Recall shooting mode. Once you have set up the RX10 with the menu options and other settings you want to store to one of the two numbered slots on the mode dial, you select the Memory menu option, and choose one of the two numbered registers, as shown in FIGURE 4-108.

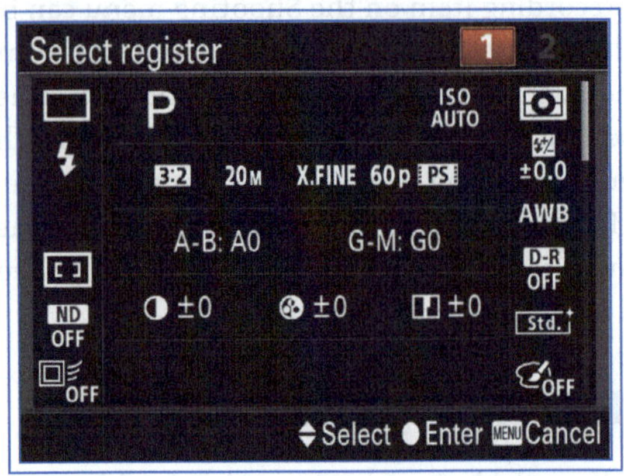

Figure 4-108. Select Register Screen for Memory Menu Option

Then press the Center button, and all of the camera's current settings will be stored to that numbered slot on the mode dial. You then recall the stored settings by turning the mode dial to the numbered slot you saved them to—1 or 2.

With the Memory option, you can scroll down to additional screens using the Down button to see other settings currently in effect, such as ISO Auto Maximum and Minimum, High ISO NR, Smile/Face Detection, and several others.

CHAPTER 5: Physical Controls

The Sony RX10, like many compact cameras, does not have as many physical controls as an advanced DSLR camera like, for example, the Sony Alpha A99. But the RX10 has more controls than most compact cameras, and the ones it has give you many options for customization. You can assign your most-used functions to various buttons and dials to a greater extent than with most other cameras in this class.

In this chapter, I'll discuss each of the camera's physical controls and how they can be used to best advantage, starting with the controls on the right side of the top of the camera, shown in FIGURE 5-1.

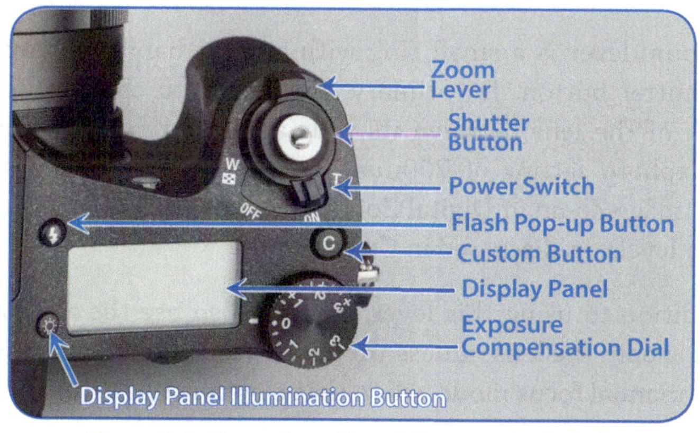

Figure 5-1. Controls on Top of Camera - Right Side

Shutter Button

The shutter button is the single most important control on the camera. When you press it halfway, the camera evaluates exposure and focus (unless you're using manual exposure or manual focus). Once you are satisfied with the settings, press the button all the way to take the picture. When the camera is set for continuous shooting, you hold this button down while the camera fires repeatedly. You also can press this button halfway to exit from playback mode, menu screens, and help screens to get the camera set to take its next picture. You can half-press this button to wake the camera up after it has powered down because of the Power Save Start Time option on the Setup menu.

One somewhat unusual feature with the RX10 is that the shutter button is threaded, so you can screw in a standard, mechanical cable release that can trip the shutter or lock it down for a long time exposure. I will discuss cable releases in Appendix A. You also can screw in a "soft release"—a button that provides a softer, smoother surface for your finger to press.

Zoom Lever

The zoom lever is a small ring with a short handle surrounding the shutter button. Its primary function is to change the focal length of the lens between its wide-angle setting of 24mm and its telephoto setting of 200mm. If you have the camera set for Clear Image Zoom or Digital Zoom, the lever will take the zoom to higher levels, as discussed in Chapter 7.

In addition to using this lever, you can also use the zoom/focus ring to zoom the lens, unless the camera is set to manual focus or direct manual focus mode, when that ring controls focus.

In playback mode, moving the zoom lever to the right enlarges the current image, and moving the lever to the left reduces the size of enlarged images and produces index screens with multiple images. Those operations are discussed in CHAPTER 6.

Power Switch

This switch behind the shutter button is used to turn the camera on and off.

Flash Pop-up Button

This small button to the right of the RX10's built-in flash, marked with a lightning bolt, has just one function—to release the flash so it can pop up. The flash on this camera will not operate until you use this button to pop it up out of the camera's housing. If you think you may have a need for the flash, be sure to press this button to pop it up. On the other hand, if you definitely do not want the flash to fire, such as when you are in a museum or other setting where flash is not permitted, just don't press this button, and the flash will not pop up. When you have finished with the flash, press it gently back into the camera until it clicks into place.

Custom Button

This small button labeled C, for Custom, is a powerful control. By default, with the factory settings, this button is programmed to bring up the ISO menu so you can quickly change the ISO sensitivity for your shooting session. However, Sony has made this button available for you to assign to another function.

Using the Custom Key Settings option on screen 4 of the Custom menu, you can assign any one of numerous settings to this button, including Drive Mode, Flash Mode, ND Filter, and many others. I will discuss all of the options in CHAPTER 7, where I discuss the Custom menu. Because of the convenient location of this button, in easy range of the index finger of your right hand, it is a good idea to choose your most-used option to be operated by the Custom button.

Exposure Compensation Dial

Another very convenient control on the RX10 is this dial, which gives you a straightforward way to control exposure compensation. Rather than having to use a menu screen, you just turn this dial to one of the clearly marked values for positive or negative exposure compensation.

Here is an example of the use of this dial to adjust exposure. In FIGURE 5-2, I photographed a horse figurine using the Program shooting mode.

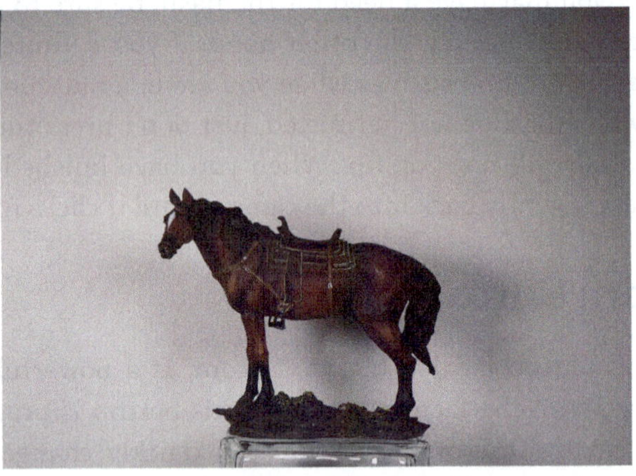

Figure 5-2. Image in Need of Exposure Compensation

The horse was dark, but the background was bright white. The camera's autoexposure system measured the light from the overall scene, and because of that bright background, it reduced the exposure, making the horse appear too dark.

I turned the exposure compensation dial to add 2.0 EV (exposure value) of positive exposure. The changed value appears in numbers at the lower right of the screen, to the left of the ISO value, as shown in FIGURE 5-3.

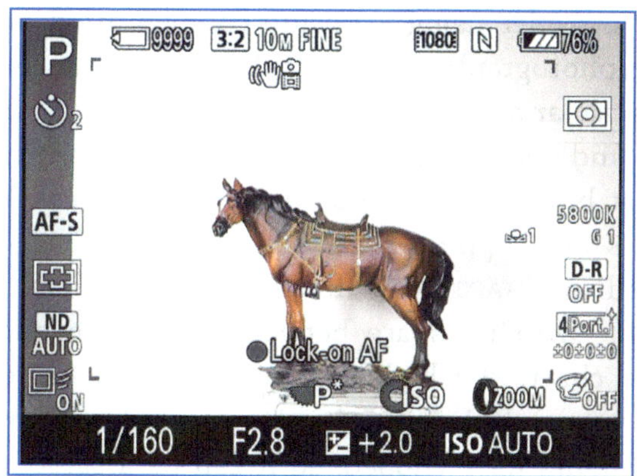

Figure 5-3. Display Showing +2.0 EV Exposure Compensation Added

With a negative value, the image will be darker than it otherwise would; with a positive value, it will be brighter. The camera's display will change to show the effect of the adjustment, if you have set the camera to show the effect. To see the effect as you adjust exposure compensation, go to screen 2 of the Custom menu, select Live View Display, and choose Setting Effect On. If you choose the other possibility, Setting Effect Off, you will not see the effect of exposure compensation on the shooting screen, though it will appear in the final image. In this case, with exposure compensation adjusted upward by 2.0 EV units, the horse became lighter and was no longer underexposed, as shown in FIGURE 5-4.

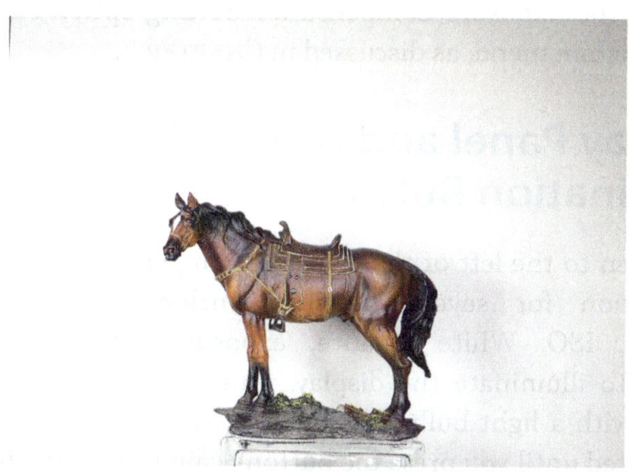

Figure 5-4. Image After Exposure Compensation Adjusted

You might consider using exposure compensation on a routine basis. Some photographers generally leave exposure compensation set at a particular amount, such as negative 0.6 EV. You could do this if you find your images often look slightly overexposed or if you see that highlights are clipping in many cases. (You can tell if highlights are clipping by checking the playback histogram, as discussed in Chapter 6. If the histogram chart is bunched to the right, with no space between the graph and the right side of the chart, the highlights are clipping, or reaching the maximum value.) It is difficult to recover details from images whose highlights have clipped, so it can be a safety measure to underexpose your images slightly to avoid that situation.

If you don't plan to leave a permanent exposure compensation setting in place, you should return the setting to the zero point when you are finished with it, so you won't inadvertently change the exposure of later images that don't need the adjustment. (The exposure compensation setting will remain in place even after the camera has been turned off and back on again.)

In Manual exposure mode, exposure compensation has no effect unless ISO is set to Auto ISO. Exposure compensation is not available in Intelligent Auto or Scene mode. You can control whether this dial adjusts flash output as well as exposure settings by using the Exposure Compensation Setting option on screen 3 of the Custom menu, as discussed in Chapter 7.

Display Panel and Display Panel Illumination Button

The screen to the left of the exposure compensation dial displays information for several settings, including shutter speed, aperture, ISO, White Balance, exposure compensation, and others. To illuminate the display, press and release the button labeled with a light bulb, to the left of the panel. The panel will stay lighted until you press the button again to turn the light off.

Now I will discuss the items on the left side of the camera's top, as shown in Figure 5-5.

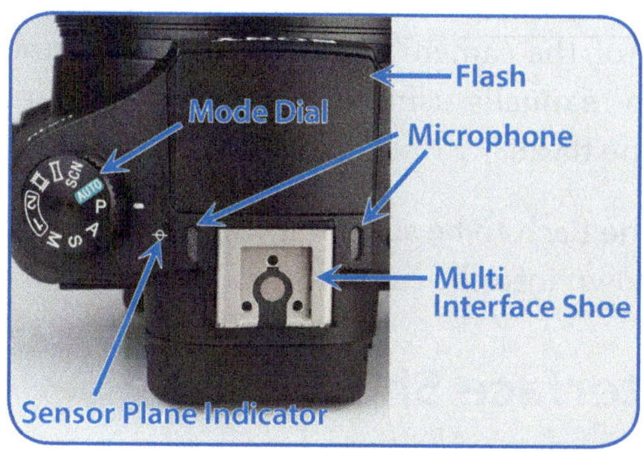

Figure 5-5. Controls on Top of Camera - Left Side

Mode Dial

The mode dial, at the far left side of the camera's top, has just one function—to set the shooting mode for capturing still images or videos. I discussed those modes in Chapter 3. To take a quick still picture, turn this dial to the green AUTO label and fire away. To take a quick video sequence, turn the dial to that position and then press the red Movie button, to the right of the viewfinder at the top of the camera's back. You can record a movie with the mode dial set to any position. There is a Movie mode on this dial, marked by a movie-film icon, but you do not have to select that icon to record movies.

Note, though, that screen 4 of the Custom menu has an option called Movie Button that can lock out the use of the Movie button unless the camera is set to Movie mode. If the mode dial is set to Intelligent Auto, Program, or any setting other than Movie mode, the Movie button will not work if that menu option is set to Movie Mode Only.

If the mode dial is set to Movie mode, the camera will not take still images. In that mode, you can only record videos.

Built-in Flash

The camera's built-in flash unit is normally retracted and hidden in the center of the camera's top. The camera cannot use it until you pop it up manually using the flash pop-up button located to the right of the flash.

If you want the flash to be stowed away again, you need to press it gently back down into the camera until it clicks into place.

Multi Interface Shoe

The shoe on top of the RX10 comes with a protective cap; slide that cap out, and the shoe is ready to accept several accessories. The most obvious accessory for this shoe is an external flash. I will discuss some available flash units in Appendix A, where I discuss accessories.

This shoe has special circuitry built into it so it can accept certain other accessories that are designed to interact with the camera. Sony makes microphones that can work with the shoe, including model ECM-XYST1M. Sony also offers an accessory kit, model XLR-K1M, that lets you use professional-level, balanced microphones with XLR connections. I will discuss those items in Appendix A. Sony undoubtedly will release other accessories that can take advantage of this interface as time goes by.

Microphone

The two openings for the camera's built-in stereo microphone are located on either side of the Multi Interface Shoe. This microphone provides excellent quality for everyday video recording. However, if you need greater quality, there are several options available for using higher-quality external microphones, as discussed in Appendix A.

Sensor Plane Indicator

This small symbol located to the right of the mode dial shows the position of the digital sensor within the RX10. This indicator is provided in case you need to measure the exact distance from the sensor plane to your subject for macro photography.

Next, I will discuss the items on the front of the camera, as seen in FIGURE 5-6, before turning to the controls on the back.

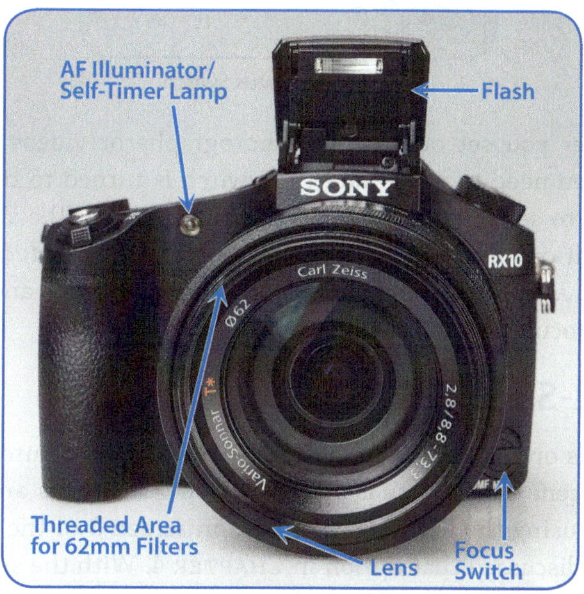

Figure 5-6. Items on Front of Camera

Focus Switch

The focus switch, one of the most important controls on the camera, is located at the extreme bottom of the camera's front, to the right of the lens as you face the camera. This small control is difficult to see in the general view of the camera's front, so I am including a detailed view of it in FIGURE 5-7.

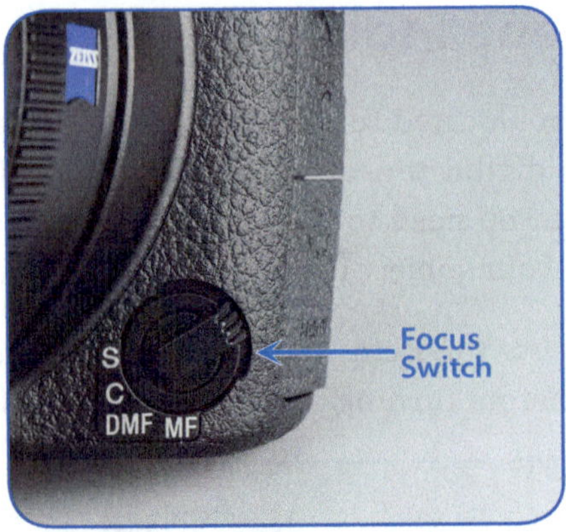

Figure 5-7. Focus Switch

Whenever you set out to take photographs or videos with the RX10, you need to make sure this switch is turned to the proper position to set the focus mode you intend to use. The switch has four positions for focus mode: S, for single-shot autofocus; C, for continuous autofocus; DMF, for direct manual focus; and MF, for manual focus. I will discuss these four settings below.

Single-Shot AF

With this option, the camera does its best to focus automatically on the scene the camera is aimed at, using the focus area that is selected using the Focus Area option on screen 3 of the Shooting menu. I discussed that option in Chapter 4. With the single-shot AF setting, the focus will be locked in when you press the shutter button halfway down.

At that point, you will see one or more green focus brackets on the screen indicating the point or points where the camera achieved sharp focus, as shown in Figure 5-8, and you will hear a beep (unless beeps are turned off through the Setup menu). In addition, a green disc in the lower-left corner of the display will light up steadily indicating that focus is confirmed. If focus cannot be achieved, the green disc will blink and no focus brackets will appear on the screen.

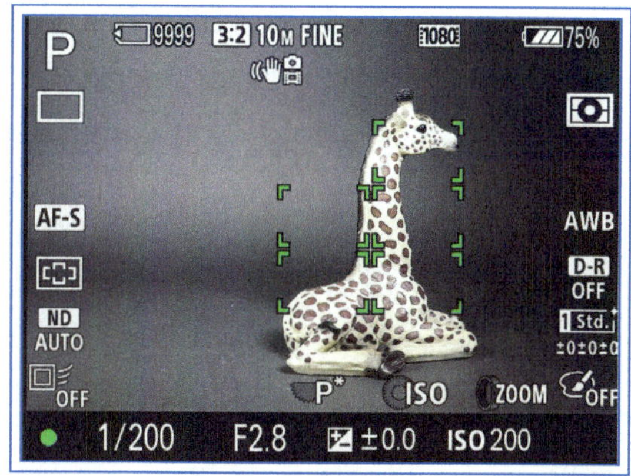

Figure 5-8. Green Frames and Disc Showing Good Focus

Once you have pressed the shutter button halfway to lock focus (and exposure), you can use the locked focus on a different subject at the same distance as the one the camera originally locked focus on. For example, if you focus on a person at a distance of 15 feet (4.6 m), and then you decide to include another person or object in the scene, once you have locked the focus on the first person by pressing the shutter button halfway, you can move the camera to include the other person or object in the scene as long as you keep the camera at about the same distance from the subject. The focus will remain locked at that distance until you press the shutter button the rest of the way down to take the picture.

Continuous AF

The second option for focus mode, continuous AF, is designated by the C setting for the focus switch. With this option, as with single-shot AF, the RX10 focuses continuously from the time you half-press the shutter button until you press the button all the way to take the picture. The difference with this mode is that the camera does not lock focus when you press the shutter button halfway. Instead, the camera continues to adjust focus if the subject or camera moves. You will not hear a beep or see any focus brackets to confirm focus. Instead, the green disc in the lower-left corner of the display will change its appearance to show the focus status.

If the green disc is surrounded by curved lines, as in Figure 5-9, that means focus is sharp but is subject to adjustment if needed.

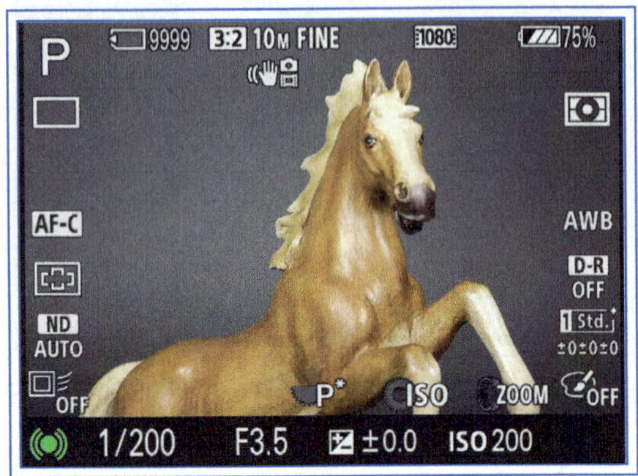

Figure 5-9. Green Disc with Curves for Continuous Focus

If only the curved lines appear, that means the camera is still trying to achieve focus. If the green disc flashes, that means the camera is having trouble focusing.

This focusing mode is useful when you are shooting a moving subject. With this option, you can get the RX10 to fix its focus on the subject, but you don't have to let up the shutter button to refocus; instead, you can keep holding the button halfway until you take the picture; in this way, you may save some time, rather than having to keep starting the focus and exposure process over by pressing the shutter button halfway again.

Before I leave the topic of autofocus modes, I will mention one menu option that has an important impact on the focusing operation of the RX10. That option, called Pre-AF, is the last item on screen 2 of the Custom menu. When you turn that option on while an autofocus mode (single-shot or continuous) is in effect, the camera will constantly attempt to bring the image into focus without any action on your part. That is, when you just aim the camera at the subject, without touching the shutter button, the camera will continue to adjust its focus.

The camera will take into account the Focus Area setting (Wide, Center, or Flexible Spot) as well as settings such as Face Detection, and attempt to focus on any object that appears to qualify as the main subject. With this option turned on, the camera should be ready to make its final focus adjustments more quickly when you press the shutter button to lock focus or to capture an image. I will discuss this option again in CHAPTER 7.

Direct Manual Focus

The third option for focus mode is DMF, which stands for direct manual focus. This feature lets you use a combination of autofocus and manual focus. One area in which DMF is useful is when you are shooting an extreme closeup of a small object, in which case focusing can be critical and hard to achieve. After you choose DMF, start the focusing process by pressing the shutter button halfway. The camera will make its best attempt to focus sharply using the autofocus mechanism. Then you can use the camera's manual focusing mechanism (turning the focus ring, as discussed below in this chapter) to fine-tune the focus, concentrating on the parts of the subject that you want to be most sharply focused.

Another time DMF is useful is when you are shooting a scene with objects at varying distances, and you want to focus on one of the more distant ones. You can start out using manual focus to get an approximate focus on the object you want to focus on, thereby letting the camera know the location of the main subject. Then you can press the shutter button halfway to let the camera take over and use autofocus to improve the sharpness of the focus.

When DMF is activated, you can turn on the Peaking feature on screen 2 of the Custom menu, as discussed below, and it will assist you with autofocus operations using DMF as well as with manual focus. The MF Assist feature also will enlarge the screen to help you with manual focusing, if you have turned it on through screen 2 of the Custom menu. However, with DMF, you have to keep the shutter button pressed halfway down while turning the focus ring for MF Assist to function. (With Manual Focus, you can just turn the focus ring without half-pressing the shutter button.)

When DMF is in effect, the zoom/focus ring is dedicated to manual focus, and cannot be used to zoom the lens.

Manual Focus

The final position on the focus mode switch is MF for manual focus. As I discussed for DMF, there are times when you may achieve sharper focus by adjusting it manually. Those situations include shooting extreme closeups, when focus is critical; shooting a group of objects at differing distances, when the camera will not know which one to focus on; and shooting through a barrier such as glass or a wire fence, which may interfere with focusing.

Also, manual focus gives you the freedom to use a soft focus effect purposely. As I discussed in Chapter 4, the RX10 has a Picture Effect setting called "Soft Focus," which adds a pleasing blurriness to images. If you would rather achieve this effect on your own by controlling focus directly, you can set the camera for manual focus and defocus your subject in precisely the way you want.

Using manual focus with the RX10 is a pleasure. All you have to do is turn the zoom/focus ring—the large ring around the lens, just beyond the aperture ring. The action is intuitive, and it is similar to the way most lenses were focused before autofocus existed.

There are several menu options available to help with manual focusing. I discussed one in Chapter 4 and I will discuss the others in Chapter 7, but I will briefly describe these aids here because you very well may need them when focusing manually.

First, the Focus Magnifier menu item, the final entry on screen 4 of the Shooting menu, puts an orange frame on the display, as shown in Figure 5-10.

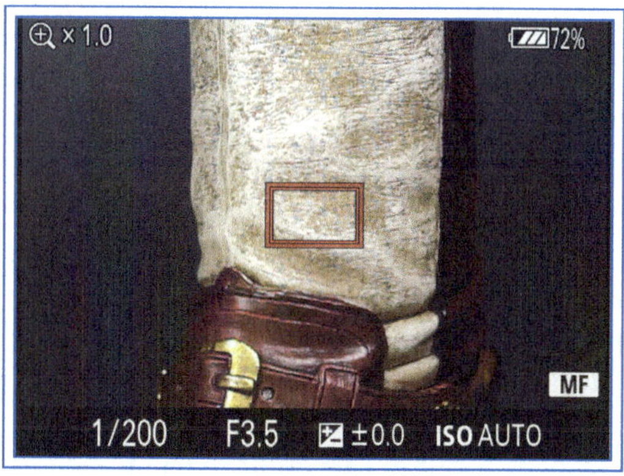

Figure 5-10. Focus Magnifier Frame on Display

Move the frame using the direction buttons, Control wheel, or Control dial. Press the Center button to enlarge the view within the frame to 8.6 times; press again to double the magnification, and a final time to return it to normal size. You can focus with the focus ring while the display is enlarged. If DMF is in use, you can half-press the shutter button for autofocus, but the display will not stay enlarged; it will return to normal if you press the shutter button.

The next manual focus aid, MF Assist, is the second option on screen 1 of the Custom menu. When MF Assist is on, whenever you turn the focus ring to adjust focus in manual focus mode, the image on the display is automatically magnified 8.6 times, as shown in Figure 5-11, so you can more clearly check the focus.

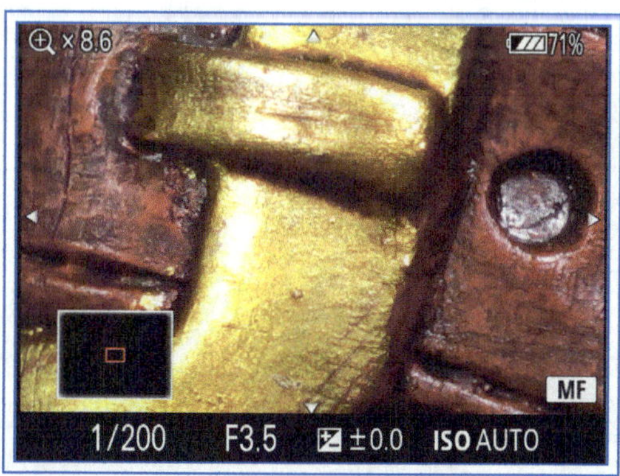

Figure 5-11. MF Assist in Use - Display Enlarged 8.6x

Once the magnified image is displayed, if you press the Center button, the image is magnified to 17.1 times normal. Press the Center button again to return to the 8.6-times view. You can control how long the magnified display stays on the screen using the Focus Magnification Time option, directly below MF Assist on screen 1 of the Custom menu. I prefer to set the time to No Limit, so the magnification does not disappear just as I am getting the focus adjusted. With No Limit, the magnification stays on the screen until you dismiss it by pressing the shutter button halfway.

If you don't want the camera to enlarge the image as soon as you start focusing, you can use the Focus Magnifier option, discussed above, instead of MF Assist. Or, you can use both the MF Assist and Focus Magnifier options, though I see no need to do so. In most cases, my preference is to use only the MF Assist option, which is sufficient for my needs.

The RX10 provides another aid to manual focusing, Peaking Level, which is the second item on screen 2 of the Custom menu. Peaking Level can be left turned off, or it can be set to Low, Mid, or High. When Peaking Level is turned on, then, when you are using manual focus, the camera places bright lines around the areas of the image that it judges to be in focus, as shown in FIGURE 5-12 (without Peaking) and FIGURE 5-13 (with Peaking Level set to Mid).

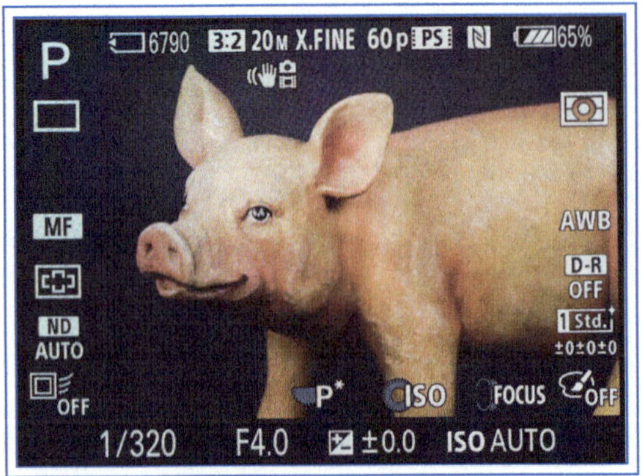

Figure 5-12. Peaking Off

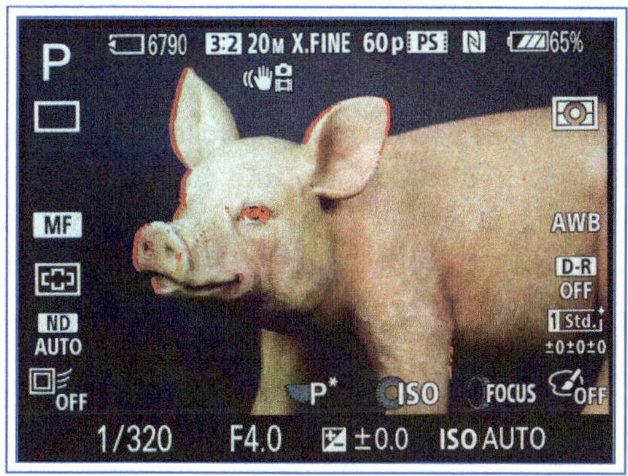

Figure 5-13. Peaking Mid and Red

Besides setting the intensity of this display, as discussed above, you can set the color the camera uses—either white, red, or yellow—using the Peaking Color option on the Custom menu. I have found this feature especially useful when focusing in dark conditions, because the Peaking color is illuminated and contrasts nicely with the dark display. Also, as noted above, Peaking Level works with both the autofocus and manual focus aspects of the DMF option. I will discuss Peaking further in CHAPTER 7.

Finally, there is another way to customize the use of manual focus with the RX10. On screen 2 of the Custom menu, you can assign the Center, Left, Right, Down, AEL, or Custom button to control any one of a long list of functions. One of those functions, called AF/MF Control Toggle, is useful if you anticipate a need to switch between autofocus and manual focus frequently. When this function is assigned to a button, you can press that button whenever you want to switch instantly between these two focus modes. This is more convenient than reaching down to find the focus switch and turning it to the new position, and it may be worthwhile assigning a button to this use.

The RX10 has a strong array of aids for manual focus. With some compact cameras, manual focus is hard to use because you have to turn a very small dial or the magnification options are not helpful.

I find that with the RX10, I prefer using manual focus to autofocus in some situations because it is so powerful and easy to use.

One reminder: When you use manual focus (or DMF), the zoom/focus ring is dedicated to that use, and you cannot use the ring to zoom the lens. You must use the zoom lever for that purpose.

AF Illuminator/Self-Timer Lamp

The lamp on the front of the camera next to the lens has two uses. Its reddish light blinks to signal use of the self-timer and it turns on in dark conditions to assist with autofocusing. You can control the lamp's autofocus function with the AF Illuminator item on screen 3 of the Shooting menu, as discussed in Chapter 4. If you set that menu item to Auto, the lamp will light as needed for autofocus; if you set it to Off, the lamp will never light for that purpose, though it will still illuminate for the self-timer.

Aperture Ring and Aperture Click Switch

The aperture ring, located next to the camera's body and labeled with numbers from 2.8 to 16, has a single purpose. You use this ring to set the aperture when the camera is in Aperture Priority or Manual exposure mode for still shooting, or in Movie mode with the movie exposure mode set to Aperture Priority or Manual Exposure. In other shooting modes, the ring has no function.

To set the aperture, turn the ring so the selected f-stop, such as f/2.8 or f/5.6, is aligned with the white indicator line on the lens. The ring is labeled with the major settings, and it has unlabeled white lines that indicate the intermediate settings of one-third of an f-stop. For example, between the labeled settings of f/2.8 and f/4 are unlabeled lines for the settings of f/3.2 and f/3.5.

There are a couple of other points to note about this ring. First, because it is a physical control on a camera with many electronic features, including automatic exposure, there will be times when the reading on the ring does not agree with the actual aperture setting. For example, when the camera is in Program mode, Shutter Priority mode, or Intelligent Auto mode, the camera will set the aperture, regardless of the position of the aperture ring.

The other point is that you can change the behavior of the ring with the aperture click switch. This small switch is hard to see; it is located near the camera's body on the lower left of the lens as you face the camera. When the switch is set to the On position, the ring moves with a reassuring click and stops cleanly at each setting on the aperture scale. I always leave this switch turned on when I'm using the camera for shooting still images.

When shooting videos, though, it's a good idea to turn the clicks off using this switch, if there's any chance you'll be turning the ring during the video recording. The reason for doing this is to avoid recording the sounds of the clicks on the audio track. With the switch turned off, the ring will rotate smoothly and quietly, with no defined stops for the various settings. This makes it harder to pick a specific aperture value, but, for shooting videos, you're probably more likely to want the smooth, silent motion of the ring, and you may not be so concerned with selecting a particular f-stop.

Zoom/Focus Ring

The other large ring around the lens, beyond the aperture ring, is the zoom/focus ring, which is covered with smooth ridges. You can use this ring to zoom the lens in and out throughout its optical focal length range of 24mm to 200mm. Those focal lengths are stated in "35mm-equivalent" terms. As you can see from the markings on the lens, the actual focal length of the zoom lens is 8.8mm to 73.3mm. However, the common practice for camera makers is to state the focal length in terms of what effect this focal length would have if the camera were a traditional model that uses 35mm film. Using this 35mm-equivalent range of 24mm to 200mm makes it easy to compare the range of this zoom lens to the zoom ranges of other digital cameras.

To use the zoom ring, just grasp it and turn it firmly in either direction to change the level of zoom. It's important to note that, if you have the focus switch set to the DMF or MF setting, for direct manual focus or manual focus, this ring becomes dedicated to manual focus, and will not zoom the lens. In that case, you have to use the zoom lever that surrounds the shutter button in order to zoom the lens.

Now it is time to discuss several important controls on the back of the RX10, as seen in Figure 5-14.

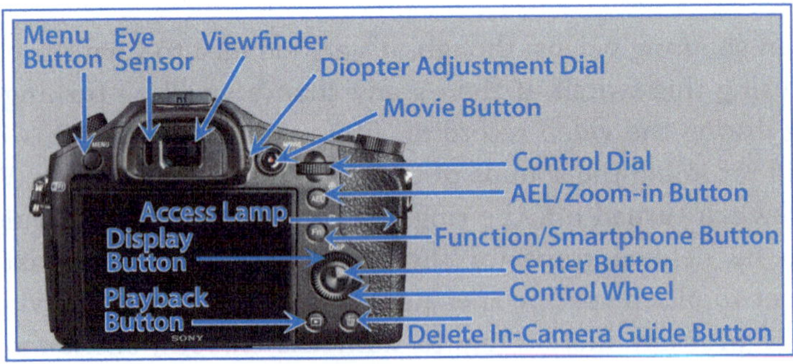

Figure 5-14. Controls on Back of Camera

Playback Button

This button to the lower left of the Control wheel, marked with a small triangle, is used to put the camera into playback mode, which allows you to view your images on the LCD screen or in the viewfinder, and gives you access to the Playback menu. When the camera is in playback mode, pressing this button will switch the camera to shooting mode. When the camera has powered down because of the Power Save Start Time menu option, you can press this button to wake the camera up into playback mode.

Movie Button

The red button at the upper right of the camera's back has just one function—to start and stop the recording of movie sequences. As I noted in discussing the mode dial earlier in this chapter, you can control how the Movie button operates. If you want to be able to start recording a movie in any shooting mode, go to the Custom menu and select the fifth option on screen 4, which is called Movie Button. If you set that menu option to Always (the default setting), then the Movie button will operate in any shooting mode. If you set that option to Movie Mode Only, then the Movie button will not operate unless the camera is set to Movie mode using the mode dial. (Movie mode is the mode marked by the movie-film icon.)

This is a fairly important decision to make, and it depends on your preferences and likely uses of the camera. If you want to be able to start recording a video at any time without delay, you should leave the Movie Button option set to Always. The reason you might not want to do this is if you believe you may press the Movie button by mistake. I have done that often myself, particularly with a smaller Sony model, the DSC-RX100, which does not have the option to limit the use of the Movie button to Movie mode. When you press the button by mistake, you have to press it again to stop the recording, and then wait for the camera to finish processing the movie before you can use any other controls. And, of course, the camera will have an unwanted file cluttering the memory card.

With the RX10, I never press the Movie button by mistake, because the button does not come within range of my thumb unless I want to press it. So, with this camera I leave the option set to Always, to avoid missing video opportunities. But you should consider whether you want to use that menu option as a precaution against unwanted footage.

There are differences in how the camera operates for video recording in different shooting modes. I will discuss movie-making in detail in Chapter 8.

Menu Button

The Menu button, at the upper left of the camera's back, has a straightforward function. Press it to enter the menu system and press it again to exit to the mode the camera was in previously (shooting or playback). The button also cancels out of sub-menus, taking you to the main menu screen. You can press the Menu button to wake the camera up into the menu system when it has powered down from the Power Save Start Time option.

Function Button

The button marked Fn, for Function, has several roles, depending on whether the camera is in shooting mode or playback mode.

Function Menu

When the camera is set to shooting mode, the Function button gives you a way to get quick access to menu options. When you press the button the camera displays the Function menu, from which you can select a setting for immediate adjustment. Using the Function Menu Settings option on screen 4 of the Custom menu (discussed in Chapter 7), you can assign up to 12 functions to this menu, from among 27 possibilities. The items that can be assigned include settings such as ISO, Drive Mode, White Balance, ND Filter, Flash Mode, Focus Area, and Picture Effect.

Once you have assigned up to 12 options to this button, it is ready for action. To use an option, press the button when the camera is in shooting mode, and a menu will appear along the bottom of the display in two rows with six choices each, as shown in Figure 5-15.

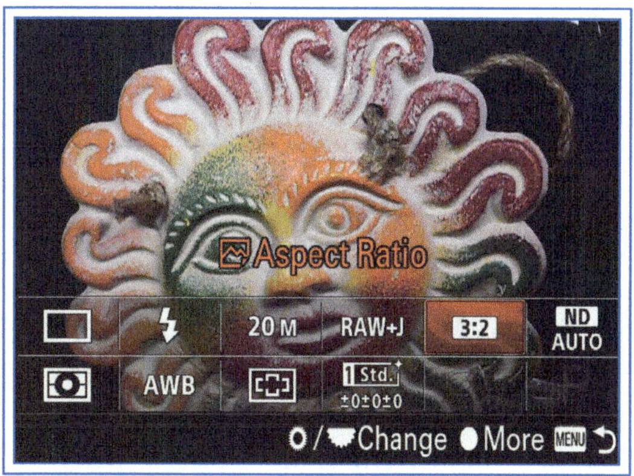

Figure 5-15. Function Menu

Use the direction buttons to move the highlight block at the bottom of the display over the item you want to select. With that setting highlighted, turn the Control wheel to cycle through the possible settings. As you do so, a circular menu will appear near the top of the display, showing the range of settings. When the one you want to select is highlighted, press the Function button to select it and exit back to the shooting screen. If there are sub-settings, use the Control dial to scroll through those before exiting the menu.

For example, if you have moved the orange highlight block to the Quality item, turn the Control wheel until the setting you want to make appears, as shown in FIGURE 5-16, where Fine is selected.

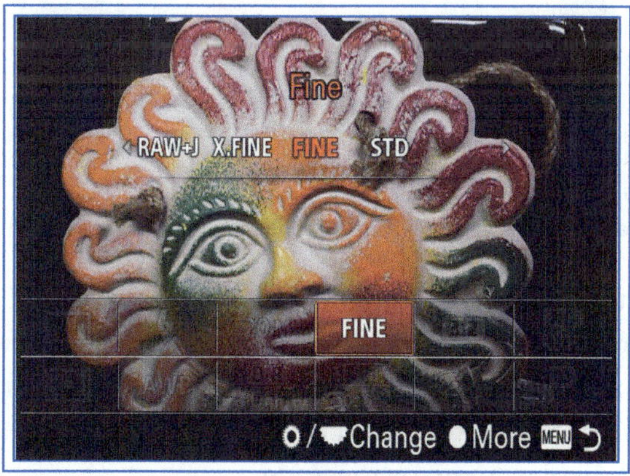

Figure 5-16. Fine Setting for Image Quality on Function Menu

Then, press the Function button to confirm the setting and exit from the Function menu screen. Or, if you want to make multiple settings from the Function menu options, after changing one setting you can press the Center button to go back to the Function menu and make more settings before you press the Function button to exit to the shooting screen.

To take an example with a sub-setting, call up the Function menu and scroll to Focus Area, then use the Control wheel to select the right-most setting, Flexible Spot. At that point, an additional line of icons will appear below the main choices, with choices for the size of the focus frame, as seen in Figure 5-17.

Use the Control dial to scroll through those choices and select small, medium, or large. When your selection is highlighted, press the Function button to confirm the selection and exit to the shooting screen. (Or, press the Center button to make more choices from the Function menu.)

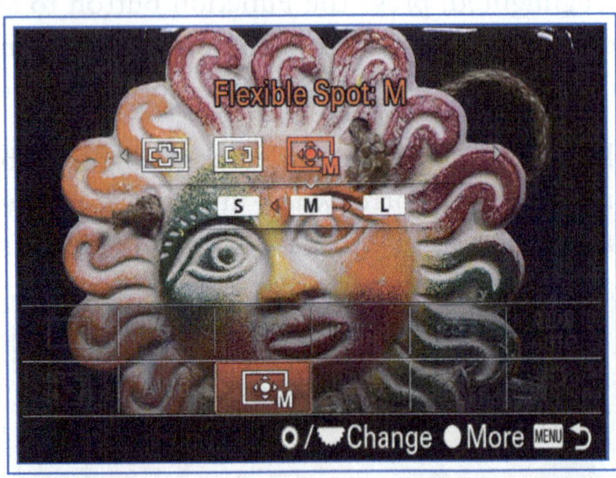

Figure 5-17. Flexible Spot Frame Size Choices on Function Menu

Note that there may be some items at the bottom of the screen whose icons are dimmed because the item is unavailable for selection in the current context. If you move the orange highlight block to one of those items and then try to change the setting, the camera will display an error message.

Also, the selections I discussed above may not be available because they have not been assigned to the Function menu. If that is the case, you can use the Function Menu Settings menu option to assign them if you want to follow the examples.

The Function menu system on the RX10 is well thought out and convenient. I strongly recommend that you experiment and develop a group of 12 items to assign to this button and make use of this speedy way to change important settings.

Quick Navi System

In shooting mode, the Function button also gives you access to the Quick Navi system for changing settings rapidly. This system has similarities to the Function menu system I just discussed, but there are significant differences.

The Quick Navi system comes into play only in one situation—when you have called up the special display screen shown in Figure 5-18, which Sony calls the "For Viewfinder" display.

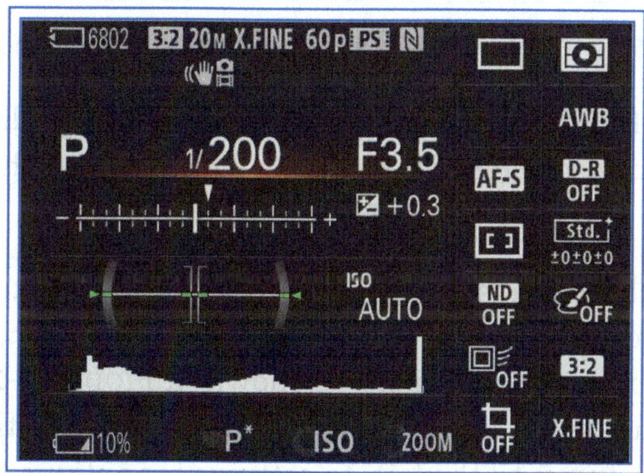

Figure 5-18. For Viewfinder Display Screen

This is the only shooting-mode display that does not include the live view. It is called "For viewfinder" because the idea is that you will use this display when you are using the viewfinder, so you can see the live view through the viewfinder and see the details of your settings on this display, which appears only on the LCD screen.

The For Viewfinder display is summoned by pressing the Display button, but only if you have selected it for inclusion in the cycle of display screens. You select it using the Display Button option on screen 2 of the Custom menu. From that menu option, select the sub-option for Monitor, and then check the box for the For Viewfinder item on the next screen, as shown in FIGURE 5-19.

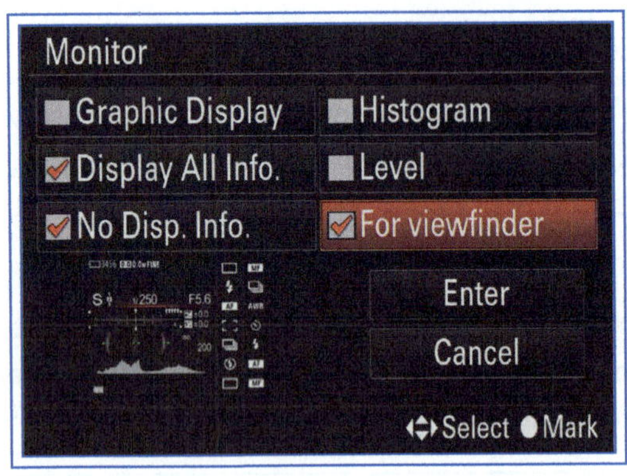

Figure 5-19. For Viewfinder Choice on Display Button Menu Screen

As seen in FIGURE 5-18, the For Viewfinder screen displays a lot of information at the right, including Drive Mode, White Balance, Focus Area, DRO, Picture Effect, and several others.

Normally, these items are displayed for information; you cannot adjust them. But, if you press the Function button, an orange highlight appears at the right, as shown in FIGURE 5-20. You can then use the direction buttons to navigate through the settings. You also can move to the left, to settings for options such as ISO, SteadyShot, and Image Size. When you have highlighted a setting to adjust, turn the Control wheel or the Control dial to scroll through the available values and make the adjustment quickly.

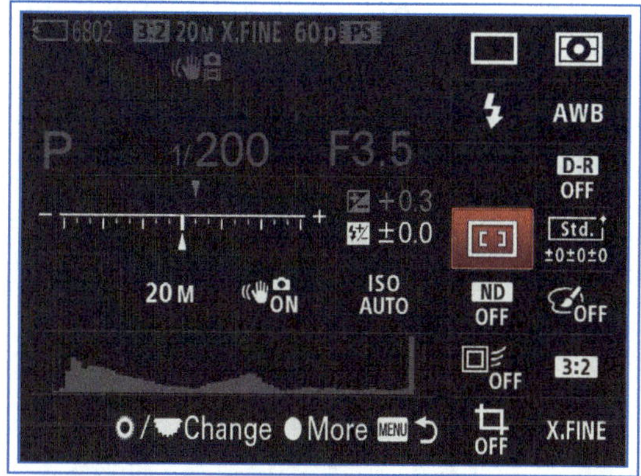

Figure 5-20. Quick Navi Menu Screen

When you adjust a setting, such as Aspect Ratio, a secondary window opens in the top part of the display, as shown in FIGURE 5-21, showing the various options available for the setting.

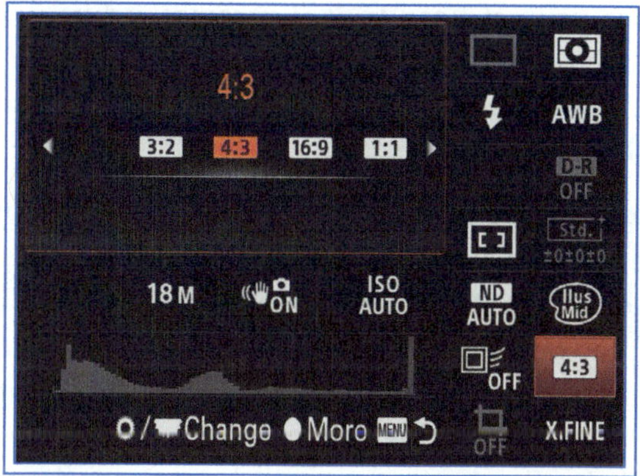

Figure 5-21. Secondary Window for Quick Navi Screen

After changing a setting, you can move to other settings using the direction buttons. Once you have made all your changes, press the Function button again to exit to the static For Viewfinder display, which will now show the new settings in place.

For sub-settings, make the main setting with the Control wheel and the sub-setting with the Control dial. For example, move the highlight to Picture Effect, turn the Control wheel to highlight

Partial Color, and turn the Control dial to highlight Blue, as shown in FIGURE 5-22. Press the Function button to exit.

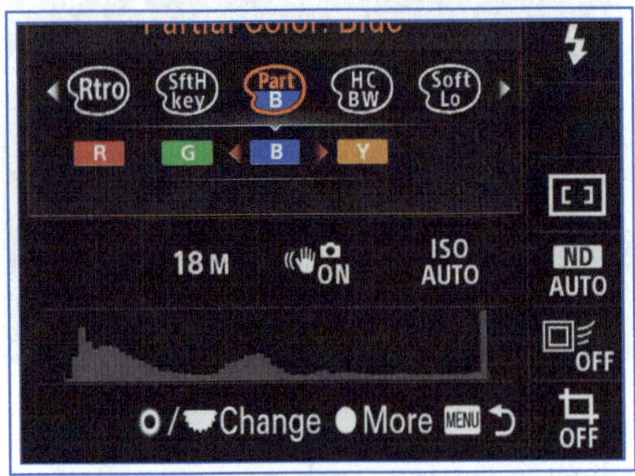

Figure 5-22. Quick Navi Adjustment of Picture Effect Option

The Quick Navi system can streamline your ability to change settings once you get used to it. I recommend you devote some time to practicing with it, if speed is important to you.

Dial/Wheel Lock

The Function button also can carry out one other operation in shooting mode, depending on how a Custom menu option is set. The final item on screen 4 of that menu is the Dial/Wheel Lock option. If that option is set to Lock, then, when you press and hold the Function button for several seconds, the shooting-related operations of the Control wheel and Control dial are locked. The wheel and dial will still operate to navigate through menu screens and menu settings, but they will not set items such as ISO and shutter speed. I will discuss that menu option in CHAPTER 7.

Send to Smartphone

When the camera is in playback mode, pressing the Function button brings up a screen allowing you to send the current image or multiple images to a smartphone or tablet. I will discuss this option in CHAPTER 9, where I discuss the camera's wireless functions.

In-Camera Guide/Delete Button

The button marked with a question mark, to the right of the Playback button, is officially called the In-Camera Guide button or the Delete button. I prefer to call it the Help button or the Trash button. When the camera is displaying a menu screen, including the Function menu or the Quick Navi screen, you can press this button to bring up a brief message with guidance or tips about the use of the option that is currently highlighted. For example, if you go to screen 2 of the Custom menu and highlight the Live View Display item, then press the Help button, the camera displays the message shown in Figure 5-23.

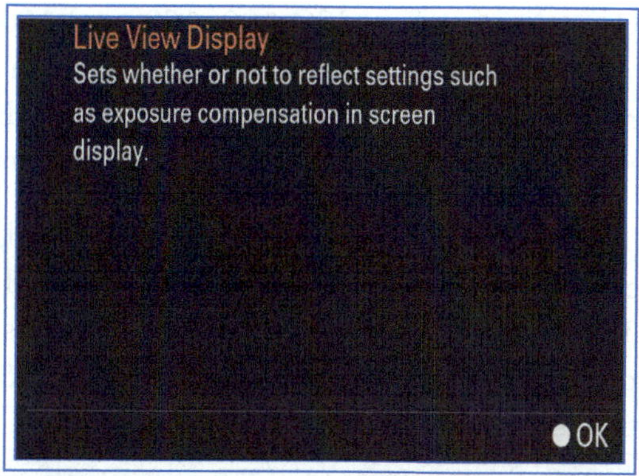

Figure 5-23. Help Message for Live View Display Menu Option

If you select a sub-option for that menu item and then press the Help button, the camera will display a different message providing details about that particular option. For example, Figure 5-24 shows the screen that was displayed when I pressed the Help button after highlighting the Speed Priority Continuous Shooting option for the Drive Mode item.

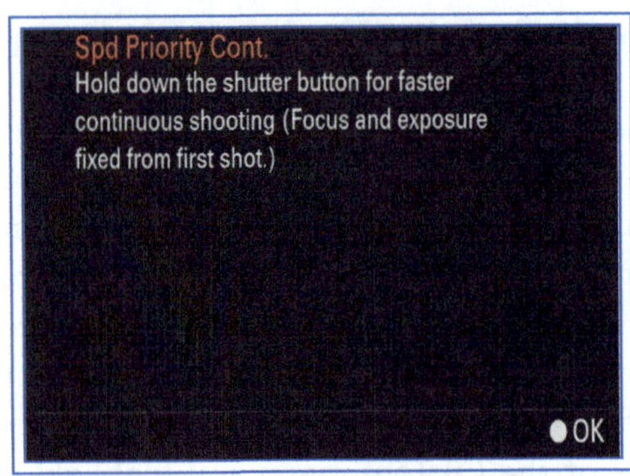

Figure 5-24. Help Message for Speed Priority Continuous Setting

This help system is quite detailed; for example, it has guidance for different ISO settings such as ISO 100, 160, and 1600, with tips about what shooting conditions might call for a given setting. The system operates with all of the menu systems, including Custom, Playback, Setup, and the others, not just the Shooting menu.

In playback mode, when an image or video is displayed, this button becomes the Delete button (Trash button), as indicated by the trash can icon to the lower right of the button. If you press the button, the camera displays the message shown in Figure 5-25, prompting you to select Delete or Cancel.

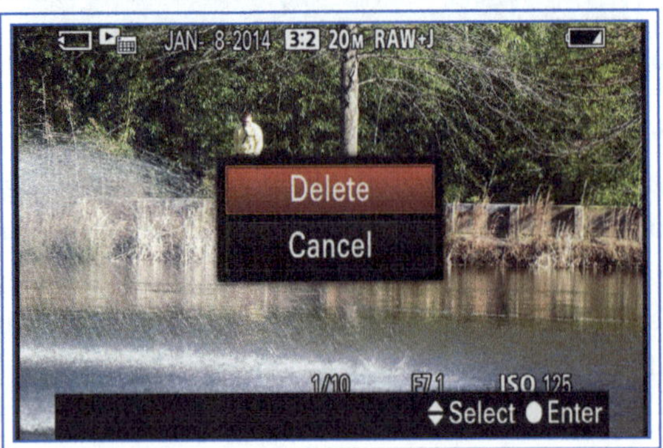

Figure 5-25. Trash Button Confirmation Screen

If you highlight Delete and press the Center button, the camera will delete the image or video that was displayed. If you choose Cancel, the camera will return to the playback mode screen.

Finally, this button has one specialized function that is not obvious. When you have activated the Flexible Spot focus frame and have moved it to a new position on the camera's display, you can press the Trash button to return the focus frame immediately to the center of the display.

Control Wheel and Its Buttons

Several important controls are within the perimeter of the Control wheel, the ridged wheel with a large button in its center. The four edges of the wheel (Up, Down, Left, and Right) function as buttons. That is, if you press the wheel's rim at any of those four points, you are, in effect, pressing a button.

On the RX10 only one of these buttons is labeled—the top button, which serves as the Display button as well as the Up button for navigating through various screens. The other three buttons also act as the Left, Right, and Down buttons for moving through screens. However, one of the powerful features of the RX10 is your ability to program each of those three buttons, as well as some other controls, with any one of numerous functions. Using this ability, you can set up the RX10 with a set of custom controls that matches your preferences for adjusting settings quickly. I will discuss these programming options for each control, as I describe the features of each button or dial below.

Control Wheel

In many cases, to choose a menu item or a setting, you can turn this wheel, which is centrally located on the camera's back. In some cases, you have the choice of using this wheel or pressing the direction buttons. In others, you can turn this wheel or the Control dial, located at the upper right of the camera's back.

The Control wheel also has many other functions. When you are viewing a menu screen, you can navigate up and down through the lists of options by turning the wheel. When you are adjusting items using the Function menu or the Quick Navi menu, you can change the value for the highlighted setting by turning the Control wheel. When you are using manual focus and you have the Focus Magnifier option turned on, you can turn the Control wheel to choose the area of the scene that is being magnified.

In playback mode, you can turn the Control wheel to navigate from one image to the next on the LCD screen. Also, when a video is being played on the screen and has been paused, you can turn the Control wheel to move the video either forward or in reverse. While a movie is playing, you can use the wheel to fast-forward or fast-reverse the footage.

Finally, with the Custom Key Settings option on screen 4 of the Custom menu, you can assign a function to each of several camera controls, including the Control wheel. Using that menu option, you can assign any one of four functions to the Control wheel: ISO, White Balance, Creative Style, or Picture Effect. I will discuss that option in CHAPTER 7, in connection with the Custom menu.

Center Button

The large button in the center of the Control wheel has many uses. On menu screens that have additional options, such as the Image Size screen, this button takes you to the next screen to view the other options. It also acts as a selection button when you choose certain options. For example, after you select Flash Mode from screen 2 of the Shooting menu and then navigate to your desired option, you can press the Center button to confirm your selection and exit from the menu screen back to the shooting screen.

When the camera is set to manual focus and the MF Assist option is turned on, once you turn the focus ring to start focusing, pressing the Center button roughly doubles the magnification of the display: from 8.6 times to 17.1 times. Pressing the button again toggles the display back to the 8.6 times magnification level. When the Focus Magnifier menu option is turned on, pressing the Center button magnifies the screen in manual focus mode.

The Center button also has several other possible uses depending on how it is set up in the menu system. Screen 4 of the Custom menu (discussed in CHAPTER 7) has an item called Custom Key Settings, with a sub-option for the Center Button. Using that sub-option, you can set the Center button to have a preset group of focus-related functions by selecting the Standard option for Function of Center Button.

If you select the Standard option, the Center button is used to activate the tracking frame for the Lock-on AF option, assuming you have turned on that menu option. When the object you want to track with autofocus is in the center of the display, press the Center button and the camera will try to keep that object in focus. Press the button again to cancel the tracking.

If Focus Area is set to Flexible Spot, pressing the Center button activates the screen to adjust the location of the focus frame.

If you prefer not to use the Standard option, you can use the Center Button option on the Custom menu to set this button to carry out any one of numerous functions. I will discuss those functions in CHAPTER 7, in connection with the Custom menu.

My strong preference is to leave the button assigned to the Standard option. If you don't, then the Lock-on AF and Flexible Spot options will not work as they normally do. Also, this button has as a primary function the selecting of menu screens, and that function may take priority even if you assign a different function to the button. For example, if you assign In-Camera Guide to this button and then press the button while a menu item is highlighted, the camera will display the next screen of the menu, if there is one, rather than the In-Camera Guide. There are several other buttons that can be assigned to handle specific options, so I recommend you leave the Center button assigned to the Standard setting.

In playback mode, you press the Center button to start playing a video whose first frame is displayed on the camera's screen. Once the video is playing, press the Center button to pause the playback and then to toggle between play and pause. When a panoramic image is displayed, press the Center button to make it scroll on the screen at a larger size using the full expanse of the display screen. When you have enlarged an image using the zoom lever, you can return it immediately to its normal size by pressing the Center button. When you are selecting images for deletion or protection using the appropriate Playback menu option, you use the Center button to mark or unmark an image for that purpose.

Direction Buttons

Each of the four edges of the Control wheel—Up, Down, Left, and Right—is also a "button" you can press to access a setting or operation, if it has had one assigned to it. This is not immediately obvious, and sometimes it can be tricky to press in exactly the right spot, but these four buttons are important to your control of the camera. You use them to navigate through menus and through screens for settings, whether moving left and right or up and down.

You also use them in playback mode to move through your images and, when you have enlarged an image using the zoom lever, to scroll around within the magnified image.

In addition to these navigational duties, the direction buttons have miscellaneous functions in connection with various settings. For example, when a movie is being played, pressing the Down button opens up the control panel for controlling playback of the movie. When a movie is displayed on the screen ready to be played, pressing the Down button brings up the camera's volume control screen. And, as with the Center button, the Right, Left, and Down buttons can be assigned to carry out other functions through the Custom menu, as discussed in Chapter 7.

Finally, one of the direction buttons, the Up button, comes pre-assigned as the Display button, as discussed below.

Up Button: Display

The Up button, marked "DISP," is used to switch among the displays of information on the camera's screen and in the viewfinder, in both shooting and playback modes. As discussed in Chapter 7, you can change the contents of the shooting mode screens using the Display Button option on screen 2 of the Custom menu. The display screens that are available in playback mode are discussed in Chapter 6. Because it is dedicated to display duties, the Up button cannot be programmed to perform any other functions.

Left Button

One of the excellent features of the RX10 is that three buttons—the Left, Right, and Down buttons—have no dedicated functions assigned to them. With many cameras, these three buttons have icons next to them on the camera's back, designating them to handle functions such as flash mode, exposure compensation, the self-timer, and the like. I greatly prefer the system with the RX10, which lets you choose the assignments for these three buttons according to your own preferences.

The Left button can be assigned to carry out any one of a number of functions, using the Custom Key Settings option on screen 4 of the Custom menu. I will discuss those options in Chapter 7.

Right Button

The choices for the Right button are the same as for the Left button.

Down Button

The Down button also has the same options as the Left button.

AEL Button

The AEL button, located above the Function button, is set by default to the AEL Hold option. With that setting, you can press and hold this button to lock the exposure as metered by the camera using the current metering method. I will discuss that option in CHAPTER 7, where I discuss all of the settings that can be assigned to this and the other control buttons.

When the camera is set to playback mode, the AEL button serves to enlarge a still image that is displayed on the camera's screen, as indicated by the plus sign next to the button on the camera's back. This function remains assigned to the button for playback mode, even if you change the button's assignment for shooting mode.

When you have set the Flash Mode to Wireless, you press the AEL button to test the connection between the triggering flash unit and the remote flash unit. I discussed that procedure in CHAPTER 4.

Control Dial

The Control dial is the small dial that sticks out from the camera's back, directly to the right of the red Movie button. The most important function of this dial is to set the camera's shutter speed when you are using either Shutter Priority or Manual exposure mode for still photos, or when you are using Movie mode and have the movie exposure mode set to Aperture Priority or Manual.

This dial also is used for selecting sub-options in some cases. For example, when you choose Picture Effect from the shooting menu, some settings, such as Toy Camera, have sub-settings that can be selected by turning the Control dial. In Program mode, turning the dial activates Program Shift, which causes the camera to pick a new pair of shutter speed and aperture settings to match the current exposure. In Panorama Sweep mode, turning this dial changes the panorama direction. In Scene mode, turning the dial changes the scene setting, such as Portrait, Landscape, and the others.

When the Control dial is available to control a particular setting, the camera displays an icon for the dial next to a label or icon for that setting. For example, in FIGURE 5-26, the display indicates that the dial is available to control shutter speed (indicated by Tv, which stands for time value).

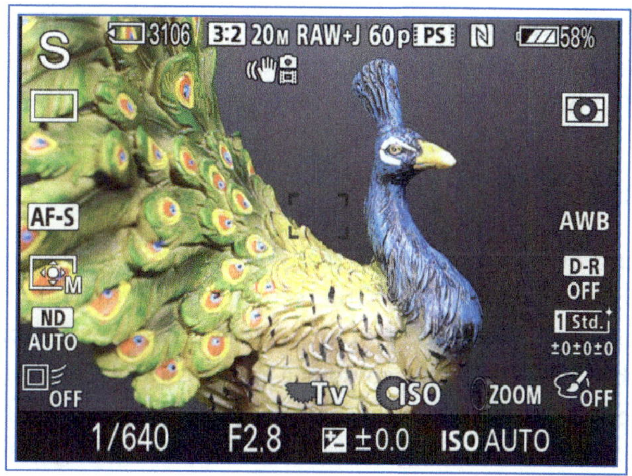

Figure 5-26. Icon Showing Control Dial Used for Shutter Speed

In playback mode, you can turn the Control dial to navigate through the images and videos stored on the camera's memory card. The dial also will zoom in and out on an image that has been enlarged using the zoom lever or the AEL button. It also will move through movies slowly when paused or rapidly when they are playing.

Diopter Adjustment Wheel

The diopter adjustment wheel is a small, ridged wheel on the right side of the viewfinder eyepiece. You can turn this wheel to adjust the viewfinder according to your vision. If you wear eyeglasses, you may find that you can adjust the setting of the viewfinder so that you can see clearly through it without your glasses.

Eye Sensor

The eye sensor is a small window in the viewfinder eyepiece to the left of the main viewfinder window. When your eye approaches this small slot and blocks the light that reaches it, the camera automatically switches from using the LCD screen to using the viewfinder, if the menu option is set for that behavior. To enable this automatic switching, go to screen 3 of the Custom menu, select the Finder/Monitor item, and choose Auto. If you don't want the automatic switching, choose Viewfinder or Monitor, to keep either one of those viewing options as the permanent setting.

Tilting LCD Screen

The tilting LCD screen is not really a "control," but it does allow some physical adjustment. This screen, even without its tilting ability, is a notable feature of the camera. It has a diagonal span of 3 inches (7.5 cm) and provides a resolution of 1.2 million dots using Sony's "WhiteMagic" technology, which adds a white sub-pixel to the normal red, green, and blue ones, giving a very clear and sharp view of your images before and after you capture them.

The screen can tilt downward as much as 43 degrees, as shown in Figure 5-27.

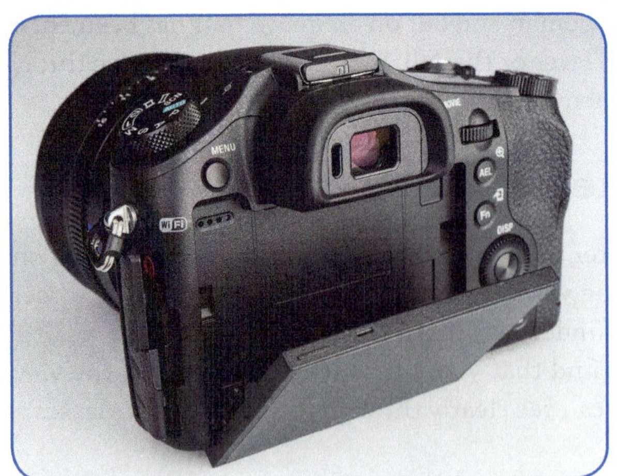

Figure 5-27. LCD Screen Tilted Down for Overhead Shots

When the LCD is tilted in this way, you can hold the camera high above your head and view the scene as if you were an arm's-length taller or were standing on a small ladder. If you attach the camera to a monopod or other support and hold it up in the air, you can extend the camera's height even further and still view the screen quite well. You can activate the self-timer before raising the camera up in the air. You also can use a smartphone or tablet connected to the camera by Wi-Fi to trigger the camera by remote control while it is raised overhead, as discussed in Chapter 9, or you can use Sony's wired remote control, which is discussed in Appendix A.

On the other hand, if you need to take images from a vantage point near ground level, you can rotate the screen so it tilts upward toward your eyes, as shown in Figure 5-28, and hold the camera down as far as you need to get a mole's-eye view of the world. The screen can tilt upward as much as 84 degrees.

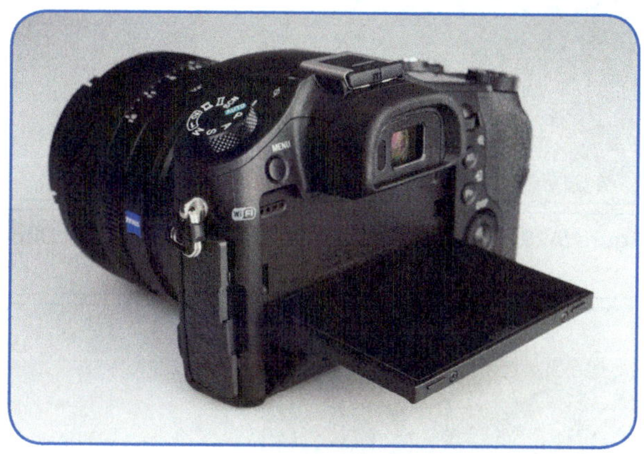

Figure 5-28. LCD Tilted Upward for Low-Angle Shots

It can be helpful to shoot upward like this when your subject is in an area with a busy, distracting background. You can hold the camera down low and shoot with the sky as your background to reduce or eliminate the distractions. (Similarly, you may be able to shoot from a high angle to frame your subject against the ground or floor to have a less-cluttered background.)

The tilting display also can be useful for street photography: you can fold the screen upward and look down at the camera while taking photos of people on the street without drawing undue attention to yourself.

Next, I will discuss the jacks and ports that are located on the left side of the camera. FIGURE 5-29 shows this side of the camera with the protective doors closed. When those doors are opened, the jacks and ports are readily accessible, as seen in FIGURE 5-30.

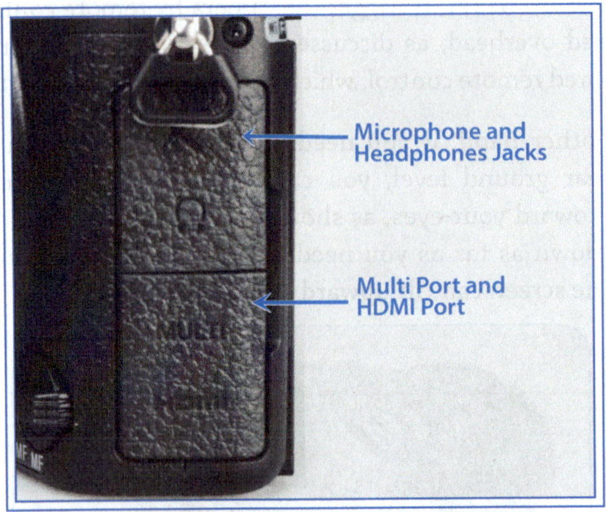

Figure 5-29. Left Side of Camera Showing Closed Port Doors

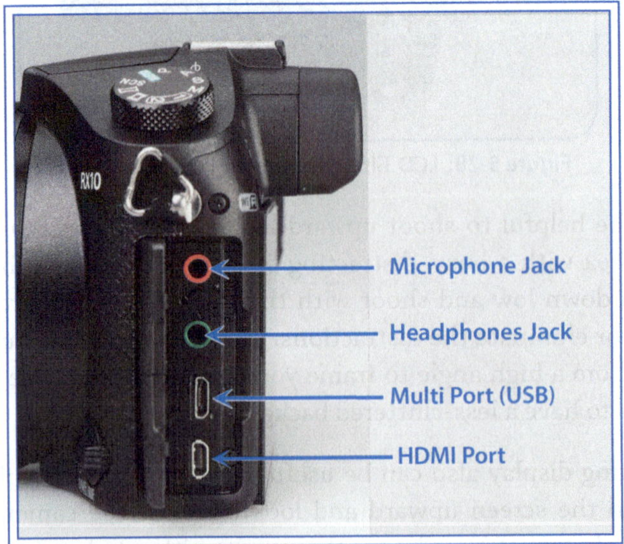

Figure 5-30. Ports on Left Side of Camera

The top jack is for an external microphone with a 3.5mm stereo plug. I will discuss external microphones in APPENDIX A. The second jack is for headphones, also using a standard 3.5mm plug, so you can monitor the audio being recorded by the camera.

The third item is the Multi port. This is where you plug in the USB cable for charging the battery, uploading images and videos to your computer, or connecting the camera directly to a printer to print images. You also can plug in other accessories that are compatible with this special terminal, including Sony's wired remote control, model RM-VPR1, which I discuss in APPENDIX A.

The last item in this area is the HDMI port, where you plug in an optional micro-HDMI cable to connect the camera to an HDTV for viewing images and videos. You also can view the shooting display from the camera through this connection, so you can connect the camera to an HDTV to act as a monitor for your shooting of still images or videos. I will discuss this process in CHAPTER 9.

The right side of the camera, shown in FIGURE 5-31, is where the memory card slot is located, under a protective door. As discussed in CHAPTER 1, you need to insert either an SD card or a Sony Memory Stick into this slot in order to store your images and videos.

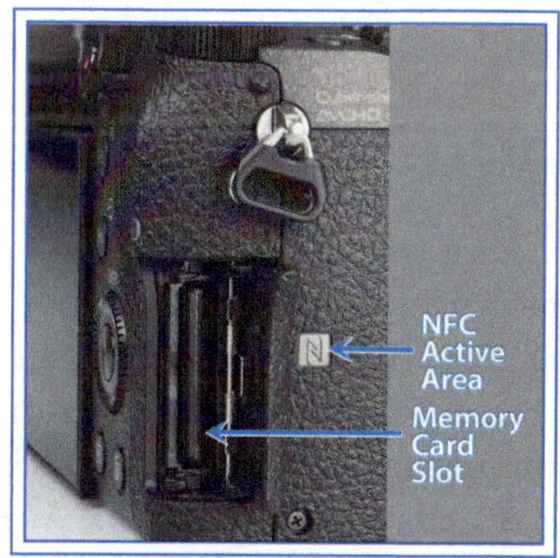

Figure 5-31. Items on Right Side of Camera

To the right of the memory card area is a decorative letter N, which marks the NFC active area for the RX10. This is where you touch the camera against the similar area on a compatible Android smartphone or tablet that uses the near field communication protocol. As discussed in CHAPTER 9, when the two devices are touched together at their NFC active areas, they should automatically connect through a Wi-Fi connection. Once the connection is established, they can share images and the phone or tablet can control the camera in some ways.

The final items are on the bottom of the RX10, seen in FIGURE 5-32.

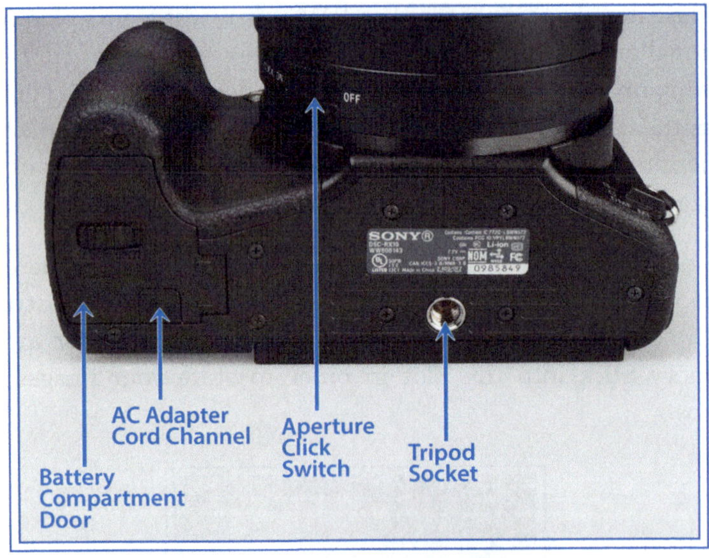

Figure 5-32. Items on Bottom of Camera

The major items here are the tripod socket and the battery compartment. The battery compartment door has a small flap located at its edge. That flap is provided so you can insert an AC adapter into the battery compartment and run its cord through the flap, so the compartment's door can be latched securely shut. I will discuss the AC adapter in APPENDIX A. In this view, you also can see the aperture click switch, which I discussed earlier in connection with the aperture ring.

Chapter 6: Playback and Printing

You may not spend a lot of time viewing your images and videos in the camera, but even if you don't, it's useful to know how the various in-camera playback functions work. You may need to examine an image closely in the camera to check focus, composition, and other aspects, or you may want to share images with friends and family. So it's worth taking a good look at the various playback functions of the Sony RX10. I'll also discuss options for printing images in this chapter.

Normal Playback

First, you should be aware of the Auto Review option on screen 1 of the Custom menu. This setting determines whether and for how long the image stays on the screen for review when you take a new picture. If your major interest for viewing images in the camera is to check them right after they are taken, this setting is all you need to be concerned with. As discussed in Chapter 7, you can leave Auto Review turned off or set it to 2, 5, or 10 seconds.

To control how your images are viewed later on, you need to work with the options that are available in playback mode. For plain review of images, the process is simple. Once you press the Playback button (marked with a triangle icon), the camera is in playback mode, and you will see the most recent image or video saved to the camera's memory card. To move back through older items, press the Left button or turn the Control wheel or Control dial to the left. To see more recent ones, use the Right button or turn the Control wheel or Control dial to the right. To speed through the images, hold down the Left or Right button.

Index View and Enlarging Images

In normal playback mode, you can press the zoom lever on top of the camera to view an index screen of your images and videos or to enlarge a single image. When you are viewing an individual image, press the zoom lever once to the left, and you will see a screen showing either 9 or 25 images, one of which is outlined by an orange frame, as shown in Figure 6-1. (You can choose whether this screen shows 9 or 25 images using the Image Index option on the Playback menu, discussed later in this chapter.)

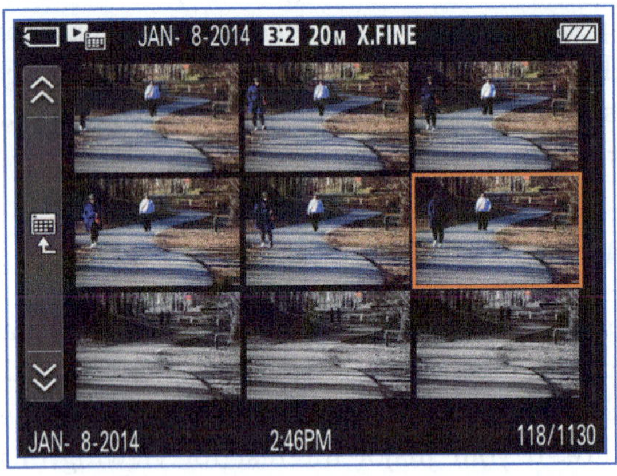

Figure 6-1. Index Screen with 9 Images

You can press the Center button to bring up the outlined image as the single image on the screen, or you can move through your images on the index screen by pressing the Left and Right buttons or by turning the Control wheel. If you move the orange highlight to the far left of the display, as seen in Figure 6-2, you then can use the Up and Down buttons to move through your images a screen at a time.

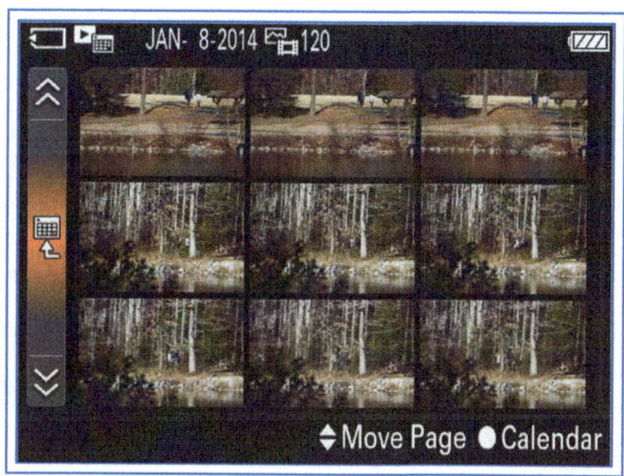

Figure 6-2. Index Screen with Far Left Strip Highlighted

At any time when you are viewing the index screen, you can turn the Control dial to move through the images a screen at a time.

When you are viewing the 9-image or 25-image index screen, one more press of the zoom lever to the left brings up a calendar display, as shown in FIGURE 6-3.

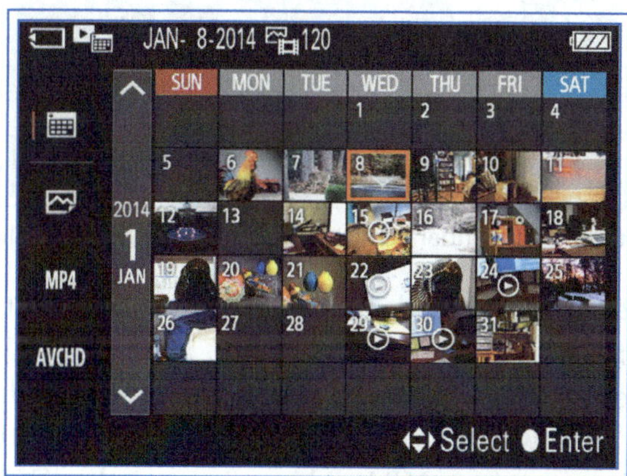

Figure 6-3. Calendar Display Screen

On that screen, you can move the orange highlight frame to any date and then press the Center button to bring up a view with all images from that date. If you move the orange highlight to the narrow strip at the left of the screen, as shown in FIGURE 6-4, you can navigate through your images by months.

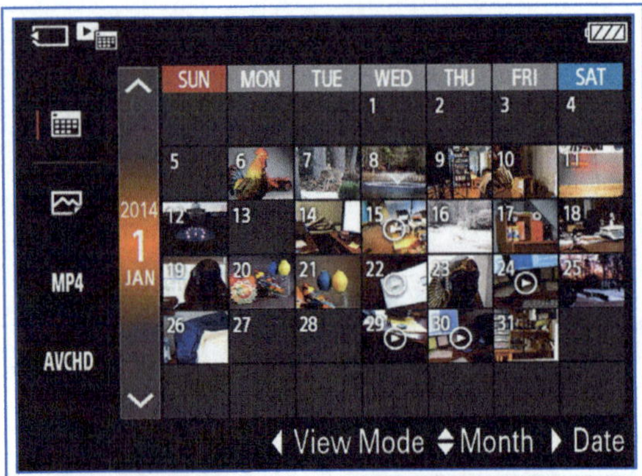

Figure 6-4. Calendar Screen with Month Strip Highlighted

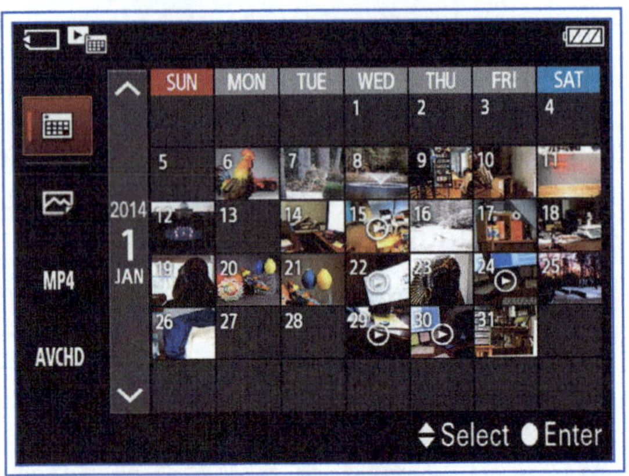

Figure 6-5. Calendar Screen with View Mode Strip Highlight

If you press the Left button or turn the Control wheel to move the cursor to the extreme left of the screen, as shown in Figure 6-5, you can use the Up and Down buttons to move through the line of four icons, from which you can choose, from the top, the calendar view, still-images view, MP4 videos view, or the AVCHD videos view. I will discuss those options later in this chapter, in connection with the View Mode menu option on the Playback menu.

When you are viewing a single image, one press of the zoom lever to the right or a press of the AEL button enlarges that image. You will then see a display in the lower-left corner of the image showing a thumbnail of the image with an inset orange frame that represents the portion of the image that is now filling the screen in enlarged view, as shown in FIGURE 6-6.

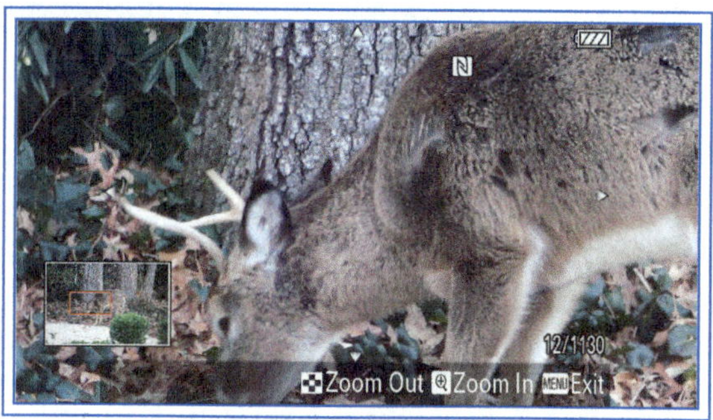

Figure 6-6. Image Enlarged in Playback Mode

If you press the zoom lever to the right repeatedly or keep pressing the AEL button, the image will be enlarged to increasing levels. While it is magnified, you can scroll in it with the four direction buttons; you will see the orange frame move around within the thumbnail image. To reduce the image size again, press the zoom lever to the left as many times as necessary or press the Center button to revert immediately to normal size. You also can zoom the image in and out using the Control dial. To move to other images while the display is magnified, turn the Control wheel.

Playback Display Screens

When you are viewing an image in single-image display mode, pressing the Display button (Up button) repeatedly cycles through the three playback screens that are available: (1) the full image with no information; (2) the full image with basic information, including date and time it was taken, image number, Aspect Ratio, aperture, shutter speed, ISO, and Image Size and Quality, as shown in FIGURE 6-7; and (3) a reduced-size image with detailed recording information, including aperture, shutter speed, ISO, shooting mode, White Balance, and other data, plus a histogram, as shown in FIGURE 6-8.

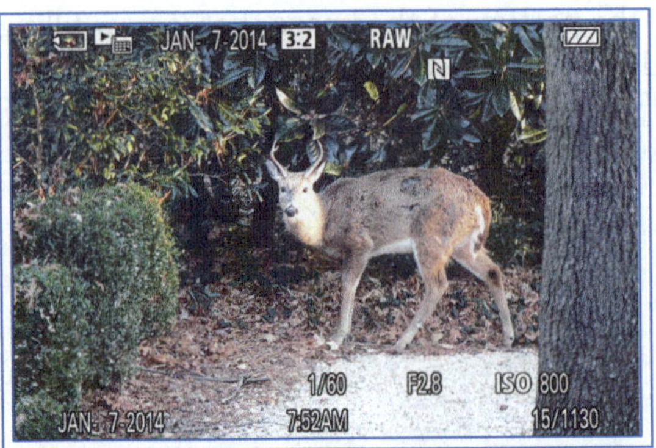

Figure 6-7. Basic Information Playback Screen

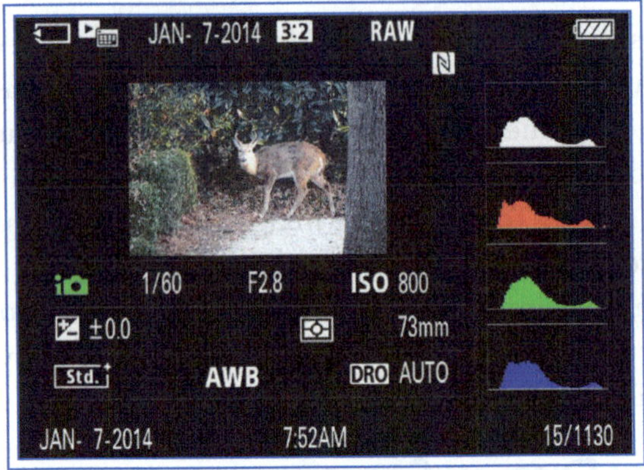

Figure 6-8. Detailed Information Playback Screen

A histogram is a graph showing the distribution of dark and bright areas in the image. The darkest blacks are represented by peaks on the left and the brightest whites by peaks on the right, with continuous gradations in between. With the RX10, the playback histogram includes four boxes with information. The top box gives information about the overall brightness of the image. The three lower boxes contain information about the brightness of the basic colors that make up the image: red, green, and blue.

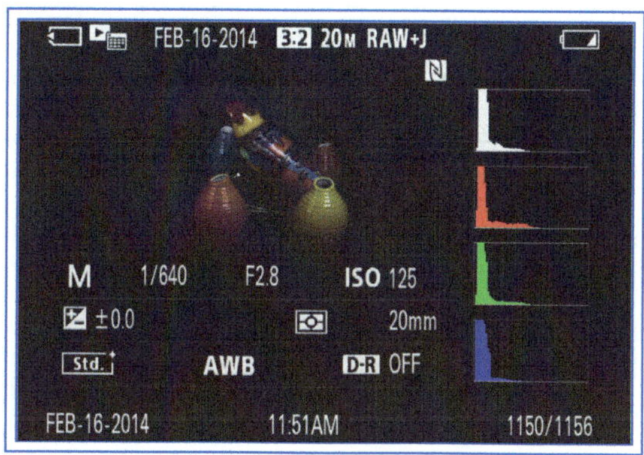

Figure 6-9. Histogram for Underexposed Image

If a histogram has brightness values bunched at the left side, there is an excessive amount of black and dark areas (high points on the left side of the histogram) and very few bright and white areas (no high points on the right). If the graph runs into the left side of the chart, it means the shadow areas are "clipped"; that is, the image is so dark that some details have been lost in the dark areas. The histogram in Figure 6-9 illustrates this degree of underexposure.

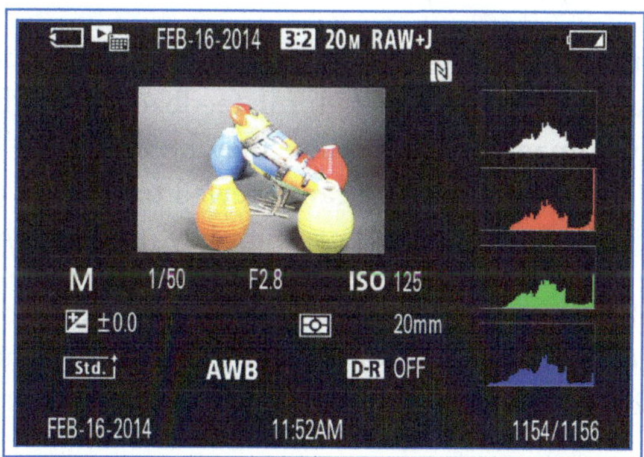

Figure 6-10. Histogram for Overexposed Image

A histogram with its high points bunched on the right side means the opposite—too bright, as shown in Figure 6-10. If the lines of the graph run into the right side of the chart, that means the highlights are clipped and the image has lost some details in the bright areas.

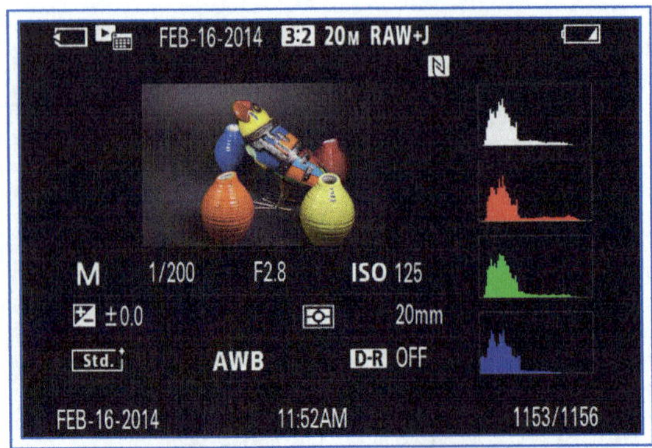

Figure 6-11. Histogram for Normally Exposed Image

A histogram for a normally exposed image has high points arranged evenly in the middle. That pattern, illustrated by Figure 6-11, indicates a good balance of light, dark, and medium tones.

When the playback histogram is on the screen, any areas containing highlights that are excessively bright will blink to indicate possible overexposure, alerting you that you might need to take another shot with the exposure adjusted to avoid that situation.

The histogram is an approximation and should not be relied on too heavily. It can give you helpful feedback as to how evenly exposed your image is. Also, there may be instances in which it is appropriate to have a histogram skewed to the left or right for intentionally "low-key" (dark) or "high-key" (brightly lit) scenes.

If you want to see the histogram when the camera is in shooting mode, you can turn that option on using the Display Button option on screen 2 of the Custom menu, as discussed in Chapter 7.

Deleting Images with the Trash Button

As I mentioned in Chapter 5, you can delete individual images by pressing the Delete button, also known as the Trash button or Help button, at the bottom right of the camera's back. If you press this button when a still image or a video is displayed, whether individually or highlighted on an index screen, the camera will display the Delete/Cancel box shown in FIGURE 6-12.

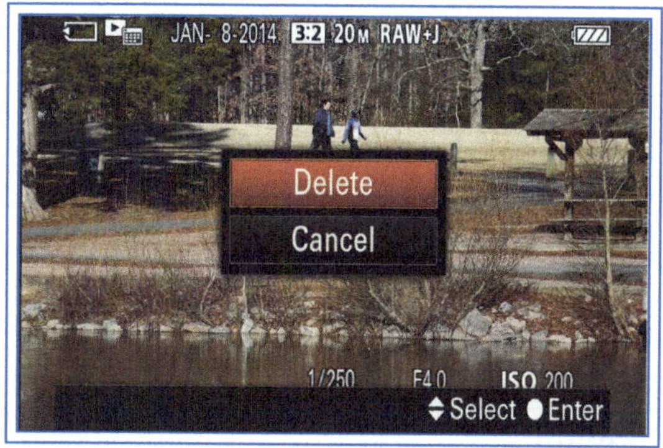

Figure 6-12. Trash Button Confirmation Screen

Highlight your choice and press the Center button to confirm. You can delete only single images or videos in this way. If you want to delete multiple items, you need to use the Delete option on the Playback menu, discussed next in this chapter.

Playback Menu

The other options that are available for controlling playback on the RX10 appear as items on the Playback menu, whose first screen is shown in FIGURE 6-13.

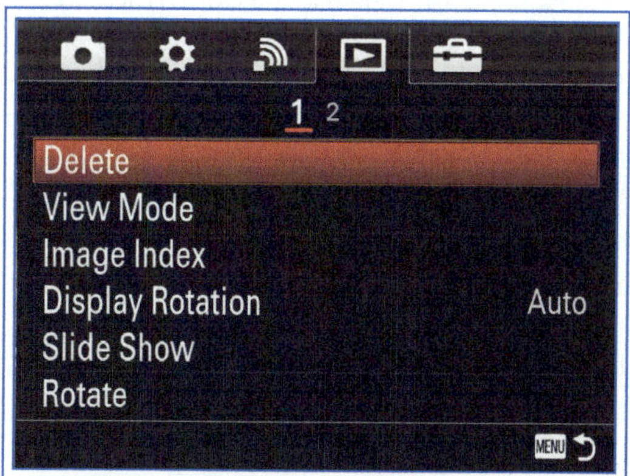

Figure 6-13. Screen 1 of Playback Menu

You get access to this menu by pressing the Menu button when the camera is in playback mode. You enter playback mode by pressing the Playback button when the camera is turned on in shooting mode. Following is information about each item on this menu:

Delete

The Delete command lets you erase multiple images from your memory card in one operation. (If you just want to delete one or two images, it's usually easier to display each image on the screen, then press the Trash button and confirm the erasure.) When you select the Delete command, the menu offers you various choices, as shown in Figure 6-14.

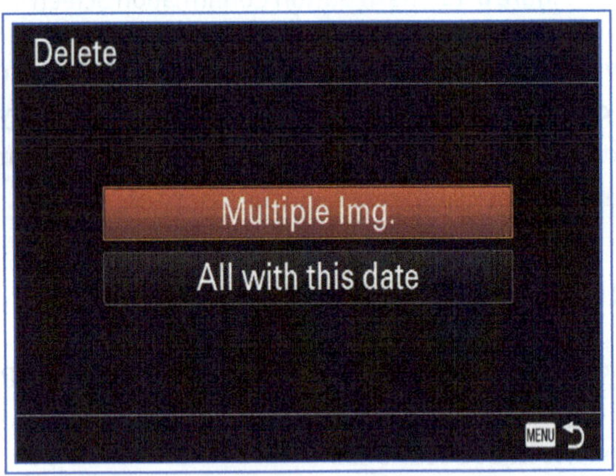

Figure 6-14. Delete Menu Options Screen

These choices may include Multiple Images, All in this Folder, or All with this Date, depending on the current view that has been selected with the View Mode option, discussed below.

If you choose Multiple Images, the camera will display either an individual image or an index screen showing the still images or videos with a check box at the left side of each image, as shown in Figure 6-15.

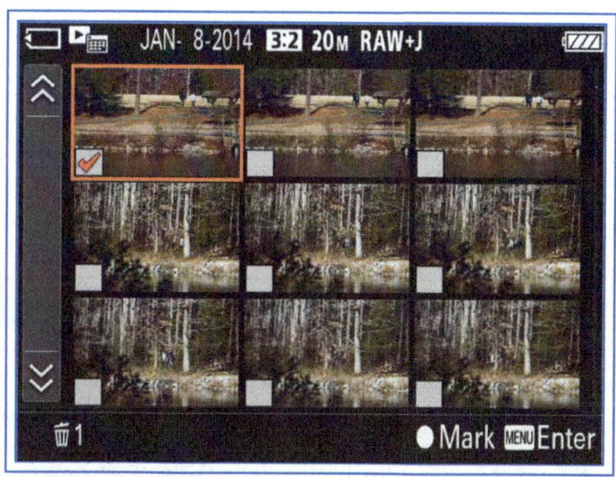

Figure 6-15. Screen with Check Boxes for Delete Menu Option

The images and videos may be shown individually or on an index screen depending on whether you started from an individual image or an index screen. You can change between full-screen and index views using the zoom lever, even after choosing the Delete option.

Scroll through the images with the Control wheel or the Left and Right buttons. When you reach an image you want to delete, press the Center button to place a check mark in the check box on that image. Continue with this process until you have marked all images you want to delete. Then, press the Menu button to move to the next screen, where the camera will prompt you to highlight OK or Cancel, and press the Center button to confirm. If you select OK, all of the marked images will be deleted. If you want to cancel before you have marked any images, press the Playback button to return to normal playback mode.

If, instead of Multiple Images, you choose All in this Folder or All with this Date, the camera will display a screen asking you to confirm deletion of all of those files.

If any images have a key icon displayed at the top, those images are protected, and cannot be deleted using this option unless you first unprotect them, as discussed later in this chapter.

View Mode

This second option on the Playback menu lets you choose which images or videos are currently viewed in playback mode. The options are Date View, Folder View (Still), Folder View (MP4), and AVCHD View, as shown in Figure 6-16.

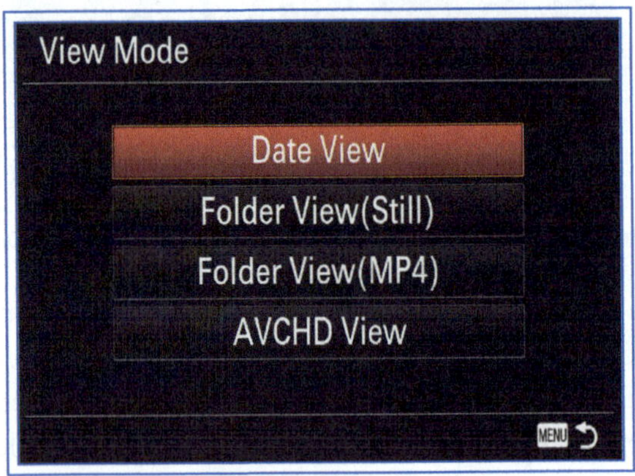

Figure 6-16. View Mode Menu Options Screen

If you select Date View, the camera will display the same calendar screen shown earlier in Figure 6-3. You can navigate through that screen using the Control wheel or the direction buttons. Highlight a date and press the Center button; the camera will then display all images and videos from that date. When the calendar screen is displayed, you can move to other months using the Control dial.

If you select Folder View (Still), the camera will display the screen shown in Figure 6-17, which displays the folders available for selection. Highlight the folder you want (there may be only one) and press the Center button; the camera will display all still images in that folder. You can navigate through the index screens for those images and select the image or images you want to view.

If you select Folder View (MP4), the process is the same, except that the camera will display only the MP4 videos from the folder you select, if there are any such videos.

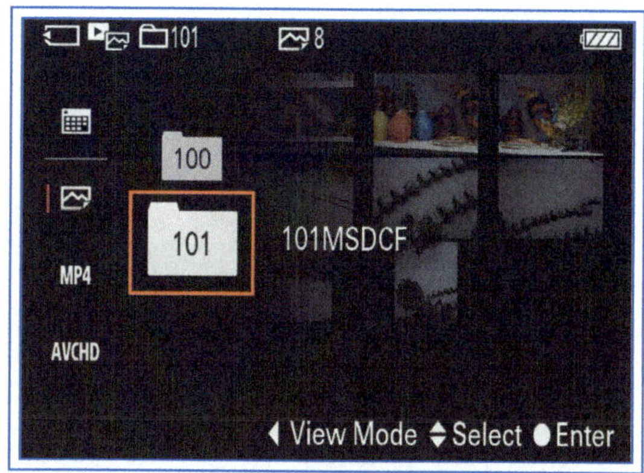

Figure 6-17. Folder View Stills Index Screen

If you select AVCHD View, the camera will display a calendar screen with thumbnail images indicating which dates have AVCHD files associated with them. You can then highlight any date with a thumbnail image to move to an AVCHD video from that date.

My general preference is to use the Date View option, because then I can view both images and videos from any date. However, if I want to locate a particular video, it can be quicker to choose one of the video views so I can limit my search to videos only.

You can select a view option from an index screen without using the Playback menu. After moving the zoom lever to the left to call up the calendar display, you can move the highlight to the extreme left of the screen to the line of four icons that represent these four view modes, and select one of the modes from that display.

Image Index

This menu option, shown in Figure 6-18, gives you the choice of having the camera include either 9 images or 25 images when it displays an index screen.

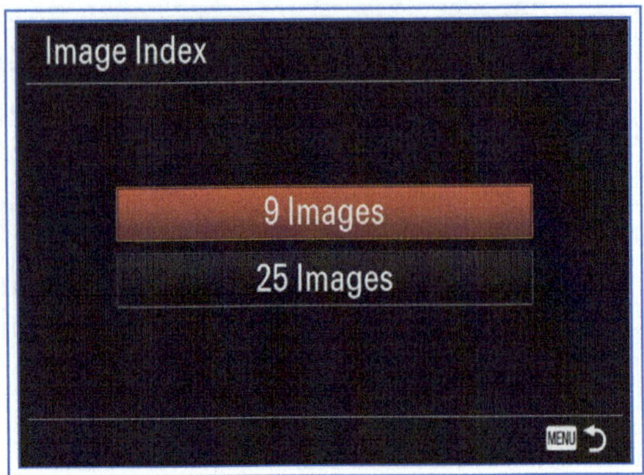

Figure 6-18. Image Index Menu Options Screen

When you make this selection, the camera displays the index screen you chose, and it will display that screen whenever you call up the index screen using the zoom lever, as discussed earlier.

Whether you choose the 9-image screen or the 25-image screen depends on your personal preference as well as some other factors, including how many images you have altogether and how easy it is to distinguish one from another by looking at the small thumbnail images. The thumbnails on the 9-image screen are considerably larger than those on the 25-image screen, and it may make sense to choose the 9-image screen unless you have so many images that it would be burdensome to scroll through them 9 at a time.

Display Rotation

This next item on the Playback menu controls whether images shot with the camera held vertically appear that way when you play them back on the camera's screen. By default, this option is set to Auto, meaning images taken vertically are automatically rotated so that the vertical shot appears in portrait orientation on the horizontal display, as shown in Figure 6-19. What is unusual about this setting is that, if you tilt the camera sideways so one side is up, a vertical image will rotate to fill the screen. In this way, you get the best of both worlds: Vertical images display in proper orientation (but smaller than normal) within the horizontal display, and, when you tilt the camera, they display at full size.

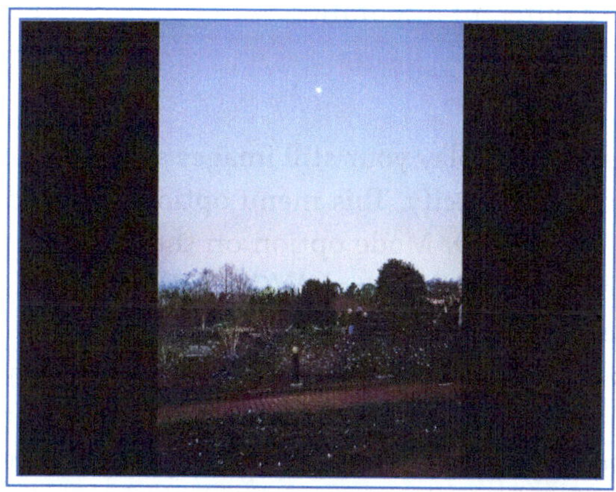

Figure 6-19. Vertical Shot Autorotated on Horizontal Display

If you change the setting to Manual, a vertical image will appear vertically on the horizontal screen, in the same way as shown in FIGURE 6-19. The difference with this setting from Auto is that, if you tilt the camera, the image will not change its orientation.

If you set this option to Off, then a vertical image will display in landscape orientation on the display, as shown in Figure 6-20, so you would have to tilt the camera to see it in its proper orientation.

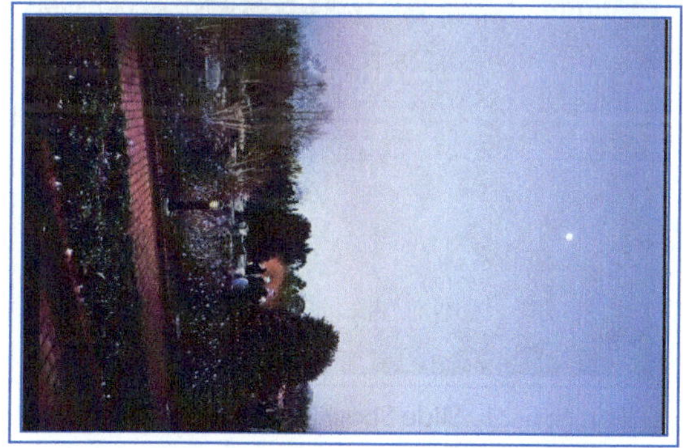

Figure 6-20. Vertical Shot with No Rotation

With all of these settings, you can use the Rotate option on the Playback menu, discussed later in this chapter, to rotate an image manually to a different orientation.

Slide Show

This feature lets you play your still images and videos in sequence at an interval you specify. This menu option will be dimmed and unavailable if the View Mode option on the Playback menu is set to either Folder View (MP4) or AVCHD View. If that is the case, use the View Mode menu option to select either Date View or Folder View (Still). The Slide Show option will display all of your movies, in both MP4 and AVCHD formats, along with your still images, if you select Date View from the View Mode menu option.

When you select the Slide Show option, the next screen has two options you can set: Repeat and Interval, as seen in Figure 6-21. If Repeat is turned on, the show will keep repeating; otherwise, it will play only once. The camera will not power off automatically in this mode, so be sure to stop the show when you are done with it. The Interval setting, which controls how long each image stays on the screen, can be set to 1, 3, 5, 10, or 30 seconds.

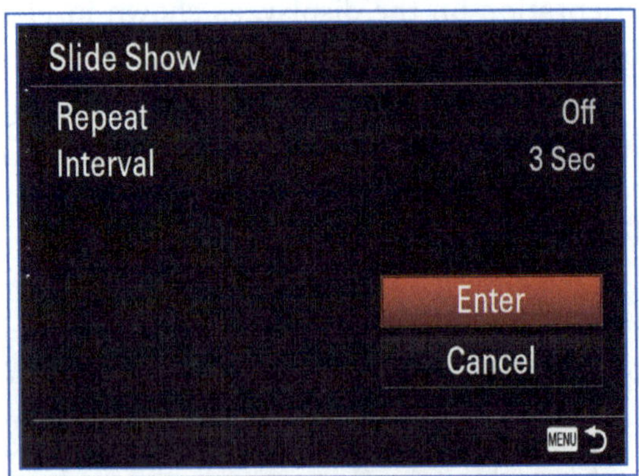

Figure 6-21. Slide Show Menu Options Screen

Once the options are set, navigate to the Enter box at the bottom of the screen using the Control wheel, the Control dial, or the direction buttons, and press the Center button to start the show. You can move forward or backward through images (and videos, if included) with the Right and Left buttons. Hold the buttons down to fast-forward or fast-reverse through the images and videos.

You can stop the show by pressing the Menu button or the Playback button. There is no way to pause the show and resume it. When a movie is playing as part of the show, you can control its volume by pressing the Down button and then adjusting the sound with the direction buttons, Control wheel, or Control dial. Each movie plays fully before the next movie or image is displayed, but you can skip to the next movie or image using the Right button.

The Slide Show option does not provide settings such as transitions, effects, or music. You cannot select which images to play; this option just lets you play all of your still images from the selected folder, if you are using Folder View, or all still images and videos from the selected date, if you are using Date View.

Rotate

The Rotate menu option gives you a way to rotate an image. Select this menu item, and you will see a screen like that in Figure 6-22, prompting you to press the Center button to rotate the image.

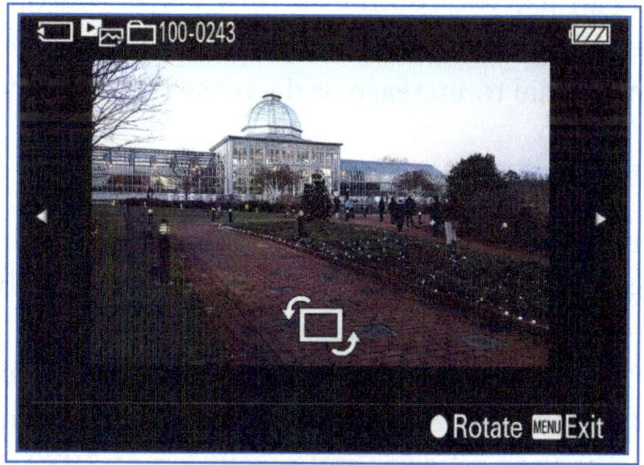

Figure 6-22. Rotate Screen

Each time you press the button, the image will rotate 90 degrees counter-clockwise. You can use this option for images taken vertically, when Display Rotation option, discussed above, is off.

The remaining options on the Playback menu are on its second and final screen, shown in FIGURE 6-23.

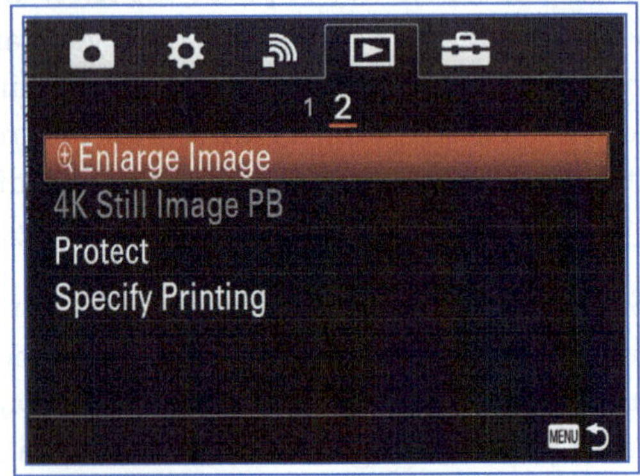

Figure 6-23. Screen 2 of Playback Menu

Enlarge Image

This option does the same image magnification discussed above, which you can also do with the zoom lever or AEL button. When you select this option, the enlarged image will appear on the screen; you can use the zoom lever or the AEL button to change the enlargement factor. Once the image is enlarged, you also can use the Control dial to increase or decrease the magnification.

4K Still Image Playback

This option is dimmed and cannot be selected unless the camera is connected to a TV set that supports 4K resolution. The standard known as 4K is a relatively recent option for HDTVs. The 4K stands for 4,000, meaning each frame has a horizontal resolution of about 4,000 pixels. A standard HD (high-definition) TV set outputs frames with a horizontal resolution of 1920 pixels and a vertical resolution of 1080 pixels. A 4K TV frame has a horizontal resolution of 3840 and a vertical resolution of 2160. The overall resolution of the 4K TV image is about 8 megapixels, while the resolution of full HDTV is about 2 megapixels, so a 4K picture has 4 times the resolution of full HDTV. So, if you have a 4K TV available, you can connect your RX10 using an optional HDMI cable and enjoy your still images at the highest possible resolution.

Protect

With the Protect feature, you can "lock" selected images or videos so they cannot be erased with the normal erase functions, including using the Trash button and using the Delete option on the Playback menu, discussed above. However, if you format the memory card using the Format command, all data on the card will be erased, including protected images.

To protect images or videos using this menu item, the procedure is similar to the one for deleting images, discussed above. When you select this option, the camera will display a screen like that shown in Figure 6-24, with the choices to select multiple images; all from the same date as the current image; all from the current folder, depending on the current setting for View Mode; or to cancel protection for all images with this date or from this folder.

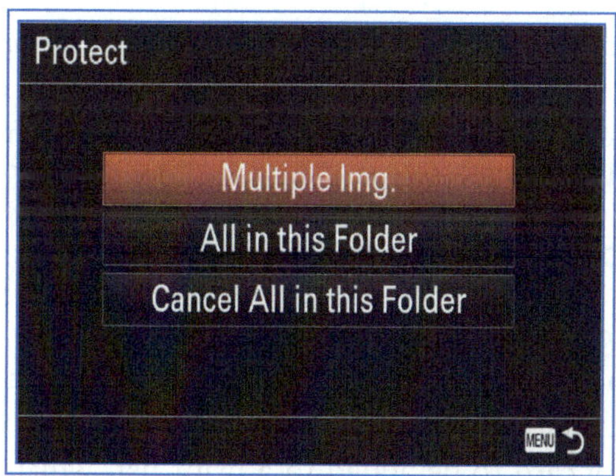

Figure 6-24. Protect Menu Options Screen

If you select Multiple Images, the camera will present you with either index screens or individual images. As with the Delete option, you can scroll through your images and mark any image's check box for protection by pressing the Center button. When you have finished marking them, press the Menu button and the camera will display a confirmation screen. If you select OK to confirm, the marked images will be protected. Any image that is protected will have a key icon in the upper-right corner to the left of the battery icon, as shown in FIGURE 6-25.

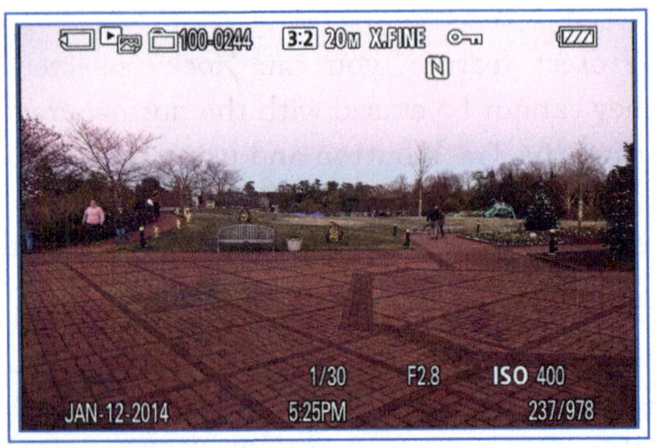

Figure 6-25. Protected Image with Key Icon at Upper Right

The key icon will be visible when the image is viewed with the detailed information screen or the basic information screen, but it will not appear in the image-only view.

To unprotect all images or videos in one operation, select the appropriate Cancel option from the Protect item on the Playback menu. That option will prompt you to Cancel All with this Date or to Cancel All in this Folder, depending on the View Mode setting.

Specify Printing

This menu option lets you use the DPOF (Digital Print Order Format) function, a standard printing protocol that is built into the camera. The DPOF system lets you mark various images on your memory card to be added to a print list, which can then be sent to your own printer. Or, you can take the memory card to a commercial printing company to print out the selected images.

To add images to the DPOF print list, select the Specify Printing option from the Playback menu. On the next screen, shown in Figure 6-26, set the DPOF Setup option to Multiple Images.

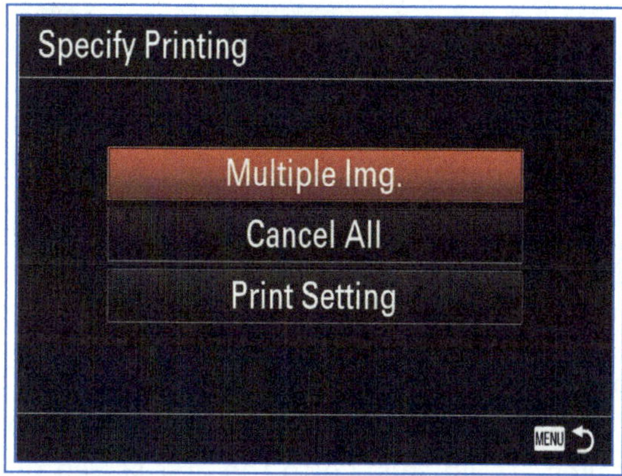

Figure 6-26. Specify Printing Menu Options Screen

The camera will display the first image with a check box at the left, as shown in Figure 6-27, or an index screen with an orange frame around the currently selected image and a check box in the lower-left corner of each image thumbnail, as with the Delete and Protect functions discussed earlier.

You can choose to display individual images or index screens using the zoom lever. There will be a small printer icon in the lower left with a zero beside it at first, meaning no copies of any images have been set for printing yet. Use the Control wheel, Control dial, or direction buttons to move through the images. When an image you want to have printed is displayed, press the Center button to mark it for printing or to unmark it. You can then keep browsing through your images and adding (or subtracting) them from the print list. As you add various images to the print list, the DPOF counter in the lower-left corner of the display will show the total number of images selected for printing.

When you have finished selecting images to be printed, press the Menu button to move to a screen where you can confirm your choices by selecting OK.

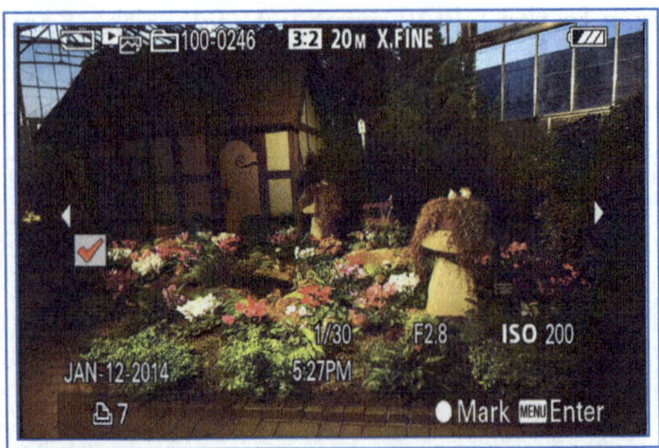

Figure 6-27. Image Marked for Specify Printing Option

You also can turn the Date Imprint option on or off to specify whether or not the pictures will be printed with the dates they were taken. To do this, go to the first screen of the Specify Printing menu option and select Print Setting. On the next screen, shown in Figure 6-28, the camera will let you select Enter, to specify that the date should be printed on each image.

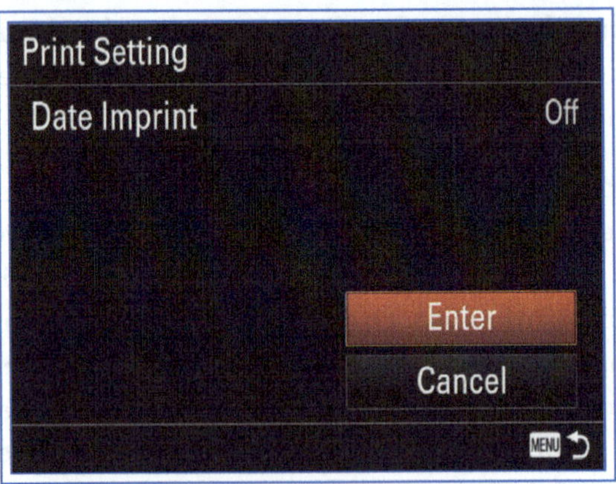

Figure 6-28. Date Imprint Menu Options Screen

You can take the memory card with the DPOF list to a service that prints photos using this system, or you can connect the camera to a PictBridge-compatible printer to print the images. If you want to cancel a DPOF order, go to the Specify Printing menu item, select DPOF Setup, and select the Cancel All option.

Chapter 7: The Custom and Setup Menus

In earlier chapters, I discussed the options available in the Shooting and Playback menu systems. The Sony RX10 has two other menu systems that help you set up the camera and customize its operation: Custom and Setup. In this chapter, I will discuss all of the options on those menus. I'll discuss menu options for Movie mode in Chapter 8 and I'll discuss the options on the Wi-Fi menu in Chapter 9.

Custom Menu

The Custom menu gives you control over numerous items that affect the ways you use the camera to take pictures and videos, but that do not change the basic photographic settings such as White Balance, ISO, focus modes, and matters of that nature. The items to be adjusted on this menu are more in the categories of control and display options, although several of them are quite important for your daily image-making operations. Details about the options on the four screens of this menu follow. The first screen of the menu is seen in Figure 7-1.

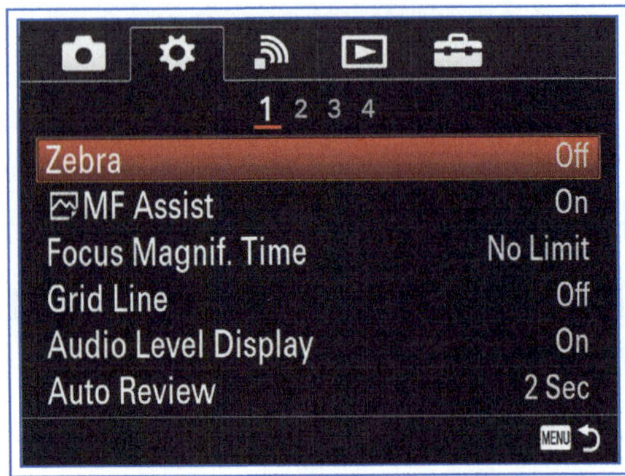

Figure 7-1. Screen 1 of Custom Menu

ZEBRA

This first Custom menu option gives you a tool for gauging whether your image or video will be overexposed. When you turn this menu option on, you can select a value from 70 to 100 in 5-unit increments, or 100+ for values greater than 100. FIGURE 7-2 shows the screen for selecting values up to 90.

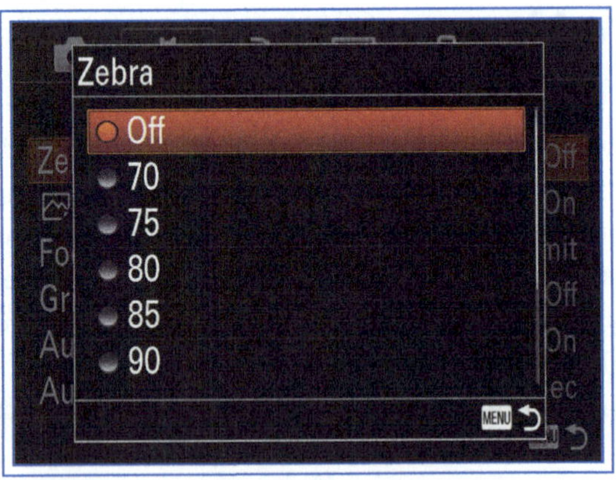

Figure 7-2. Zebra Menu Options Screen

When you turn this option on to any level, you very likely will see, in some parts of the display, the black-and-white "zebra" stripes that give this feature its name.

The numerical units from 70 to 100+ are IRE units. Those initials stand for the Institute for Radio Engineers, an organization that has since merged into the Institute of Electrical and Electronics Engineers (IEEE). The IRE units are a measure of relative brightness or exposure, with 0 representing black and 100 representing white.

Zebra stripes originally were created as a feature for professional video cameras, so the videographer could see whether the scene would be properly exposed. This tool often is used in the context of taping an interview, when proper exposure of a human face is the main concern.

There are various approaches to using these stripes. Some videographers like to set the zebra function to 90 IRE and adjust the exposure so the stripes just barely start to appear in the brightest parts of the image. Another recommendation is to set the option to 75 IRE for a scene with Caucasian skin, and expose so that the stripes just barely appear in the area of the skin.

In Figure 7-3, I set IRE to 75 and exposed to have the stripes barely begin to appear on the mannequin's head.

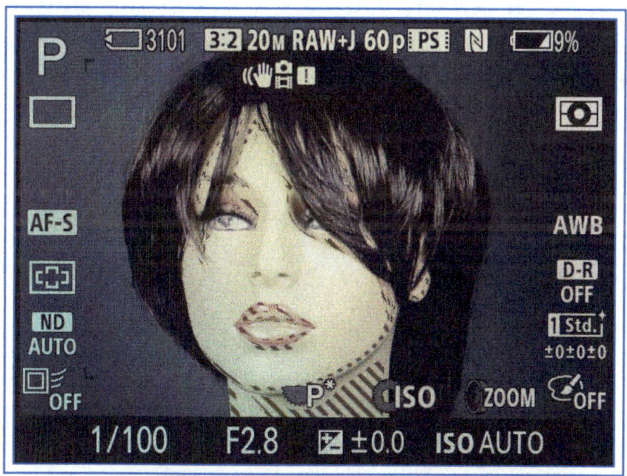

Figure 7-3. Zebra Option Set to IRE 75

As the brightness of the lighting increases for a subject, there may be no stripes at first, then they will gradually appear until they cover the subject, then they will seem to disappear, because the exposure is so bright that the subject is surrounded by an outline of "marching ants" rather than having stripes in its interior.

Zebra is a feature to consider, especially for video recording, but the RX10 has an excellent metering system, including both live and playback histogram histograms, so you can manage without this option if you don't want to deal with its learning curve.

MF Assist

The MF Assist option provides a useful function when manual focus or DMF is in effect. When MF Assist is turned on in manual focus mode, the RX10 enlarges the image on the display screen as soon as you start turning the focus ring, as shown in Figure 7-4. This feature is helpful in judging whether a particular area is in sharp focus. If you turn this option off, you can use another focusing aid, such as Focus Magnifier, discussed in Chapter 4, or Peaking, discussed later in this chapter. Or, you can use this option and Peaking at the same time, to provide even more assistance.

When DMF is in effect, you have to keep the shutter button pressed halfway down while turning the focus ring to use the MF Assist enlargement feature.

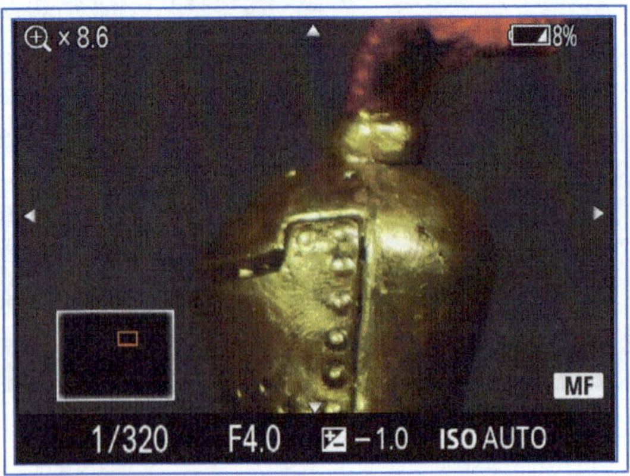

Figure 7-4. MF Assist Option with Screen Magnified to 8.6x

I find MF Assist to be very helpful, especially because I can set the camera to leave the enlarged screen in place indefinitely using the Focus Magnification Time option, discussed immediately below. However, the Focus Magnifier also is helpful, and may be preferable in one way because the screen does not become magnified until you press the Center button, select the area to be magnified using the orange frame, and then magnify the screen.

In some cases, where a subject (like the moon) does not have clear edges or other features to focus on, enlarging the view may not be that much help. In those situations, Peaking may be more useful. Or, you may find that using Peaking in conjunction with MF Assist is the most useful approach of all. You should experiment with the various options to find what works best for you.

Focus Magnification Time

This option lets you select how long the display will stay magnified when you use either the MF Assist option, discussed directly above, or the Focus Magnifier option, discussed in Chapter 4. The choices are 2 or 5 seconds or No Limit, as shown in Figure 7-5. The default option is 2 seconds.

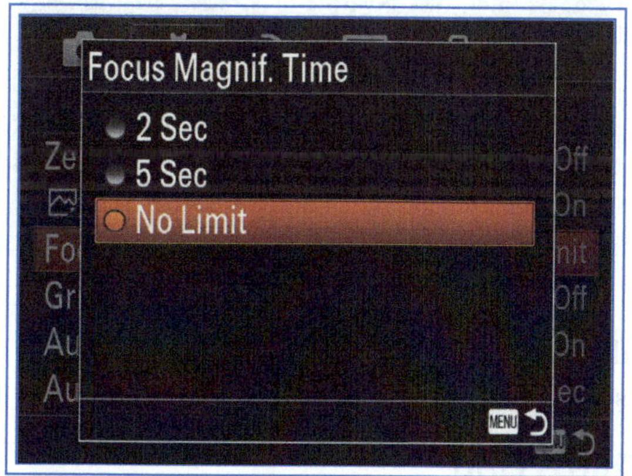

Figure 7-5. Focus Magnification Time Menu Options Screen

With No Limit, the image will stay magnified until you press the shutter button all the way to take the picture, or press it halfway to dismiss the enlarged view. My preference is to use the No Limit option, so I can take my time in adjusting manual focus precisely. Note, though, that with the No Limit option, whenever you turn the focus ring, the image will be enlarged, and you may want to be able to keep adjusting focus with a view of the unenlarged subject. If that is the case, select one of the options with a time limit.

Grid Line

With this option, you can select one of four settings for a grid to be superimposed on the shooting screen. By default, there is no grid. If you choose one of the options to use a grid, the lines will appear in your chosen configuration whenever the camera is showing the live view in shooting mode, whether the detailed display screen is selected or not. Of course, the grid does not appear when the For Viewfinder display, with its black screen full of shooting information, is displayed. The four options are seen in Figure 7-6.

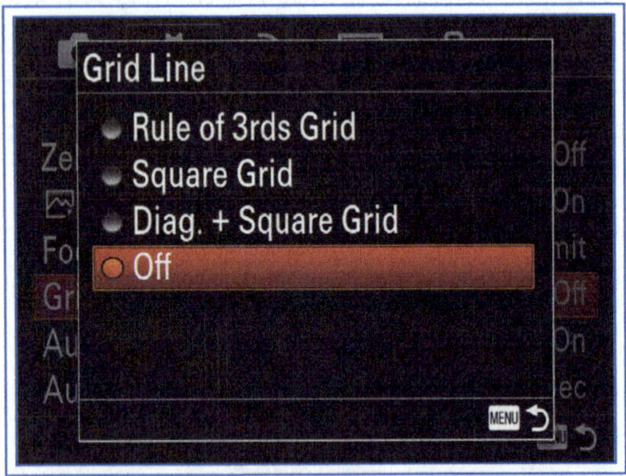

Figure 7-6. Grid Line Menu Options Screen

Here are descriptions of these choices, other than Off, which leaves the screen with no grid.

Rule of Thirds Grid

This arrangement has two vertical lines and two horizontal lines, dividing the screen into nine blocks, as shown in Figure 7-7.

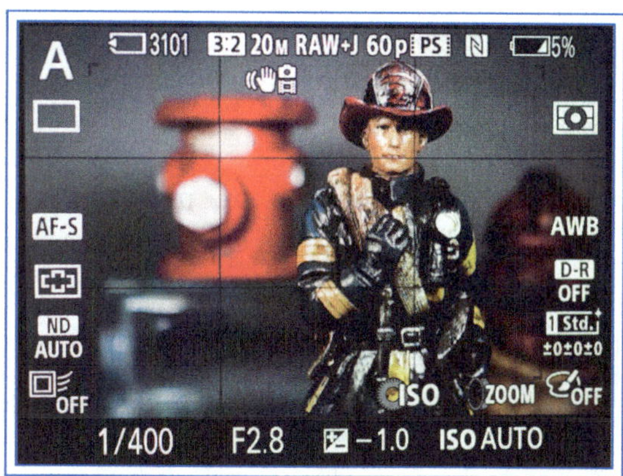

Figure 7-7. Rule of Thirds Grid Example

This grid follows a rule of composition that calls for locating an important subject at an intersection of these lines, which will place the subject one-third of the way from the edge of the image. This arrangement can add interest and asymmetry to an image.

Square Grid

With this setting, the grid has 5 vertical lines and 3 horizontal lines, dividing the display into 24 blocks, as seen in FIGURE 7-8.

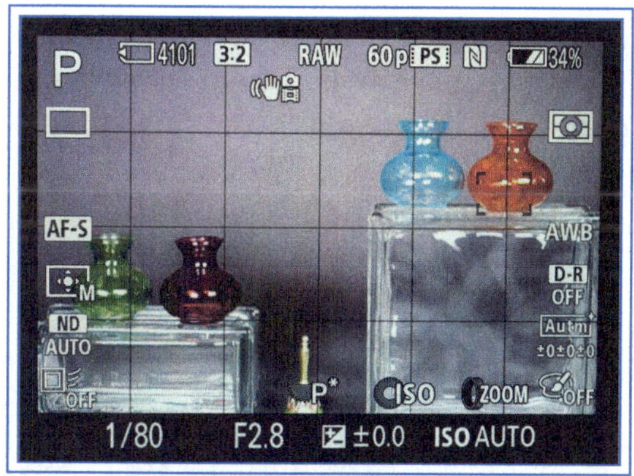

Figure 7-8. Square Grid Example

In this way, you can still use the Rule of Thirds, but you have additional lines available for lining up items, such as the horizon or the edge of a building, that need to be straight.

Diagonal Plus Square Grid

The last option gives you a square grid of four blocks in each direction and adds two diagonal lines, as shown in Figure 7-9.

The idea is that placing a subject or, more likely, a string of subjects along one of the diagonals can add interest to the image by drawing the viewer's eye into the image along the diagonal line.

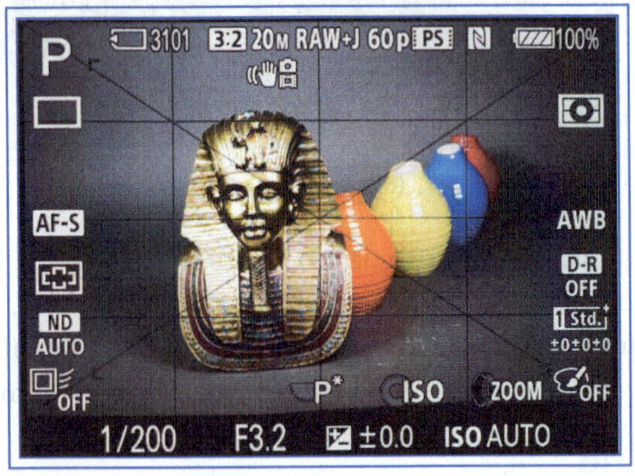

Figure 7-9. Diagonal Plus Square Grid Example

Audio Level Display

This option controls whether audio meters appear during movie recording. The meters have green bars that rise and fall with the volume of audio being recorded, as shown in Figure 7-10.

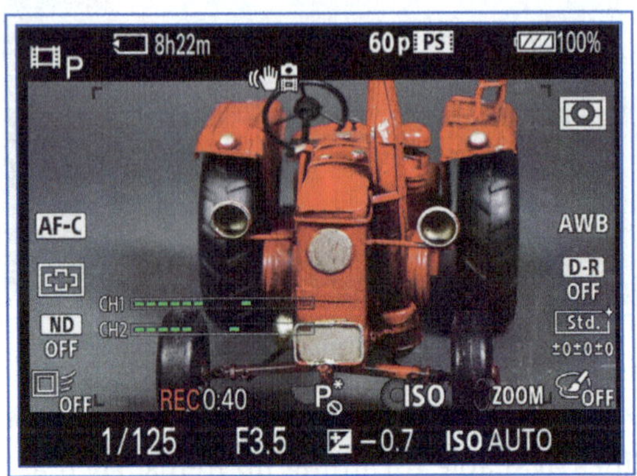

Figure 7-10. Audio Level Meters on Display

The meters appear on detailed information screens; if this option is on and you don't see the meters when recording a video, press the Display button to call up one of the other screens. Also, check to see if the Audio Recording option on screen 7 of the Shooting menu is on; if that option is off, the meters will not be displayed. I generally leave this option turned on; seeing the rise and fall of the meters reassures me that the audio is being recorded successfully.

Auto Review

The Auto Review option, shown in Figure 7-11, lets you set the length of time that an image appears on the display screen immediately after you take a still picture.

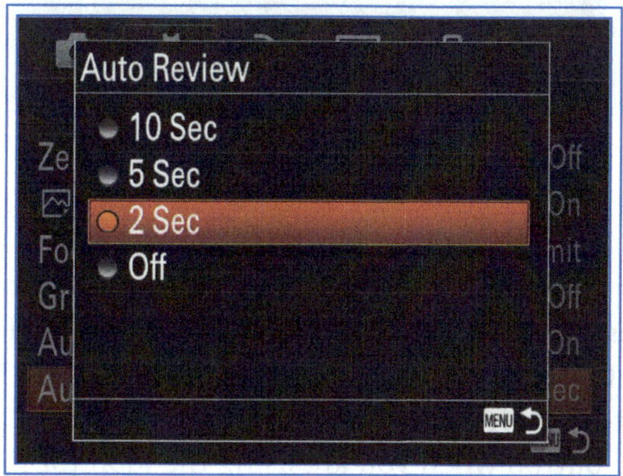

Figure 7-11. Auto Review Menu Options Screen

The default is 2 seconds, but you can set the time to 5 or 10 seconds, or you can turn the function off. If you turn it off, the camera will return to shooting mode as soon as it has saved a new image to the memory card. When this option is in use, you can always return to the live view by pressing the shutter button halfway. The Auto Review option does not apply to movies; the camera does not display the beginning frame of a movie that was just recorded until you press the Playback button.

While the new image is being displayed, you can use the various functions of playback mode, such as enlarging the image, bringing up index screens, and moving to other images. If you start one of these actions before the camera has reverted to shooting mode, the camera will stay in playback mode.

The second screen of the Custom menu is shown in FIGURE 7-12.

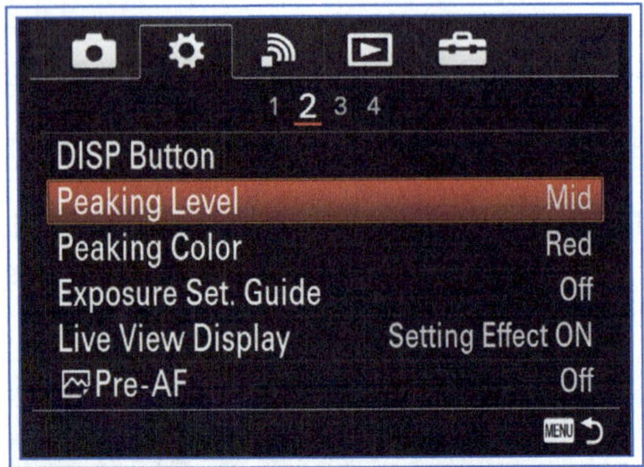

Figure 7-12. Screen 2 of Custom Menu

Display Button

This option lets you choose what screens appear in shooting mode as you press the Display button. There are sub-options for the monitor (LCD) and viewfinder, as seen in FIGURE 7-13. You can make different choices for the LCD and the viewfinder, so pressing the Display button when you are using the monitor may bring up a different set of screens than when you are using the viewfinder.

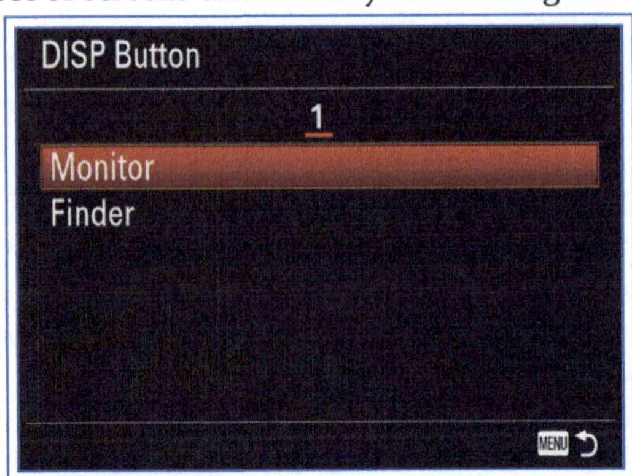

Figure 7-13. Display Button Menu Options Screen

After you decide to choose display screens for the monitor or the viewfinder, you will see a screen like that shown in Figure 7-14.

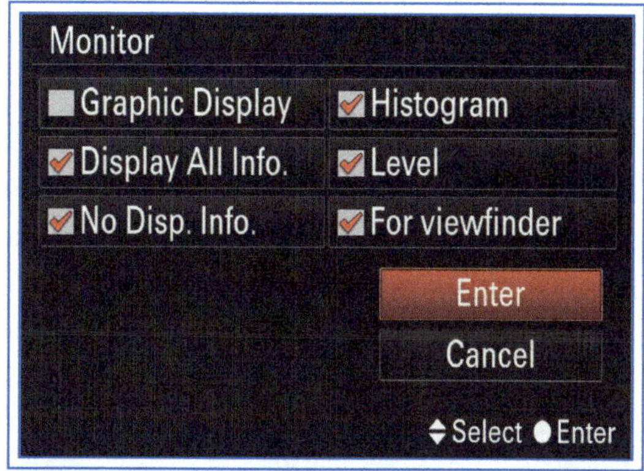

Figure 7-14. Display Button Screen Showing Display Screen Options

This screen shows the six display screens you can select for the monitor. The selection screen for the viewfinder is identical to this one, except that the sixth choice, For Viewfinder, is not available as a choice to appear in the viewfinder. That display screen is designed to appear on the monitor to provide shooting information when you are viewing the live view through the viewfinder.

Five of the six display screens available for the monitor are shown in Figure 7-15 through Figure 7-19. The screen displaying just the image with no information is not shown here.

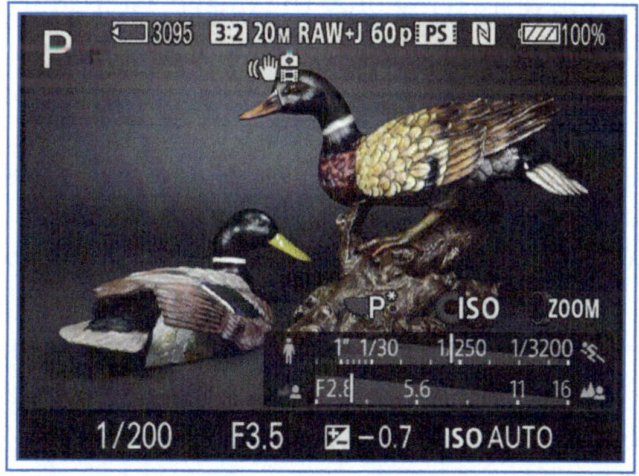

Figure 7-15. Graphic Display Screen

FIGURE 7-15 shows the version of the screen with the Graphic Display in the lower-right corner; that display is supposed to illustrate the use of faster shutter speeds to stop action and the use of wider apertures to blur backgrounds. I find it distracting and not especially helpful, but if it is useful to you, by all means select it.

I find the Display All Information screen, shown in FIGURE 7-16, to be cluttered, but it has useful information. You can always move away from this screen by pressing the Display button (if there is at least one other display screen available), and I like to have it available for times when I need to see what settings are in effect.

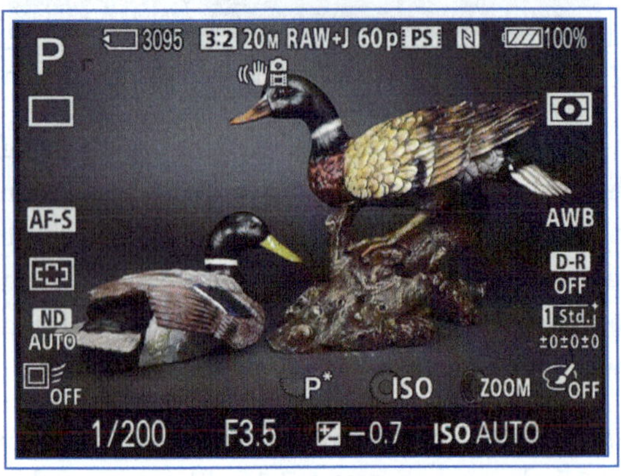

Figure 7-16. Display All Information Screen

The third option, displaying only the image, isn't shown here. This display is helpful for focusing and composing your shot, and I always include it in the cycle of display screens.

The fourth screen, shown in FIGURE 7-17, displays the histogram. This shooting-mode histogram, unlike the one displayed in playback mode, shows only basic exposure information with no color data. However, it gives you an idea of whether your image will be well exposed, letting you adjust exposure compensation and other settings as appropriate while watching the live histogram on the screen. If you can make the histogram display look like a triangular mountain centered in the box, you are likely to have a good result.

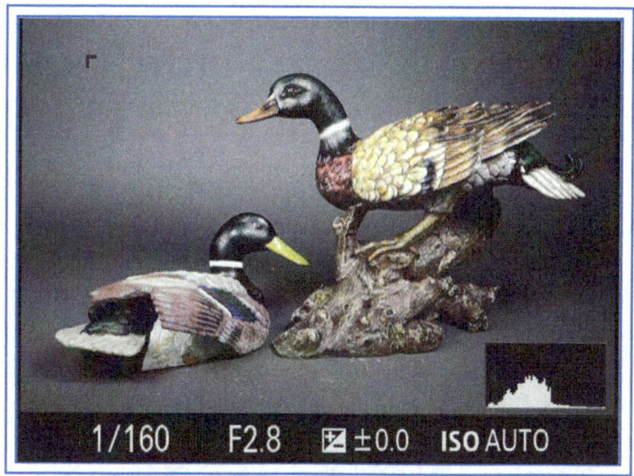

Figure 7-17. Histogram Screen

You should try to keep the body of the histogram away from the right and left edges of the graph, in most cases. If the histogram runs into the left edge, that means shadow areas are clipping and details in those areas are being lost. If it hits the right edge, you are losing details in highlights. If you have to choose, it is best to keep the graph away from the right edge because it is harder to recover details from clipped highlights than from clipped shadows.

The fifth available display screen, shown in FIGURE 7-18, includes the RX10's level, which is a useful tool for leveling the camera both side-to-side and front-to-back.

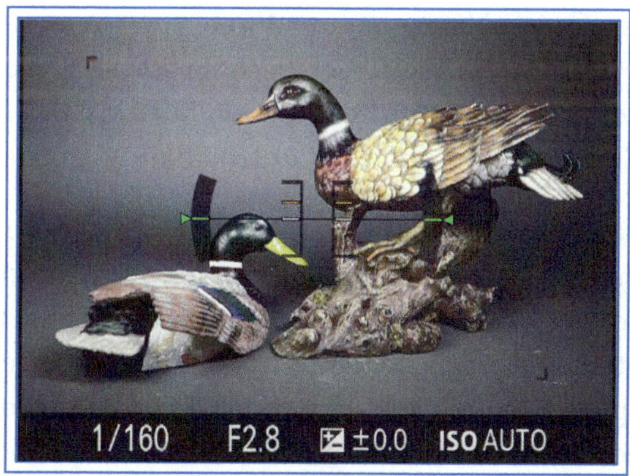

Figure 7-18. Level Screen

Watch the small orange lines on the screen; when the outer two ones have turned green, the camera is level side-to-side; when the inner two lines are green, the camera is level front-to-back.

The sixth choice, shown in FIGURE 7-19, which is available only for the monitor, is called For Viewfinder.

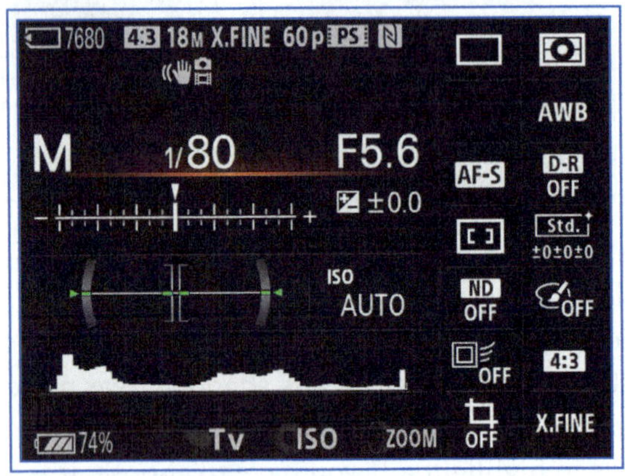

Figure 7-19. For Viewfinder Screen

This option is the only one that does not include the live view in shooting mode. Instead, it displays a black screen with detailed information about the camera's settings, so you can check your settings after (or before) you look at the live view in the viewfinder. In addition, as I discussed in CHAPTER 5, this screen includes the Quick Navi system. When you press the Function button, the settings on the screen become active. You can navigate through the settings using the direction buttons and adjust them using the Control wheel and the Control dial.

Once you select the Display Button option and choose whether to select screens for the monitor or viewfinder, you can scroll through the six (monitor) or five (viewfinder) choices using the Control wheel, Control dial, or direction buttons. When a screen you want to have displayed is highlighted, press the Center button to put an orange check mark in the box to the left of the screen's label, as seen in FIGURE 7-14.

You can also press that button to unmark a box. The camera will let you un-check all six of the items (or all five for the viewfinder), but if you do that, you will see an error message as you try to exit the menu screen. You have to check at least one box so that some screen will display when the camera is in shooting mode.

After you select one to six screens for the monitor and one to five for the viewfinder, highlight the Enter block and press the Center button. Then, whenever the camera is in shooting mode, the selected screens will be displayed; you cycle through them by pressing the Display button (Up button). If you have selected only one screen, pressing the Display button will have no effect in shooting mode when the live view is displayed.

Even if you select only the one screen that includes no information, the camera will still always display the shutter speed, aperture, exposure compensation, and ISO; all of those values are displayed in the black strip below the area where the image is displayed.

Peaking Level

The Peaking Level option, shown in Figure 7-20, controls the camera's use of the Peaking display to assist with manual focus.

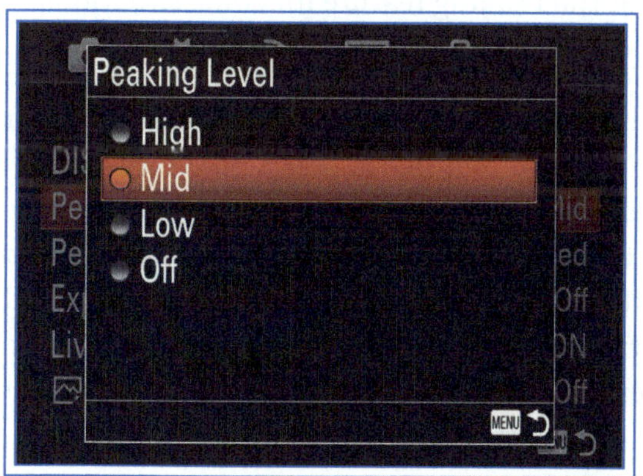

Figure 7-20. Peaking Level Menu Options Screen

By default, this option is turned off. You can turn the feature on with a level of Low, Mid, or High. When it is on and you are using manual focus, the camera places an outline with the selected intensity around any areas of the image that have edges the camera can distinguish. FIGURE 7-21 illustrates this feature with a composite image in which Peaking Level is turned off for the left image and set to Mid for the right image.

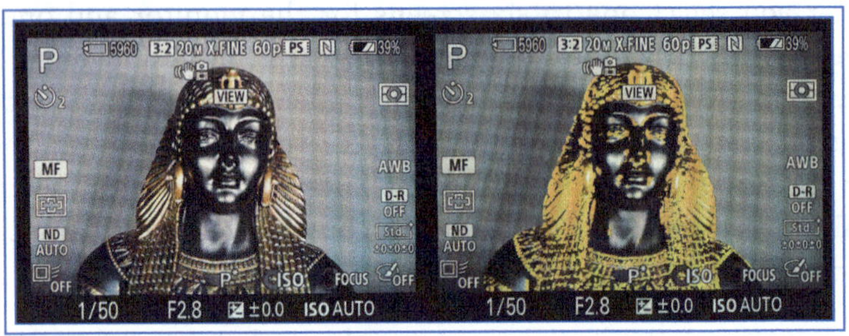

Figure 7-21. Left: Peaking Off, Right: Peaking Mid

The idea is that these lines provide a more definite indication that the focus is sharp than just relying on your judgment of sharpness. When I first used a camera with this feature, I found it distracting and not as useful as options such as MF Assist and Focus Magnifier that enlarge the screen for a clearer view when using manual focus. However, after further experience, I have come to appreciate the usefulness of the Peaking feature for some situations.

For example, as discussed in CHAPTER 9, I took some shots of the moon through a telescope connected to the RX10. I used manual focus mode and had to finish adjusting the focus using the controls on the telescope. The image on the camera's screen was unsteady because of the high magnification, and the moon did not have any features with edges that I could see clearly in the enlarged view. When I turned on Peaking with the red color selected, I found it much easier to focus; the camera displayed a broad band of red around the edge of the moon when focus was sharp.

Some photographers set Creative Style to black and white while focusing so the Peaking color will stand out, and some like to set Peaking Level to Low so the color is not overwhelming, letting them see when the color just starts to appear. Some like to turn on MF Assist to enlarge the screen when using Peaking. You should experiment to find what approach works best for you.

For an excellent demonstration of how Peaking works, see this YouTube video posted by a participant in the Sony Cyber-shot Talk forum at dpreview.com at http://youtu.be/jMAlMQev7Kw.

Note that Peaking also works with DMF, even if you are using the autofocus function of that setting.

Peaking Color

This option lets you choose red, yellow, or white for the color of the lines that the Peaking Level feature places around the edges of in-focus areas of the image. The default color is white. It is useful to be able to change the color depending on the colors present in your image. The Peaking Level feature is likely to be most useful when the color you choose for the effect contrasts with the main colors in your subject. As noted above, I found that the red color worked very well for shots of the moon; yellow or white may work well with darker subjects.

Exposure Settings Guide

The next option on the Custom menu places a circular display on the screen to simulate one or two rotating wheels showing the settings for aperture, shutter speed, or both. The display varies according to the shooting mode. In Program mode, the wheels display aperture and shutter speed when you activate Program Shift. In Shutter Priority and Manual exposure modes, a single wheel displays shutter speed as you adjust it using the Control dial. Figure 7-22 shows the display when shutter speed is being adjusted. In Aperture Priority and other shooting modes, this menu option has no effect.

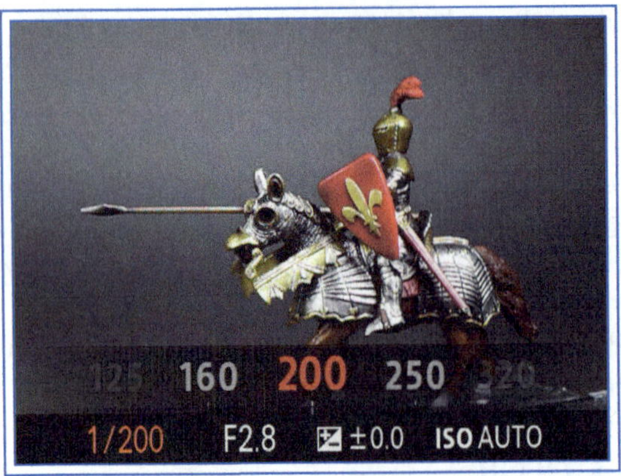

Figure 7-22. Exposure Settings Guide Display on Screen

I find this display distracting so I leave it turned off, but it might be useful to see this large display to let you know what value is being set, in some circumstances.

Live View Display

This menu option can be very important for getting results that match your expectations. It lets you choose whether or not the camera displays the effects that certain settings will have on your final image, while you are composing the image.

When you select this option, you will see two sub-options on the next screen: Setting Effect On and Setting Effect Off, as shown in Figure 7-23. If you select Setting Effect On, then, when you are using Program, Aperture Priority, Shutter Priority, or Manual exposure mode, the camera's display in shooting mode will show the effects of the following settings: exposure compensation, White Balance, Creative Style, and Picture Effect, with some limitations. In addition, it will show the effects of exposure changes in Manual exposure mode and other advanced modes, to some extent.

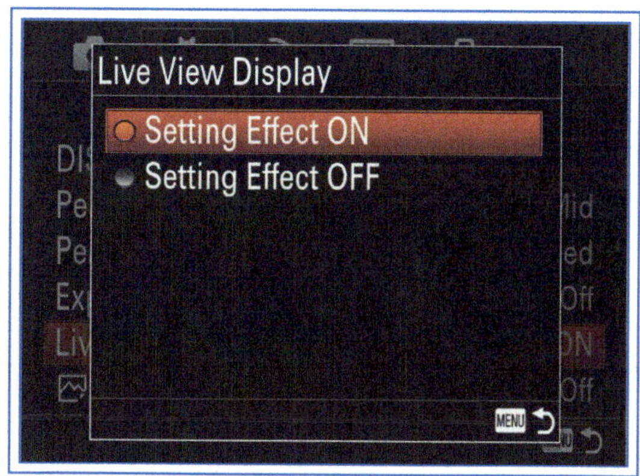

Figure 7-23. Live View Display Menu Options Screen

This menu option gives you considerable flexibility. In some cases, it may be helpful to see what effect a particular setting will have on the final image, and in other cases that feature might be distracting or might even make it difficult to take the shot.

For example, when you are setting White Balance, it can be quite helpful to see how the various options will alter the appearance of your final images. If you have selected Setting Effect On, then, as you scroll through the White Balance menu options, you will instantly see the effect of each setting, such as Daylight, Cloudy, Shade, and Incandescent. That change in the display is not distracting; it is actually very informative.

However, if you are using the Picture Effect option and experimenting with a setting such as Posterization, which drastically alters the appearance of your images, you might find it difficult to compose the image with Setting Effect On selected.

There is one particular use for the Live View Display menu option that I find practically indispensable. On occasion, I use the RX10 to trigger external, non-Sony flash units, with the camera set to Manual exposure mode. For some of these shots, I use settings such as f/16.0, 1/200 second, and ISO 80. This shot will be exposed properly with the flash units I am using, but, with Setting Effect On selected, the camera's screen is completely dark as I compose the shot. That is because the camera's programming does not account for the fact that flash units will be fired.

If I use the Setting Effect Off setting, then the camera displays the scene using the available ambient light, ignoring the settings I have made. In this way, I can see the scene on the camera's display in order to compose the shot properly.

The Setting Effect On option, though, can be useful when using Aperture Priority, Shutter Priority, or Manual exposure mode when you are shooting in unusually dark or bright conditions, because the camera's display screen will change its brightness to alert you that a normal exposure may not be possible with the current settings. (You should see the aperture, shutter speed, or M.M. value flashing to alert you to this situation, also.)

With the Picture Effect setting, some of the options will not change the appearance of the display, even with this setting activated. Those options are Soft Focus, HDR Painting, Rich-tone Monochrome, Miniature, Watercolor, and Illustration.

When the Setting Effect Off option is selected, the camera will display a VIEW icon on the screen, as shown in Figure 7-24, to remind you that you the camera's display is not showing the effects of all your settings.

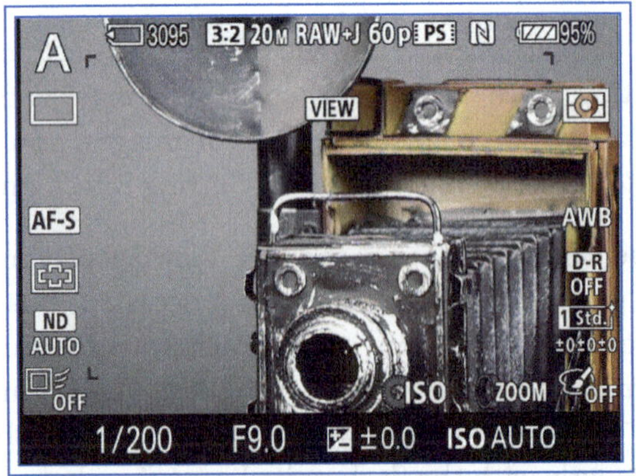

Figure 7-24. VIEW Icon on Screen for Setting Effect Off

My recommendation is to leave this option at Setting Effect On unless you are faced with a situation in which it is difficult to compose a shot, either because the display is too dark or light, or because a setting such as Picture Effect interferes with your ability to view the subject clearly.

In Intelligent Auto, Scene, Sweep Panorama, and Movie modes, this option is forced to Setting Effect On and cannot be changed.

Pre-AF

The Pre-AF setting affects the way the RX10 uses autofocus. When this option is turned on and the focus switch is set to the S or C position, for single-shot or continuous autofocus, the camera continuously tries to focus on a subject, even before you press the shutter button halfway. With this setting, the camera's battery is depleted more quickly than normal, but the final focusing operation may be speeded up because the camera can reach an approximate focus adjustment before you press the shutter button to evaluate focus and take the picture.

If this setting is turned off, then the camera makes no attempt to use its autofocus mechanism until you press the shutter button to check focus and take the picture.

I usually leave this setting off to avoid running the battery down too soon. But, if I were taking pictures of moving subjects, I might activate this setting to speed up the focusing process.

Screen 3 of the Custom menu is shown in Figure 7-25.

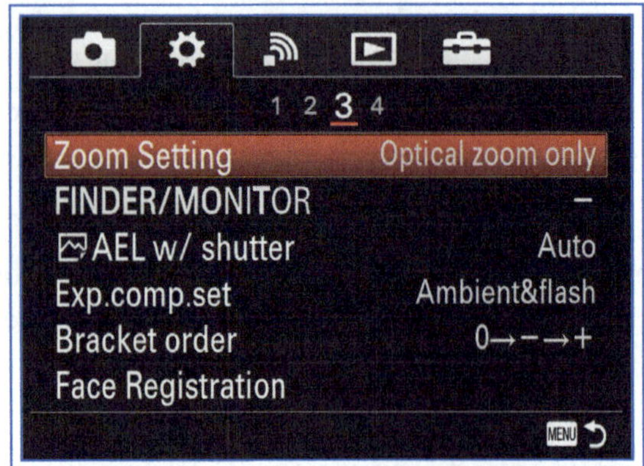

Figure 7-25. Screen 3 of Custom Menu

Zoom Setting

The first option on screen 3 of the Custom menu, Zoom Setting, provides two ways to give the RX10 extra zoom range, using features called Clear Image Zoom and Digital Zoom. To explain these features in context, I will discuss all three zoom methods that the camera offers—optical zoom, Clear Image Zoom, and Digital Zoom. (I will also discuss a fourth feature that is related to these, called Smart Zoom.)

Optical zoom is the camera's "natural" zoom capability—moving the lens elements so they magnify the image, just as binoculars do. You can call optical zoom a "real" zoom because it increases the amount of information that the lens gathers. The optical zoom of the RX10 operates within a range from 24mm at the wide-angle setting to the fully zoomed-in telephoto setting of 200mm.

Just to complicate matters a bit, I should point out that the actual optical zoom range of the RX10's lens is 8.8mm to 73.3mm; you can see those numbers on the end of the lens. But the numbers that are almost always used to describe the zoom range of a compact camera's lens are the "35mm-equivalent" figures, which translate the actual zoom range into what the range would be if this were a lens on a camera that uses 35mm film. This translation is done because so many photographers are familiar with the zoom ranges and focal lengths of lenses for traditional 35mm cameras, on which a 50mm lens is considered "normal." I use the 35mm-equivalent figures throughout this book.

The Digital Zoom feature on the RX10 magnifies the image electronically without any special processing to improve the quality. This type of zoom does not really increase the information gathered by the lens; rather, it just increases the apparent size of the image by enlarging the pixels within the area captured by the lens. On some cameras, the amount of digital zoom can be very large, such as 50 times normal, but such a large figure should be considered as a marketing ploy to lure customers, rather than as a feature of real value to the photographer.

The other option on the RX10, Clear Image Zoom, is a special type of digital zoom developed by Sony. With this feature, the RX10 does not just magnify the area of the image; rather, the camera uses an algorithm based on analysis of the image to add pixels through interpolation, so the pixels are not just multiplied. The enlargement is performed in a way that produces a smoother, more realistic enlargement than the Digital Zoom feature. Therefore, with Clear Image Zoom, the camera achieves greater quality than with Digital Zoom, though not as much as with the "pure" optical zoom.

Finally, there another way the RX10 can have a zoom range greater than the normal range of 24mm to 200mm, with no reduction in image quality. The standard range of 24mm to 200mm is available when Image Size is set to Large. However, if Image Size is set to Medium or Small, then the camera needs only a portion of the pixels on the image sensor to create the image at the reduced size. It can use the "extra" pixels to enlarge the view of the scene. This process, which Sony calls Smart Zoom in its documentation, is similar to what you can do using editing software such as Photoshop. If the overall image size does not need to be of the Large size, you can crop out some pixels from the center (or other area) of the image and enlarge them, thereby retaining the same overall image size with a magnified view of the scene.

So, with Smart Zoom, if you set Image Size to M or S, the camera can zoom to a greater range than with Image Size set to L and still retain the full quality of the optical zoom. You will, of course, end up with lower-resolution images, but that may not be a problem if you are going to post them on a website or share them via e-mail.

In short, optical zoom provides the best quality for magnifying the scene; Clear Image Zoom gives excellent quality; and Digital Zoom produces magnification accompanied by deterioration of the image. Smart Zoom lets you get greater zoom range with no image deterioration, but at the expense of resolution.

Here is how to use these settings. I will assume for this discussion that you are leaving Image Size set to L, because that is the best setting for excellent results in printing and editing your images.

When you select the Zoom Setting menu option and press the Center button, the camera displays the screen shown in FIGURE 7-26, giving you the choice of Optical Zoom Only; On: Clear Image Zoom; or On: Digital Zoom. If you turn on Digital Zoom, Clear Image Zoom will automatically be activated also. Optical Zoom is always available, no matter what settings are used.

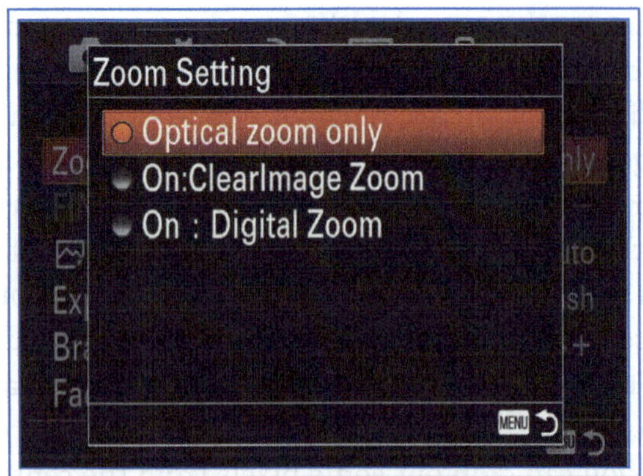

Figure 7-26. Zoom Setting Menu Options Screen

If you turn on only Clear Image Zoom, you will have greater zoom range than normal, as discussed above, with minimal quality loss. If you also turn on Digital Zoom, you will get even greater zoom range, but quality will suffer as the lens is zoomed past the Clear Image Zoom range. When these various settings are in effect, you will see different indications on the camera's display.

In FIGURE 7-27, Image Size is set to L and both Clear Image Zoom and Digital Zoom are turned off. The zoom indicator at the top of the screen goes only as far as 200mm.

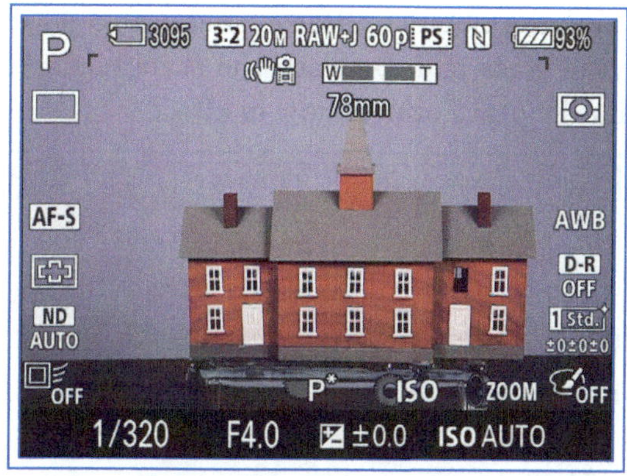

Figure 7-27. Indicator for Optical Zoom Only

In FIGURE 7-28, Clear Image Zoom is turned on. The zoom indicator shows the lens is zoomed to 1.2 times the normal range.

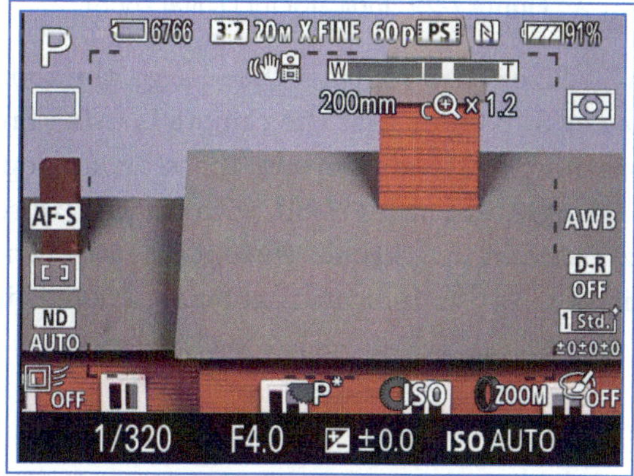

Figure 7-28. Indicator for Clear Image Zoom

There is a small vertical line in the center of the zoom scale marking the point where the zoom changes from optical-only to expanded (either Clear Image Zoom or Digital Zoom, depending on the settings). The magnifying glass icon with the "C" beneath the scale means Clear Image Zoom is turned on. Also, once the lens zooms past the optical zoom range, the sound of the zoom mechanism stops, so you can tell by listening when the camera has entered the range of Clear Image Zoom and Digital Zoom.

In FIGURE 7-29, both Clear Image Zoom and Digital Zoom are turned on, and the zoom indicator goes up to 4 times normal. The magnifying glass icon beneath the scale has a "D" beside it, indicating that Digital Zoom is now in effect.

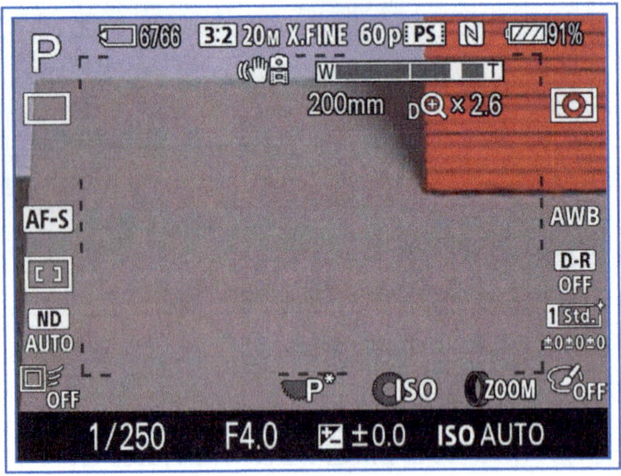

Figure 7-29. Indicator for Digital Zoom

With an Image Size setting smaller than Large, the zoom indicator will use a letter S to show that the camera is using Smart Zoom, as the zoom range extends beyond the standard optical zoom range. For example, in FIGURE 7-30, with Image Size set to Small, the lens is zoomed in to 1.4 times the optical range, and the zoom indicator displays an S to indicate that Smart Zoom is in effect.

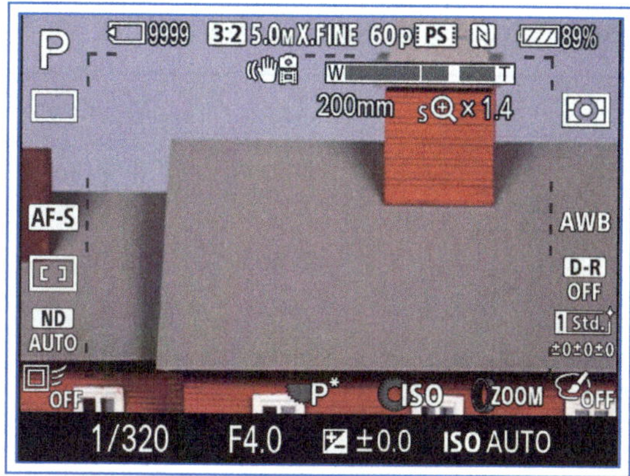

Figure 7-30. Indicator for Smart Zoom

With smaller image sizes, the ranges of Clear Image Zoom and Digital Zoom also are expanded. For example, as shown in Figure 7-31, with Image Size set to Small and Digital Zoom turned on, the lens can be zoomed in to 8.0 times the normal optical range.

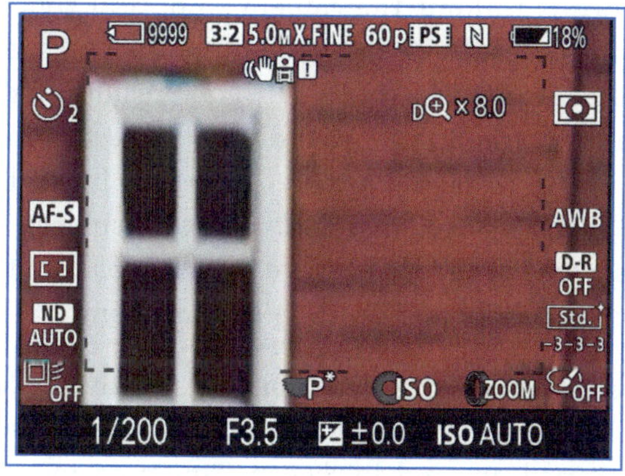

Figure 7-31. Digital Zoom with Small Image Size

Table 7-1 shows the zoom ranges that are available when Image Size is set to Large, Medium, and Small, with settings of Optical Zoom, Clear Image Zoom, and Digital Zoom. In all cases, Aspect Ratio is set to 3:2; with other Aspect Ratio settings, results would be different.

Table 7-1. Zoom Ranges at Various Image Sizes

	Large	Medium	Small
Optical Zoom (with no deterioration)	200mm	300mm	400mm
Clear Image Zoom (with minimal deterioration)	400mm	600mm	800mm
Digital Zoom (with significant deterioration)	800mm	1200mm	1600mm

To summarize the situation with zoom, when Image Size is set to Large, you can zoom up to 200mm with no deterioration using optical zoom; you can zoom to about 400mm with minimal deterioration using Clear Image Zoom; and you can zoom to about 800mm using Digital Zoom but with significant deterioration.

My preference is to limit the camera to optical zoom and avoid any deterioration. However, many photographers have found that Clear Image Zoom yields surprisingly good results, and it is worth using when you cannot get close to your subject. I do not like to use Digital Zoom to take a picture. However, it can be useful to zoom in to meter a specific area of a distant subject, or to check the composition of your shot before zooming back out and taking the shot using Clear Image Zoom or optical zoom.

Clear Image Zoom and Digital Zoom are not available in several situations, including when shooting Raw images, when the Smile Shutter is turned on, and in Sweep Panorama mode. They also are unavailable when the Smart Teleconverter option has been assigned to a control button. The Smart Teleconverter option, discussed later in this chapter, is itself a form of Digital Zoom.

Whenever the lens is zoomed into the range of Clear Image Zoom or Digital Zoom, the Focus Area option is disabled and the camera uses a broad focus frame, which is represented by the dotted area seen in Figure 7-30 and Figure 7-31.

Finder/Monitor

This next option on the Custom menu, shown in Figure 7-32, lets you choose whether to view shooting and playback displays on the RX10's LCD screen or in the viewfinder.

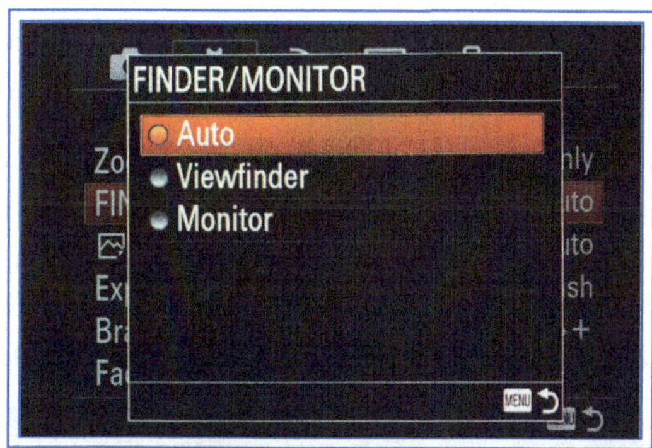

Figure 7-32. Finder/Monitor Menu Options Screen

The viewfinder provides the same information as the LCD screen, but its display is viewed inside an eye-level window that is shaded from daylight, giving you a very clear view of the shooting, playback, and menu screens.

By default, this menu option is set to Auto, which means the camera switches the view to the viewfinder automatically when you move your head near the camera. The camera turns on the viewfinder display and blacks out the LCD. (The viewfinder has an eye sensor at its left side that detects the presence of an object nearby.)

If you prefer to use either the viewfinder or the LCD screen at all times, set this menu option to Viewfinder or Monitor, according to your preference. With either of those settings, the camera will not switch to the other method of viewing unless you go back to this menu option and change the setting.

For me, the Auto option works well, and I have not found a reason to use the other settings. But if you will be working with your head (or another object) very close to the camera's viewfinder, you might want to use the Monitor option so the screen does not blank out unexpectedly.

AEL with Shutter

This menu item, whose options screen is shown in Figure 7-33, controls how the shutter button handles autoexposure lock. There are three possible settings for this feature: Auto, On, and Off.

With the default option, Auto, pressing the shutter button halfway locks exposure when the focus switch is set to S for single-shot autofocus or DMF for direct manual focus. When the focus switch is set to C for continuous focus or MF for manual focus, pressing the shutter button halfway does not lock exposure.

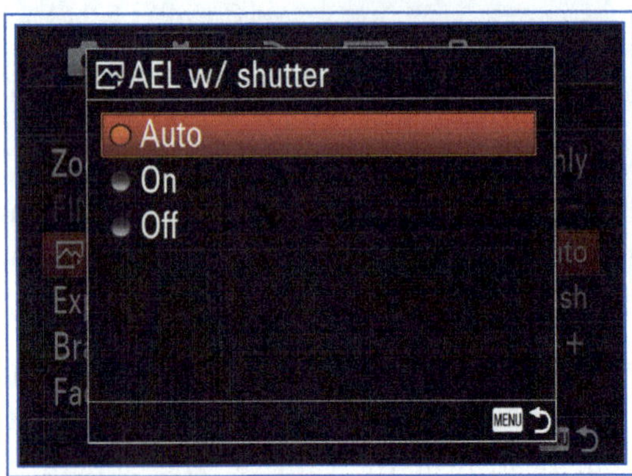

Figure 7-33. AEL with Shutter Menu Options Screen

If AEL with Shutter is set to On, then pressing the shutter button halfway locks exposure in all situations, regardless of what focus mode is in place. So, for example, if the focus switch is set to the C position for continuous autofocus, pressing the shutter button halfway locks exposure, though the focus mechanism will continue adjusting focus.

If this menu option is set to Off, then pressing the shutter button halfway never locks exposure, in any focus mode. You may want to use this setting when you need to press the shutter button halfway to lock focus and then move the camera to change the composition somewhat. You might want the camera to re-evaluate the exposure, even though you have already locked the focus.

Another important use for the Off setting is when you are using the continuous shooting settings of Drive Mode. As I discussed in Chapter 4, if you want the camera to adjust its exposure for each shot in a continuous burst, you need to set AEL with Shutter to Off. Otherwise, the camera will lock exposure with the first shot, and will not adjust it if the lighting changes during the burst.

Of course, you may not want to use the Off setting in that scenario, because it can slow down the burst of shots, and, depending on the situation, it may not be likely that the lighting will change during a brief burst of shots. But this option is available for those times when you want the camera to keep evaluating and adjusting exposure while you take a burst of shots.

Exposure Compensation Setting

This next option has two possible settings, as shown in Figure 7-34: Ambient & Flash, or Ambient Only.

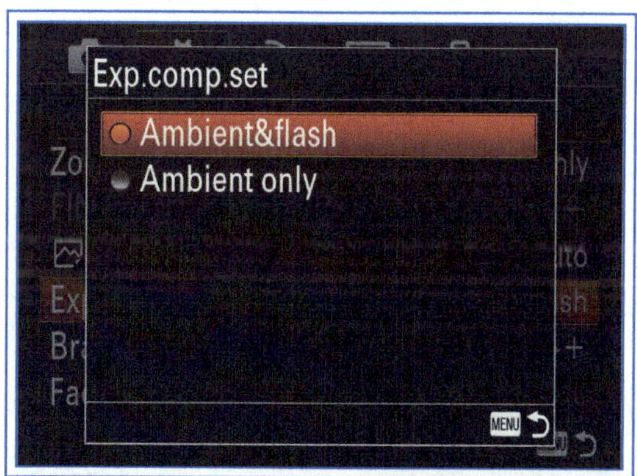

Figure 7-34. Exposure Compensation Setting Menu Options Screen

With Ambient & Flash, the default setting, when you turn the exposure compensation dial the camera will adjust not only its exposure settings, but also the intensity of the flash. If you choose Ambient Only, then turning that dial will control only the exposure settings, and not the flash.

I have not found this setting to make much difference in any situations I have encountered. If you want to give the RX10 maximum flexibility in adjusting exposure compensation, leave the setting at Ambient & Flash. Remember, though, that the camera has a separate adjustment for Flash Compensation on the shooting menu, and you can set that value separately if you see a need to adjust the output of the flash. I recommend using the Ambient Only setting unless you have a particular reason for using the Ambient & Flash option.

Bracket Order

As I discussed in Chapter 4, the RX10 offers several varieties of bracketing. When you turn on one of the bracketing settings, the camera takes multiple shots at different settings for the option being bracketed—exposure, White Balance, or DRO. The Bracket Order menu option lets you change the order in which the bracketed exposures are taken for exposure bracketing and White Balance bracketing. This option has no effect on the order of shots for DRO bracketing.

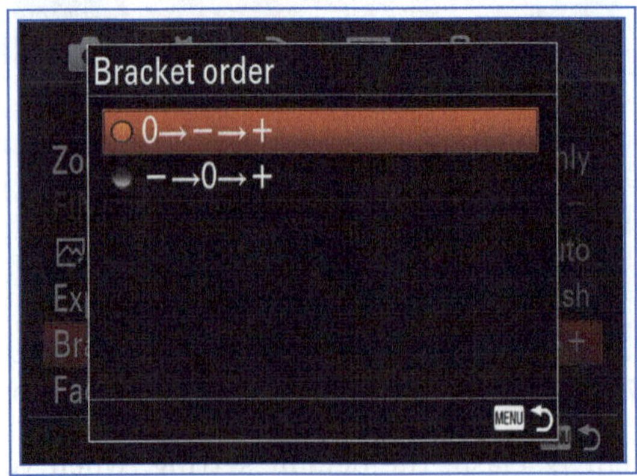

Figure 7-35. Bracket Order Menu Options Screen

The default option, seen on the first line in FIGURE 7-35, records three shots as follows: normal, low, high. When the camera is set to take five shots, it records them as follows: normal, low, high, even lower, even higher.

If you choose the second option, then the camera records three shots as follows: low, normal, high. When it takes five shots, it records them as follows: low, normal, high, higher, highest.

I do not use bracketing all that much, and I have never had occasion to change the bracket order. If you do a lot of bracketing, you might prefer to have the exposures all in ascending order of settings, rather than having the normal shot come first.

Face Registration

This last option on screen 3 of the Custom menu lets you register human faces so the RX10 can give those faces priority when it uses face detection. You can register up to eight faces and assign each one a priority from one to eight, with one being the highest. Then, when you set the Shooting menu option for Smile/Face Detection to On (Registered Faces), the camera will try to detect the registered faces first in the order you have assigned them.

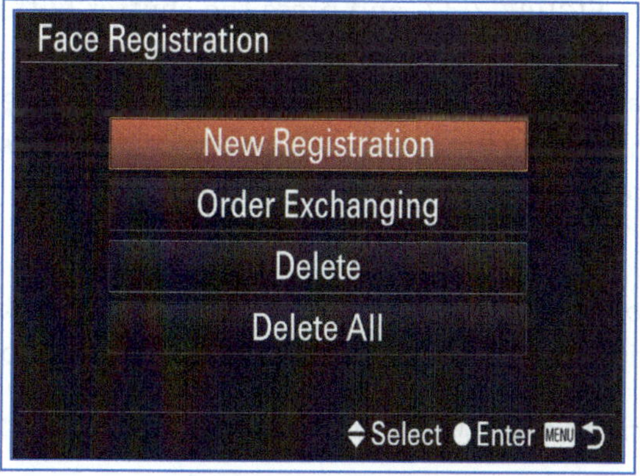

Figure 7-36. Face Registration Menu Options Screen

This feature is not one that I find any need for, but it could be useful if, for example, you take pictures at school functions and you want to make sure the camera focuses on your own children rather than on other kids.

To use this setting, select this menu option, and then on the next screen, shown in Figure 7-36, select New Registration. Press the Center button, and the camera will place a large square on the screen.

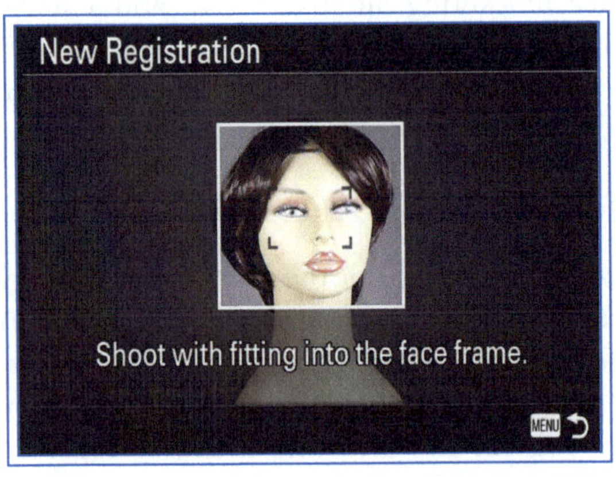

Figure 7-37. New Registration Screen for Face Registration Menu Option

Compose a shot with the face to be registered inside that frame, as shown in Figure 7-37, and press the shutter button to take a picture of that face. If the process is successful, the camera will display that face inside the frame with the message "Register face?" Highlight the Enter bar on that screen and press the Center button to complete the registration process.

Later, you can use the Order Exchanging option to change the priorities of the registered faces, and you can delete registered faces individually or all at once using other menu options.

The final screen of the Custom menu is shown in Figure 7-38.

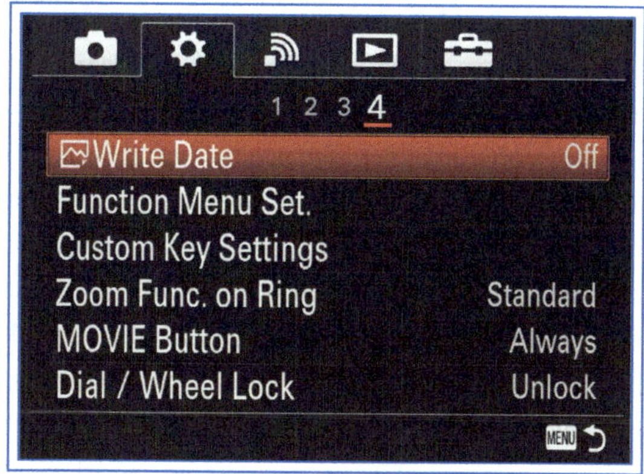

Figure 7-38. Screen 4 of Custom Menu

Write Date

This first setting on screen 4 of the Custom menu can be used to embed the current date in orange type in the lower-right corner of your images, as shown in Figure 7-39.

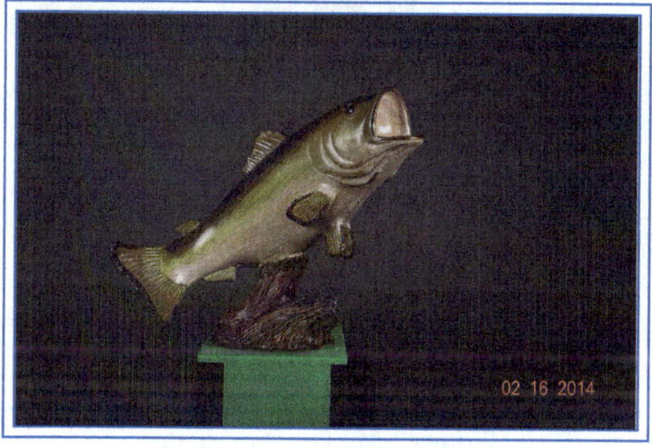

Figure 7-39. Write Date Option Example

This embedding is permanent, which means the information will appear as part of your image and cannot be deleted, other than through cropping or other editing procedures. You should not use this function unless you are certain that you want the date recorded on your images, perhaps for pictures that are part of a scientific research project.

You can always add the date in other ways after the fact in editing software if you want to, because the camera records the date and time internally with each image (if the date and time have been set accurately), so think twice before using this function. When you are shooting with this option activated, the word "DATE" appears in the upper-right corner of the screen as you compose your shot if you are using a shooting screen that displays detailed information. This option is not available when Quality is set to Raw or Raw & JPEG, with panoramas, bracketing, continuous shooting, or in Movie mode.

Function Menu Settings

As I discussed in Chapter 5, when you press the Function button in shooting mode, the camera displays up to 12 options in blocks at the bottom of the display, as shown in Figure 7-40.

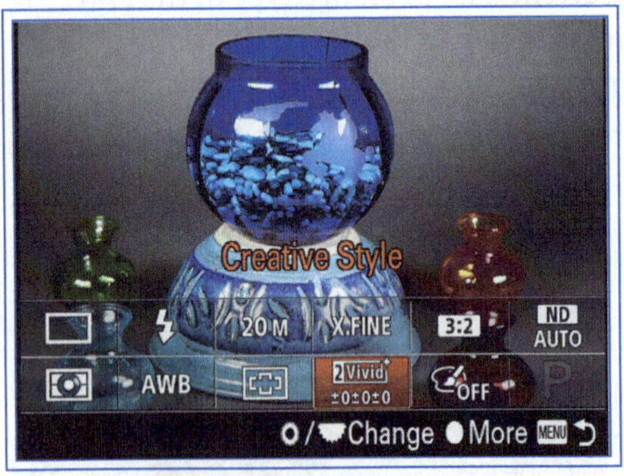

Figure 7-40. Function Menu

You move through those options with the direction buttons. Adjust the main settings with the Control wheel and secondary settings with the Control dial. Use the two screens of the Function Menu Settings menu item to assign options to the 12 blocks of the Function menu. When you select this menu option, the camera displays the screen shown in Figure 7-41, showing the assignments for the upper 6 blocks of the Function menu.

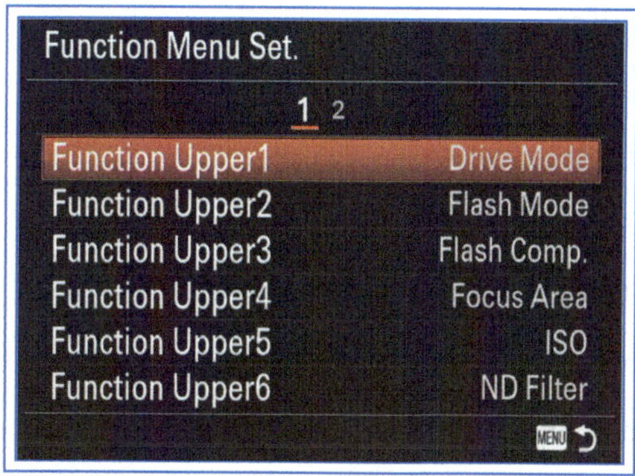

Figure 7-41. Function Menu Settings Menu Options Screen

When you press the Center button on any one of those lines, you will see a screen like that in Figure 7-42, listing the options that can be assigned to that block.

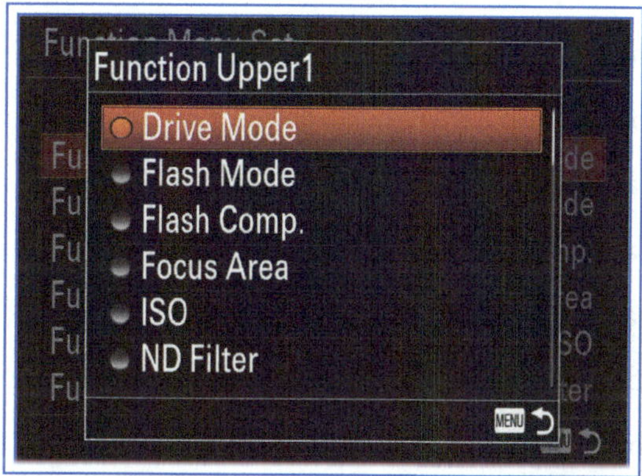

Figure 7-42. Settings Screen for Function Upper 1 Slot for Function Button

For each menu block, the options that can be assigned are:

- Drive Mode
- Flash Mode
- Flash Compensation
- Focus Area
- ISO

- ND Filter
- Metering Mode
- White Balance
- DRO/Auto HDR
- Creative Style
- Shoot Mode
- Picture Effect
- Lock-on AF
- Smile/Face Detection
- Soft Skin Effect
- Auto Object Framing
- Image Size
- Aspect Ratio
- Quality
- SteadyShot (Still Images)
- SteadyShot (Movies)
- Audio Recording Level
- Zebra
- Grid Line
- Audio Level Display
- Peaking Level
- Peaking Color
- Not Set

Press the Center button when the option you want to assign to a given block is displayed, and the camera will place an orange dot on that line to indicate that that feature is assigned to that block.

I recommend you assign a function to each of the 12 blocks and experiment to find the best setup. Remember that you can use the Control wheel and the Custom, AEL, Center, Left, Right, and Down buttons for your most important settings, such as, perhaps, ISO, AEL Toggle, Drive Mode, ND Filter, White Balance, and Focus Area, so you can reserve these 12 blocks for other options.

Custom Key Settings

I described this menu option in Chapter 5, in discussing controls that can have settings assigned to them. Now I will discuss the details of the settings that can be assigned to these controls.

When you select the Custom Key Settings menu option, you will see the screen shown in Figure 7-43. That screen includes all of the controls that can be assigned except the Down button, which is the only entry on the second screen of this menu option.

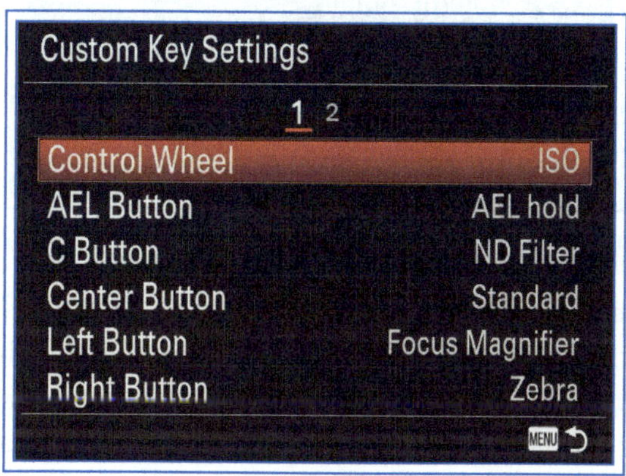

Figure 7-43. Custom Key Settings Menu Options Screen

Navigate to the line for a control and press the Center Button. You will see a screen listing all the options that can be assigned to that control. In most cases, these assignments are self-explanatory. When you assign a function, such as ISO, to a button, pressing the button calls up the menu screen for ISO, which lets you set the ISO just as if you had selected ISO from the Shooting menu. However, there are differences for some controls, and there are some items that can be assigned through this option that are not available through any menu. I will discuss these details below, as I provide information about each of the items for this menu option.

Control Wheel

The first control on the Custom Key Settings menu screen is the Control wheel. This control is a special case, because, of course, it is not a button but a wheel. The options that can be assigned to the wheel are ISO, White Balance, Creative Style, Picture Effect, or Not Set, as shown in FIGURE 7-44.

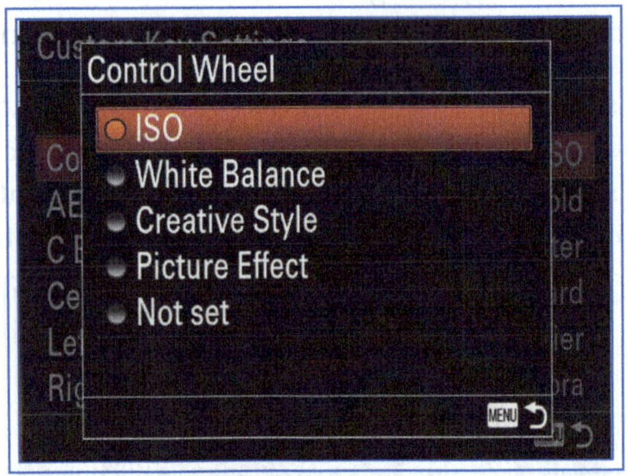

Figure 7-44. Screen for Assigning Function to Control Wheel

This feature is powerful because, when you assign a setting such as ISO to this wheel, you can use the wheel to instantly adjust the setting. For example, if you choose ISO, then, when the camera is in shooting mode, all you have to do is turn the Control wheel and the ISO setting will change. You can then immediately press the shutter button to take a picture with the new setting.

However, you cannot get access to all aspects of these settings by turning the wheel. For example, if you assign ISO to the wheel, you can select a numerical ISO value or Auto ISO, but you cannot set the Minimum and Maximum settings for Auto ISO, and you cannot select Multi Frame Noise Reduction from the ISO menu.

Similarly, if you assign White Balance to the Control wheel, you can select a White Balance setting, including Custom or Color Temperature, but you cannot set a new Custom White Balance or choose a new Color Temperature setting, and you cannot fine-tune the White Balance setting using the color axes. For those options, you need to use the White Balance menu option. Likewise, with Creative Style assigned to the wheel, you cannot adjust the contrast, sharpness, and saturation parameters of a selected setting.

However, if you choose Picture Effect, you can select any of the settings or sub-settings, because the Control wheel will cycle through all of the options, including, for example, the sub-settings for Toy Color, including Normal, Cool, Warm, Green, and Magenta.

When the Control wheel has been assigned to a function through this menu item, the camera places a gray icon representing the wheel in the bottom right of the screen next to an icon or label indicating what setting is currently assigned to the wheel. For example, Figure 7-45 shows the screen as it appears when ISO has been assigned to the Control wheel.

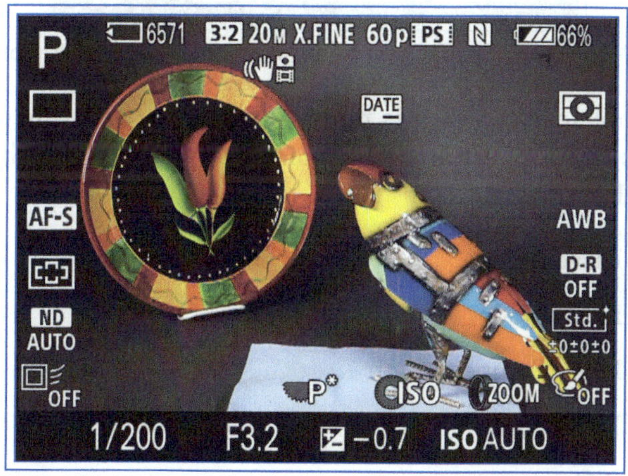

Figure 7-45. Icon Showing ISO Assigned to Control Wheel

Assigning one of these few shooting-related functions to the Control wheel does not interfere with any other operations of the wheel, because turning the wheel ordinarily does not have any effect unless a menu screen or a special screen like the MF Assist enlarged screen is displayed.

AEL Button

If you select AEL button from the Custom Key Settings menu screen, the camera will display the screen shown in Figure 7-46, which lists the first 6 options that can be assigned to the AEL button.

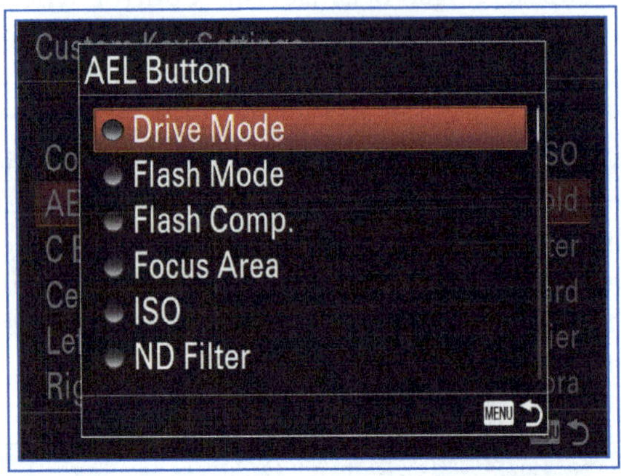

Figure 7-46. Screen 1 of Possible Assignments for AEL Button

The complete list, which is much longer than that single screen, includes all of the following choices, any one of which can be assigned to this button:

- Drive Mode
- Flash Mode
- Flash Compensation
- Focus Area
- ISO
- ND Filter

- Metering Mode
- White Balance
- DRO/Auto
- HDR
- Creative Style
- Picture Effect
- Smile/Face Detection
- Soft Skin Effect
- Auto Object Framing
- SteadyShot (Still Images)
- SteadyShot (Movies)
- Audio Recording Level
- Image Size
- Aspect Ratio
- Quality
- In-Camera Guide
- Memory
- AEL Hold
- AEL Toggle
- Spot AEL Hold
- Spot AEL Toggle
- AF/MF Control Hold
- AF/MF Control Toggle
- Lock-on AF
- Eye AF

- Smart Teleconverter
- Focus Magnifier
- Deactivate Monitor
- Zebra
- Grid Line
- Audio Level Display
- Peaking Level
- Peaking Color
- Send to Smartphone
- Control with Smartphone
- Monitor Brightness
- Not Set

Just scroll through the list and press the Center button to make your selection. The dot next to the chosen option will turn orange to mark the choice.

Many of these options are self-explanatory because, when the button has the option assigned, pressing the button will simply call up the menu screen for that option, if the option is available in the current shooting mode. For example, if the AEL button is assigned to Drive Mode, then, when you press the button, the camera displays the Drive Mode menu, just as if you had used the Menu button to get access to that option. (In some cases the screen looks different from the menu screen called up with the Menu button, but the regular menu options are available in every case.) I will not discuss those options here; see CHAPTER 4 for discussion of the Shooting menu, CHAPTER 7 for discussion of the Custom and Setup menus, and CHAPTER 9 for discussion of the Wi-Fi menu.

However, there are several other selections for the AEL button (and the other control buttons) that do not call up a menu screen. Instead, they perform a particular function that does not come from a menu option. I will discuss those selections below.

AEL Hold

If you set the AEL button to the AEL Hold (Autoexposure Lock Hold) option, then, when the camera is in shooting mode, pressing this button will lock exposure at the current setting as metered by the camera, as long as you hold down the button. If the camera is set to Manual exposure mode, pressing the button to activate AEL Hold will lock the M.M. (Metered Manual) setting while you hold the button down. The exposure will already be "locked" because you have set it manually, so using the AEL Hold function will just keep the M.M. setting from changing further. (The M.M. setting does not function when ISO is set to Auto.)

When exposure is locked in this way, a large asterisk will appear in the lower-right corner of the display and remain there until the AEL button is released.

Here is an example to illustrate the use of the AEL Hold function. You might want to use AEL Hold to make sure your exposure is calibrated for an object that is part of a larger scene, such as a dark painting on a light wall. You could lock exposure while holding the camera close to the painting, then move back to take a picture of the wall with the locked exposure ensuring the painting will be properly exposed.

To do this, assuming the camera is in Program mode, hold the camera close to the painting until the metered aperture and shutter speed appear on the screen. Press and hold the AEL button and an asterisk (*) will appear on the screen, as shown in FIGURE 7-47, indicating that exposure lock is in effect.

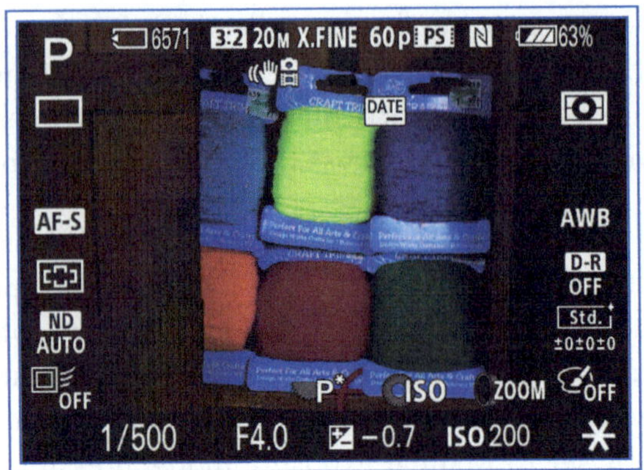

Figure 7-47. Asterisk on Screen When AEL Hold in Effect

Now you can move back (or anywhere else) and take your photograph using the exposure setting that you locked in. Once you have finished using the locked exposure setting, release the AEL button to make the asterisk disappear. The camera is now ready to measure a new exposure reading.

AEL Toggle

If you set the AEL button to the AEL Toggle option, then, in shooting mode, pressing the AEL button will lock exposure just as with AEL Hold. The difference with this setting is that you just press and release the AEL button; the exposure will remain locked until you press the button again to cancel the exposure lock.

Spot AEL Hold

The next option for the AEL button is listed on the menu as AEL Hold with a spot icon before the name. The icon means that, with this setting, when you press the AEL button and hold it, the camera will lock exposure as metered by the spot-metering area in the center of the display, no matter what metering method is currently in effect. This option can be quite useful if you think you will want to switch to spot-metering just for one or two shots. You can press the AEL button, make sure the center of the display covers the area that you want to use for evaluating the exposure, and take the shot with the exposure adjusted for that spot.

Spot AEL Toggle

The Spot AEL Toggle option is similar to the AEL Toggle option, except that the camera meters only in the spot area in the very center of the display.

AF/MF Control Hold

If you select AF/MF Control Hold for the AEL button's function, pressing the button switches the camera between autofocus and manual focus, but only while you hold down the button. If the camera is set to any autofocus mode, pressing and holding the AEL button will switch the camera into manual focus mode. Releasing it will switch to the autofocus mode that was originally set. If the camera is set to manual focus mode, pressing and holding the button will switch to single-shot AF mode. In this situation, when you press the AEL button, the camera will also evaluate the focus and lock focus, if possible. Releasing the button will switch back to manual focus mode. If the camera is set to DMF mode, the button will toggle between DMF and manual focus.

This function is useful in situations when it is difficult to use autofocus, such as dark areas, extreme close-ups, or areas where you have to shoot through obstructions such as glass or wire cages. You can switch very quickly into manual focus mode and back again, as conditions warrant.

Also, this capability is helpful if you want to set "zone" focusing, so you can shoot quickly without having to wait for the autofocus mechanism to operate. For example, if you are doing street photography, you can set the camera to single-shot autofocus mode and focus on a subject at about the distance you expect to be shooting from—say, 25 feet (7.6 meters). Then, once focus is locked on that subject, press and hold the AEL button to switch the camera to manual focus mode, and the focus will be locked at that distance in manual focus mode. You can then take shots of subjects at that distance without having to refocus. If you need to set another focus distance, just release the AEL button to go back to autofocus mode and repeat the process.

Finally, it is convenient to be able to quickly get the camera to use autofocus when it is set to manual focus mode. With this function, as noted above, when you press and release the AEL button, the camera will quickly focus using autofocus, and then go back to manual focus mode for any further adjustments you may want to make.

AF/MF Control Toggle

If you select AF/MF Control Toggle for the setting of the AEL button's function, pressing the button switches the camera between autofocus and manual focus. This option works the same as AF/MF Control Hold, except that you do not hold down the AEL button; you just press it and release it. The switched focus mode then stays in effect until you press the button again.

Eye AF

If you assign Eye AF to the AEL button, then, when the camera is set to single-shot autofocus mode, it will look for human eyes and focus on them if possible. If the camera detects an eye, it will display a small green frame to show that it has focused on the eye, as shown in FIGURE 7-48.

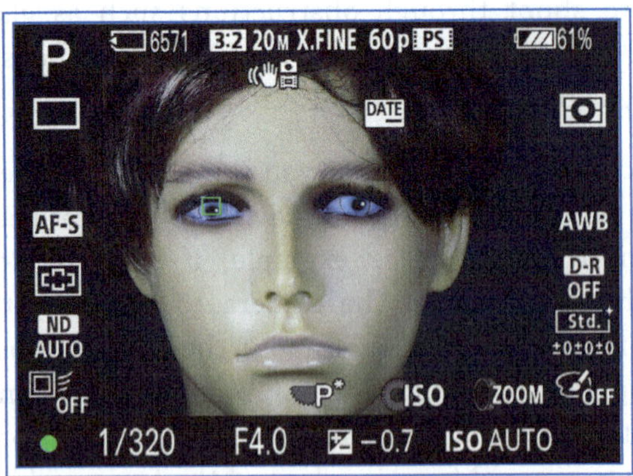

Figure 7-48. Green Eye AF Frame Showing Focus on Eye

Continue to hold down the assigned button to lock focus on the eye while you press the shutter button to take the picture.

This option can be especially useful when depth of field is shallow, such as when the lens is zoomed in to a long focal length or you are shooting a close-up, to make sure the focus is sharpest on the subject's eyes rather than on the nose or some other feature. A portrait generally looks best when the eyes are in sharp focus.

Smart Teleconverter

The next choice for the AEL button is Smart Teleconverter. With this option, when you press the button and release it, the camera enlarges the current image by a factor of 1.4 times and crops the enlarged image to fill the frame. If you press the button again, the magnification increases to 2.0 times. The camera does not do any enhancement of the image; it just crops away some of the pixels in the image, which results in a loss of some resolution.

Some users like this feature because it gives them a quick way to get an enlarged view of the scene—just press a button and you immediately get a 1.4x or 2.0x magnification. With the 20-megapixel sensor of the RX10, you can afford to lose some resolution. Some people like to be able to compose a shot while looking at a magnified view, and then go back to the normal view to capture it. They may want to have the camera's metering system evaluate the exposure for the enlarged area before capturing the final image. In any event, if you find this feature useful, it is available here and easy to use. It is not available when Quality is set to Raw. Also note that this feature conflicts with some other features, such as Digital Zoom.

Deactivate Monitor

This is the next non-menu option for the AEL button. (Remember that I'm skipping over settings that are just duplicates of menu options, such as Focus Magnifier.)

If you assign the AEL button to the Deactivate Monitor option, pressing the button while the camera is in shooting mode will turn off the LCD, leaving only a single line of information at the bottom of the screen. You might want to use this option if you are in a darkened area and don't want to distract others or attract attention with the brightness of the monitor. This feature can also help you save power if your battery is running down. By pressing the assigned button, you can quickly turn off the monitor temporarily, and recall it just as quickly with the same button.

If you want to deactivate the monitor on a longer-term basis, you can use the Finder/Monitor option on screen 3 of the Custom menu. If you select Viewfinder for that option, then the monitor will be turned off at all times, and will not display even the single line of information that appears when the Deactivate Monitor option is used.

Not Set

The last option that can be assigned to the AEL button is called Not Set. If you choose this option, then the AEL button will not be assigned any special function. I cannot think of any reason to use this option, unless you will be using a limited number of settings and don't want to risk activating a different setting by pressing the button accidentally.

Custom Button

The next item on the main screen of the Custom Key Settings menu option is the C button, or Custom button. This button can be assigned to any of the same items discussed above for the AEL button.

Center Button

Next, you can assign the Center button to any of the same options as for the AEL or Custom button. Because of the location and other duties of this button, though, there are a few differences in how this assignment operates.

Most importantly, the first item on the list of possible assignments for the Center button is called Standard, as shown in FIGURE 7-49.

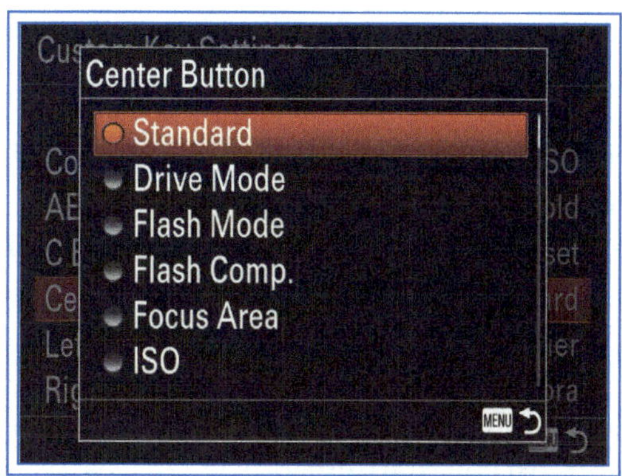

Figure 7-49. Screen 1 of Possible Assignments for Center Button

This option is not available for any other control. As I noted in CHAPTER 5, if you select Standard, the Center button is used for two purposes. First, it activates the tracking frame for Lock-on AF, assuming you have turned on that menu option on screen 5 of the Shooting menu. Second, if Focus Area is set to Flexible Spot on screen 3 of the Shooting menu, pressing the Center button activates the screen for adjusting the location of the spot-focusing bracket.

If you don't want to assign the Standard option to the Center button, then you can select any one of the other options on the list that is available for the AEL button, discussed above. If you do that, then, of course, the Center button will no longer carry out the actions that can be assigned to it with the Standard option. It still will operate to select menu options, but it will not operate to lock on a subject when Lock-on AF is selected, and it will not activate the focus frame so it can be moved when Flexible Spot is selected for the Focus Area menu option.

If you assign the Center button to one of the AEL functions (locking exposure by holding or toggling the button), then, if you are using manual focus, you will still be able to use the Center button for changing the magnification on the MF Assist screen without affecting the exposure lock function. To activate or cancel the exposure lock, press the Center button when the shooting screen is in its normal mode (that is, when the MF Assist magnification screen is not displayed).

I strongly recommend that you leave the Center button assigned to the Standard option so it will carry out its focus-related duties. There are plenty of other controls that can have settings assigned to them without disrupting the normal uses of the Center button.

Left Button

For the Left button, the choices of assignment are the same as for the AEL button, except that four of the choices are not available. The unavailable options are AEL Hold, Spot AEL Hold, AF/MF Control Hold, and Eye AF. So, if you want to set the Left button to lock exposure or to switch between autofocus and manual focus, the button will act only as a toggle, not as one that you have to hold down. Presumably, Sony made this choice because it would be awkward to hold down the Left button while pressing the shutter button. (Eye AF also requires that you hold down the button while pressing the shutter button.)

Right Button

The choices of assignment for the Right button are the same as those for the Left button.

Down Button

The option to assign a function to the Down button is located on screen 2 of the Custom Key Settings menu option. The assignment choices are the same as those for the Left and Right buttons.

Zoom Function on Ring

This next item on the Custom menu controls the way the zoom/focus ring around the lens operates when you are using it to zoom the lens in and out. The two choices are Standard and Step, as shown in Figure 7-50.

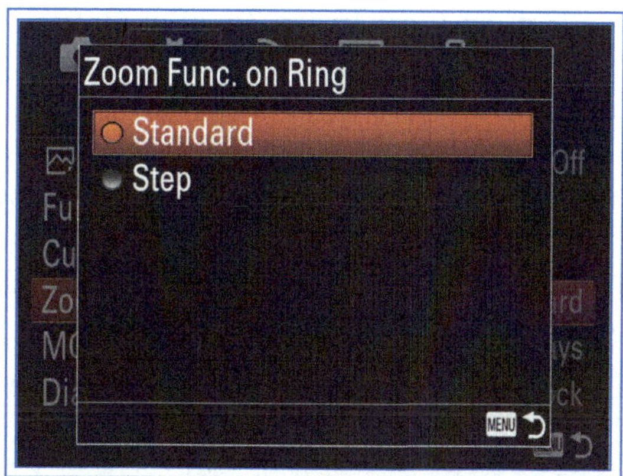

Figure 7-50. Zoom Function on Ring Menu Options Screen

With Standard, when the zoom/focus ring is used to zoom the lens, it does so continuously, just as the zoom lever does. That is, as you turn the ring, the lens zooms through all focal lengths that are available. With optical zoom, that means it will zoom from the 24mm wide-angle setting to the 200mm telephoto setting in continuous increments. With Clear Image Zoom and Digital Zoom, the zoom levels increase beyond the 200mm point.

If you set this option to Step, then the zoom/focus ring zooms the lens only to certain preset values. Those values are 24mm, 35mm, 50mm, 70mm, 100mm, 135mm, and 200mm. When you nudge the ring toward the wide-angle or telephoto side, the zoom will move to the next preset focal length. You should give the ring a quick nudge and then release it; if you keep turning it, it will move past the next value and go on to the one after that.

There are some important limitations to note about the step zoom function on the RX10. First, if you set the camera for manual focus or DMF using the focus switch, the zoom/focus ring will control manual focus and will not zoom the lens.

Second, the step zoom feature works only for the zoom/focus ring; the zoom lever will always zoom the lens continuously. Also, the step zoom feature does not work when shooting movies.

Finally, if you turn on Clear Image Zoom or Optical Zoom using the Zoom Setting option on screen 3 of the Custom menu, the step zoom feature will not include specific increments for the zoom range beyond the optical limit of 200mm. Instead, as shown in FIGURE 7-51, the camera will display the range of preset increments with an area at the right side of the range extending from the 200mm mark to a magnifying glass icon at the far right, showing a general area of extended zoom range.

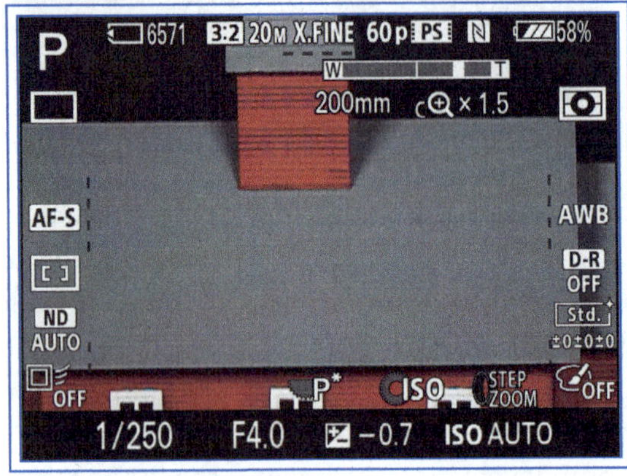

Figure 7-51. Indicator When Step Zoom and Clear Image Zoom in Use

Having the ability to turn on step zoom is a valuable feature in some situations. For example, if you want to set a specific focal length for a shot, using the step zoom feature is an excellent way to make sure you have the lens zoomed to the exact focal length you want. Of course, this feature is of use only if your desired focal length is 35mm, 50mm, 70mm, 100mm, or 135mm; it is easy to set the focal length to 24mm or 200mm using the normal zoom method because those focal lengths are at the two extremes of the camera's optical zoom range.

You might want to choose a focal length of 35mm, for example, to compare shots from the RX10 against shots from another camera using that specific focal length for the comparisons.

I do not often use the step zoom feature, but it is good to have it available as an option.

Movie Button

This option, shown in Figure 7-52, lets you lock out the operation of the red Movie button to avoid accidentally starting a video recording. The two choices are Always and Movie Mode Only.

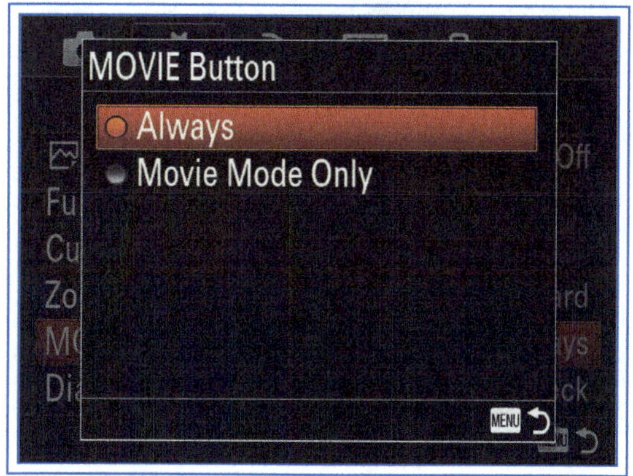

Figure 7-52. Movie Button Menu Options Screen

If you want to be able to start recording a video at any time without delay, you should leave the Movie Button option set to Always. With this setting, you can start recording a movie by pressing this button, no matter what shooting mode is set on the mode dial. This is a very convenient system, because you can start shooting a video at a moment's notice without having to turn the mode dial to the Movie position.

As I discussed in Chapter 5 in the section on the Movie button, the main reason to choose the Movie Mode Only option is if you are afraid you may press the Movie button by mistake. With the RX10, I have never pressed the Movie button by mistake, because the camera is large enough that the button does not come within range of my thumb unless I want to press it. So, with this camera I leave the menu option set to Always, to avoid missing any video opportunities. But you should consider whether you want to use this option protect against unwanted footage. Of course, if you have no interest in video recording, you can set this option to Movie Mode Only to avoid unwanted uses of the button.

Dial/Wheel Lock

This final option on the Custom menu has two possible settings, Lock and Unlock, as seen in Figure 7-53.

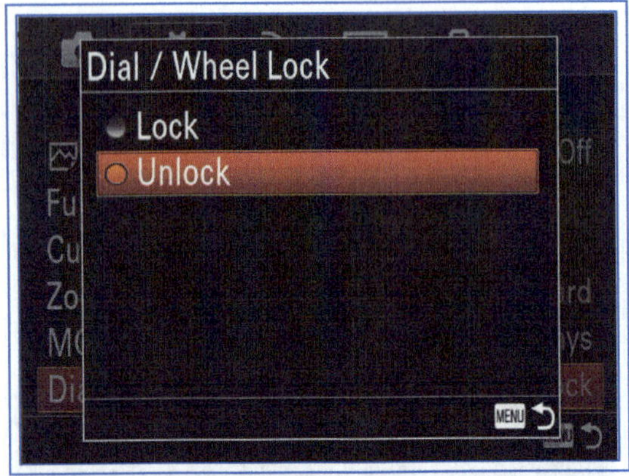

Figure 7-53. Dial/Wheel Lock Menu Options Screen

If you select Lock, you can lock the functioning of the Control wheel and Control dial. To engage the actual lock, after this menu item is set to Lock, press and hold the Function button for several seconds until a Locked message appears on the screen. After that, you will see an icon in the lower right corner of the display, indicating that the lock is in effect, as shown in Figure 7-54.

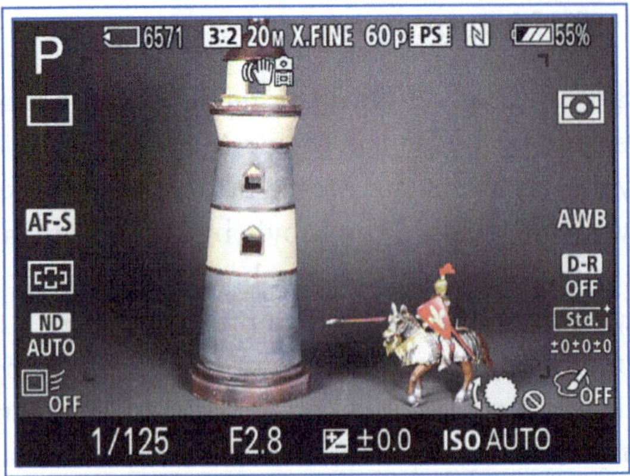

Figure 7-54. Icon Showing Control Wheel Lock in Effect

Once the lock is in effect, turning the Control wheel or Control dial will not have any effect on the camera's settings. For example, if the Control wheel has been set to adjust ISO using the Custom Key Settings menu option, turning the dial will not adjust ISO while the lock is in effect. Similarly, when the camera is in Shutter Priority or Manual exposure mode, turning the Control dial will not change the shutter speed, as it normally would.

However, the dial and wheel will still carry out their functions of navigating through menu screens, even with the lock in effect.

The purpose of this menu option is to give you a way to prevent these dials from accidentally moving and changing your settings. If you have made an important adjustment to your settings, you can lock both of these dials so the settings will stay in place. When you are ready to change settings, you can just press and hold the Function button again to remove the lock.

I have not had occasion to use this feature myself, but I can see its value for situations in which you need to keep a setting locked in and want to guard against accidental slipping of the wheel or dial.

Even when the Lock option is turned on, the Function button can still be used to call up the Function menu. A quick press of the button will call up that menu, and a longer press-and-hold will lock or unlock the wheel and dial.

Setup Menu

The next menu to be discussed, whose tab is found to the right of the tab for the Playback menu, is the Setup menu, whose first screen is shown in FIGURE 7-55.

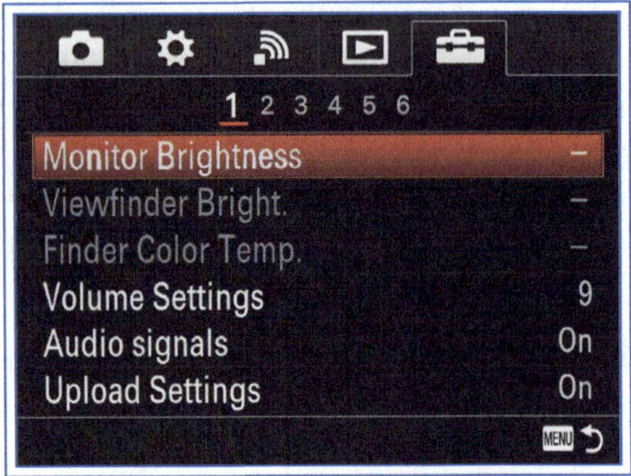

Figure 7-55. Screen 1 of Setup Menu

This six-screen menu contains options that control technical matters such as computer connections, display brightness, audio volume, file numbering, formatting a memory card, and others. I will discuss each menu item below.

Monitor Brightness

When you select this option, the camera displays a screen that shows the current setting, as seen in Figure 7-56.

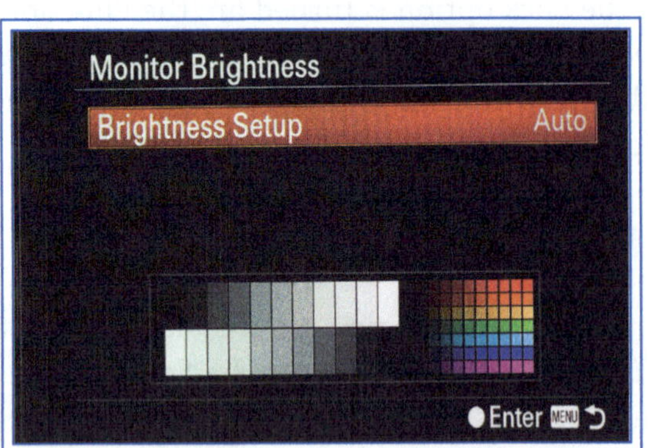

Figure 7-56. Brightness Setup Set to Auto

If you press the Center button on that screen, you will see a screen where you can choose one of three available settings for controlling the brightness of the LCD display: Auto, Manual, or Sunny Weather, as seen in FIGURE 7-57.

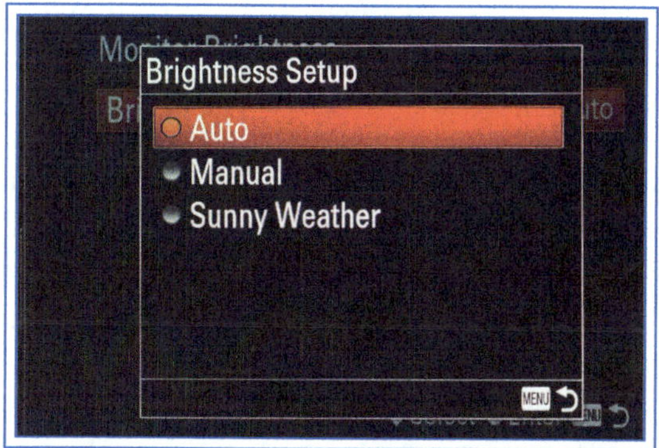

Figure 7-57. Screen Showing 3 Choices for Brightness Setup Option

If you choose Auto, the camera adjusts the screen's brightness using a small light sensor at the upper-left corner of the LCD screen to gauge the amount of ambient light. As the ambient light grows dimmer, the screen grows dimmer also, and vice-versa.

If you choose Manual, the camera displays the screen in FIGURE 7-58.

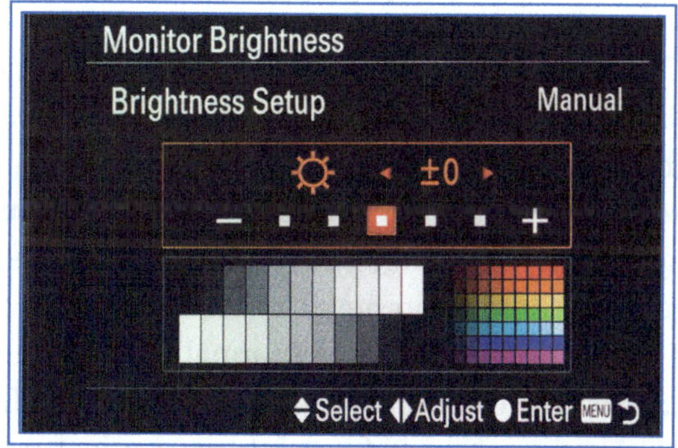

Figure 7-58. Scale for Manual Setup of Monitor Brightness

Using the controls indicated on this screen, you can adjust the brightness to one or two units above or below normal. After moving the orange highlight block into the scale with a plus and minus sign, press the Left or Right button or turn the Control dial to make your desired adjustment. If your battery is running low and you don't have a spare, you may want to set the monitor to its minimum brightness to conserve power. Conversely, you can increase the brightness if you're finding it difficult to compose the image on the screen.

If you are shooting outdoors in bright conditions, you can choose the third setting, Sunny Weather, which sets the display to a very bright level that helps you see the screen despite the bright sunshine. I have found the Sunny Weather setting to be useful in some situations, because the screen can be very difficult to see when the sun is shining. Of course, you can always switch to viewing through the viewfinder in bright conditions, but there may be times when you want to hold the camera away from your head as you compose the shot, even in bright sunlight. Or, you may want to play back your images for friends while outdoors.

The Sunny Weather setting drains the camera's battery fairly rapidly, so you should turn it off when it is no longer needed. For everyday shooting, I use the Auto setting, which has been quite adequate for me.

Viewfinder Brightness

This second option is similar to the Monitor Brightness selection, discussed above, but it has some differences. With this option, you have to be looking into the viewfinder to make adjustments. There is no Sunny Weather setting, because the viewfinder is shaded from the sun and there is no need for a super-bright setting. You can set the brightness to Auto or Manual. If you select Manual, you can make the same adjustments as with the LCD screen. Again, there is not much need for brightness adjustments because the view is always shielded from outside light.

Finder Color Temperature

This option lets you adjust the color temperature of the view through the viewfinder. As with the Viewfinder Brightness setting, you have to look into the viewfinder to make the adjustments. You can use the camera's controls to adjust the color temperature downward by one or two units, which will make the view appear slightly more reddish, or "warmer," or you can adjust upward by one or two units to make it more bluish, or "cooler."

I have not found a reason to take advantage of this adjustment, but, if it is helpful to you, it is easy to use.

Volume Settings

This option lets you set the volume for playback of movies at a level anywhere from 0 to 15. You can also set this level when a movie is playing by pressing the Down button to get access to the detailed controls, which include a volume setting option. When a movie is displayed on the screen in playback mode before playback starts, pressing the Down button calls up the volume adjustment screen immediately. Pressing that button when a still image is displayed in playback mode also calls up the volume screen, if View Mode is set to show both videos and still images.

Audio Signals

This option lets you choose whether or not to activate the various sounds the RX10 makes when an operation takes place, such as pressing the shutter button, confirming focus, or pressing a control button. By default, the sounds are turned on, but it can be helpful to silence them in a quiet area or during a religious ceremony, or when you are doing street photography and want to avoid alerting your subjects that a camera is being used.

Upload Settings

This option is the last item on the first screen of the Setup menu as shown in Figure 7-55, but only when an Eye-Fi card is inserted in the camera. If no Eye-Fi card is present, this menu option is not dimmed; it just does not display at all, leaving a blank space at the bottom of the menu screen.

As discussed in Chapter 1, an Eye-Fi card is a memory card that includes a transmitter to send images to a computer over a Wi-Fi network or directly to a wireless device if you use Direct Mode. This menu item has only two settings—On and Off. You might want to use the Off setting if you are on an airplane where you may be required to turn off radio transmitters. Or, if you know you will not be using the Eye-Fi uploading capability for a while, you can turn this menu option off to save some battery power.

Of course, the RX10 has its own built-in Wi-Fi capability, which makes it less likely you will use an Eye-Fi card for the transfer of images.

The second screen of the Setup menu is shown in Figure 7-59. Following are details about the options on this screen.

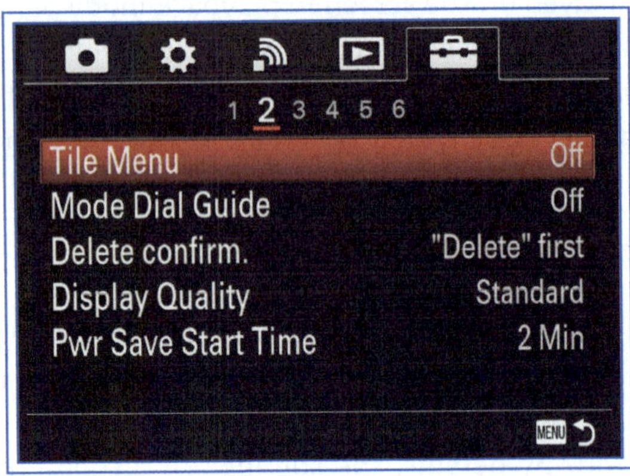

Figure 7-59. Screen 2 of Setup Menu

Tile Menu

If you turn this option on, the camera displays a screen with five tiles representing the various menu systems, as shown in Figure 7-60, when you press the Menu button.

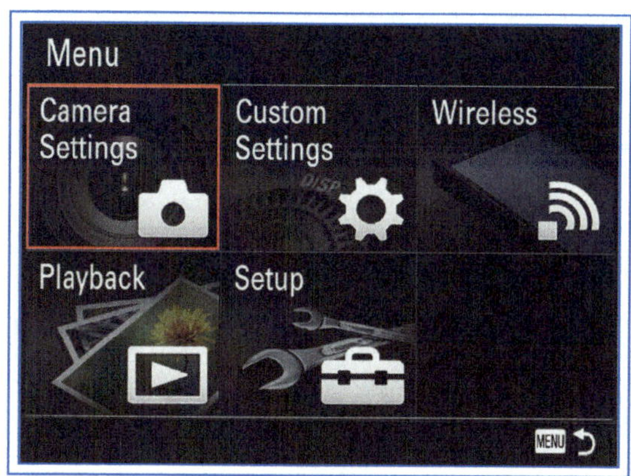

Figure 7-60. Five Menu Tiles for Tile Menu Option

This screen is helpful because it gives you a graphic representation of which menu is which, and lets you choose a menu and get quick access to it. You navigate through the 5 blocks using the direction buttons, the Control wheel, or the Control dial.

I prefer to leave this option turned off, because, without it, pressing the Menu button takes me right into the last menu option I was using. From there, I can navigate quickly to any other menu system. But for those who are new to this camera or who like having a large display to show the menu choices clearly, the Tile Menu option may be worth using.

Mode Dial Guide

This menu item gives you a way to turn on or off the mode dial guide, a graphic display that appears on the camera's screen when you turn the mode dial to select a shooting mode, as shown in Figure 7-61.

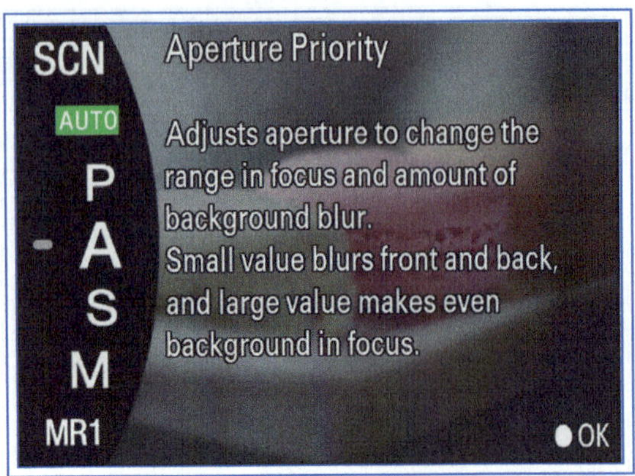

Figure 7-61. Mode Dial guide for Aperture Priority Mode

This guide can is helpful when you first get the camera, but it can be annoying if you don't need the reminder, and you have to press the Center button or press the shutter button halfway to dismiss the screen. I leave this option turned off to speed up my shooting.

Delete Confirmation

This menu item has two options as shown in Figure 7-62: "Delete" First or "Cancel" First.

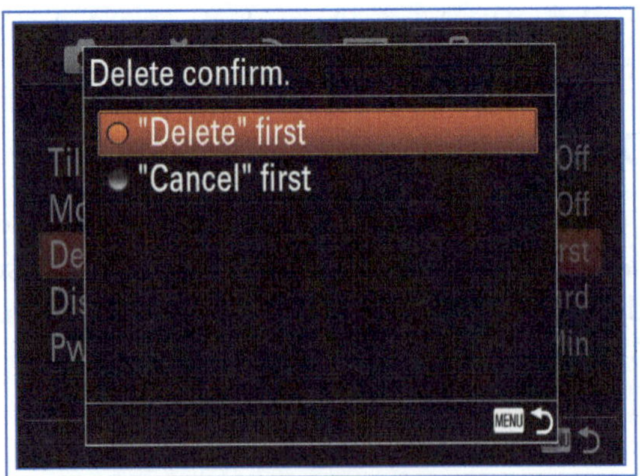

Figure 7-62. Delete Confirmation Menu Options Screen

This option lets you fine-tune the way the menu system operates for deleting images. Whenever you press the Trash button to delete an image in playback mode, the camera displays a confirmation screen, as shown in Figure 7-63, with two choices: Delete or Cancel. One of those choices will be highlighted when the screen appears; you can then just press the Center button to accept that choice and the operation will be done. Of course, you also can use the Control wheel, Control dial, or Up or Down direction button to highlight the other choice before you press the Center button to carry out your choice.

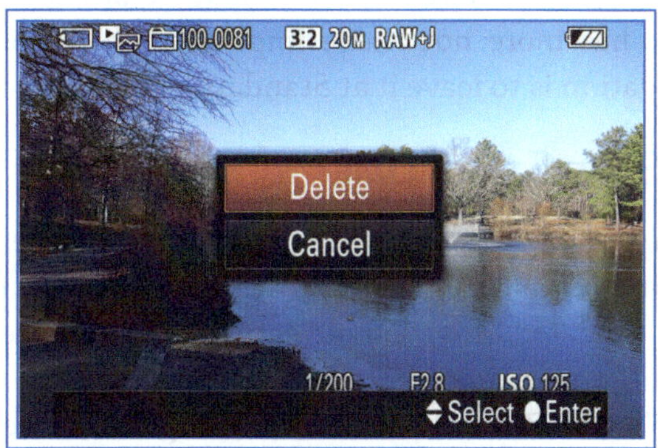

Figure 7-63. Delete Button Confirmation Screen

Which option you choose depends on your habits, and how careful you want to be to guard against the accidental deletion of an image. If you like to move quickly in deleting images, choose "Delete" first. Then, as soon as the confirmation screen appears you can press the Center button to carry out the deletion. If you prefer to have some insurance against an accidental deletion, choose "Cancel" first, so that, if you press the Center button too quickly when the confirmation screen appears, you will only cancel the operation, rather than deleting an image.

Unless you use this process often and need to save time, I recommend you leave this menu item set at the "Cancel" First setting to be safe.

Display Quality

This menu item lets you choose Standard or High for the quality of the display. According to Sony, with the High setting the camera displays the live view on the LCD screen or in the viewfinder at a higher resolution than with the Standard setting, at the expense of additional drain on the battery.

I have tried several experiments with these settings, viewing small print from a catalog using both the viewfinder and the LCD display with both Display Quality settings, and I have not found a noticeable difference. There may be situations in which this option has more noticeable impact on the display, but my recommendation is to leave it at Standard to conserve battery life.

Power Save Start Time

This menu option lets you set the amount of time before the camera turns off automatically to save power, when no controls have been operated. The default setting is 1 minute; with this option you can also choose 2, 5, or 30 minutes, or 10 seconds, as shown in Figure 7-64. When the camera goes to sleep with this option, you can wake it up by half-pressing the shutter button, or by pressing the Menu button or the Playback button. These presses will place the camera into shooting mode, playback mode, and the menu system, respectively.

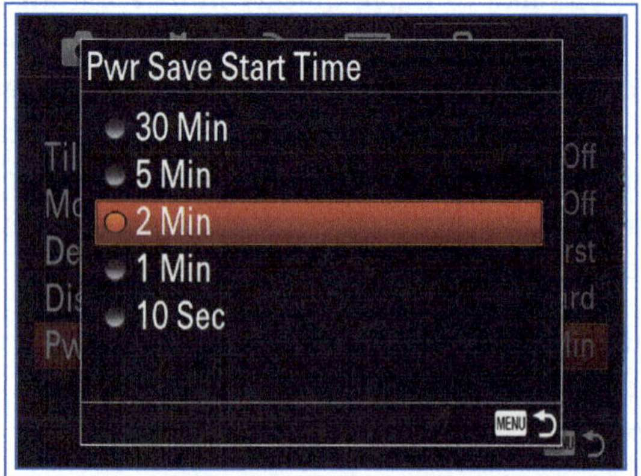

Figure 7-64. Power Save Start Time Menu Options Screen

You cannot turn the power-saving function off. However, the camera will not power off automatically when you are recording movies, when a slide show is playing, or when the camera is connected to a computer.

The setting you use depends on your habits and needs. In my case, I am usually well aware of the camera's status, and I like to use the maximum 30-minute period for this option so the camera does not power down just when I am about to use it again. I always have extra batteries available and I'm not too concerned if I have to replace the battery. If you are out in the field and running low on battery power, you might want to choose a shorter time for this option to conserve battery life.

PAL/NTSC Selector

This menu option appears only on cameras that are sold in areas that use the PAL video standard and that therefore use the 1080 50i video format rather than the 1080 60i format that is used in the United States, Canada, and other areas with the NTSC video standard. As I noted in the Introduction, I live in the United States and have the NTSC version of the RX10, so my information about this menu option is secondhand.

The 50i version of the camera, which has a "50i" label on the bottom, can be switched to record video with the NTSC standard, using the 60i format, using the PAL/NTSC Selector menu option. So, if you purchased your camera in Europe or another area where the PAL version is sold, you will have the option to record your videos in either the PAL (50i) or NTSC (60i) format. However, if, like me, you have the 60i (NTSC) version of the camera, you can record and play back video only in the NTSC formats.

If you have the PAL version of the camera, you should note that you cannot record NTSC video on a memory card that was previously formatted using the PAL system. If you try to do so, you will receive an error message. You will have to re-format the card with the PAL/NTSC Selector set to NTSC or use a different card that has been formatted under that system.

Next, I'll discuss the options on screen 3 of the Custom menu, shown in Figure 7-65.

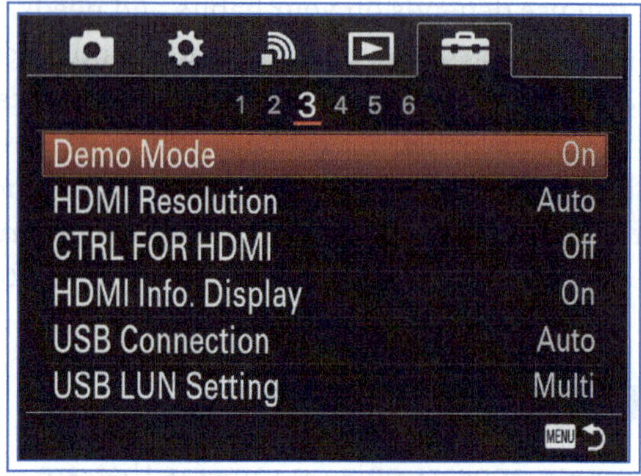

Figure 7-65. Screen 3 of Setup Menu

Demo Mode

The Demo Mode menu item automatically plays a movie if the camera has not had any controls operated for about one minute. This feature is designed for use by retail stores, so they can leave the camera turned on with a continuous demonstration on its screen. But you can use it for your own purposes, if you want to create a movie that demonstrates the camera's features for friends, for example, or if you just like the idea of having the camera play a movie when it's not otherwise occupied.

For this feature to be available for selection on the menu screen, as shown in Figure 7-65, the camera has to be plugged into AC power using an AC adapter. Otherwise, this line on the menu will be dimmed. (As noted in Chapter 1 and Appendix A, the charger that ships with the RX10 does not work as an AC adapter; you can purchase one from Sony as an optional accessory.)

When the Demo Mode option is turned on and the camera is in shooting mode, after one minute of inactivity the camera enters Demo Mode. At that point, the camera will automatically play a movie, which you have to provide. It cannot be just any movie.

The movie the camera will play in Demo Mode must be recorded in the AVCHD format, it must be protected using the Protect option on the Playback menu, and it must be the oldest AVCHD movie on the memory card. So, if you have a reason to use this option, you may want to use a fresh memory card and record a single AVCHD movie on the card, and then use the Protect function to protect it. When the movie plays, it plays audio as well as video, and it will keep repeating in a loop. To exit from Demo Mode, you can press the Center button or just turn the camera off.

HDMI Resolution

The HDMI Resolution menu item can be set to Auto, 1080p, or 1080i. This option controls how the camera displays images and videos on an HDTV. Ordinarily, the Auto setting will work best; the camera will set itself for the optimum display according to the resolution of the HDTV it is connected to. If you experience difficulties with that connection, you may be able to improve the image on the HDTV's screen by trying one of the other settings.

CTRL for HDMI

This menu option is of use only when you have connected the camera to an HDTV and you want to control the camera with the TV's remote control, which is possible in some situations. If you want to do that, set this option to On and follow the instructions for the TV and its remote control. This option is intended to be used when you connect the camera to a Sony Bravia model HDTV.

HDMI Information Display

This is an interesting feature, which I have not encountered before. It controls the behavior of the camera when you connect it to an HDTV set using an optional HDMI cable. However, unlike other HDMI-related menu options, this one does not control what happens when the camera is in playback mode, playing your images and videos on the HDTV. Instead, it controls what happens in shooting mode when the HDMI connection is active.

If this menu option is set to On, which is the default setting, then, when the camera is connected to an HDTV in shooting mode, the HDTV's screen displays exactly what you would see on the camera's display in that mode if the camera were not connected to the HDTV. With the On setting, the HDTV acts as a large, external monitor for the RX10, and the screen of the RX10 is blank. I use this setting a great deal myself, because this is how I capture screen shots for this book. Once the camera is connected, I can capture all of the shooting screens and menu screens of the camera, with a few exceptions for special settings that are not output through the HDMI port, such as the zebra stripes.

If this menu option is set to Off, then, when the camera is connected to an HDTV in shooting mode, the HDTV's screen displays only the image that is being viewed by the camera, with no shooting information displayed at all. If you press the Display button, nothing will happen on the TV; the view will not switch to another display with more information on it. However, at the same time, the RX10's screen continues to display all of the shooting information it normally would, including the image and whatever information is chosen by presses of the Display button.

You might use the Off setting when you have need to display images from the camera's shooting mode on a large HDTV screen, possibly at a wedding or other gathering, and not have the images cluttered or marred by any shooting information at all. For example, I have seen occasions where a camera is used to focus on an unsuspecting person in the audience, and that person's image suddenly appears on the large screen for everyone to see.

Also, this option is useful for video production when you need to output a "clean" video signal that does not include any shooting information from the camera. That signal could be used for recording to another medium, or for display on a large monitor being viewed by the production team.

With the On setting, you can press the Display button to show a screen with very minimal shooting information, but that screen still shows the basic information of aperture, shutter speed, exposure compensation, and ISO value at the very bottom of the screen. If you don't want even that minimal level of information to interfere with the video footage, choose the Off setting.

This setting does not change the behavior of the camera for playback of images; its only effect is for using the camera in shooting mode through an HDMI connection.

USB Connection

This menu item sets the technical standard that the camera uses for transferring images and videos to your computer using the USB cable. This option has three choices, as shown in Figure 7-66: Auto, Mass Storage, and MTP, which stands for Media Transfer Protocol, a standard developed by Microsoft for transferring media files over a USB connection.

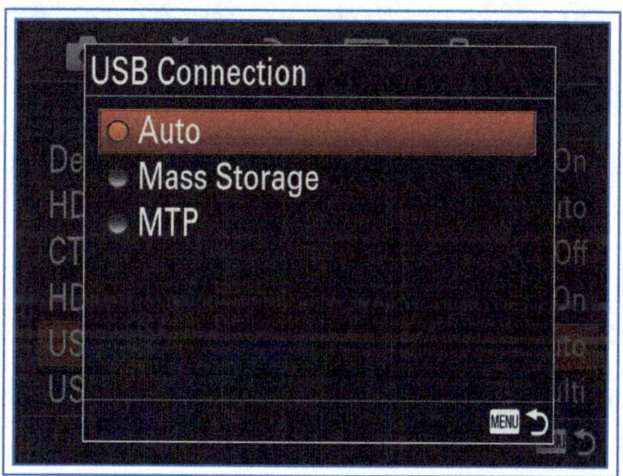

Figure 7-66. USB Connection Menu Options Screen

You ordinarily should select Auto, and the RX10 should detect which standard is used by the computer you are connecting the camera to. If the camera does not automatically select a standard and start transferring images, you can try one of the other settings to see if it works better than the Auto setting.

USB LUN Setting

This option is a technical one that should not often be used. LUN stands for logical unit number. This option has two possible settings—Multi or Single. Ordinarily, it should be set to Multi, the default. In particular, it should be set to Multi when the RX10 is connected to a Windows-based computer and you are using Sony's PlayMemories Home software to manage your images. If you ever encounter a problem with a USB connection to a computer, you can try the Single setting to see if it solves the problem.

The next options to be discussed are on screen 4 of the Setup menu, shown in Figure 7-67.

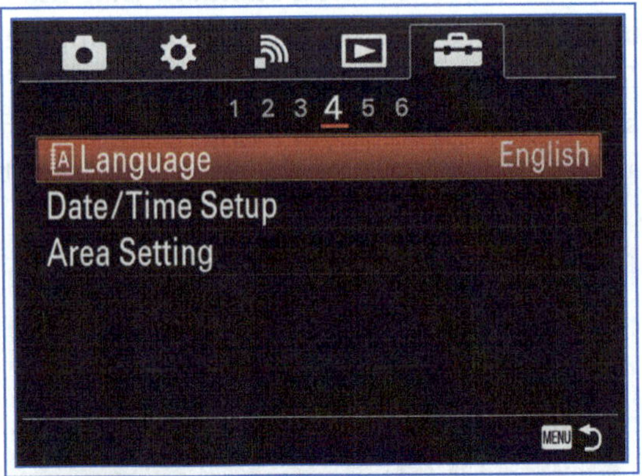

Figure 7-67. Screen 4 of Setup Menu

Language

This option gives you the choice of language for the display of commands and information on the camera's LCD screen.

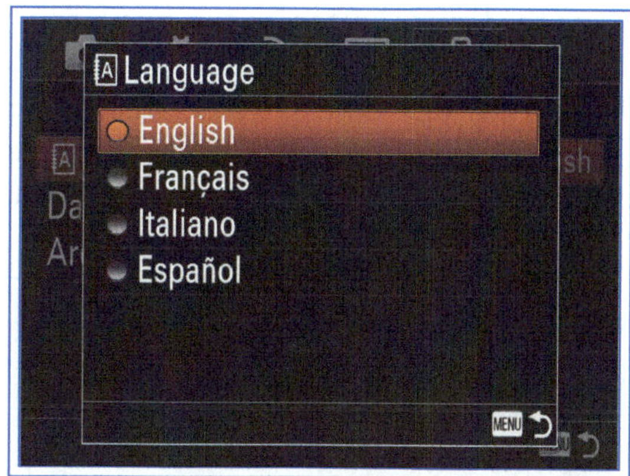

Figure 7-68. Language Selection Screen

Once you have selected this menu item, as shown in FIGURE 7-68, scroll through the language choices using the Control wheel or the direction buttons and press the Center button when your chosen language is highlighted.

DATE/TIME SETUP

I discussed this item in CHAPTER 1. When the camera is new or has not been used for a long time, it will prompt you to set the date and time and will display this menu option. If you want to call up these settings on your own, you can do so at any time.

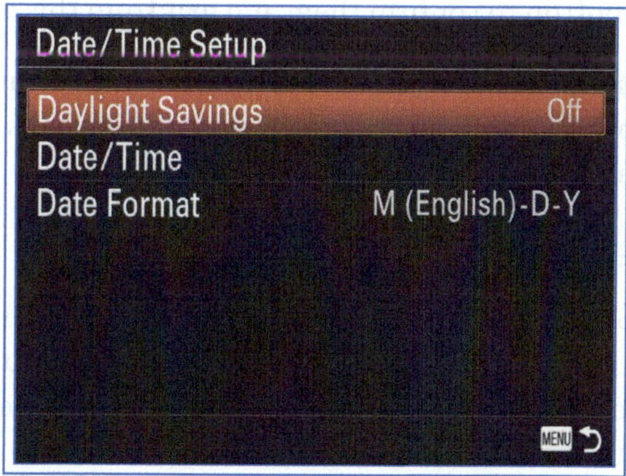

Figure 7-69. Date/Time Setup Menu Options Screen

When you press the Center button on this menu line, you will see a screen like that in FIGURE 7-69, which gives you the choice of adjusting Daylight Savings Time (On or Off), Date/Time, or Date Format. To adjust Date/Time, select that option and press the Center button. The camera will display a screen like that shown in FIGURE 7-70.

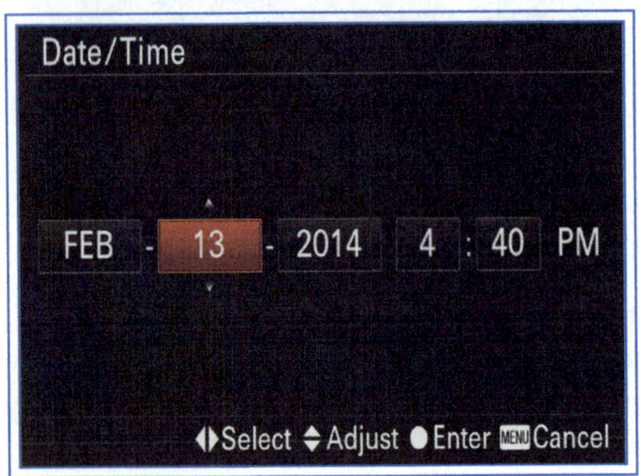

Figure 7-70. Date/Time Settings Screen

Scroll through the various options for setting Daylight Savings Time, month, day, year, and other items by turning the Control wheel or pressing the Left and Right buttons. As you reach each item, adjust its value by using the Up and Down buttons or by turning the Control dial. When all of the settings are correct, press the Center button to confirm them and exit from this screen.

You can also go back to the first menu screen and turn Daylight Savings Time on or off depending on the time of year, and you can choose a date format according to your preference.

Area Setting

The next option on screen 4 of the Setup menu, Area Setting, lets you select your current location so you can adjust the date and time for a different time zone when you are traveling. When you highlight this item and press the Center button, the camera displays the map shown in FIGURE 7-71.

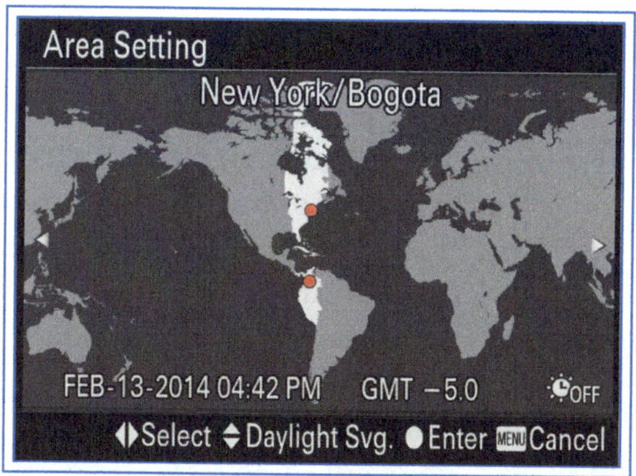

Figure 7-71. Area Setting Menu Screen

Turn the Control wheel or press the Left and Right buttons to move the light-colored highlight over the map until it covers the area of your current location, then press the Center button. The date and time will be adjusted for that location until you change the location again using this menu item.

The fifth screen of the Setup menu is shown in Figure 7-72.

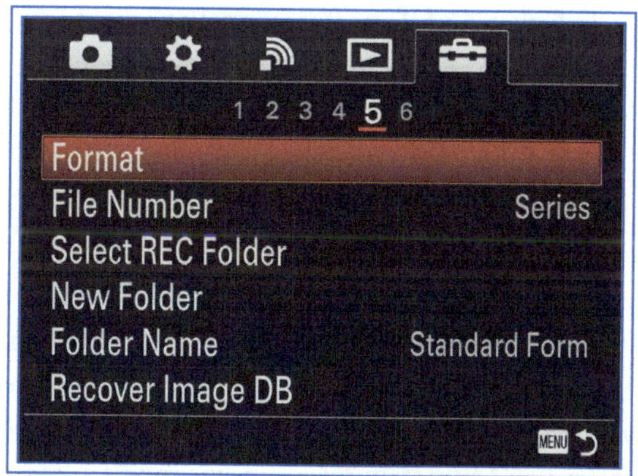

Figure 7-72. Screen 5 of Setup Menu

Format

The first option at the top of the fifth screen—Format—is an extremely important one. This command is used to prepare a new memory card with the appropriate data structure to store images and videos. The Format command also is useful when you want to wipe all the data off a card that has become full or when you have copied a card's images to your computer or other device. Choose this process only when you want or need to completely wipe all of the data from a memory card. When you select the Format option, as shown in FIGURE 7-73, the camera will warn you that all data currently on the card will be deleted if you proceed.

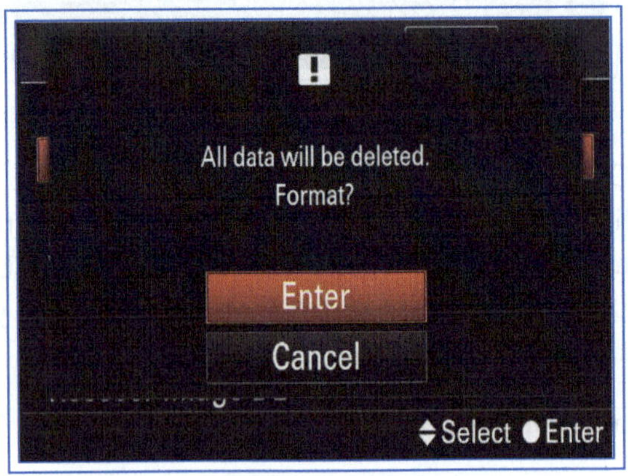

Figure 7-73. Format Confirmation Screen

If you reply by highlighting Enter and pressing the Center button to confirm, the camera will format the card that is in the camera and the result will be a card that is empty and properly formatted to store new images and videos recorded by the camera.

With this procedure, the camera will erase all images, including those that have been protected from accidental erasure with the Protect function on the Playback menu. It's a good idea to periodically save your images and videos to your computer or other device and re-format your memory card to keep it properly set up for recording new images and videos. It's also a good idea to use the Format command on any new memory card when you first insert it into the camera. Even though it likely will work without that procedure, it's best to make sure the card is set up with Sony's own particular method of formatting for the RX10.

File Number

This option controls the way the camera assigns numbers to your images and videos. There are two choices: Series and Reset, as shown in Figure 7-74.

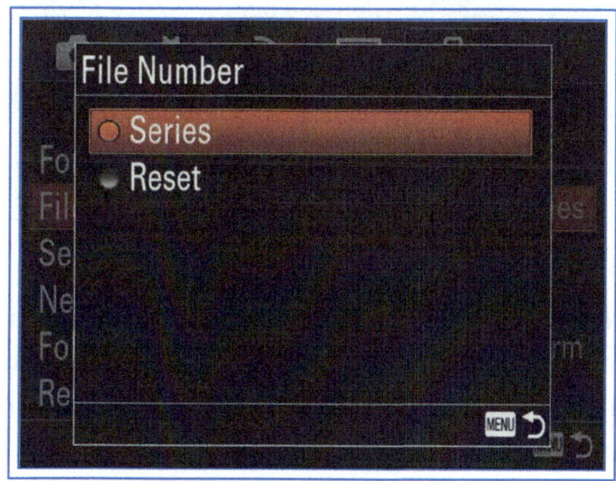

Figure 7-74. File Number Menu Options Screen

With Series, the camera continues numbering where it left off, even if you put a new memory card in the camera. For example, if you have 112 images on your first memory card, the last image likely will be numbered 100-0112: 100 for the folder number and 0112 for the image number. If you then switch to a new memory card with no images on it, the first image on that card will be numbered 100-0113 because the numbering scheme continues in the same sequence. If you choose Reset instead, the first image on the new card will be numbered 100-0001 because the camera resets the numbering to the first number.

Select REC Folder

When you select this item, the camera displays an orange bar with the name of the current folder, as shown in Figure 7-75.

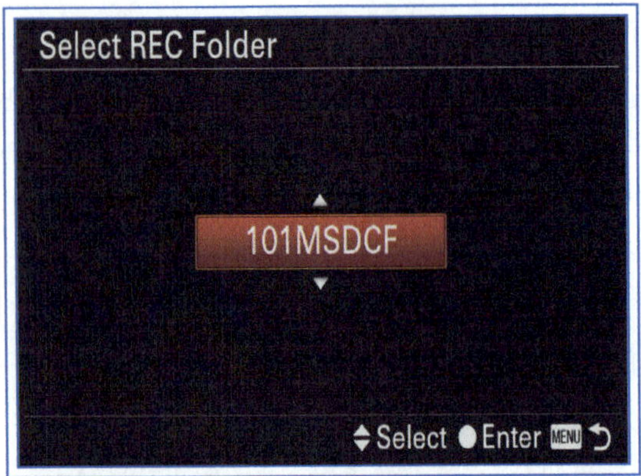

Figure 7-75. Select REC Folder Menu Screen

You can use the Up and Down buttons or turn the Control wheel to scroll to the name of another folder if one exists, so you can store future images and videos in that folder. It might be worthwhile to use this function if you are taking photos or movies for different purposes during the same outing. For example, if you are taking some photos for business and some for pleasure, you can create a new folder for the business-related shots (see the next menu item, below). The camera will then use that folder. Afterward, you can use the Select REC Folder option to select the folder where your personal images are stored and take more personal images that will be stored in that folder.

New Folder

This menu item lets you create a new folder on your memory card for storing images and videos. Highlight this item on the menu screen and press the Center button; you will then see a message announcing that a new folder has been created, as shown in Figure 7-76. Creating a new folder can be an excellent way to organize the images and videos from a particular shooting session. If you are going to view and process the files on your computer, it can be useful to have images from different locations arranged in different folders, for example.

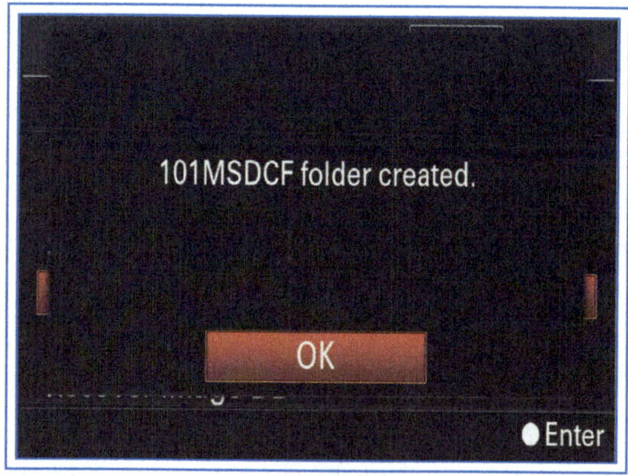

Figure 7-76. New Folder Option Confirmation Screen

Folder Name

This menu option gives you a choice of two methods for naming the folders used for storing still images on your memory card, as shown in Figure 7-77: Standard Form or Date Form. The Standard Form option uses the folder number, such as 100, 101, or higher, followed by the letters MSDCF. An example is 100MSDCF. If you choose Date Form, folder names will have the same 100 or higher number followed by the date, in a form such as 10040128 for a folder created on January 28, 2014, using only one digit to designate the year.

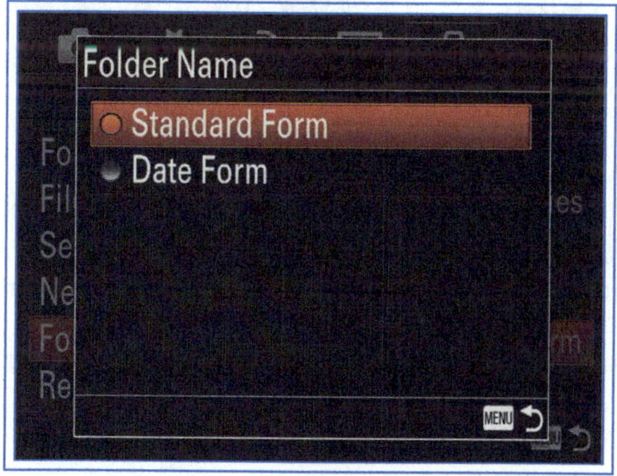

Figure 7-77. Folder Name Menu Options Screen

I find the date format confusing and hard to read, and I am used to the MSDCF format. If you use the date format, you will end up having a folder for every date on which you record still images. You may prefer having your image folders organized in that way so you can quickly locate images from a particular date. I prefer having fewer folders and organizing the images using software on my computer according to my own preferences.

Recover Image Database

This menu item activates the Recover Image Database function. If you select this option and press the Center button to confirm it on the next screen, as shown in Figure 7-78, the camera runs a check to test the integrity of the file system on the memory card.

This option displays automatically when you insert in the camera a new memory card or a card that contains images that were recorded in a different camera. I have never used this menu option, but if the camera is having difficulty reading the images on a card, using this option might recover the data.

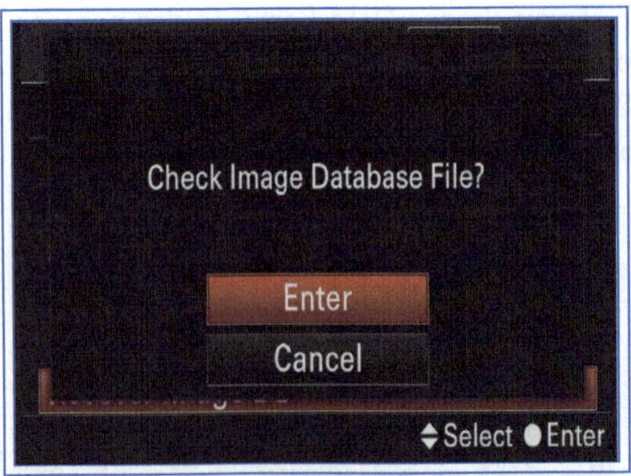

Figure 7-78. Recover Image Database Confirmation Screen

The sixth and final screen of the Setup menu is shown in Figure 7-79.

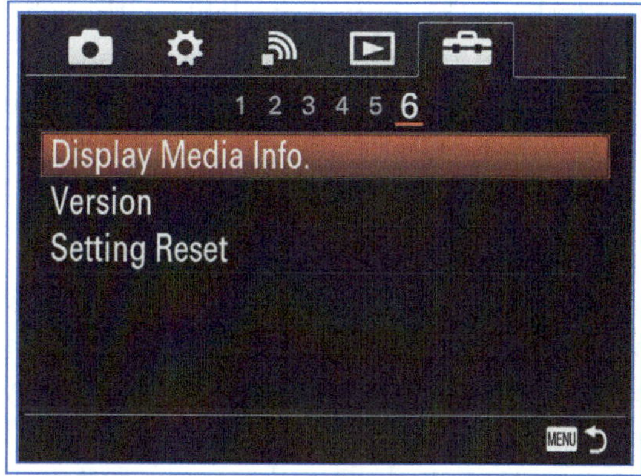

Figure 7-79. Screen 6 of Setup Menu

Display Media Info

The first item on the final Setup menu screen gives you another way to see how much storage space is remaining on the memory card that is currently in the camera. When you select Display Media Info and press the Center button, the camera displays a screen like that in Figure 7-80, with information about the number of still images and the hours and minutes of video that can be recorded using the current settings for Image Size, Quality, and video format.

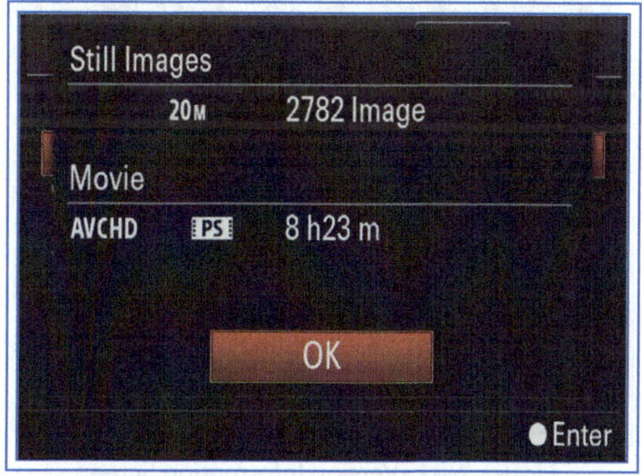

Figure 7-80. Display Media Info Screen

It may be nice to have this option available, although the number of images that can be recorded is also displayed on the detailed shooting screen, and the available video recording time appears on the video recording screen once a recording has been started.

VERSION

This option tells you the current version of the firmware in your camera. The RX10, like other cameras, is programmed at the factory with firmware, which is a set of electronically implanted computer instructions. These instructions control all aspects of the camera's operation, including the menu system, functioning of the controls, and in-camera image processing.

You may want to see what version is installed because the manufacturer may release an updated version of the firmware to fix problems or bugs in the system, provide minor enhancements, or, in some cases, provide major improvements, such as adding new shooting modes or menu options.

To determine the firmware version installed in your camera, highlight this menu option, then press the Center button, and the camera will display the version number, as shown in FIGURE 7-81.

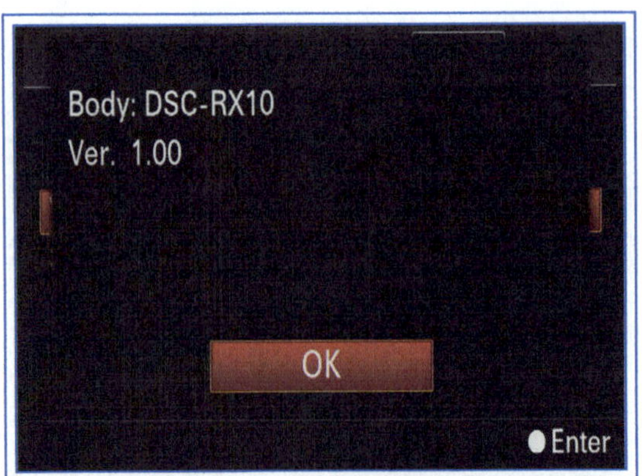

Figure 7-81. Version Information Screen

To see if firmware upgrades have been released, I recommend you visit Sony's support website at http://esupport.sony.com. Find the link for Drivers and Software, then the link for Cyber-shot Cameras, and then a link to any updated version for the DSC-RX10. The site will provide instructions for downloading and installing the new firmware.

Setting Reset

This final option on the Setup menu is useful when you want to reset some or all of the camera's settings to their original (default, or factory) values. This action can be helpful if you have been experimenting with different settings and you find that something is not working as expected.

When you select this item, the camera displays two choices: Camera Settings Reset and Initialize, as shown in Figure 7-82.

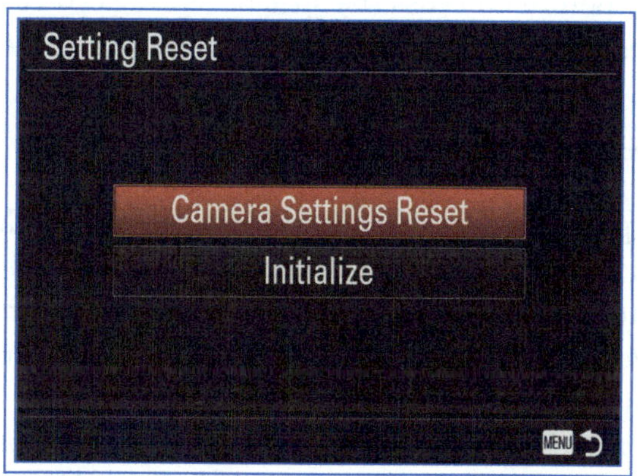

Figure 7-82. Setting Reset Menu Options Screen

If you choose Initialize, the camera resets all major settings to their original values and deletes registered data, such as faces. With Camera Settings Reset, only the values from the Shooting menu are reset.

CHAPTER 8: Motion Pictures

You may have purchased the Sony RX10 because of its advanced features for capturing still images, but you should not overlook the camera's options for recording movies. The RX10's video abilities are quite strong for a compact camera; they provide you with an excellent level of flexibility in recording video, including several features more common in professional equipment. Before I discuss the specific settings you can make for your movies, I'll begin with a brief overview of the process.

Movie-Making Overview

The basic procedure for making videos with the RX10 can be reduced to four words: "Push the red button." (That is, the red Movie button to the right of the viewfinder on the camera's back.) Having a dedicated movie recording button makes things easy for users of this camera. Anytime you see a reason to take some video footage, just press and release the red button while aiming at your subject, and you are likely to get decent results. You do not need to worry about making any particular settings, if you have set the camera to one of the more automatic shooting modes, such as Intelligent Auto or Scene. To stop recording, press the red button again. (If you prefer not to run the risk of recording unwanted movies by pressing the red button accidentally, you can change the button's operation, so it activates movie recording only when the camera is in Movie mode, as discussed in CHAPTER 7.)

If you're mainly a still photographer and not that interested in movie-making, you don't need to read any further. Be aware that the red button exists, and if a newsworthy event starts to unfold before your eyes, you can get some excellent footage to post on YouTube or elsewhere with a minimum of effort.

But for RX10 users who want to delve further into their camera's excellent motion picture capabilities, there is considerably more information to discuss.

The RX10, like most cameras in its class, has built-in limitations that prevent it from recording any sequence longer than about 29 minutes (15 minutes for the MP4 HD format). You can, of course, record multiple sequences adding up to any length depending on the amount of storage space available on your memory cards.

If you plan to record a significant amount of HD video, you should get one of the highest-capacity and fastest memory cards you can find. For example, a 16 GB card can hold about 70 minutes of the highest quality of AVCHD video, about 90 minutes of lower-quality AVCHD video, or about 2 hours 45 minutes of MP4 HD video. (I will discuss these video formats later in this chapter.)

If you want to fit both still images and HD video sequences on a card, you might be better off with a 32 GB card or even an SDXC card with a capacity of up to 128 GB. (As noted in Chapter 1, there are 256 GB cards available at this writing, but they are very expensive.) You should try to get a card rated at Class 6 or higher, so it will have the necessary speed for recording HD video. I like to use a card rated at Class 10; that speed helps not only with recording video but also with shooting continuous still images at the best possible rate.

Details of Settings for Shooting Movies

As I noted above, the one step that is needed for recording a movie with the RX10 is to press the red Movie button. However, there are numerous settings that affect the way the camera records a movie when that button is pressed. I will discuss four categories of settings: (1) the movie-related selections you make on the Shooting menu; (2) the position of the mode dial on top of the camera; (3) the other selections you make on the Shooting menu and other menus; and (4) the settings you make with the camera's physical controls. I will discuss these four areas in turn.

Movie-Related Shooting Menu Options

First, I will discuss the movie-related options on the Shooting menu, because those options control the format and several other important settings for all movies you record with the RX10. I discussed this menu in Chapter 4, but I did not provide details about the movie-oriented options in that chapter.

As noted above, you can press the Movie button to start a video recording any time and in any shooting mode as long as the Movie Button option on the fourth screen of the Custom menu is set to Always. Because of this ability to shoot movies in any shooting mode, you can always change the settings for movie recording using the Shooting menu, no matter what shooting mode the camera is set to. I will discuss each item on the Shooting menu that has an effect on your shooting of videos.

At this point, I am going to discuss the Shooting menu options that apply only to movies; later in this chapter, I will discuss the options on this menu and other menus that affect movies as well as still images, such as White Balance, ISO, Creative Style, Picture Effect, and others.

File Format

The first item on screen 2 of the Shooting menu, File Format, gives you a choice of the two available movie recording formats on the RX10—AVCHD and MP4, as shown in Figure 8-1.

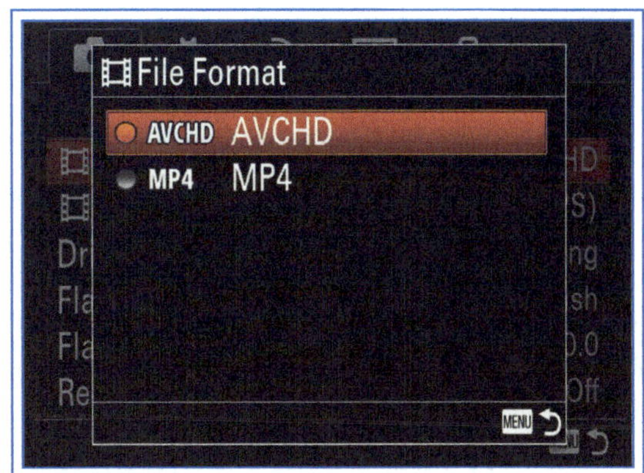

Figure 8-1. File Format Menu Options Screen

If you want the highest-possible quality of video for viewing on an HDTV set, you should choose AVCHD. This format, developed jointly by Sony and Panasonic, has become increasingly common in advanced digital cameras. It provides excellent quality, and movies recorded in this format on the RX10 can be used to create Blu-ray discs.

However, files recorded in the AVCHD format can be complicated to edit on a computer. In fact, just finding the AVCHD video files on a memory card can be a challenge. When you take a memory card from the RX10 camera and insert it into a card reader for viewing on your computer, you can find the still-image files within the folder labeled DCIM and then within sub-folders with names such as 100MSDCF. The AVCHD files, however, are not within that folder; they are within a different folder named PRIVATE. Inside that folder you will find another one called AVCHD, and within that one another one called BDMV. Open that folder and you will see more files or folders, including a folder called STREAM. With the card whose contents I am looking at now on my Macintosh, that folder contains numerous files with the extension .mts. Those .mts files are the actual AVCHD files that can be edited with compatible software packages, such as Adobe Premiere Pro. (You don't have to worry about finding the files if you connect your camera to the computer using the USB cable or the Send to Computer menu option, only if you use a card reader, as I do.)

If you want to record movies with excellent video quality but in a video format that is easier to edit with a computer, you can choose MP4. The MP4 format is compatible with Apple Computer's QuickTime software, and the files can be edited with various software programs, including QuickTime, iMovie, Windows Movie Maker, and many others. The MP4 files also are found in a different folder on your memory card, not within the DCIM folder. On my memory card, the MP4 files are located in a folder named 100ANV01, which is inside a folder named MP_ROOT.

Record Setting

The Record Setting item on the Movie menu lets you set another quality-related option for recording video.

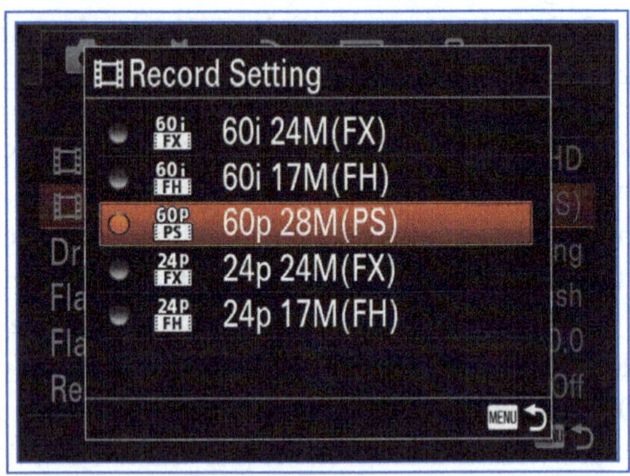

Figure 8-2. Record Setting Menu Options Screen

(The accent is on the second syllable of "Record.") The choices for this item are different depending on whether you choose AVCHD or MP4 for File Format. (I will be discussing these formats for cameras sold in the United States and other areas that use the NTSC video system, which uses the 1080 60i format. Cameras sold in Europe and other areas that use the PAL video system will have different options, although they can be switched to use

NTSC video formats using the PAL/NTSC Selector option on the Setup menu, as discussed in Chapter 7.)

If you choose AVCHD, the five choices for Record Setting are 60i 24M(FX), 60i 17M(FH), 60p 28M(PS), 24p 24M(FX), and 24p 17M(FH), as shown in Figure 8-2. In each case, the number 60 or 24 stands for the number of video fields or frames recorded per second. (Cameras sold in countries using PAL video rather than NTSC use 50i and 50p formats instead of 60i and 60p.)

60i and 60p Video Formats

First, I will discuss the three formats using 60 fields, or frames per second. The letter that comes after the number 60, either "i" or "p," stands for interlaced or progressive. With interlaced video, the camera records 60 fields per second; a field is equal to one-half of a frame, and the two halves are interlaced together to form 30 full frames. The video frame rate of about 30 frames per second (fps) is the standard video playback rate in the United States.

If the letter is "p," for progressive, that means the camera records 60 full frames per second, which yields higher quality than interlaced video. The 60 frames are later translated into 30 frames for playback at the standard rate of 30 fps. However, if your video-editing software has this capability, you can play back your 60p footage in slow motion at one-half the normal speed and still maintain full HD quality. This possibility exists because, as noted above, the 60p footage is recorded with twice the number of full frames as 60i footage, so the quality of the video does not suffer if it is played back at one-half speed. (With other video formats, playback at half speed will appear choppy or jerky because not enough frames were recorded to play back smoothly at that speed.) So, if you think you may want to slow down your footage significantly for playback, you should choose the 60p setting.

The next number-letter combination, either 28M, 24M, or 17M, provides the "bit rate," or volume, of video information that is recorded—either 24 megabits per second or 17 megabits per second. Not surprisingly, the higher-numbered settings provide greater quality at the cost of using more storage capacity on the memory card and requiring greater computer resources to edit.

The final designations, FH, FX, and PS, are proprietary labels used by Sony for these various qualities of video. They have no particular meanings; they are just labels for various levels of video quality—PS is the highest, then FX, and then FH.

Choose 60p 28M if you want the highest quality (including slow-motion capability), 60i 24M for excellent quality, or 60i 17M for excellent quality that takes up fewer resources.

24p Video Formats

If you select either of the 24p video formats, your video will be recorded at 24 fps. This is not a substantially slower rate than for the 60i and 60p formats, because the video playback rate in the United States is about 30 fps, and the 60i and 60p formats are converted to about 30 fps for playback. The 24p rate is considered by some people to be more "cinematic" than the 60i and 60p formats. This may be because 24 fps is the standard speed for movie cameras that shoot with film. My personal practice is to use the 60p format, but if you find that 24p suits your purposes better, you have that option with the RX10.

MP4 Formats

If, instead of AVCHD, you choose MP4 for File Format, you are presented with just two choices for Record Setting: 1440 x 1080 12M and VGA 3M, as shown in FIGURE 8-3.

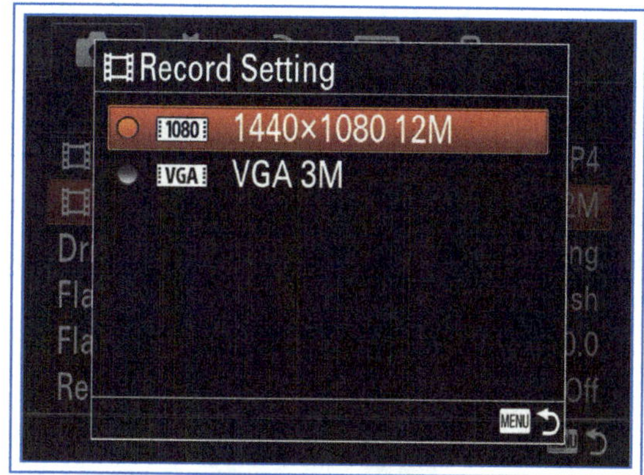

Figure 8-3. Record Setting Options for MP4 Format

The numbers 1440 x 1080 represent the horizontal and vertical pixels in the image. An image with 1440 pixels horizontally and 1080 vertically is considered to be widescreen. The other choice, listed as VGA, has only 640 x 480 pixels; this format produces images in the shape of traditional computer monitors, which are often designated as VGA, for video graphics array. As you can see from the last numbers for these settings, 12M and 3M, they have lower data rates than any of the AVCHD settings. Therefore, the quality is not as great as for AVCHD, but the MP4 formats take up less storage space than AVCHD and, as noted above, are easier to manipulate with a computer and to send by e-mail.

If you choose the MP4 file format, I recommend you always select the 1440 x 1080 setting, because the quality of VGA video is quite low. You should use VGA only if you have a shortage of space on your memory card or you are recording the video for a purpose that does not require high quality, such as making an inventory of household possessions.

You also should recall that because of a 2 GB limitation on file size, the RX10 can record only 15 minutes of MP4 video in the HD format (1440 x 1080) in one continuous file. Of course, you can record any number of 15-minute segments, up to the storage limits of your memory card.

Movie (Exposure Mode)

The next movie-related item, on screen 6 of the Shooting menu and somewhat confusingly called simply Movie, is one of the most important options for video shooting with the RX10, because it gives you control over aperture and shutter speed. This item is available for selection only when the camera's mode dial is set to Movie mode, as shown in FIGURE 8-4.

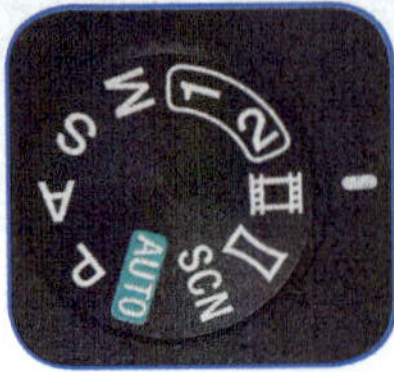

Figure 8-4. Mode Dial Set to Movie Mode

In all other shooting modes, this menu option is dimmed and cannot be selected.

When the camera is in Movie mode, the Movie option on the menu lets you select an exposure mode for shooting movies. If you have the Mode Dial Guide option turned on through screen 2 of the Setup menu, the choices for the Movie menu item, as shown in FIGURE 8-5, will appear automatically when you select Movie mode with the mode dial and then press the Center button after the initial mode dial guide screen appears.

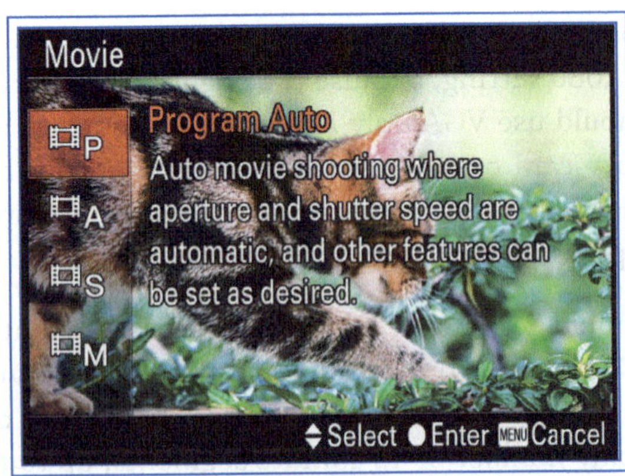

Figure 8-5. Movie Menu Options Screen

If the Mode Dial Guide option is not active, you get to this screen by selecting Movie from the Shooting menu. With the mode dial set to Movie mode, Navigate to screen 6 of the Shooting menu, select the third item, Movie, and this screen will appear with its four options: Program Auto, Aperture Priority, Shutter Priority, and Manual Exposure, as shown in FIGURE 8-5.

Move through these choices by turning the Control wheel or Control dial, or by pressing the Up and Down buttons.

You also can call up this screen of four Movie options by assigning Shoot Mode to the Function menu. If you do that, then, when the mode dial is set to Movie, you can press the Function button to activate the Function menu, scroll to the Shoot Mode item, and select your choice of Movie exposure mode.

Following are details about the behavior of the RX10 when shooting movies with each of these settings.

Program Auto

With the Program Auto setting, highlighted in FIGURE 8-5, the RX10 handles video recording the same way it does when it is set to any of the more advanced modes for still photography—Program, Aperture Priority, Shutter Priority, or Manual exposure. The camera sets the aperture and shutter speed according to its metering system, and it uses several settings from the Shooting menu that carry over to video recording, including ISO, White Balance, Metering Mode, Face Detection, and DRO. In this mode, the camera can set the aperture as narrow as f/16.0. In addition, it can use the unusually fast shutter speeds that are available in Movie mode, as fast as 1/12800 second. In normal conditions, the camera will not use a shutter speed slower than 1/30 second, 1/50 second, or 1/60 second, depending on the settings for File Format and Record Setting. It can use a slightly slower speed if you turn on the Auto Slow Shutter option, discussed later in this chapter.

With one caveat, noted below, I don't recommend using the Program setting for the movie exposure mode. It doesn't provide any options beyond those that are available when the camera is set to a still-shooting mode, such as Intelligent Auto, Program, Aperture Priority, or Shutter Priority. And it has the disadvantage that the mode dial must be set to the Movie mode. In that mode, you cannot shoot still images; if you press the shutter button, you will see an error message. So, if you want to shoot movies with the camera making all of the exposure decisions for you, I recommend that you set the camera to the Intelligent Auto or P position on the mode dial. With that setup, you have the option of taking still images with the settings you want, and you still can press the red Movie button at any time to record a video.

The one exception to this recommendation is if you use the Movie Button option on the third screen of the Custom menu to lock out the functioning of the Movie button unless the camera is set to Movie mode. You might want to do that to avoid accidentally recording a movie by pressing the Movie button inadvertently. If you have made that setting, then, of course, you cannot start recording a movie unless the camera is set to Movie mode. In that situation, you may want to have the Movie (exposure mode) menu option set to Program Auto, so you can turn the mode dial to Movie mode and start recording a movie with automatic exposure in effect. You also could set one of the two Memory Recall slots on the mode dial to call up Movie mode with the Program Auto setting, for quick access to this setting.

Aperture Priority

With this setting for Movie mode, shown in Figure 8-6, you are able to set the aperture, just as in the same-named mode for shooting still images, and the camera will set the shutter speed based on the exposure metering.

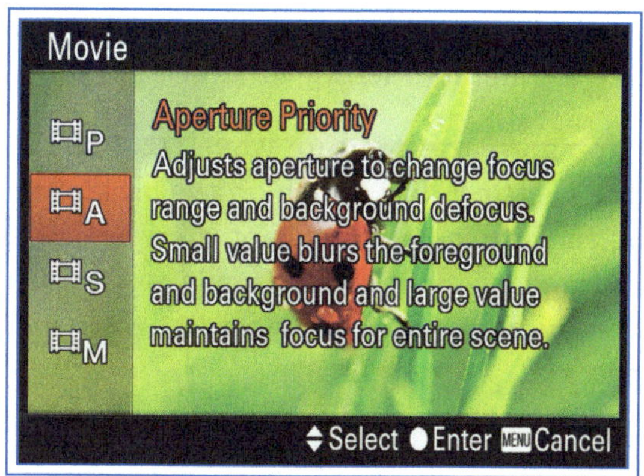

Figure 8-6. Aperture Priority Setting for Movie Option

You can set the aperture anywhere from the fully open f/2.8 to the most narrow f/16.0. However, as with the Program Auto exposure mode, discussed above, the camera will not use shutter speeds slower than 1/30 second (1/60 second for 60i or 60p settings) unless you turn on the Auto Slow Shutter option, discussed later in this chapter.

One excellent feature of the RX10 is that you can adjust the aperture during a video recording. This may not be something you need to do often, but it can be useful in some situations. For example, you may be recording at a location with a variety of subjects, such as a garden show, and at some point you may want to open the aperture wide to achieve a blurred background as you focus on a small plant or other object. Afterward, you may want to close the aperture down to a narrow value to achieve a broad depth of field to keep a large area in focus.

Also, you can use the aperture setting to accomplish a smooth fadeout of the scene. For example, in normal indoor conditions, you may start with the aperture set to f/2.8 and ISO set to 200, with Auto Slow Shutter turned off. Press the Movie button to start recording. When you're ready, start turning the aperture ring smoothly to the f/16.0 setting. You should get a nice fadeout to black. In brighter conditions, you may need to turn on the ND

Filter on screen 3 of the Shooting menu, and you may need to reduce ISO to its minimum setting for movies, which is 125.

If you plan to adjust the aperture while recording a movie, you should set the aperture click switch on the back of the lens to its Off position, so the clicking sounds of the aperture ring will not be recorded. In addition, you will be able to turn the ring more smoothly to achieve a pleasing transition with the closing (or opening) aperture.

Shutter Priority

The Shutter Priority exposure mode for movies, shown in Figure 8-7, lets you set the shutter speed using the Control dial, and the camera will set the aperture.

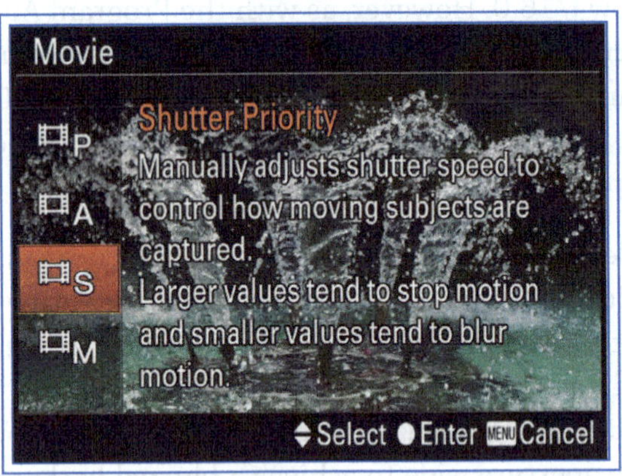

Figure 8-7. Shutter Priority Setting for Movie Option

Unlike the situation with the Aperture Priority exposure mode for movies, in which the camera normally will not set the shutter speed slower than 1/30 second (or 1/60 second for 60i or 60p video formats), you are able to set the shutter speed as slow as 1/4 second in this mode, even if Auto Slow Shutter is turned off. You can select any shutter speed from that rate all the way to the super-fast maximum shutter speed for movies, which is 1/12800 second. Of course, to expose your video normally at a shutter speed of 1/12800 second, you must have bright lighting or a high ISO setting, or both. Using a super-fast (or even moderately fast) shutter speed for video can yield a crisper appearance for your shots, especially when there is considerable movement in them, as when shooting sports or other fast-moving events. In addition, having these very fast shutter speeds gives the camera considerable flexibility when recording video in bright conditions.

With the slower shutter speeds, particularly those below the normal video speed of 1/60 second (equivalent to 60 fps), the footage can become somewhat blurry with the appearance of smearing, particularly with panning motions. If you are shooting a scene in which you want to have a drifting, dreamy appearance that looks like motion underwater, this option may be appropriate. You will not be able to achieve good lip sync at the slower shutter speeds, so this technique would not work well for realistic recordings of people talking or singing.

One interesting point is that you can preview this effect on the camera's display even before you press the Movie button to start recording. If you have the shutter speed set to 1/4 second in Movie mode, you will see any action on the screen looking blurry as if it had already been recorded with this slow shutter speed. (Note that the Live View Display option on screen 2 of the Custom menu is forced to the Setting Effect On option in Movie mode, and you cannot change it.)

With the Shutter Priority exposure mode for movies, you also can achieve a fadeout effect, as with Aperture Priority mode, discussed above. Just turn the Control dial smoothly to increase the shutter speed to its fastest speed of 1/12800 second, and the scene may go black, depending on the lighting conditions. You may need to turn on the ND Filter to achieve full darkness.

Manual Exposure

The last setting for the Movie item, shown in Figure 8-8, gives you more complete control over the exposure of your videos.

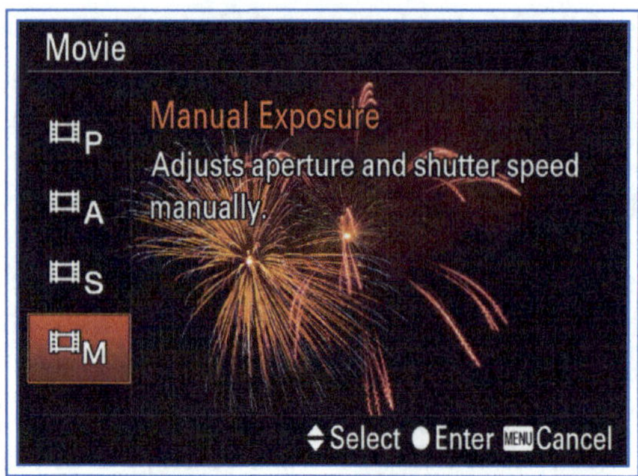

Figure 8-8. Manual Exposure Setting for Movie Option

Just as with the Manual exposure mode for shooting stills, you can adjust both the aperture and the shutter speed to achieve your desired effect. With video shooting, you can adjust the aperture from f/2.8 to f/16.0, and you can adjust shutter speed from 1/12800 second to 1/4 second. Using these settings, you can create effects such as fades to and from black as well as similar fades to and from white.

For example, if you begin a recording in normal indoor lighting using settings of 1/60 second at f/3.2 with ISO set to 800, you can start recording the scene, and, when you want to fade out, start turning the Control dial slowly to the right, increasing the shutter speed smoothly until it reaches 1/12800 second. Depending on how bright the lighting is, the result may be complete blackness. Of course, you can reverse this process to fade in from black.

If you want to fade to white, here is one possible scenario. Suppose you are recording video with shutter speed set to 1/400 second and aperture to f/2.8 at ISO 3200. When you want to start a fade to white, turn the Control dial smoothly to the left until the shutter speed decreases all the way to 1/4 second. In fairly normal lighting conditions, as in my office as I write this, the result will be a fade to a bright white screen.

There are, of course, many other uses for Manual Exposure mode when recording videos, such as shooting "day for night" footage, in which you underexpose the scene by using a fast shutter speed, narrow aperture, or both, to turn day into night for creative purposes. Also, you might want to use Manual Exposure mode when you are recording a scene in which the lighting may change, but you do not want the exposure to change. In other words, for creative purposes, you may want some areas to remain in the dark and some to be unusually bright, rather than have the camera automatically adjust the exposure. In some cases, having a constant exposure setting can be preferable to having the scene's brightness change as the metering system adjusts the exposure.

Note that you can set ISO to Auto ISO with the Manual Exposure setting if you want. With the Auto ISO setting, you can maintain a constant aperture and shutter speed, but the camera will adjust exposure using the ISO setting, to the extent that it can. You might want to use that setup if you need to maintain a narrow aperture to have a large depth of field.

SteadyShot (Movies)

The second SteadyShot item on screen 6 of the Shooting menu, shown in FIGURE 8-9, is different from the SteadyShot (Stills) item above it.

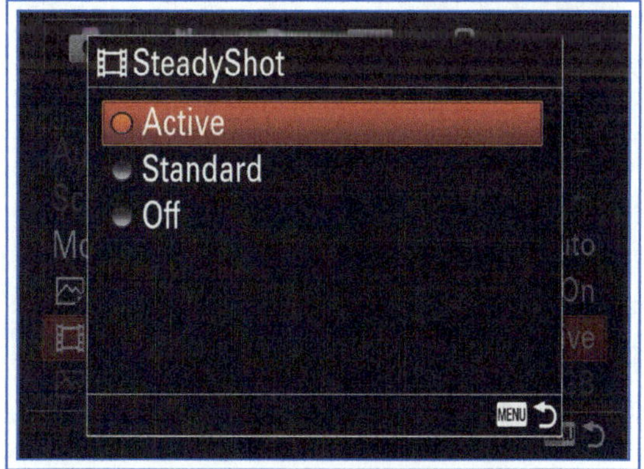

Figure 8-9. SteadyShot Menu Options Screen for Movies

(The Movies and Stills designations are indicated by icons on the menu—a movie film icon for Movies and a mountain/landscape icon for Stills.)

The SteadyShot (Movies) setting offers three options: Off, Standard, and Active, unlike the Stills version, which is limited to being turned on or off. With the Movies version, if you select Standard, the camera uses the same optical stabilization system used for shooting stills. If you select Active, the camera also uses an additional electronic stabilizing system that can compensate for unwanted camera movement to some extent. With this feature, the camera will crop out parts of the image at the edges to compensate for the required processing of the image.

If you would like to see the difference in the cropping of the video frame with and without the Active setting for SteadyShot, here is an easy way to do that. Assign SteadyShot (Movies) to one of the control buttons, such as the Custom button, using the Custom Key Settings option on screen 4 of the Custom menu. Then, aim the camera at a scene with a variety of items and press the Movie button to start recording a video. While it is recording, press the Custom button to call up the SteadyShot (Movies) menu option.

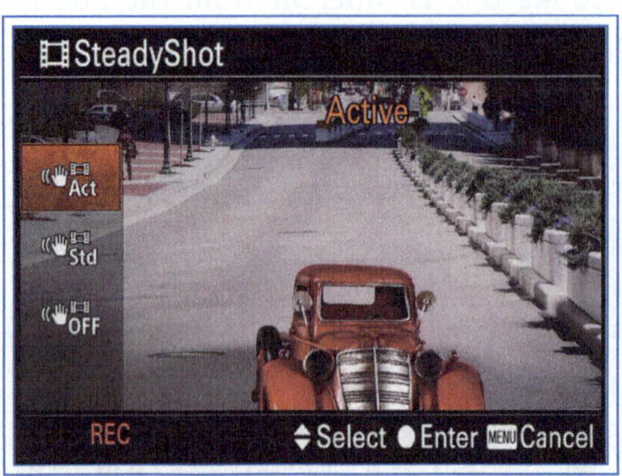

Figure 8-10. SteadyShot Menu Options Screen During Movie Recording

While that option's screen is visible, as seen in FIGURE 8-10, press the Down button to move from the Active setting at the top to the Standard or Off setting. You will immediately see the difference in the cropping of the video frame as the setting is changed.

If you are using a tripod, as I recommend for all movie shooting whenever possible, you probably should set this SteadyShot option to Off. If you are hand-holding the camera, I advise you to use the Active setting. I would use the Standard setting only if you find that the Active setting does not provide good results or if you object to the cropping that results from using this setting.

Auto Slow Shutter

The next movie-related option, found on screen 7 of the Shooting menu, is Auto Slow Shutter, which can be turned either on or off. When this option is turned on and the RX10 is recording a movie using automatic exposure, the camera will automatically use a slower shutter speed than normal if the lighting is too dim to achieve a proper exposure otherwise.

The details of this option depend on the settings for File Format and Record Setting on screen 2 of the Shooting menu. If File Format is set to AVCHD and Record Setting to a 60i or 60p setting, then the camera normally will not use a shutter speed slower than 1/60 second. (This makes sense, because, in order to record 60 fields or frames per second with good quality, a shutter speed of 1/60 second naturally is needed.) If Auto Slow Shutter is on, the camera can use a shutter speed as slow as 1/30 second.

If File Format is set to AVCHD and Record Setting is at one of the 24p settings, the camera ordinarily will use a shutter speed no slower than 1/50 second, but it will go down to 1/25 second with Auto Slow Shutter turned on. If File Format is set to MP4, the slowest shutter speed available without this option is 1/30 second. With the option turned on, the camera can use a shutter speed as slow as 1/15 second.

There are a couple of limitations to this setting. First, even with this menu option turned on, the automatic use of a slower shutter speed will take place only when the RX10 is set to a movie exposure mode in which the camera sets the shutter speed. The only movie exposure modes in which the camera sets the shutter speed are Program Auto and Aperture Priority. In addition, for the Auto Slow Shutter option to work, ISO must be set to Auto ISO.

The use of an unusually slow shutter speed can have a negative effect on your video footage, which may have a slurred or blurry appearance because the shutter speed may not be fast enough to keep up with the motion in the scene. But, if you are recording in a dimly lighted area, this option can help you achieve properly exposed footage, so it is worth considering in that situation.

Audio Recording

The Audio Recording item on the Shooting menu, shown in FIGURE 8-11, can be set either on or off.

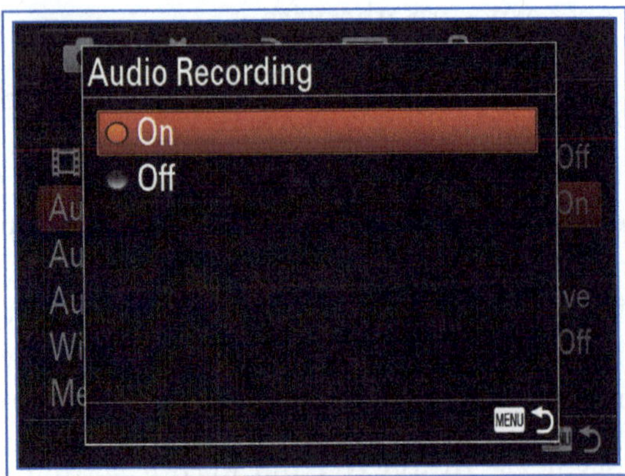

Figure 8-11. Audio Recording Menu Options Screen

If you are certain you won't need the sound recorded by the camera, then you can turn this option off. I never turn it off, because you can always turn down the volume of the recorded sound when playing the video, or if you are editing the video on a computer, you can delete the sound and replace it as needed—but you can never recapture the original audio after the fact.

Audio Recording Level

This option is available for selection only when the mode dial is set to Movie mode. If you record movies by pressing the Movie button in any other shooting mode, the camera will set the level for recording sound, and you cannot control it. In Movie mode, you can control the recording sound level using this menu option.

When you select this option, the camera displays a screen like that in FIGURE 8-12, which includes a scale with values from 0 to 31. While the scale is highlighted by the orange box, use the Control wheel, Control dial, or Left and Right arrows to select your desired value on the scale. If you highlight the Reset block and press the Center button, the level will be reset to the default value of 26.

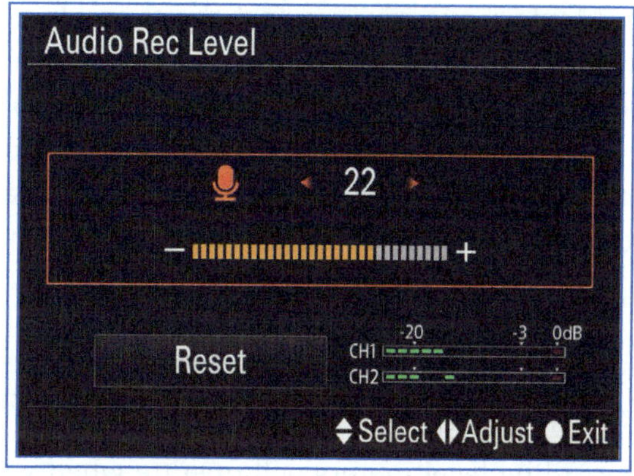

Figure 8-12. Audio Recording Level Adjustment Screen

Once the adjustment is made, press the Center button to exit to the live view. The new setting will be reflected in the behavior of the volume meters on the screen, when those meters are displayed, as shown in FIGURE 8-13. The meters will be displayed only when the Audio Level Display option is turned on through screen 1 of the Custom menu. If that menu option is turned on, the meters will appear on the screen during video recording in any shooting mode and they also will appear on the screen before the recording begins when the camera is in Movie mode.

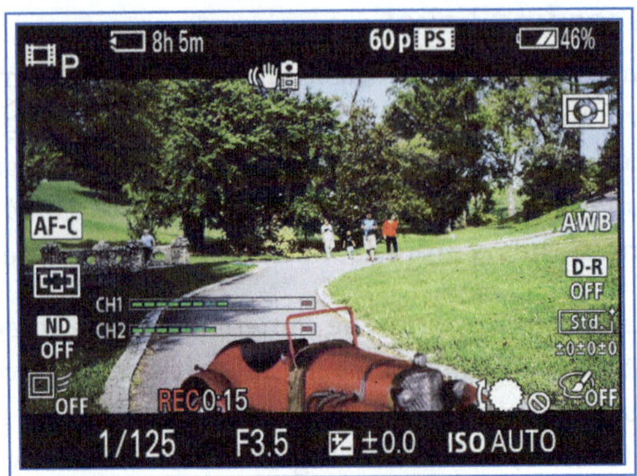

Figure 8-13. Recording Level Meters on Screen

When this screen is shown, these meters will react to sounds you make, so, in Movie mode, you can test the sound level before the recording starts. For example, if you are recording an interview, you can ask your subject to speak normally to test the level. You should try to adjust the level so the green bars never extend all the way to the right sides of the meters; if the bars reach into the red zones, the result is likely to be distorted sound. You should try to keep the ends of the bars from going beyond the -3 dB levels.

No matter what level is set, the camera uses a limiter—an electronic circuit that keeps volume from getting excessively loud.

The audio recording level meters will operate when you are using the built-in microphone or when using an external audio source, as discussed in Appendix A.

Audio Out Timing

With this option, you can set the timing for the output of audio through headphones, when you are monitoring the sound being recorded for a movie. The two possible settings are Live or Lip Sync, as shown in Figure 8-14.

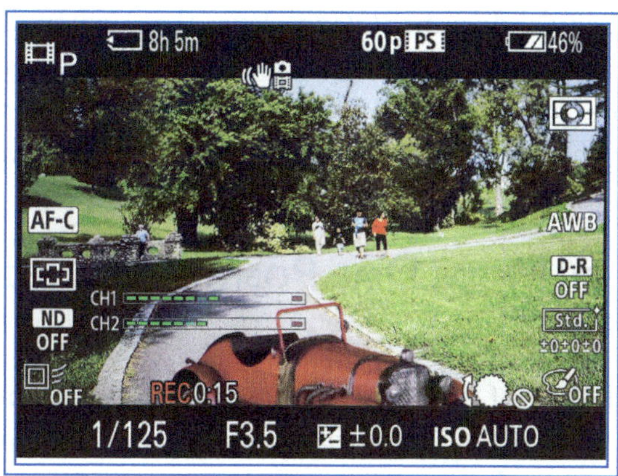

Figure 8-14. Audio Out Timing Menu Options Screen

If you choose the default setting of Live, the sound is sent through the headphones jack immediately, with no delay. If you choose the Lip Sync setting, the camera delays the sound by a small amount to account for the delay caused by the camera's processing and display of the video signal.

I have not noticed a significant difference between these two settings. If you ever notice a gap between the sound and video signals as you monitor a recording using headphones, you can try using the Lip Sync setting to see if that fixes the problem.

This setting should have no effect on how the audio and video are recorded; its purpose is only to let you monitor audio through the headphones in sync with the video.

Wind Noise Reduction

This option, if turned on, activates an electronic filter designed to reduce the volume of sounds in the low frequencies of wind noise. I recommend not activating this feature unless you are certain it will help, because it limits the sounds that are recorded. With video (or audio) editing software, you can remove sounds in the frequencies that may cause problems for the sound track, but using the camera's built-in wind noise filter may permanently remove or alter some wanted sounds.

Although Sony's documentation says that, when an external microphone is installed, this option does not function, I was able to turn it on from the menu even with an external microphone in use. It may be that the option did not function, but I was not able to verify that point.

Effects of Mode Dial Position on Recording Movies

The second type of setting that has an effect on the recording of movies with the RX10 is the position of the camera's mode dial. As I discussed above, you can shoot movies no matter what position this dial is set to (if the Movie Button menu option is set that way), and you can get access to many movie-related menu items no matter what position the dial is in. However, as I also noted above, the shooting mode does make some difference for your movie options. I will provide more details here.

First, as noted earlier, you cannot access the Movie option on screen 6 of the Shooting menu unless the mode dial is set to Movie mode. The Movie option, which I would prefer to call Movie Exposure Mode, lets you select one of the four special exposure modes for shooting movies: Program Auto, Aperture Priority, Shutter Priority, or Manual Exposure. In the last three of those modes, you have the ability to set the camera's aperture, shutter speed, or both for movie recording.

Second, the mode the camera is set to has an effect on what options are available on the Shooting menu and with the control buttons, as discussed in the next two sections. For example, if the mode dial is set to Intelligent Auto, Sweep Panorama, or Scene, the Shooting menu options are limited. If the mode dial is set to Program, Aperture Priority, Shutter Priority, or Manual exposure, the options are greater. This point is important for video shooting because, as discussed below, several important Shooting menu options carry over to movie recording. For example, if the camera is set to Program mode (P on the mode dial), you can make several settings that will control the recording of videos while the mode dial is in that position.

If the camera is set to Sweep Panorama mode, it will act as if it were set to Movie mode with the Program Auto exposure mode selected. If it is set to Scene mode, it will shoot as if it were set to Intelligent Auto mode, in which limited menu options are available. It will not recognize any specific scene settings, such as Portrait, Sports Action, or Sunset.

Effects of Other Shooting Menu Settings on Recording Movies

Next, I will discuss the details of other Shooting menu options that have an effect on the recording of movies, beyond the options that are applicable only to video recording, such as File Format, Record Setting, and the others discussed earlier in this chapter.

One of the main reasons the shooting mode is important for movies is that, just as with still photography, some menu options are not available in some shooting modes. For example, in a still-shooting mode such as Aperture Priority or Program, video recording will be affected by the settings for ISO, ND Filter, Metering Mode, White Balance, DRO, Creative Style, Picture Effect, Focus Magnifier, Lock-on AF, and Face Detection.

In some cases, you can adjust these settings while the video is being recorded. You cannot get access to the Shooting menu by pressing the Menu button; you have to use a control button or wheel to call up the item to adjust. Of course, you have to have that setting assigned to a button or wheel ahead of time.

For example, you can adjust ISO while recording a video, but only if you have assigned ISO to the Control wheel or one of the control buttons using the Custom Key Settings menu option on screen 4 of the Custom menu. Table 8-1 shows which of these settings can be adjusted while a video recording is in progress.

Table 8-1. Shooting Menu Items that Affect Movies, and Items that Can Be Adjusted During Video Recording.

Shooting Menu Item	Can Adjust During Video Recording
File Format	No
Record Setting	No
ISO	Yes
ND Filter	Yes
Metering Mode	No
White Balance	No
DRO	No
Creative Style	No
Picture Effect	No
Focus Magnifier	Yes
Lock-on AF	Yes
Face Detection	No
SteadyShot (Movies)	Yes
Auto Slow Shutter	No
Audio Recording	No
Audio Recording Level	No
Audio Out Timing	No
Wind Noise Reduction	No

There are built-in limitations with some of these settings. The ISO range is from 125 to 12800, omitting the lowest settings. Also, you cannot set ISO to Multi Frame Noise Reduction, which would cause the camera to take multiple shots. With Picture Effect, you can use some of the sub-settings, but not all. The settings that are unavailable for movie recording are Soft Focus, HDR Painting, Rich-tone Monochrome, Miniature, Watercolor, and Illustration.

There are some other options on the Shooting menu that have no effect for recording movies. Some of these settings are clearly incompatible with shooting movies, such as Drive Mode, Flash

Mode, and Auto Object Framing. Some are less obvious, including Focus Area, Soft Skin Effect, AF Illuminator and Scene Selection.

There are two other points that should be made about the ability of the RX10 to use Shooting menu settings for movies while the camera is set to a still-shooting mode. First, you have a great deal of flexibility in choosing settings for your movies, even when the camera is not set to the Movie position on the mode dial. You can set up the camera with the ISO, Metering Mode, White Balance, Creative Style, Picture Effect (to some extent), and other settings of your choice, and then press the Movie button to record using those same settings. In this way, you could, for example, record a black-and-white movie in a dark environment using a high ISO setting. Or, you could record a movie that is monochrome except for a broad selection of red objects, using the Partial Color-Red effect from the Picture Effect option, with the red color expanded using the color axis adjustments of the White Balance setting.

Second, you have to be careful to check the settings that are in effect for still photos before you press the Movie button. For example, if you have been shooting stills using the Posterization setting from the Picture Effect menu option and then suddenly see an event that you want to record on video, if you press the Movie button, the movie will be recorded using the Posterization effect, making the resulting footage practically impossible to use as a clear record of the events. Of course, you may notice this problem as you record the video, but it takes time to stop the recording, change the menu setting to turn off the Picture Effect option, and then start recording again, and you may have missed a crucial part of the action by the time you start recording again.

One way to lessen the risk of recording video with unwanted Shooting menu options is to switch the mode dial to the Intelligent Auto position before pressing the red Movie button. That action will cause the camera to use more automatic settings and will disable the Creative Style and Picture Effect options altogether. (Of course, you have to have the Movie Button item on the Custom menu set to Always for this approach to work.)

Effects of Physical Controls When Recording Movies

The next group of settings that carry over to some extent from still-shooting modes to video recording are those set by the physical controls. In this situation, as with Shooting menu items, there are differences depending on what shooting mode the camera is set to. I will not attempt to describe every possible combination of shooting mode and physical control, but I will give some examples and discuss the most important settings to be aware of.

First, you can use the focus switch to change focus mode, even while recording. So, if you are recording a performance and the RX10 is having trouble using autofocus because of darkness on the stage, you can switch the camera to manual focus mode and adjust the focus as needed. Later, if conditions get brighter, you can go back to using autofocus by moving the switch back up to the S or C mark.

When recording videos, the only focus modes available are autofocus-continuous and manual focus. If the focus switch is at the S mark for autofocus-single, the camera will use autofocus-continuous. If the switch is at the DMF mark for direct manual focus, the camera will use manual focus. The Focus Area option on screen 3 of the Shooting menu has no effect for video recording. The camera will use the Wide setting in all situations.

Second, you can use the exposure compensation dial while recording movies when the mode dial is set to the P, A, S, M, Movie, or Sweep Panorama setting. The dial has no effect in Auto or Scene mode. The range of exposure compensation adjustments for movies is plus or minus 2.0 EV, rather than the plus or minus 3.0 EV that is available when shooting still images. If you set exposure compensation to a value greater than 2.0 (plus or minus), the camera will set it back to 2.0 after you press the red Movie button to start shooting a movie.

Third, the Function button operates normally depending on the shooting mode that is currently set. For example, if the mode dial is set to P for Program mode, then, after you press the Movie button to start recording a movie, you can press the Function button and the Function menu will appear on the screen. This menu will let you control only those items that can be controlled under current conditions, as seen in FIGURE 8-15.

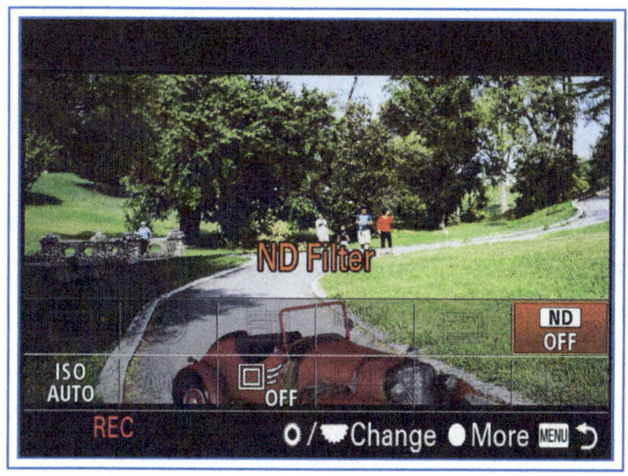

Figure 8-15. Function Menu for Video Recording in Program Mode

If you start recording a movie while the mode dial is set to a mode such as Intelligent Auto in which most functions on the Function Button menu are not available, the RX10 will display the menu, but few of the items can be selected, as shown in FIGURE 8-16.

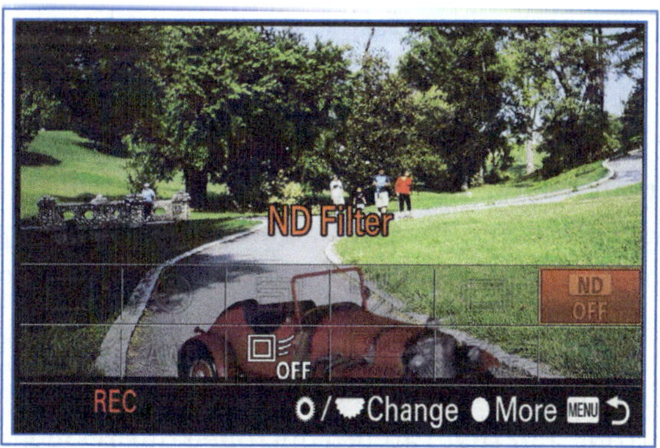

Figure 8-16. Function Menu for Video Recording in Auto Mode

Fourth, if you assign the AEL, Custom, Center, Left, Right, or Down button or the Control wheel to carry out a particular operation using the Custom Key Settings option on screen 4 of the Custom menu, you can use that button or wheel to perform the operation while recording a movie if the action is compatible with movie recording in the current shooting mode.

For the Control wheel, the only function that can be assigned and controlled during video recording is ISO. Although White Balance, Creative Style, or Picture Effect can be assigned to the wheel and controlled before the recording starts, ISO is the only value that can be controlled during the recording.

However, there are numerous options that can be assigned to a control button that will function during video recording, if the current context permits that control. For example, if the Left button is set to control ISO and you are shooting a movie with the mode dial set to P, pressing the Left button will bring up the ISO menu and you can select a value while the movie is recording. If the mode dial is set to Auto, though, pressing the button will have to effect, because ISO cannot be adjusted in that shooting mode.

If the Center button is assigned its Standard setting through the Custom Key Settings menu option and the Lock-on AF option is turned on through screen 5 of the Shooting menu, you can press the Center button during video recording to activate tracking focus. Of course, to use tracking focus, you have to have an autofocus mode selected using the focus switch on the front of the camera.

If you set the AEL button (or some other button) to the AEL Toggle function, you can press that control while recording a movie to lock the exposure setting. This ability can be quite useful when recording a movie, if you don't want the exposure to change as you move the camera over different areas of a scene.

Following is a list of functions that can be assigned to one of the control buttons and that can be controlled during video recording by pressing the button:

- ISO
- ND Filter
- SteadyShot (Movies)
- Audio Recording Level
- AEL Hold
- AEL Toggle
- Spot AEL Hold
- Spot AEL Toggle
- AF/MF Control Hold
- AF/MF Control Toggle
- Lock-on AF
- Focus Magnifier
- Zebra
- Grid Line
- Audio Level Display
- Peaking Level
- Peaking Color

Finally, the aperture click switch can be used while recording a video. As mentioned earlier, it's a good idea to set that switch to the Off position when recording movies, so the sounds of the aperture ring don't get recorded. If you start recording and have forgotten to move that switch, you can still do so at any time.

Summary of Options for Recording Movies

As I have discussed, there is some complication in trying to explain all of the relationships among the controls and settings of the RX10 for recording movies. To cut through that complication, here is a summary of your options for recording movies with the RX10.

To record a video clip with standard settings, set the mode dial to the Auto or Scene position and press the Movie button. The camera will adjust exposure automatically, and you can use either autofocus-continuous (S or C position of focus switch) or manual focus (DMF or MF position). You cannot use many shooting options, such as ISO, White Balance, DRO, Creative Style, or Picture Effect. You can use options such as Lock-on AF, Face Detection, and SteadyShot (Movies). You can choose File Format and Record Settings options to control the video quality.

For more control over video shooting, set the mode dial to the P, A, S, or M position. Then you can control several additional Shooting menu options, including ISO, White Balance, Metering Mode, Creative Style, and Picture Effect, among others. You can choose continuous autofocus or manual focus in the same way as for the more automatic shooting modes. The camera will adjust exposure automatically.

For maximum control over movie recording, set the mode dial to the movie film icon for Movie mode. Then select an option for the movie exposure mode from the Movie item on screen 6 of the Shooting menu. To control aperture, choose Aperture Priority; to control shutter speed, choose Shutter Priority; to control both aperture and shutter speed, choose Manual Exposure. Other options can be selected from the Shooting menu.

Control buttons operate during movie recording if the context permits, as discussed earlier. There are many possibilities for assigning settings to them. If you want a good set of functions tailored for video recording, use the list in Table 8-2 to start, and adjust it for your own needs:

Table 8-2. Suggested Control Assignments for Video Recording

CONTROL	FUNCTION
Control wheel	ISO
AEL button	AEL Toggle

Custom button	ND Filter
Center button	Standard
Left button	Audio Recording Level
Right button	Zebra
Down button	Focus Magnifier

If you want the RX10 to be ready to record good, standard video footage at a moment's notice without having to remember a lot of settings, I recommend that you set up one of the two registers (I use register 2) of the Memory Recall shooting mode with a solid set of movie-recording settings. Table 8-3 lists the settings I recommend. (Settings not listed here can be set however you like.)

Table 8-3. Suggested Settings for Recording Movies

PHYSICAL CONTROLS	
Mode Dial	Movie
Focus Switch	AF-S
Aperture Click Switch	Off
SHOOTING MENU	
File Format	AVCHD
Record Setting	60p 28M (PS)
ISO	ISO Auto
ND Filter	Off
Metering Mode	Multi
White Balance	Auto White Balance
DRO/Auto HDR	DRO Off
Creative Style	Standard
Picture Effect	Off
Lock-on AF	On
Smile/Face Detection	Off
SteadyShot (Movies)	Active
Auto Slow Shutter	On
Audio Recording	On

Table 8-3. Suggested Settings for Recording Movies

Audio Recording Level	26
Audio Out Timing	Live
Wind Noise Reduction	Off

Other Settings and Controls for Movies

There are several other points to be made about recording and playing back videos that don't concern the Shooting menu or the major physical controls. Here are brief notes about these issues.

- The step zoom function is not available for video recording, even if the Zoom Function on Ring option is turned on through screen 4 of the Custom menu. The zoom operates continuously for movies.
- The Display button operates normally to change the information that is viewed during video recording. The screens that are displayed are controlled by the Display Button option on screen 2 of the Custom menu. However, the For Viewfinder screen does not appear for video shooting, even if it was selected through that menu option.
- In playback mode, the Display button operates normally for movies, but the screen with a playback histogram does not display.
- The MF Assist option on screen 1 of the Custom menu does not operate for video recording, so the camera will not magnify the display when you turn the focus ring to carry out manual focus. However, you can assign the Focus Magnifier function to one of the control buttons, and use that capability to enlarge the screen when using manual focus.
- The Setting Effect Off choice for the Live View Display option on screen 2 of the Custom menu does not function for video recording; the Setting Effect On choice is locked in. So, for

example, if you are shooting movies in Movie mode using Manual Exposure for the Movie setting and you have the aperture and shutter speed set for strong underexposure, you cannot adjust this option to make the display more visible.

Movie Playback

As with still images, you can transfer your movies to a computer for editing and playback, or play them back in the camera, either on the camera's LCD screen or on a TV connected to the camera by an optional HDMI cable.

If you want to play your movies in the camera, there is one basic aspect of the RX10 you need to be mindful of. As I discussed in CHAPTER 6, the View Mode option on screen 1 of the Playback menu controls what images or videos you will see in playback mode. If you don't see the video you are looking for, check to make sure this menu option is set to display all files from a certain date (Date View), Folder View (MP4), or AVCHD View, depending on what format your video is in.

Once you have selected the proper mode to view your video, navigate to that file by pressing the direction buttons, turning the Control wheel, or turning the Control dial. Once the first frame of the selected video is displayed on the screen, you will see a playback triangle inside a circle, as shown in FIGURE 8-17.

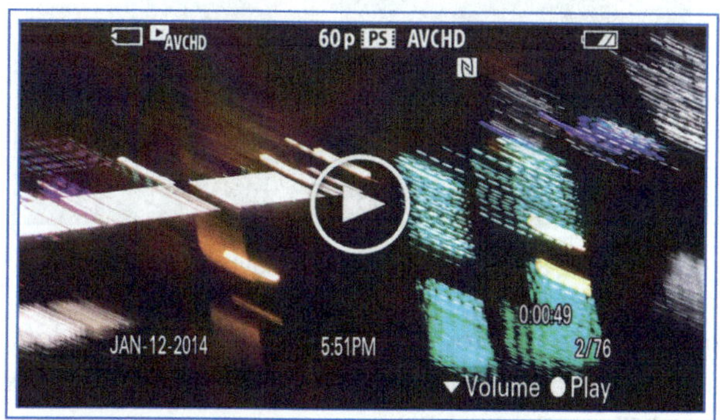

Figure 8-17. Movie Ready for Playback in Camera

In the lower right corner of the screen will be a Play prompt with a white circle icon indicating that you can press the Center button to play the video. (If you don't see that prompt, press the Display button one or more times until it appears.)

After you press the Center button to start the playback, you will see more icons at the bottom of the screen, as seen in FIGURE 8-18.

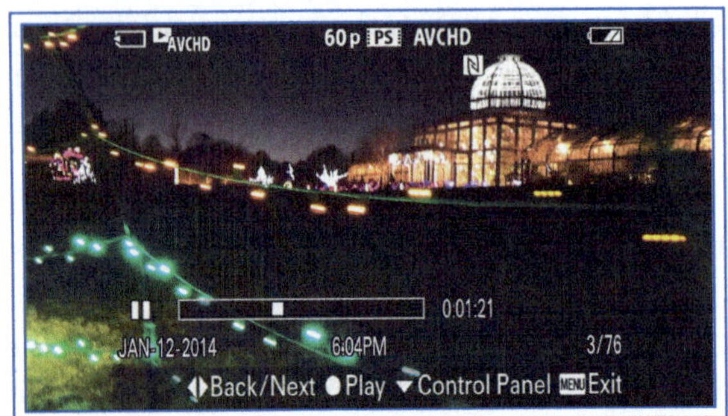

Figure 8-18. Initial Movie Playback Controls

One icon indicates that you can press the Down button to bring up the Control Panel. While the video is still playing, press the Down button, and you will see a new line of controls at the bottom of the screen, as shown in FIGURE 8-19.

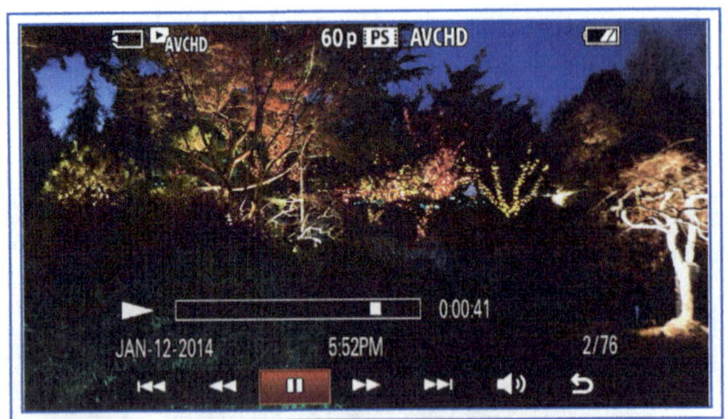

Figure 8-19. Detailed Movie Playback Controls

When the movie is playing, the icons indicate, from left to right: Previous Movie; Fast Reverse; Pause; Fast Forward; Next Movie; Volume; and Close Control Panel.

When the movie is paused, the icons change, as shown in Figure 8-20. Those icons indicate, from left to right: Previous Frame; Reverse Slow; Normal Playback; Forward Slow; Next Frame; Volume; and Close Control Panel.

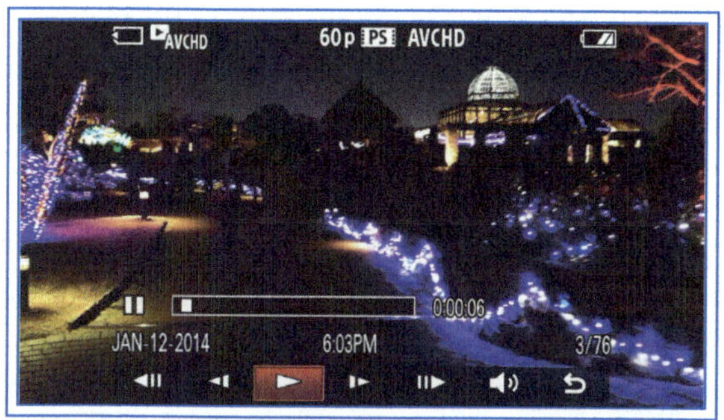

Figure 8-20. Detailed Movie Playback Controls When Paused

In either case, move through the icons with the Left and Right buttons, and press the Center button to select the function for that icon.

When a movie is playing, you can fast-forward or fast-reverse through a video at increasing speeds by turning the Control wheel or the Control dial to the right or left.

Editing Movies

The RX10 cannot edit movies in the camera. If you want to do any editing, you will have to do it with a computer. For Windows, you can use software such as Windows Movie Maker. If you are using a Mac, you can use iMovie or any other movie editing software that can deal with MP4 and AVCHD files. I use Adobe Premiere Pro on my Mac, and it handles these files very well.

You also can use the PlayMemories Home software that comes with the RX10. To install PlayMemories Home on your computer, you need to download the software from the internet. For

Windows-based computers, go to http://www.sony.net/pm. For Macintosh computers, go to http://www.sony.co.jp/imsoft/Mac/.

One issue you may encounter when first starting to edit movie files from the RX10 is finding the files. When you insert a memory card into a card reader, the still images are easy to find; on my computer, the SD card shows up as No Name or Untitled; then, beneath that level, there is a folder called DCIM; inside it are folders with names such as 100MSDCF, which contain the still images.

The movie files are a bit trickier to find. As I mentioned earlier in this chapter, the AVCHD files that you need to find and import into your software are the files with the .mts extension. Here is the pathway to a sample file, assuming the file name at the level of the SD card is Untitled: Untitled\Private\AVCHD\BDMV\Stream\0006.MTS. The file called 0006.MTS is an AVCHD file that can be imported directly into compatible software for editing.

To find your MP4 files, locate the files using a pathway such as Untitled\MP_ROOT\100ANV01\MAH1430.MP4. The file named MAH1430.MP4 is an MP4 file that can be played by Apple's QuickTime software or imported into iMovie for editing.

You can avoid the complications of finding the movie files on a memory card by connecting the camera to your computer using the USB cable. With most video-editing software, the camera should be detected and the software should import the movie files automatically, ready for you to edit them.

Also, of course, with the RX10, you can transfer your files to your computer using the Wi-Fi capabilities that are built into the camera, as discussed in Chapter 9.

Chapter 9: Using Wi-Fi and Other Topics

Connections Using Wi-Fi and NFC

One useful feature of the RX10 is the camera's ability to connect to computers and other devices using a Wi-Fi network. As noted in Chapter 1, you can transfer images wirelessly using an Eye-Fi card or other memory card that includes Wi-Fi connectivity, but having Wi-Fi circuitry built into the camera gives you features that are not available with a card. In addition, with Android devices the RX10 can use NFC technology to establish a Wi-Fi connection without using menu options. In this section, I will provide an introduction to these features with some examples of how you can use them.

First, here is a note to remember when using any of the camera's Wi-Fi features: The Wi-Fi menu (discussed later in this chapter) has an option called Airplane Mode near the bottom of its first screen. If that option is turned on, no Wi-Fi features will work. Make sure that setting is turned off when using the Wi-Fi options.

Sending Images to a Computer

If you want to print your images from a software program, edit them, or organize them for long-term storage, you need to transfer the images to a computer. The traditional way to do this involves connecting the camera to the computer using the camera's USB cable or connecting a memory card reader to the computer using a USB port and inserting the camera's memory card into the reader for the transfer operation. However, there are two methods you can use to transfer your images to a computer over a wireless network, eliminating the need for any USB connection.

First, as discussed in Chapter 1, you can use an Eye-Fi card or a similar memory card with the capability to transfer your images wirelessly to the computer. This system works well, but it requires the purchase and use of this special type of memory card. One drawback of that system is that you cannot use one of the high-capacity or high-speed memory cards that are now available; you must use one of the Wi-Fi–enabled cards.

The other approach for wireless transfer is to take advantage of the Wi-Fi capability built into the RX10. Once you have the camera and computer set up to communicate over a wireless network, you can use the Send to Computer menu option to transfer images and videos from the camera's memory card over that network, regardless of what type of memory card is installed. The steps to set up the camera and computer are quite straightforward; here are the actions to take:

1. Install the appropriate Sony software on the computer.

   For Windows-based computers, the software is PlayMemories Home, available for download at http://www.sony.net/pm/.

   –or–

   For Macintosh computers, you need to install Wireless Auto Import, available for download at http://www.sony.co.jp/imsoft/Mac/.

2. Make sure the camera is within range of a wireless access point, also known as a Wi-Fi router. Normally, this will be a private, secured network at your home or office.

3. If the router has a button labeled WPS (for Wi-Fi–protected setup), you can use the button to connect. First, select the WPS Push option on the Wi-Fi menu, as shown in FIGURE 9-1.

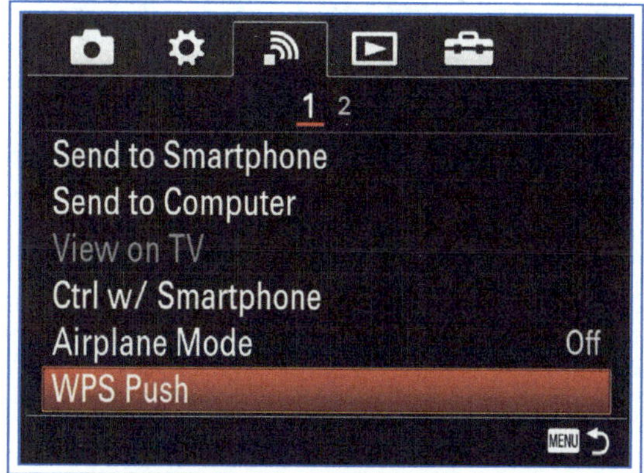

Figure 9-1. WPS Push Menu Option

4. Then, within two minutes, press the WPS button on the router. FIGURE 9-2 shows an example of that sort of button.

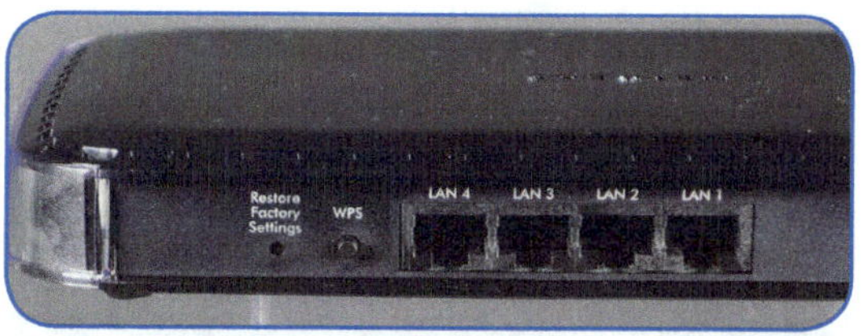

Figure 9-2. WPS Button on Router

If the setup is successful, proceed to STEP 8.

–or–

If the router does not have a WPS button, or if pushing the button does not work, proceed to STEP 5.

5. Locate the name of the network and its password. (This information may be on a label on the bottom or side of the router or modem, particularly if the device is provided by your Internet company, such as Comcast, Verizon, or others.)

6. Select the Access Point Settings option on the second screen of the Wi-Fi menu, as shown in FIGURE 9-3.

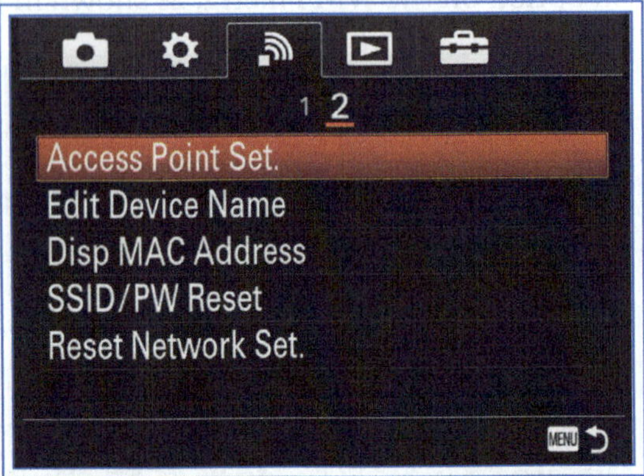

Figure 9-3. Access Point Settings Menu Option

7. If the name of your network soon appears on the camera's screen, as shown in FIGURE 9-4, enter the network's password, as shown in FIGURE 9-5.

Figure 9-4. Network Name on Camera's Screen

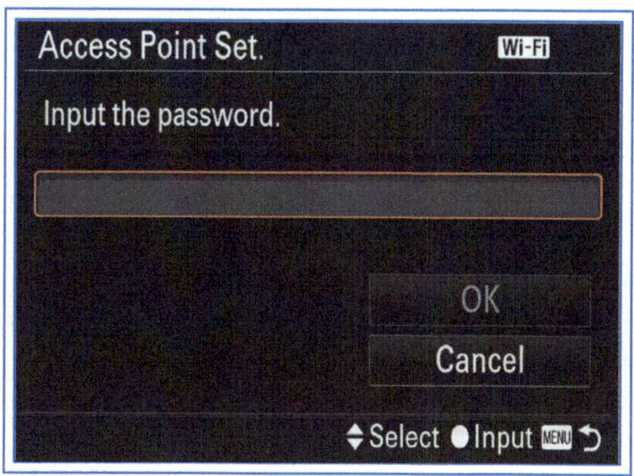

Figure 9-5. Password Input Screen

–or–

If the access point does not appear on the camera's screen, select the Manual Setting option on the menu screen, as shown in FIGURE 9-6, and then enter the network's SSID, as shown in FIGURE 9-7.

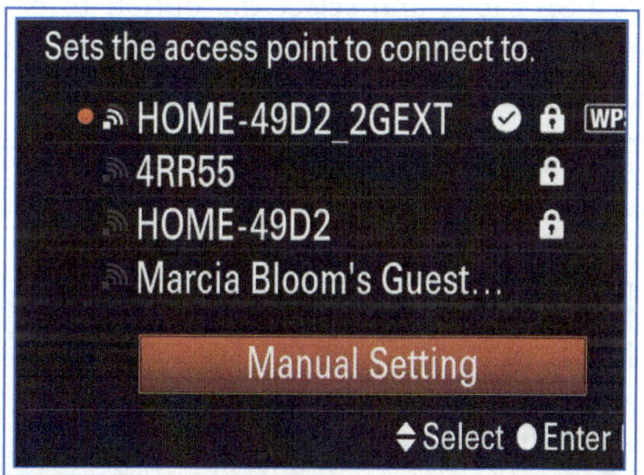

Figure 9-6. Manual Setting Option for Access Point

After that, follow any prompts on the camera's screen for entering passwords or other information.

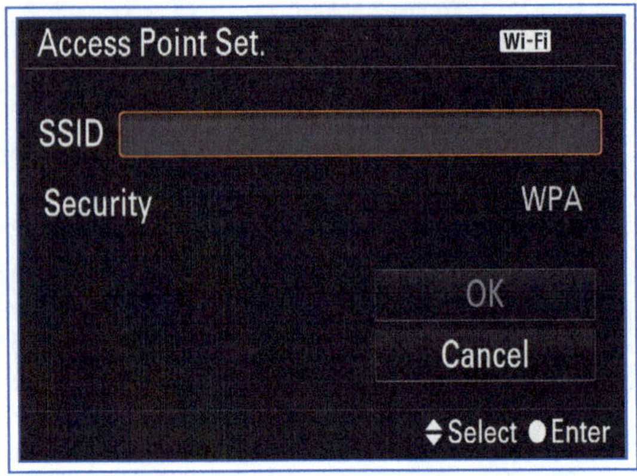

Figure 9-7. Screen for Entering SSID

8. To send images from the RX10 to the computer, first you have to set the computer as the device to receive images. To do that, run the software you downloaded in STEP 1 (PlayMemories Home for Windows or Wireless Auto Import for Mac). Then connect the camera to the computer using the camera's USB cable, and select the option to designate this computer as the device to receive images from the camera. (That needs to be done only once, unless you later switch to a different computer.) Then you can disconnect the cable.

9. On screen 1 of the Wi-Fi menu, select Send to Computer, as seen in FIGURE 9-8.

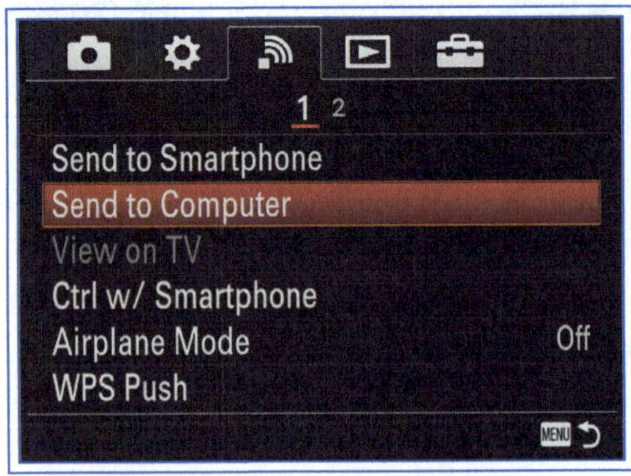

Figure 9-8. Send to Computer Menu Option

10. The camera will display a screen like that in FIGURE 9-9, reporting the name of the computer it is connecting to.

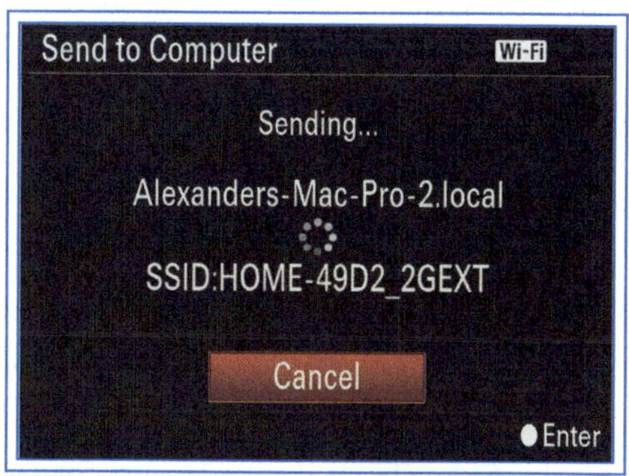

Figure 9-9. Screen When Camera Sending Files to Computer

11. The computer will display a Preparing to Import dialog box, and then an Importing dialog box. The images and videos will be uploaded to the appropriate folder on your computer. You can designate what folder they are transferred to using the software installed in STEP 1. On my Macintosh, the default folder was the Pictures folder; the computer placed the images in a folder bearing the date of the transfer. The camera will only transfer files that have not previously been transferred wirelessly to the computer. The transfer may take a long time if there are many large files to upload.

Sending Images to a Smartphone

If you don't need to print your images or do heavy editing, you may want to transfer them to a smartphone or tablet, so you can send them to social networks, display them on the larger screen of your tablet, or otherwise share and enjoy them.

You can transfer your images and MP4 videos (not AVCHD videos) wirelessly from the RX10 to a smartphone or tablet that uses either the iOS (iPhone and iPad) or the Android operating system. These two systems have different capabilities. With the iPhone and other iOS devices (such as the iPad), you have to use the camera's menu system to connect, just as with a computer, as discussed above. With many Android devices, you can use NFC technology, which establishes a Wi-Fi connection automatically when the camera is placed very close to, or touching, the smartphone or tablet.

Here are the steps for connecting using the menu system, using an iPhone as an illustration:

1. Install Sony's PlayMemories Mobile app on the phone; it can be downloaded from the App Store for the iPhone and from Google Play for Android devices.
2. Put the camera into playback mode and select an image or MP4 video to be transferred to the phone.
3. On screen 1 of the Wi-Fi menu, select Send to Smartphone, and from that option choose Select on This Device, as shown in FIGURE 9-10. On the next screen, you can choose to transfer This Image; All Images (or All Movie (MP4)) on Date; or Multiple Images. (Details of those menu options are discussed later in this chapter.)

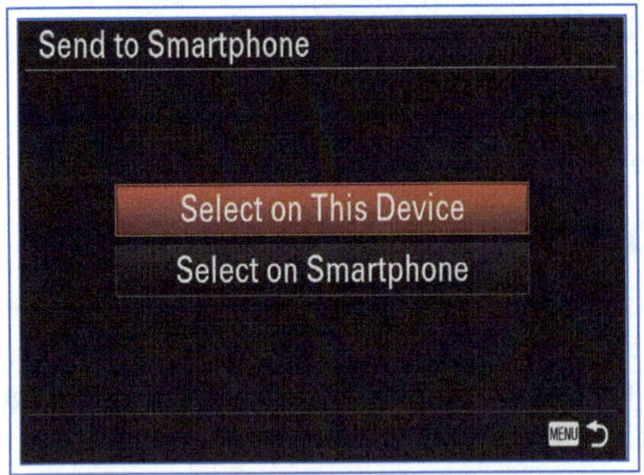

Figure 9-10. Send to Smartphone Menu Options Screen

4. On the next screen, as shown in FIGURE 9-11, the camera will display the SSID (name) of the Wi-Fi network it is generating.

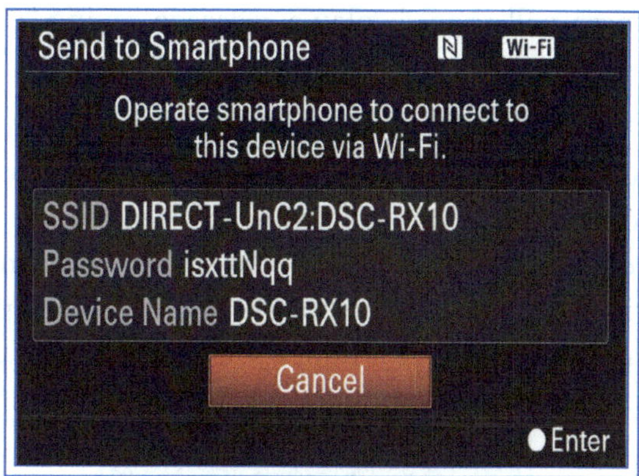

Figure 9-11. Camera's Display of its SSID for Send to Smartphone Option

5. On the iPhone, go to the Settings app, select Wi-Fi, and then select the network that displays on the camera's screen, as shown in Figure 9-12. The first time you connect to that network, you will have to enter the password displayed on the camera's screen. After that initial connection, you can connect to that network without entering the password.

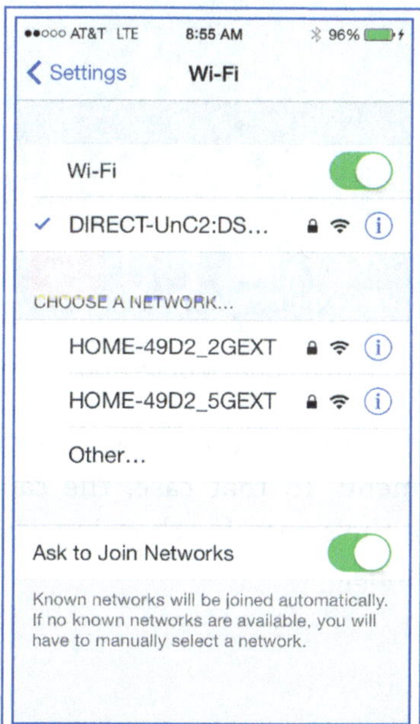

Figure 9-12. Camera's SSID on iPhone's Wi-Fi Screen

6. The camera will then display a message saying "Connecting." At this point, start the PlayMemories Mobile app, shown by the arrow in FIGURE 9-13 on the iPhone.

7. The phone will display a message saying it is copying the selected images or videos from the camera to the phone, and then a message that the contents have been copied, as shown in FIGURE 9-14. The images or videos will appear in the Camera Roll area on an iPhone; you can see them by selecting the Camera app on the phone.

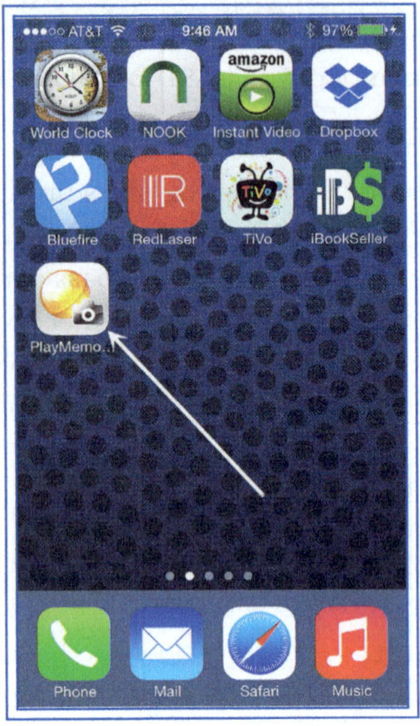

Figure 9-13. PlayMemories Mobile App on iPhone Screen

8. For STEP 3, you can just press the Function button instead of using the menu. In that case, the camera will take you immediately to the screen for choosing which images to send to the smartphone.

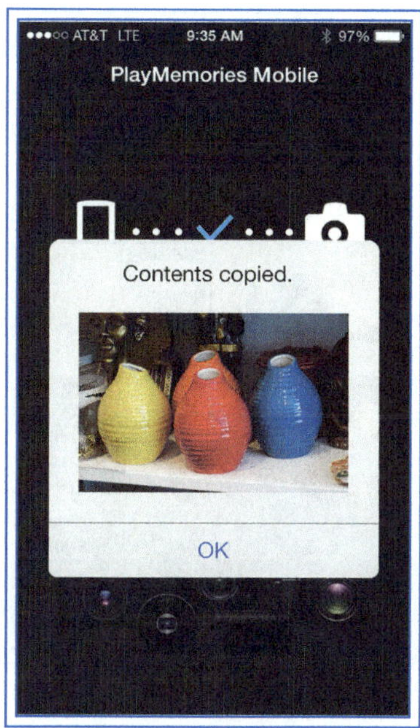

Figure 9-14. Screen Showing Image Was Copied to iPhone

Connecting with NFC

If you are using an Android phone or tablet that has NFC capability built in, the steps for connecting that device to the RX10 are considerably easier. I tested the procedure using a Google Nexus 7 tablet, but the same process should work with many Android devices that have NFC included. Here are the steps:

1. On the Android device, go to the Google Play Store and find and install the PlayMemories Mobile app, as shown in Figure 9-15.

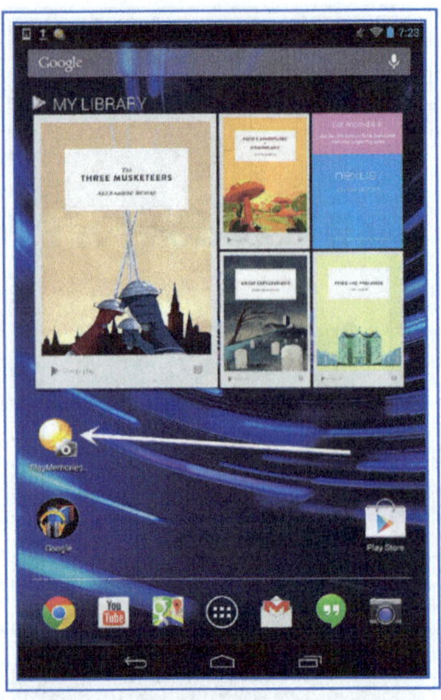

Figure 9-15. PlayMemories Mobile App on Nexus 7 Tablet Screen

2. On the Android device, go to the Settings app, and under the Wireless and Networks area, choose More. On the next screen, make sure there is a check mark next to the NFC item, as shown in FIGURE 9-16.
3. Put the RX10 into playback mode and display an image that you want to send to the Android device.
4. Find the NFC icon on the right side of the camera, which looks like a fancy "N," as shown in FIGURE 9-17.
5. While both devices have their screens active, touch the N on the camera to the similarly marked NFC area on the Android device. (On the Nexus tablet, this area is on the back of the tablet, as shown in FIGURE 9-18.) Be sure these two areas actually touch; the distance tolerance for NFC is tight, and you cannot have the two NFC spots separated by anything more than about a millimeter, if that.

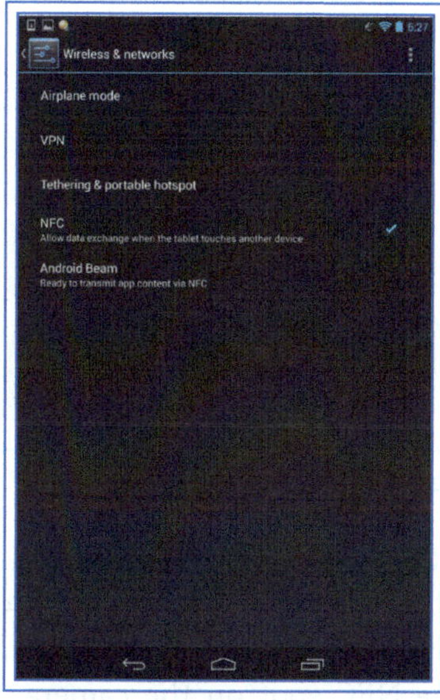

Figure 9-16. NFC Settings Screen on Nexus 7 Tablet

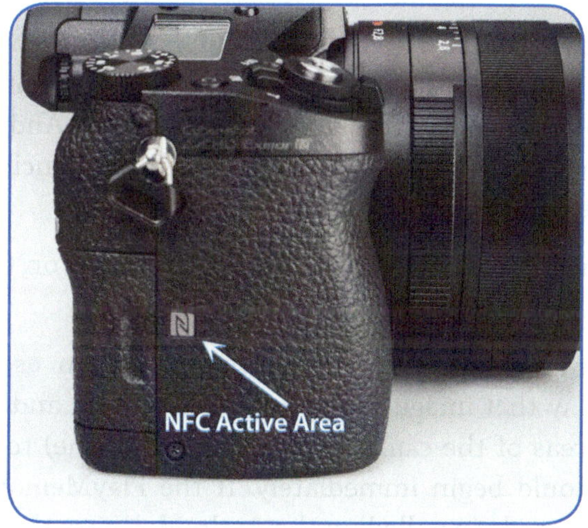

Figure 9-17. NFC Active Area on RX10

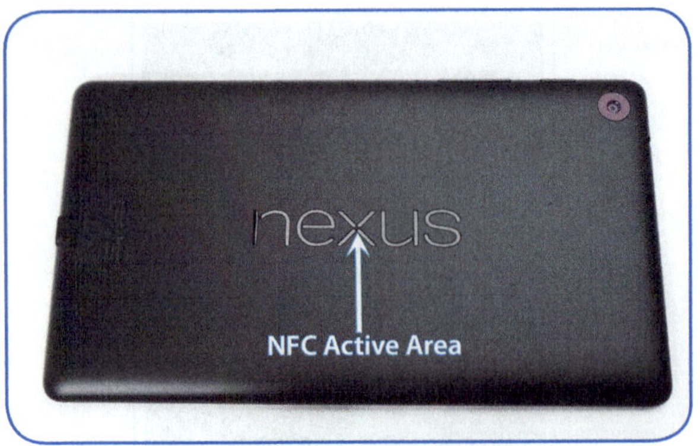

Figure 9-18. NFC Active Area on Nexus 7 Tablet

One slight design issue with the RX10 is that the shoulder strap lug on the right side of the camera makes it difficult to place the NFC spot of a larger device, such as a tablet, flat against the NFC spot on the camera. With some effort, though, it is possible to get the two devices close enough together to make the NFC connection.

6. Hold the devices together without moving them. Within a couple of seconds, you should hear a confirmation sound, and the camera will transfer the image to the Android device; you should see a display on its screen announcing that the transfer is complete, as shown in Figure 9-19.
7. The image will then appear in the Gallery app on the Android device.

If you want to transfer a single image, you can use a simpler method. Play that image on the camera's display, and then touch the NFC areas of the camera and tablet (or phone) together. The transfer should begin immediately. If the PlayMemories Mobile app is not already installed on the Android device, the device may display a screen that prompts you to install the app.

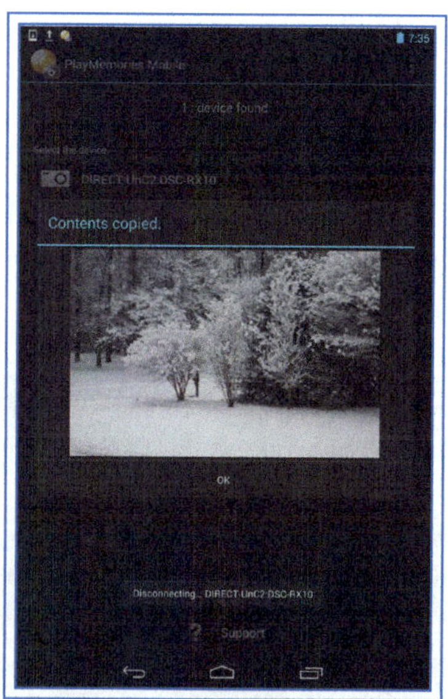

Figure 9-19. Nexus 7 Screen After Receiving Image from RX10

By default, when you transfer images to a smartphone or tablet, the maximum image size will be 2 MP. That is, if the image originally was larger than that, it will be reduced to that size. You can change this setting to send the images at their original size or at the smaller VGA size, if you want. To do that on your device, find the settings for the PlayMemories Mobile app. (On an iPhone, go to Settings, then scroll to find PlayMemories Mobile. On an Android device, open PlayMemories Mobile, then tap the Settings icon.) If the images were taken with Raw quality, they will be converted to JPEG format before being transferred to the smartphone or tablet, even if the device is set for transfer at the original size.

Using a Smartphone or Tablet as a Remote Control

You can use a smartphone or tablet as a remote control to operate the RX10 in a few limited ways from a distance of up to about 33 feet (10 meters), as long as the devices are in sight of each other. Here are the steps to do this with an iPhone:

1. On screen 1 of the camera's Wi-Fi menu, select Control with Smartphone, as shown in Figure 9-20. The camera will display the identification of its own Wi-Fi network, as shown in Figure 9-21. (To get quicker access to this option, you can assign Control with Smartphone to one of the camera's control buttons using the Custom Key Settings menu option on screen 4 of the Custom menu.)

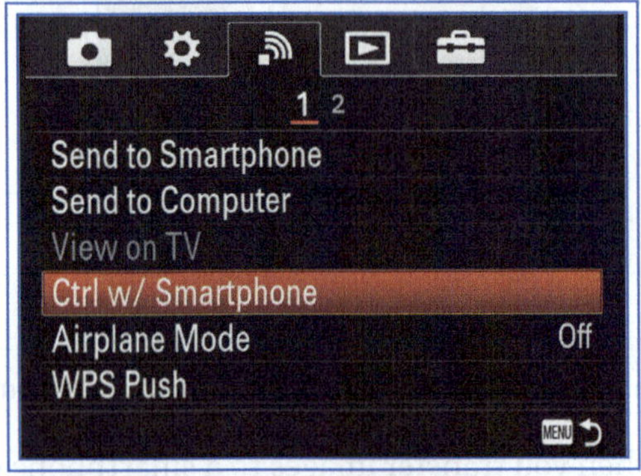

Figure 9-20. Control With Smartphone Menu Option

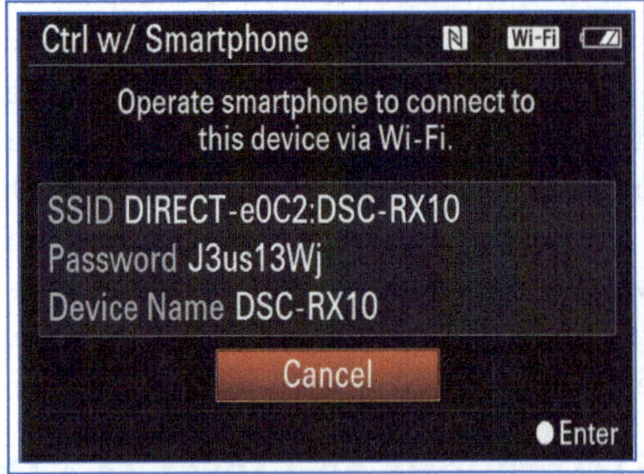

Figure 9-21. Camera's Display of its SSID for Control with Smartphone

2. On the phone, go to the Wi-Fi tab of the Settings app and select the network ID displayed by the camera, as shown in Figure 9-22. If this is the first time you are making this connection, you will have to enter the network password on

the phone; you will not have to enter the password for future connections unless the network ID is changed.

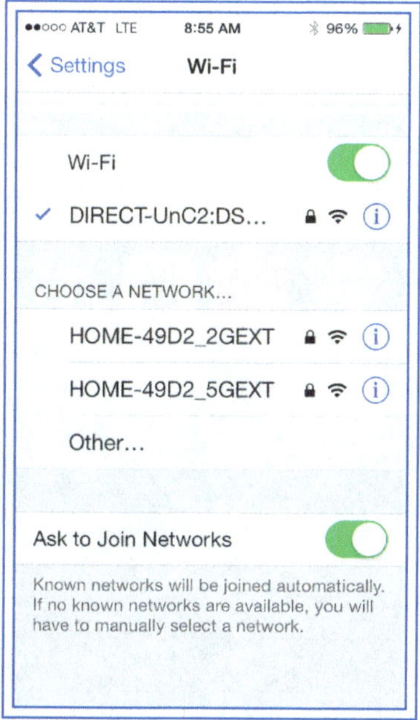

Figure 9-22. iPhone's Display of Camera's SSID

3. The camera will display a screen like that in FIGURE 9-23, saying that the camera is now being controlled by the phone, and you cannot control the camera with its own controls.

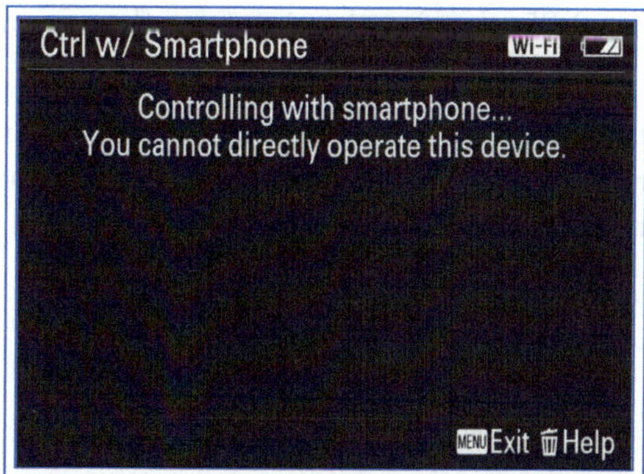

Figure 9-23. RX10's Screen When Controlled by Smartphone

4. Set up the camera on a tripod or just place it where you want it, aiming at your intended subject.
5. Open the PlayMemories Mobile app on the iPhone, as shown in FIGURE 9-24.

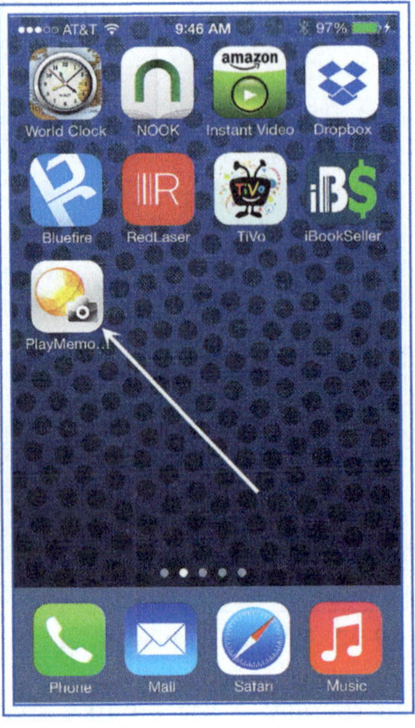

Figure 9-24. PlayMemories Mobile App on iPhone

6. After a few seconds, the phone will display a screen like that in FIGURE 9-25, showing the view from the camera's lens and several control icons.
7. Using these controls, you can zoom the lens in and out, and you can use the settings icon and its sub-menu to control the self-timer, flash, and options for reviewing and saving the images on the phone, as shown in FIGURE 9-26.

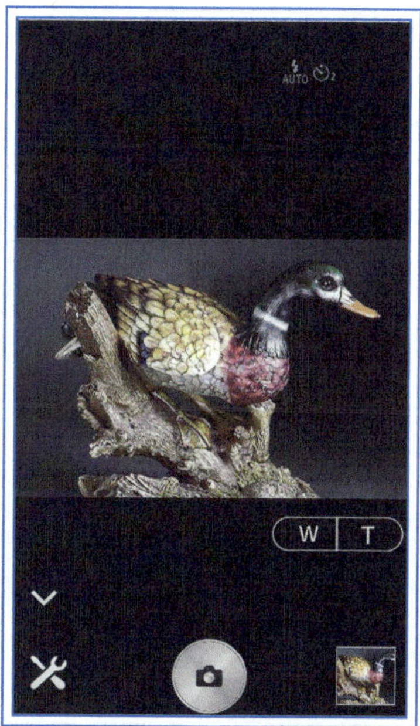

Figure 9-25. iPhone Screen to Control Camera

8. If you turn on Review Image, the image will appear on the phone's display after it is captured. If you turn on the Save option, the image will be saved to the phone. Otherwise, it will be saved only to the camera, provided the camera has a memory card in it.

9. By default, images saved to the phone will be resized to 2 MP unless they already were that small or smaller. If you want to change that setting, on the iPhone, go to the Settings app and scroll down to the settings for the PlayMemories Mobile app, where you can select Copy Image Size and set it to Original; 2M (2 megapixels, the default setting); or VGA (a smaller size).

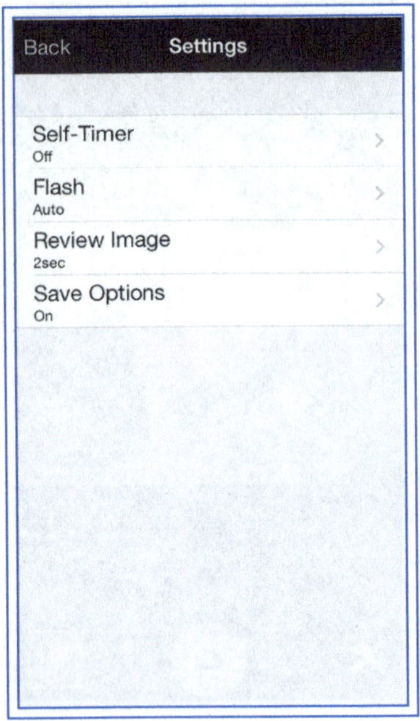

Figure 9-26. Main Settings Screen on iPhone for Controlling Camera

10. When you have set up the shot as you want it, press the camera icon to take the picture.

If you are using an Android device with NFC capability, you can connect it to the camera by touching the device to the camera, as discussed above in connection with transferring images. Once the connection has been made, you can separate the devices up to the maximum remote-control distance of up to about 33 feet (10 meters). The camera can then be controlled using the PlayMemories Mobile app on the Android device, as noted in the numbered steps above.

Obviously, the remote-control function using Wi-Fi is quite limited. You cannot use any menu settings at all; the camera will shoot as if in Intelligent Auto mode. You can control only the zoom level, flash (turning it off or setting it to Auto), and self-timer, apart from the review and saving options. So, for example, even if you have the camera set to Aperture Priority mode with a Picture Effect such as Posterization selected, the camera will take a picture with no special effect, just as if it were set to Intelligent Auto mode. If you have the camera set for manual focus, though, the manual focus setting will not be changed by the camera when you take the picture.

Despite its considerable limitations, this wireless remote capability is quite useful for certain situations.

For example, you can use this setup if you want to place your camera on a tripod in an area where birds or other wildlife may appear, so you can control the camera from a distance without disturbing the animals. (The wireless remote will work through glass if you are indoors behind a window.)

Also, you can try pole aerial photography, which involves attaching the camera to a painter's pole or other pole about 10 to 16 feet (3 to 5 meters) tall, as shown in Figure 9-27, to get shots from a higher vantage point than would otherwise be possible.

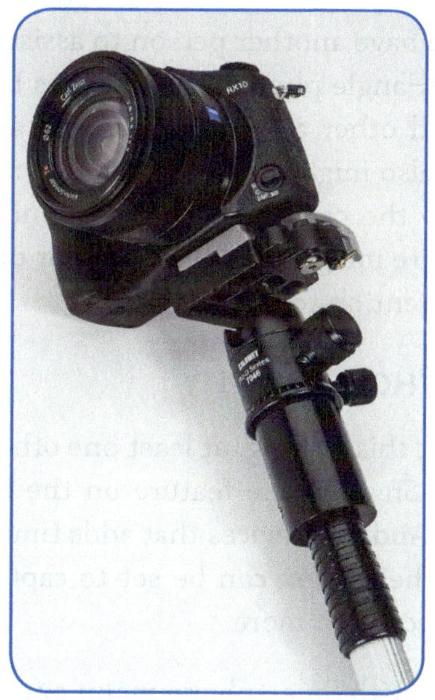

Figure 9-27. Camera Mounted on Pole

I took the image shown in FIGURE 9-28 using this pole, to get a shot of the chimney on the roof of my house.

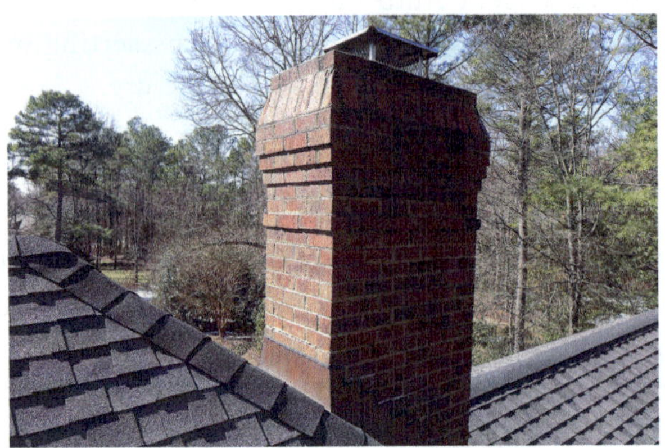

Figure 9-28. Image Taken with Camera Mounted on Pole

I stood on a small balcony below the roof, held the pole up as high as I could, and controlled the camera using my iPhone. With this system, I could see exactly where the camera was being aimed. I had some difficulty holding the pole steady while using the iPhone, but if you have another person to assist, this setup can be helpful for higher-angle photos of properties being sold, viewing above crowds, and other applications. Being able to control the camera remotely also might be useful in other situations in which you want to have the camera set up unattended, such as when you want to capture images in a classroom or other group setting without calling attention to the camera.

Time-Lapse Photography

Finally, there is, at this writing, at least one other option for using the Control with Smartphone feature on the RX10. An app has been released for Android devices that adds time-lapse capabilities to the RX10, so the camera can be set to capture still images at intervals of one second or more.

Using the Control with Smartphone menu option, you establish a connection between the camera and the Android phone or tablet, using NFC if the Android device supports it. After the camera takes a series of images at the specified interval, the images can be combined with software into a time-lapse video sequence that greatly speeds up an event such as a sunrise, construction of a building, filling up of parking lot with cars, and the like.

The app is called TimeLapse. Its description can be found at the following location: https://play.google.com/store/apps/details?id=com.thibaudperso.sonycamera&hl=en. A YouTube video that shows how the app operates can be found at: http://www.youtube.com/watch?v=imbHgAyO9R8.

I tested the app using my RX10 with a Nexus 7 tablet, and it worked well.

Wi-Fi Menu Options

The RX10 camera includes a special menu for its wireless functions, designated by a wireless network icon, between the Custom and Playback menus. I have discussed the use of several of the options on this menu earlier in this chapter. Now I will go through each menu option to cover any points I have not already mentioned. The first screen of this menu is shown in Figure 9-29.

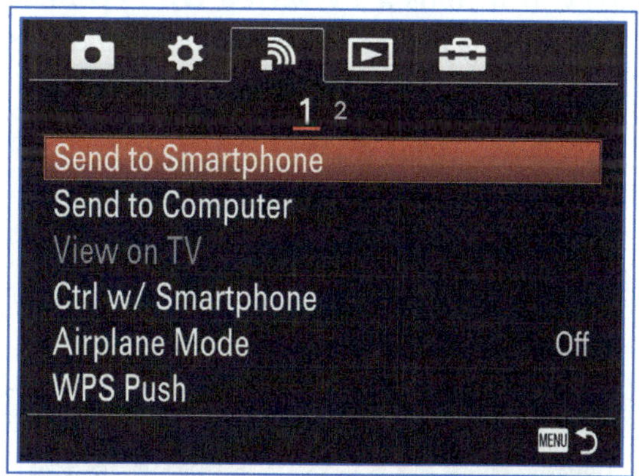

Figure 9-29. Screen 1 of Wi-Fi Menu

Send to Smartphone

This first option lets you use the RX10's built-in wireless capability to send still images or MP4 videos from the camera to an iOS (Apple) or Android device, including smartphones and tablets. I discussed the steps for using this feature earlier in this chapter.

Send to Computer

This next option lets you send still images or movies directly from the RX10 to your computer via a Wi-Fi network. Before you can do this, you have to register your network and computer with the camera using the WPS Push or Access Point Settings menu option on the Wi-Fi menu, as described earlier in this chapter. You also have to install Sony's PlayMemories Home software if you are using a Windows-based computer or Sony's Wireless Auto Import software if you are using a Macintosh. Then follow the steps that I outlined earlier in this chapter.

View on TV

This option lets the camera transmit still images (not movies) to a Wi-Fi-enabled TV. The procedure varies with the TV set you are using. Once the TV is set up properly, select this menu option and the camera will display a screen showing that it is attempting to connect to a TV. If it finds a TV with a Wi-Fi connection, it will display the name of the device, as shown in FIGURE 9-30.

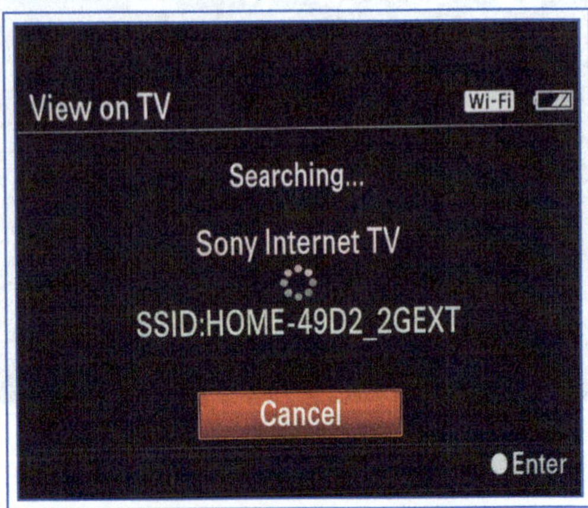

Figure 9-30. View on TV Screen When Camera Connecting to TV

Once the connection is established, you should see a screen like that in FIGURE 9-31, with the camera displaying icons showing that the images on the memory card are being sent wirelessly to the TV.

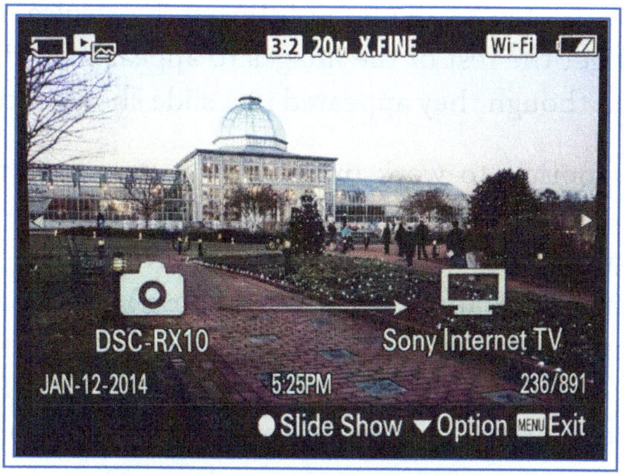

Figure 9-31. Camera Display When Sending Images with View on TV

At this point, you can browse through the images using the Left and Right buttons, or you can start a slide show by pressing the Center button. You also can get access to a screen with more options, shown in FIGURE 9-32, by pressing the Down button.

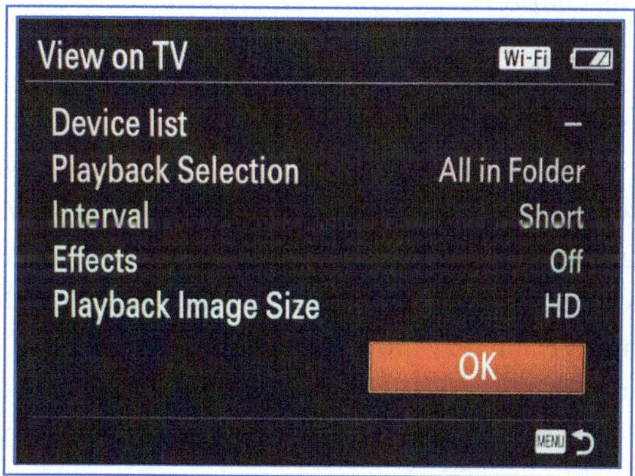

Figure 9-32. Additional Settings for View on TV Menu Option

I don't recommend you try this option unless you already have set up an Internet-enabled TV on your home network and are quite familiar with its operation. I worked for a considerable time to configure a Sony NSZ-GT1 Wi-Fi–enabled Blu-ray player and Internet TV device to use this option. I eventually was able to get a few images from my RX10 camera to appear on the TV screen that was connected to the Sony Internet TV device, but I never was able to get the rest of the images to appear in a slide show on the TV, even though they appeared in a slide show on the camera.

To get this option to work properly, you may have to set up a DLNA server on your computer, which I found to be difficult to do successfully with my Macintosh. (DLNA stands for Digital Living Network Alliance; see www.dlna.org.) If you are familiar with setting up a DLNA server, this option may be great for you. Otherwise, I recommend you view your images on a TV using an HDMI cable, a USB flash drive, or some other direct connection.

Control with Smartphone

This next option is for use with the built-in Wi-Fi features of the RX10. This menu option is what you use to set up the camera to be controlled remotely by a smartphone or tablet—either an Apple iPhone or ipad or an Android device. I discussed this process earlier in this chapter.

Airplane Mode

This option gives you a quick way to disable all of the camera's functions related to Wi-Fi, including Eye-Fi card activity and the camera's own internal Wi-Fi network, including NFC. As indicated by its name, this option is useful when you are on an airplane and you are required to disable electronic devices. In addition, this setting can save battery power, so it may be useful to activate it when you are on an outing with the camera and you won't be needing to use any Wi-Fi capabilities for a period of time.

If you are trying to use any of the camera's built-in Wi-Fi functions, such as Control with Smartphone, Send to Computer, and the like, and notice that the menu options are dimmed, it may be because this option is turned on. Just turn it back off and the Wi-Fi options should be available again.

WPS Push

The WPS Push option gives you an easy way to set up your camera to connect to a computer over a Wi-Fi network. Ordinarily, to connect to a wireless network you have to set your device to find the network and then enter the network password to establish the connection. The WPS Push option gives you a shortcut if the wireless access point or wireless router you are connecting to has a WPS button. This option, if it is present, is likely to be a small button on the back or top of the router, and it is likely to have the WPS label next to it or on it. For example, the router I connect to has the button shown earlier in this chapter in FIGURE 9-2.

If the router has such a button, you will not have to make any manual settings or enter a password. All you have to do is select the WPS Push menu option on the RX10, and then within two minutes after that, press the WPS button on the router. If the operation is successful, the camera's display screen will show that the connection has been established, as shown in FIGURE 9-33.

Figure 9-33. WPS Push Successful Registration Screen

Once that connection has been made, you will be able to connect your camera to a computer on that network in the future to transfer images using the Send to Computer option on the first screen of the Wi-Fi menu.

If the connection does not succeed using the WPS Push option, you will need to use the Access Point Settings option, which is the first option on the second screen of the Wi-Fi menu, shown in FIGURE 9-34.

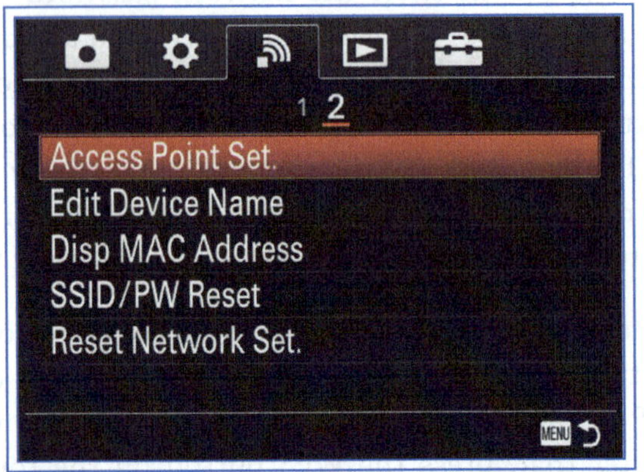

Figure 9-34. Access Point Settings Menu Options Screen

Access Point Settings

This option on the second screen of the Wi-Fi menu is for connecting your camera to a wireless router if the WPS Push option, discussed above, is not available or does not work. To use this option, you will need to know the SSID (service set identifier or identifying name) of the Wi-Fi network you will be connecting the camera to. For routers that are provided by a service provider such as Comcast or Verizon, this name may be printed on the bottom or back of the router. In other cases, the name may be one you or a system administrator has assigned.

Once you know the SSID of the network, select the Access Point Settings menu option, and the camera will display a screen showing that it is searching for networks. When it finds one or more networks, it will display a single name, as shown in FIGURE 9-35, or a list of networks, and you should select the network you want to connect to.

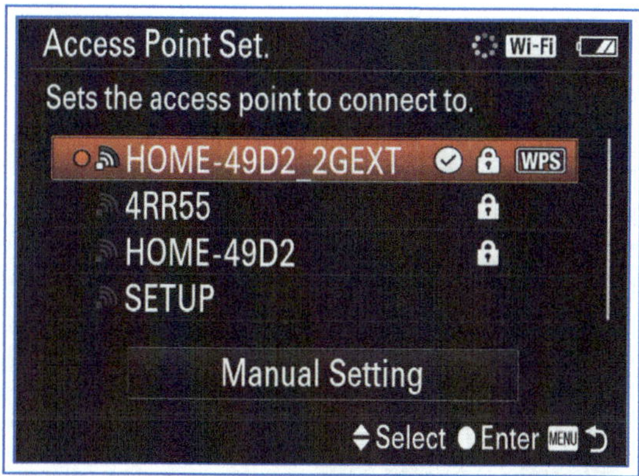

Figure 9-35. Access Point Settings Screen Showing Available Networks

If you have not previously connected to it, the camera will display a screen asking you to enter the network password, as shown in Figure 9-36.

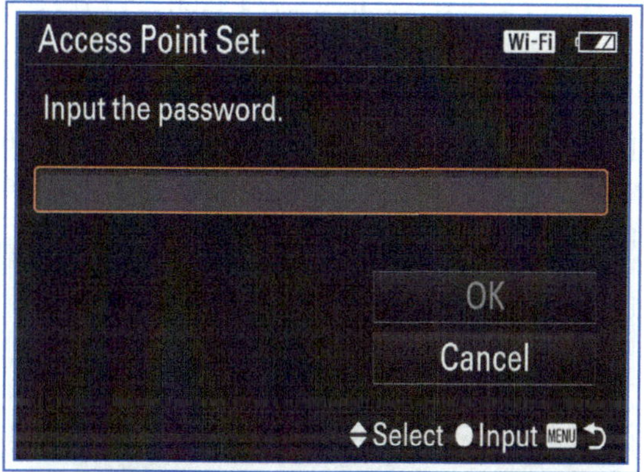

Figure 9-36. Password Input Screen

To do that, use the text-entry functions of the camera's on-screen keyboard, shown in Figure 9-37, which operates somewhat like the data-entry options on a cell phone.

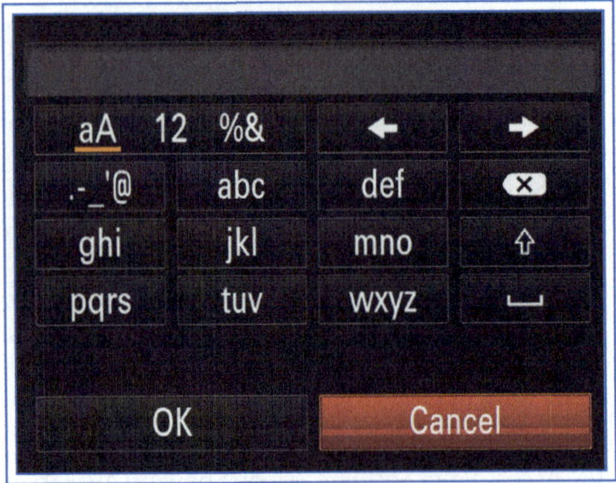

Figure 9-37. Text Input Screen

Once the password has been entered, the connection will be established just as if you had used the WPS Push option, and you can proceed to use the Send to Computer option on the first screen of the Wi-Fi menu, as discussed earlier in this chapter.

Edit Device Name

This next option, whose main screen is shown in Figure 9-38, lets you change the name of the camera as displayed on the network.

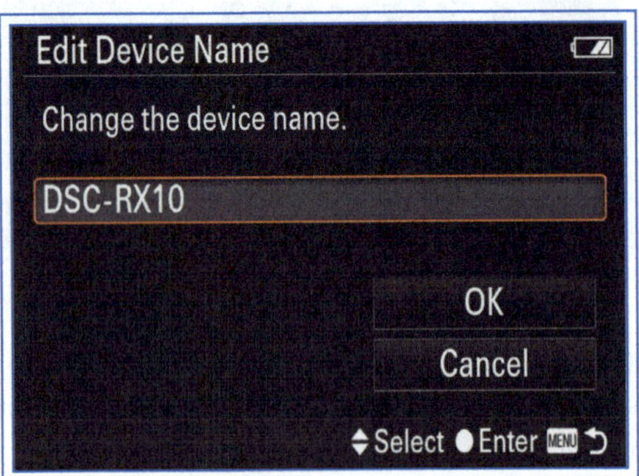

Figure 9-38. Edit Device Name Screen

The default name is DSC-RX10, and I have found no reason to change it, especially because doing so would require me to use the camera's laborious data-entry system. This option could be useful if you are in an environment where other RX10 cameras are present and you need to distinguish one camera from another with different names.

Display MAC Address

If you select this menu option, the camera will display a screen like that seen in FIGURE 9-39, which provides the MAC address of your camera.

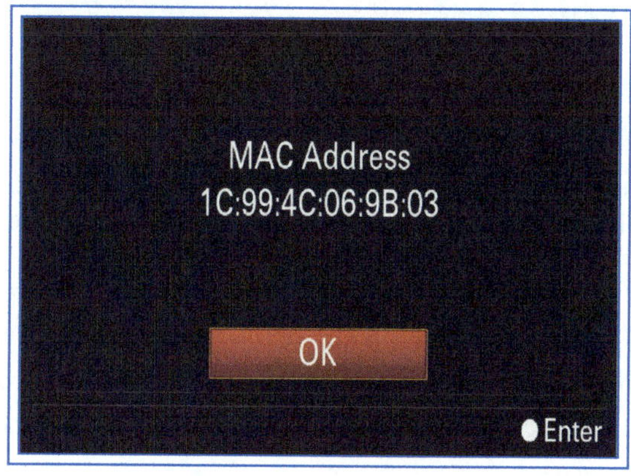

Figure 9-39. Display MAC Address Screen

The MAC (media access control) address is a string of characters that identifies a physical device connected to a network. In some cases, a router can be configured to reject or accept devices with specified MAC addresses. If you are having difficulty connecting your camera to your Wi-Fi router using the menu options discussed above, you may want to try configuring your router to specifically recognize the MAC address of the camera. With this menu option, you can find out what that MAC address is. I have not had to use this option, but it is available in case you need it.

SSID/PW Reset

When you connect your RX10 to a smartphone or tablet, either to transfer images or to have the camera controlled remotely by the other device, the camera generates its own Wi-Fi network internally. With this option, whose main screen is shown in

FIGURE 9-40, you can force the camera to change the SSID (name) and password of its own wireless network.

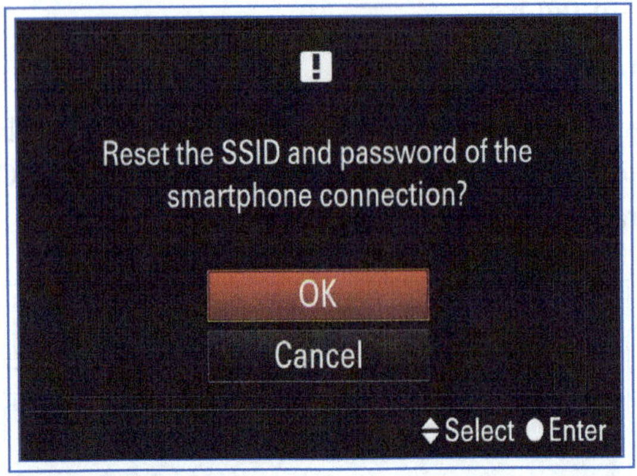

Figure 9-40. SSID/Password Reset Confirmation Screen

You might want to do this if, for example, you have been to a conference where you allowed other people to connect their smartphones to your camera, and now you want to reset the camera's network ID, so they will no longer have access to the camera's network.

Reset Network Settings

This final item on the Wi-Fi menu lets you reset all of the camera's Wi-Fi network settings, not just the SSID and password. This option is useful if you are having problems and need to get a fresh start with the wireless functions, if you are switching to a new wireless network where you use the camera, or if you are selling the camera and want to erase these settings.

Macro (Closeup) Shooting

Macro photography is the art or science of taking photographs when the subject is shown at actual size (1:1 ratio between size of subject and size of unenlarged image) or magnified (greater than 1:1 ratio). So, if you photograph a flower using macro techniques, the image on the camera's sensor will be about the same size as the actual flower. You can get wonderful detail in your images using macro photography, and you may discover things about the subject you hadn't noticed before taking the photograph.

There are several ways to take macro photographs with the RX10. First, you can set the mode dial to the Scene mode setting and select the Macro option, as shown in FIGURE 9-41.

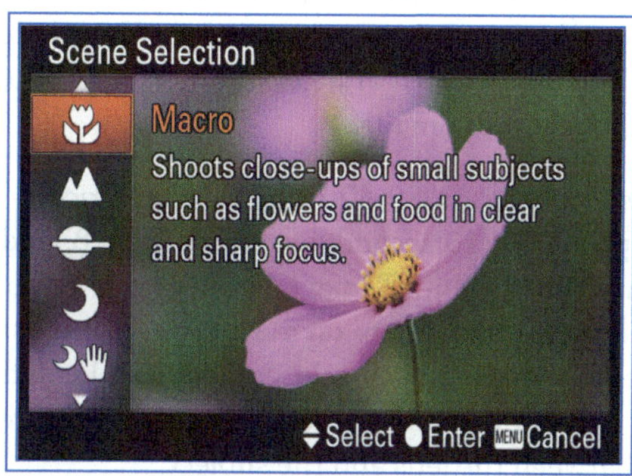

Figure 9-41. Macro Setting of Scene Mode

With this setting, as discussed in CHAPTER 3, the camera will be set up for closeup shots, and you can still make a number of advanced settings, including choosing Raw or Raw & JPEG for the Quality setting. However, you will not be able to select several other important Shooting menu items, including continuous shooting, Focus Area, ISO, White Balance, DRO/Auto HDR, Metering Mode, Creative Style, and others.

Another way to take closeups is to set the camera to the Intelligent Auto mode, in which case, when you get close to the subject, the camera is likely to select the Macro mode using its scene recognition technology. Here, again, you will likely get good results, but you will not be able to make advanced settings.

The best way to take macro shots with the RX10, in my opinion, is to use one of the advanced shooting modes—Program, Aperture Priority, Shutter Priority, or Manual exposure. In that way, you will have the full range of Shooting menu options available. Also, depending on the subject, you can choose a shooting mode that makes the most sense.

For example, if you are photographing flowers or other items that are not moving significantly, you may want to use Aperture Priority for one of two reasons: so you can use a wide aperture to focus sharply on the subject while blurring the background, or so you can use a more narrow aperture to get the whole subject in focus, with expanded depth of field. In other cases you may prefer to use another shooting mode.

I took the shot in FIGURE 9-42 using Shutter Priority mode with a shutter speed of 1/10 second, aperture of f/2.8, and ISO set to 400. I wanted to maximize image quality with a fairly low ISO setting, so I placed the camera on a firm tripod and used this slow shutter speed. I focused at the closest distance I could and added light using a small flashlight whose beam I could direct into the small area between the lens and the subject.

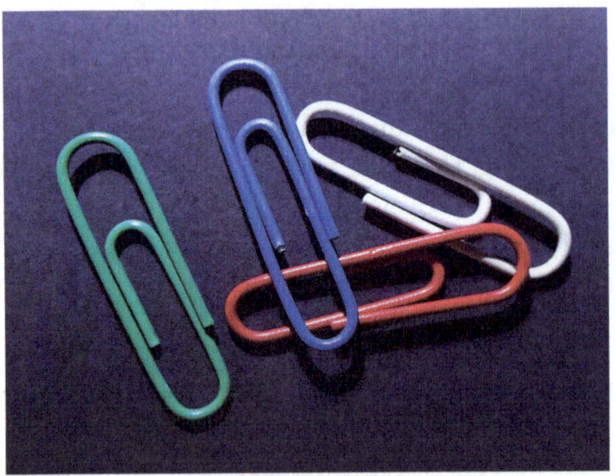

Figure 9-42. Macro Example Image

There is one aspect of the RX10's focusing system that makes macro photography particularly easy: There is no special "macro" focusing mode, as there is on many other cameras. If you set the camera to one of its autofocus modes—either single-shot AF or continuous AF—it will focus on objects as close as 1.2 inch (3 cm) when the lens is zoomed out and as close as 12 inches (30 cm) when the lens is zoomed in to its maximum telephoto range.

You don't have to use autofocus for macro shots; if you set the camera to manual focus, you can focus on objects very close to the lens. You do, however, lose the benefit of automatic focus, and it can be tricky finding the correct distance manually. If you use the DMF setting, though, you have the ability to check your manual focusing by pressing the shutter button halfway and having the camera use its autofocus system. You also can take advantage of the several excellent aids to manual focusing that the RX10 provides: Peaking, MF Assist, and the Focus Magnifier option, discussed in CHAPTER 4 and CHAPTER 7.

When shooting extreme closeups, you should use a tripod if possible, because the depth of field is very shallow and you need to keep the camera steady to take a usable photograph. It's also a good idea to take advantage of the 2-second self-timer setting. If you take the picture using the self-timer, you will not be touching the camera when the shutter is activated, so the chance of camera shake is minimized. You also can use Sony's wired remote control or a cable release, as discussed in APPENDIX A.

If you need artificial illumination, consider using some sort of diffuser over the built-in flash, such as a handkerchief or piece of translucent plastic. Using the flash without some diffusion is likely to result in uneven illumination caused by a shadow from the lens at such a close range. You might consider using a small lamp or flashlight that can illuminate the subject without overwhelming it, as I did for FIGURE 9-42. Another approach is to use off-camera flash triggered by Sony's wireless flash protocol, or by a radio transmitter or optical slave system, with a softbox to diffuse the light, as discussed in APPENDIX A.

Using Raw Quality

I've discussed Raw a couple of times. Raw is a setting for Quality on the Shooting menu. It applies only to still images, not to movies. When you set the image type to Raw, as opposed to JPEG, the camera records the image without extensive in-camera processing; essentially, it takes in the "raw" data and records it.

There are both advantages and drawbacks to using Raw in this camera. First, the drawbacks. A Raw file takes up a lot of space on your memory card, and if you copy it to your computer, it takes up a lot of space on your hard drive. Second, there are various functions of the RX10 that won't work when you're using Raw. The menu options that don't work with Raw mode include Image Size, Soft Skin Effect, Auto HDR, Picture Effect, Zoom Setting, High ISO Noise Reduction, and Write Date. In addition, you cannot use Raw quality with the Sweep Panorama mode, and you cannot use the DPOF feature to mark Raw images for printing directly from a memory card.

The main advantage is that Raw files give you an amazing amount of control and flexibility with your images. When you open up a Raw file (those from the RX10 have an .arw extension) in a compatible software program, the software gives you the opportunity to correct problems with exposure, White Balance, contrast, color tints, and other settings.

For example, the image in FIGURE 9-43 is shown being opened in Adobe Camera Raw before being opened in Photoshop. On the right side of the image, you may be able to see the broad range of control sliders available for adjusting various aspects of the image before it is even opened in Photoshop for editing.

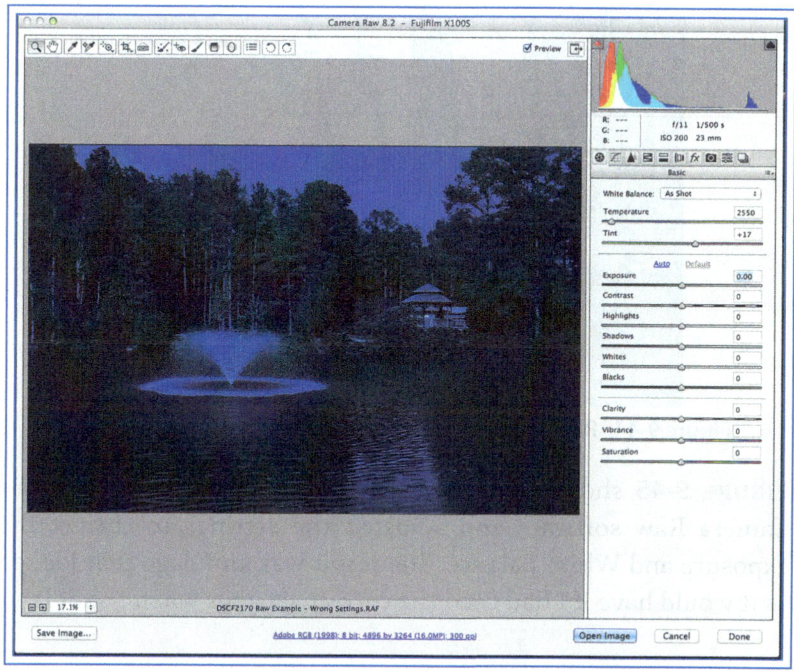

Figure 9-43. Image Being Opened in Adobe Camera Raw Software

If you had the aperture of the camera too narrow when you took the picture and it looks underexposed, you can move the Exposure slider in the software and recover the image to a proper exposure level. Similarly, you can adjust the White Balance after the fact and correct color tints. You can even change the amount of fill lighting. In effect, you get a second chance at making the correct settings, rather than being stuck with an unusable image because of unfortunate settings when you pressed the shutter button.

Figure 9-44 is an image I took with the RX10 using the Raw format, with the exposure purposely set too bright and the White Balance set to a custom setting based on a green surface, even though I took the picture in normal daylight conditions.

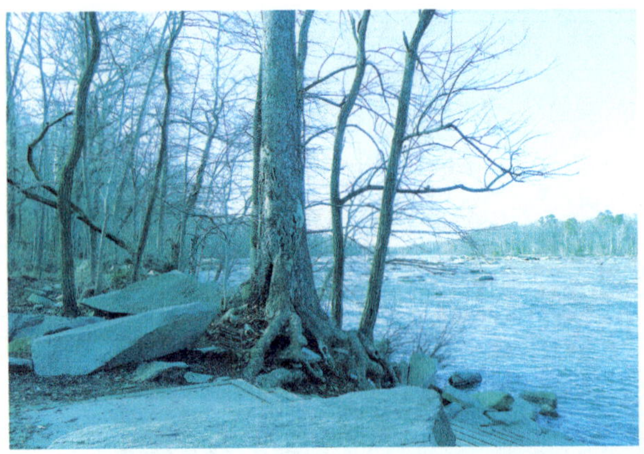

Figure 9-44. Raw Image with Improper Settings, Before Corrections

FIGURE 9-45 shows the same image after I opened it in Adobe Camera Raw software and adjusted the settings to correct the exposure and White Balance. The result was an image that looked as it would have if I had used the correct settings when I shot it.

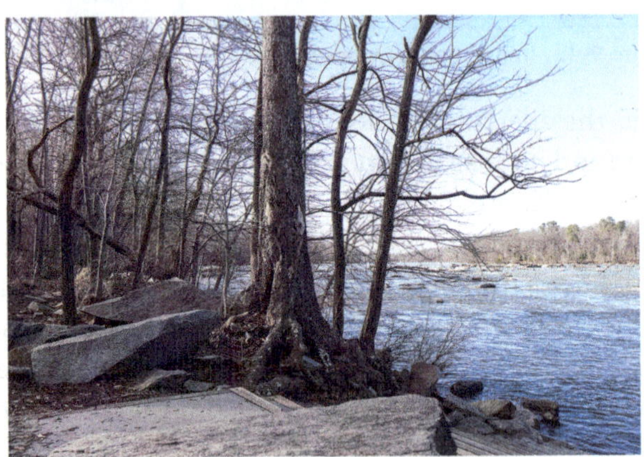

Figure 9-45. Raw Image with Improper Settings, After Corrections

The drawbacks of using the Raw format are either not too severe or they are counterbalanced by the great flexibility Raw gives you. The large file size may be inconvenient, but the increasing size of hard drives and SD cards with steadily dropping prices makes file size less of a concern than previously.

I have had problems with Raw files not loading when I didn't have the latest Camera Raw plug-in for Adobe Photoshop or Photoshop Elements, but with a little effort, you can download an updated plug-in and the software will then process and display your Raw images. Sony provides users of the RX10 with Image Data Converter, a computer program for processing Raw files and converting them to JPEG or other formats that you can use for sending photos by e-mail and manipulating them with editing software. The bottom line is you certainly don't have to use Raw, but you may be missing some opportunities if you avoid it.

Street Photography

Many users find the RX10 well suited for street photography—that is, for shooting candid pictures in public settings, often without the subject being aware of your activity. The camera has several features that make it good for this type of work. Its 24mm equivalent wide-angle lens takes in a broad field of view, so you can shoot from the hip without framing the image carefully on the screen. You can tilt up the LCD screen and look down at it to frame your shot, which further hides your actions. The f/2.8 lens lets in plenty of light, and it performs well at high ISO settings, so you can use a fast shutter speed to avoid motion blur. You can silence the camera by turning off its beeps and shutter sounds.

As far as guidelines for settings are concerned, I will give some suggestions as a starting point. Some photographers shoot in Raw and use post-processing software like Photoshop or Lightroom to convert the images to black and white, along with any other effects they are looking for, such as extra grain to achieve a gritty look. (Of course, you don't have to produce your street photography in black and white, but that is a common practice.) If you shoot using Raw, you can't take advantage of the image-altering settings of the Picture Effect menu option. You can, however, use the Creative Style option on the Shooting menu. You might want to try using the Black and White setting; you can tweak it by increasing contrast and sharpening if you want. If you use Raw together with Creative Style, the files on your computer may not reflect the Creative Style settings, depending on the Raw software you use to process them.

You also can experiment with basic exposure settings. I suggest you try shooting in Shutter Priority mode at a fairly fast shutter speed, 1/100 second or faster, to stop action on the street and to avoid blur from camera movement. You can set ISO to Auto, or use a high ISO setting, in the range of 800 or so, if you don't mind some noise. Or, you can rely on the more automatic settings. For FIGURE 9-46, I used Program mode, because this man appeared fairly suddenly. I turned on continuous shooting and took a series of shots to get a clear view as he approached me under the bridge.

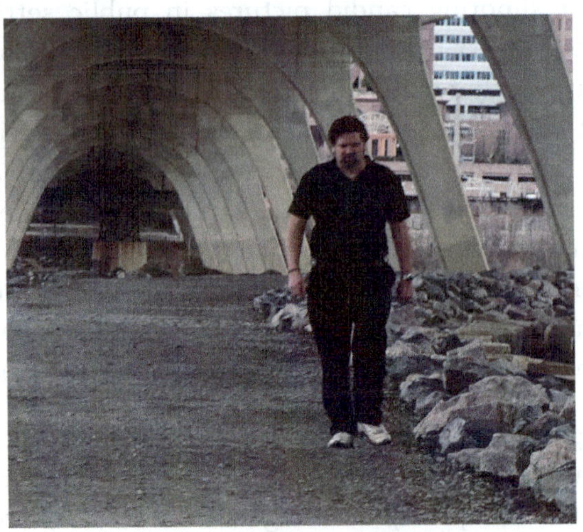

Figure 9-46. Street Photography Example 1

Alternatively, you can set the image type to JPEG at Large size and Extra Fine quality to take advantage of the camera's image-processing capabilities. To get the gritty "street" look, try using the High Contrast Monochrome setting of the Picture Effect item on the Shooting menu, with ISO set somewhat high, in the range of 800 or above, to include some grain in the image while boosting sensitivity enough to stop action with a fast shutter speed. For FIGURE 9-47, I again used Program mode and continuous shooting to capture an image of this woman as she walked by, but I later converted the image to monochrome in Photoshop, just to illustrate that look for street photography.

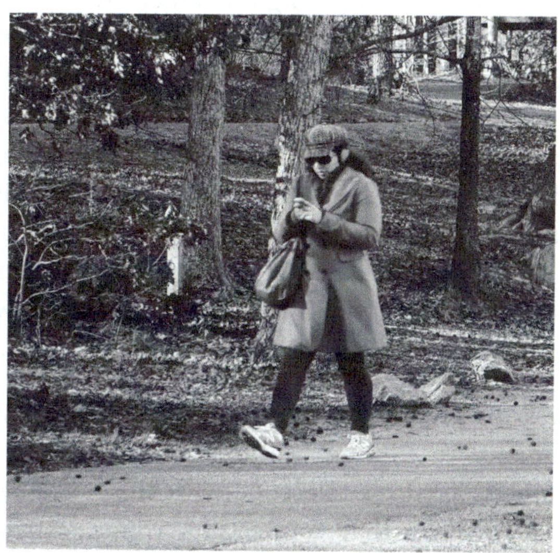

Figure 9-47. Street Photography Example 2

Although you are likely to get good results using the RX10's autofocus system, you may want to try manual focus. Here is one approach to try. In preparation for shooting, use autofocus and focus on a test subject at about the distance where you expect your actual subjects to be. Then switch the camera to manual focus; the focus distance will remain at this range for all future shots, so you will not have to refocus as long as you keep shooting subjects at the same distance. You should try to use a somewhat narrow aperture (f/5.6 or higher) to keep the depth of field broad. I suggest you leave the lens zoomed back to its full wide-angle position, unless a specific situation comes up when you have time to hold the camera very steady and zoom in on a specific subject.

Astrophotography and Digiscoping

Astrophotography involves photographing sky objects using a camera connected to (or aiming through) a telescope. Digiscoping is the practice of attaching a digital camera to a spotting scope to get shots of distant objects, often birds and other wildlife. I can't say the RX10 is the best camera for either activity. However, my goal is to suggest useful and enjoyable ways to use the Sony RX10, not to find the best possible methods for long-distance photography. The RX10 has some features that equip it nicely for taking pictures through a scope, including light weight, a large sensor for a camera of its size, a high-quality f/2.8 lens, manual exposure, manual focus with good focusing aids, Raw quality, a self-timer, and a connection for a wired remote control.

I will discuss the technique I used and hope it gives you enough general guidance to explore the area further if you want to. I used a Meade ETX-90/AT telescope with the RX10 connected to its eyepiece. To make that connection, you need adapter rings that let you connect the camera's lens to the telescope's eyepiece. You can get the proper adapter rings for the RX10 by purchasing the 62mm Digi-Kit, part number DKSR62T, from the online site telescopeadapters.com. That is the setup shown in FIGURE 9-48.

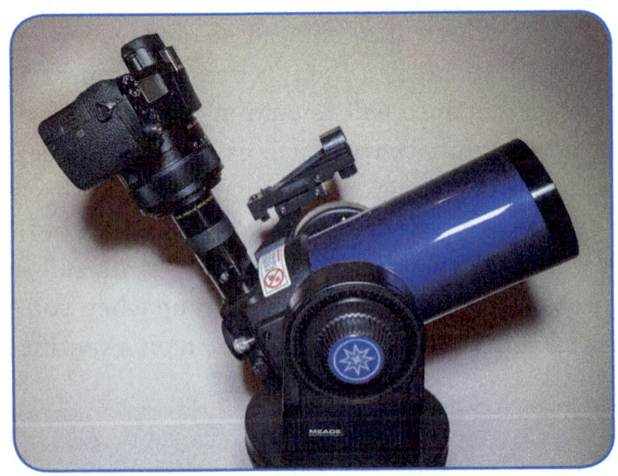

Figure 9-48. Camera Attached to Telescope

I took the image of the moon shown in FIGURE 9-49 with the RX10 connected to a 40mm eyepiece on the telescope using the adapter rings.

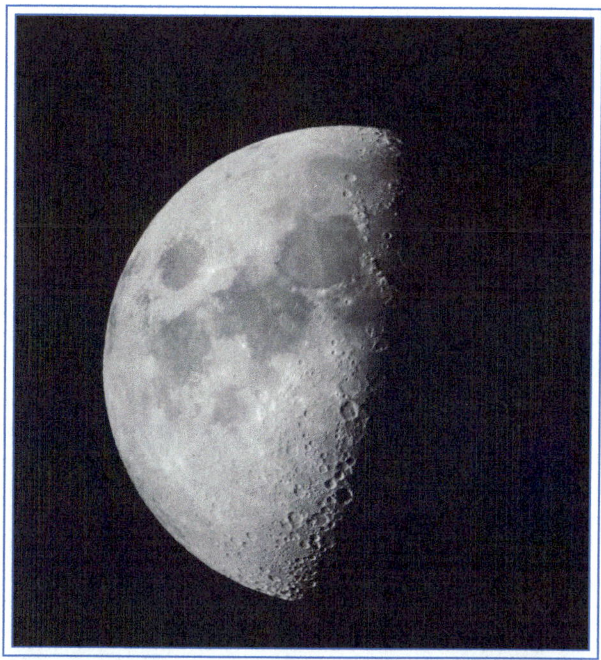

Figure 9-49. Moon, 1/160 Second, f/4.5, ISO 250

The camera was set to Manual exposure mode; through experimentation I arrived at an exposure of 1/160 second at f/4.5, with the ISO set to 250. I used manual focus mode on the camera, setting the focus approximately at first, then adjusting the telescope's focusing control until the image appeared sharp on the camera's LCD display. At first I used the MF Assist option, so I could fine-tune the focus with an enlarged view of the moon's craters. After some experimenting, though, I found that I got better results for focusing on the moon using the Peaking function, with the Peaking Color set to red. When focus was sharp, I saw a bright, red outline on the outer edge of the moon, which made focusing much easier than relying on the normal manual focus mechanism, even with MF Assist activated.

I set the self-timer to 2 seconds to minimize camera shake as the exposure was taken, with SteadyShot turned on. I set the image quality to Raw & JPEG, so I would have a Raw image to give some extra latitude in case the exposure seemed incorrect. As you can see in Figure 9-49, the RX10 did a good job of capturing the half moon. Because of the large sensor and relatively high resolution of the RX10, this image can be enlarged to a fair degree without deteriorating.

You can also use this setup for digiscoping. I tried this out by attaching the RX10 to a Celestron Regal 80F-ED spotting scope using the same eyepiece I used with the telescope. Figure 9-50 is a shot of birds gathering in the middle of the James River taken with the RX10 through this scope.

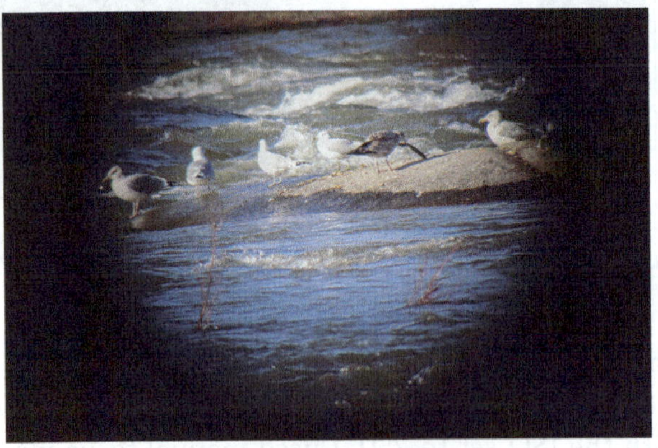

Figure 9-50. Digiscoping Example

I used Program mode with an exposure of 1/200 second at f/4.0 and ISO 200. The trickiest part was getting the focus sharp. As you can see, the scope cut off a lot of the image at the edges, but the central part still yielded a usable image.

Figure 9-51 is a shot I took from the same location as the digiscoping image using the full optical zoom of the RX10 to show how much magnification the Celestron scope provided.

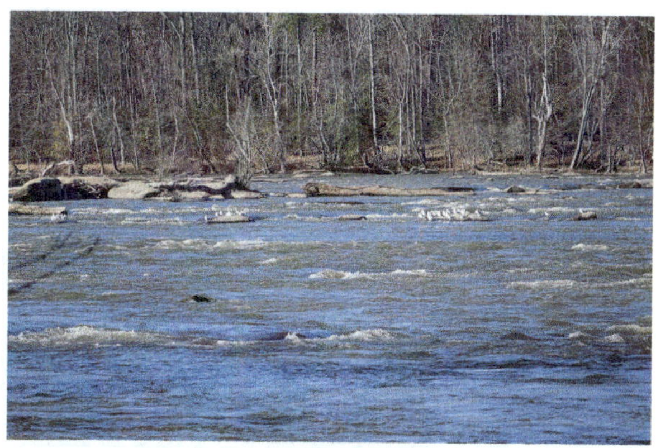

Figure 9-51. Digiscoping Comparison Image at Full Optical Zoom

Infrared Photography

Infrared photography involves recording scenes using infrared light. The results can be spectacular, producing scenes in which green foliage appears white and blue skies appear eerily dark.

To take infrared photographs, you need a camera that can "see" infrared light. Many cameras include internal filters that block infrared rays, but some do not, or block it only partially. (You can test a camera by aiming it at the light-emitting end of an infrared remote control and taking a photograph while pressing a button on the remote; if the remote's light shows up as bright white, the camera can "see" infrared light at least to some extent.)

The RX10 is capable of taking infrared photographs if you use a filter that blocks most visible light but lets infrared light reach the camera's sensor. (If you don't use a filter, the infrared light will be overwhelmed by the visible light, and you'll get an ordinary picture based on visible light.)

I use the Hoya R72 infrared filter. When you attach this very dark red filter to the RX10's lens, a great deal of the visible light from the scene is blocked. With experimentation, you can get interesting results.

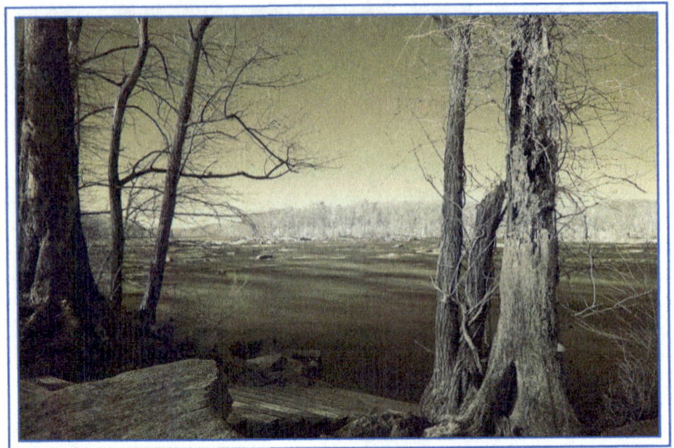

Figure 9-52. Infrared Example Image

For FIGURE 9-52, I aimed the camera at green trees in bright sunlight to set a Custom White Balance that would yield the characteristic white appearance of green grass and leaves. I used Manual exposure mode and adjusted the shutter speed until I could see the image clearly on the LCD display. I ended up with an exposure for 13 seconds at f/4.0 with ISO set at 800.

This sort of infrared photography often is most successful in the spring or summer when there is a rich variety of green subjects available outdoors.

Connecting to a Television Set

The RX10 can play back its still images and videos on an external television set, as long as the TV has an HDMI input. The camera does not come with any audio-video cable as standard equipment, so you need to purchase a cable with a micro-HDMI connector at the camera end and a standard HDMI connector at the TV end. These cables are widely available through electronics and photography retailers.

To connect the cable to the camera, open the lower flap, marked Multi and HDMI, on the left side of the camera and plug the micro-HDMI connector into the lower port underneath that flap, as shown in Figure 9-53.

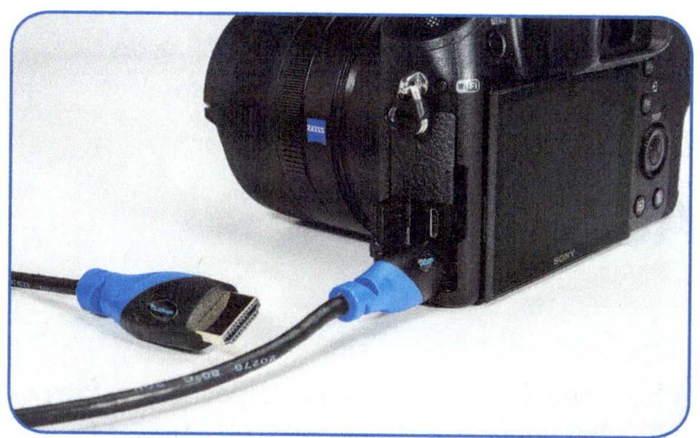

Figure 9-53. HDMI Cable Connected to Camera

Then connect the large connector at the other end of the cable to an HDMI input port on an HDTV set.

When you connect the camera to the set, the camera not only can play back images and videos, it also can record. In shooting mode, you can see on the TV the live image seen by the camera. In that way, you can use the TV as a large monitor to help compose your photos and videos. The camera's behavior will change according to how you set the HDMI Information Display option on screen 3 of the Setup menu. As I discussed in Chapter 7, if you set that option to Off, no shooting information will display on the TV in shooting mode, just the image. If you press the Display button, no other screens will appear on the TV; all that will be displayed is the image being viewed by the camera's lens.

As noted in the Wi-Fi section of this chapter, the RX10 also has an option on the Wi-Fi menu, View on TV, that is intended to let you view your images on a Wi-Fi–enabled TV. As I discussed there, I have found this option to be difficult to use effectively. Unless you are familiar with setting up the special type of network that apparently is needed for this sort of connection, I recommend that you stick to using an HDMI cable for the connection.

Appendix A: Accessories

When people buy a camera, especially a fairly expensive model like the Sony RX10, they often ask what accessories they should buy for it. I will discuss several options, sticking mostly with items I have used personally.

Cases

You don't have to get a case for your RX10, but I always use one when I'm going out for a photo session, so I can carry along filters, extra batteries, and other items. I will discuss a few of the many possible choices.

The Sony case designed for the RX10, model number LCJ-RXE, is shown in Figure A-1. I tried this case first because I always like to try the "official" option. It has the appearance of black leather, though it is made of 100% polyester. It does a good job of holding and protecting the camera, but has no room for accessories apart from a small slot to hold an extra memory card, and does not have a particularly attractive appearance, in my opinion. The RX10 will not fit in the case with the lens hood attached normally, but the camera will fit if you put the lens hood on in the reverse direction. Then, of course, you would need to remove the lens hood and put it back on in the correct orientation before taking any shots.

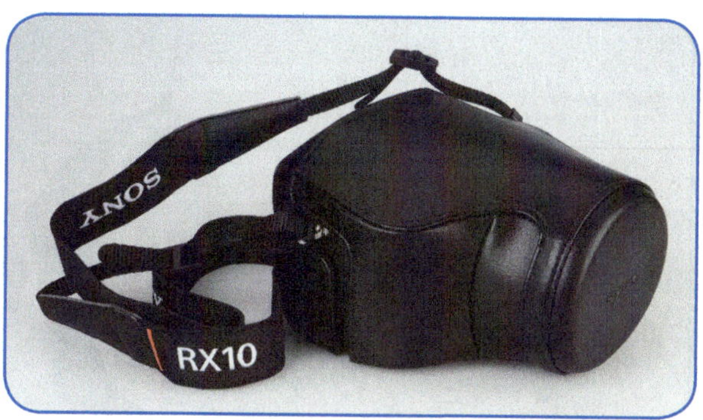

Figure A-1. Sony Case, Model No. LCJ-RXE

If you want a case with room for other items besides the camera, there are many choices. I occasionally go on a day trip using the Lowepro Inverse 100 AW waist pack, shown in Figure A-2, which has room for the camera, some accessories, and a couple of small water bottles in the two side pouches.

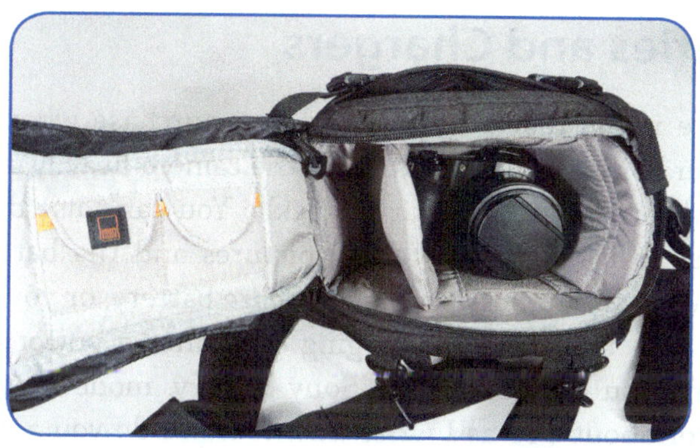
Figure A-2. Lowepro Inverse 100 AW Case

If you like the backpack style, with room for considerably more accessories, such as a large flash, external microphone, filters, batteries, battery charger, and the like, you could consider a case like the Lowepro Slingshot 200 AW, shown in Figure A-3, which can accommodate all of those items and has the advantage of riding on your back.

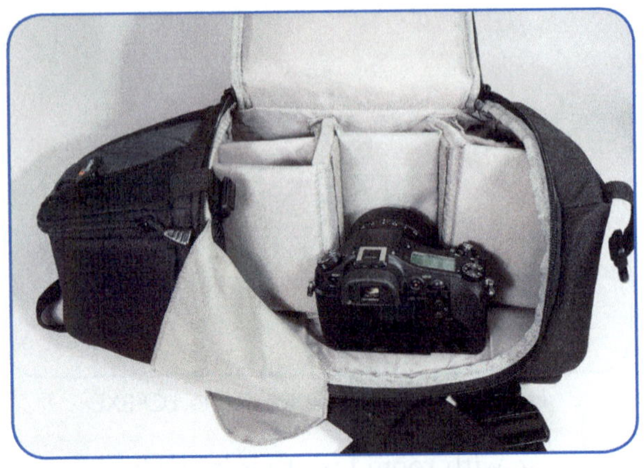

Figure A-3. Lowepro Slingshot 200 AW Case

There are many other options that photographers have found useful, such as the Tamrac 514, the Think Tank Mirrorless Mover 10, the Lowepro Apex 110 AW, and the Tamrac Zuma 4 bag.

Batteries and Chargers

These are items that I recommend you purchase when you get the camera or soon afterward. I use the camera heavily, and I find it runs through batteries fairly quickly. You can't use disposable batteries, so if you're out taking pictures and the battery dies, you're out of luck unless you have a spare battery, or you have the time to plug the camera's charging cable into a power outlet or USB port. You can get a spare Sony battery, model number NP-FW50, for about $40 as I write this. It won't do you a great deal of good by itself, though, because the battery is designed to be charged in the camera.

There is an easy solution to this problem. You can find generic replacement batteries, as well as chargers to charge the batteries outside the camera, inexpensively from eBay, B&H Photo, and elsewhere. I purchased a package including two generic replacement batteries and a charger, shown in Figure A-4, for about $27 from an online seller.

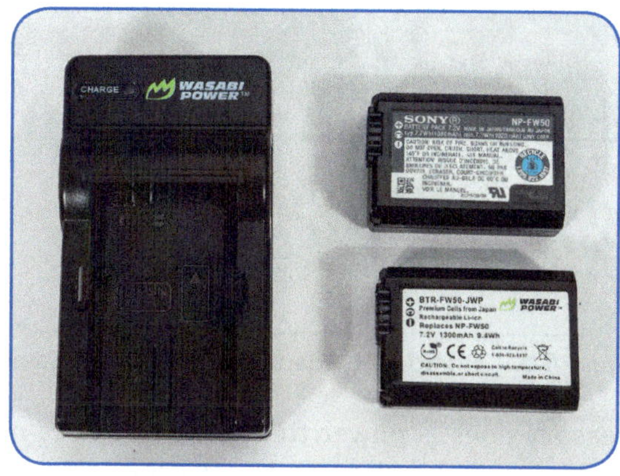

Figure A-4. Generic Charger with Sony Battery and Generic Battery

AC Adapter

Another option for powering the RX10 is the AC adapter, Model No. AC-PW20, which Sony sells as an optional accessory. As you can see in FIGURE A-5, this item is quite cumbersome.

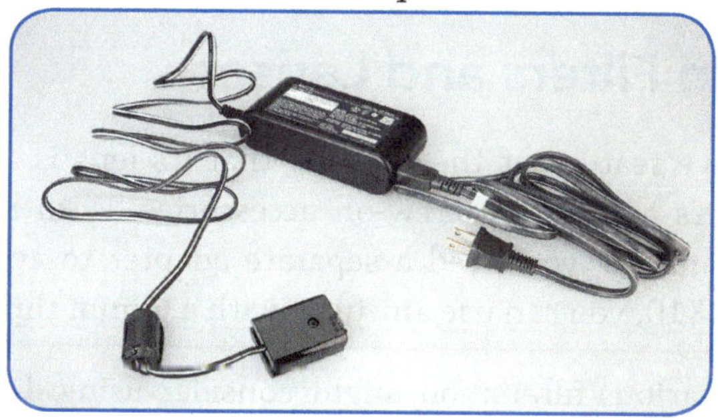

Figure A-5. Sony AC Adapter Model No. AC-PW20

It consists of a power brick with a separate cord that plugs into an AC outlet, and a smaller cord that terminates in a block shaped like the camera's battery. That block is inserted into the camera, and the cord is routed through a small flap in the battery compartment door, as shown in FIGURE A-6. You have to pull that flap out to leave room for the cord, so the door can be closed and latched.

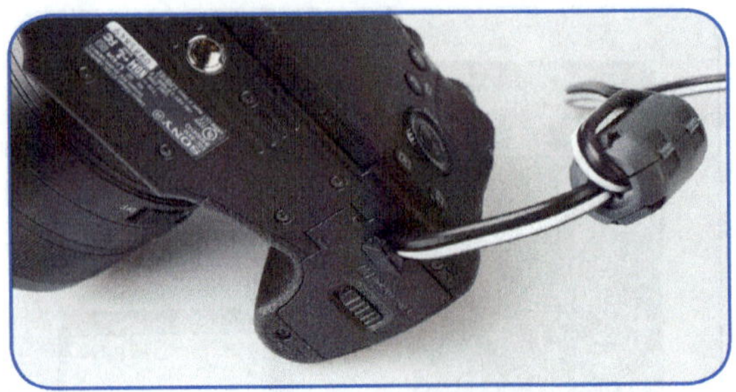

Figure A-6. Cord from AC Adapter Coming Out of Camera

All this accessory does is power the camera. It does not recharge the battery, because the battery has to be removed from the camera in order to use this setup. For many photographers, this is not an item you will need. But, if you will be uploading numerous large still and video files from the camera to a computer using the USB cable, or if you are using the camera for extended experiments or general shooting in a studio, you may find this accessory to be highly useful.

Add-On Filters and Lenses

One positive feature of the RX10 is that its lens is threaded to accept filters and other screw-on accessories. With many other compact cameras, you need a separate adapter to attach filters. With the RX10, you can use any filter with a 62mm thread.

There are various filters you might consider using. I use a Hoya R72 infrared filter, as discussed in Chapter 9, for infrared photography. Figure A-7 shows that filter attached to the camera. A neutral density (ND) filter can be useful when you need to reduce the amount of light entering the lens, but the RX10 comes with its own internal ND filter, so the need for that accessory is not so great. You might want to consider using a polarizing filter to cut down on haze and to darken skies for landscape photos.

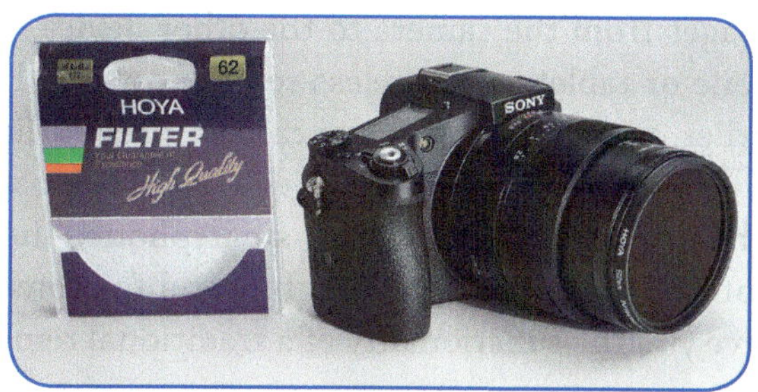

Figure A-7. Hoya Infrared Filter on RX10

You also can use close-up lenses to enhance the camera's macro shooting. I do not recommend using accessory lenses such as teleconverters and wide-angle conversion lenses, because the RX10 is not designed to withstand the weight of such an item on the end of its lens, especially when zooming. I tried several such items, including the Raynox 0.7x Wide Angle Conversion Lens, Raynox 0.3x Semi-Fisheye Wide Angle Conversion Lens, and Olympus TCON-14B teleconverter lens. These all worked to some extent, but I would not recommend any of them for regular use because of their weight. In addition, their use results in vignetting that cuts off parts of the image, at least at some focal lengths. I found the Raynox Semi-Fisheye lens to be the most useful of the ones I tested, because of the unusual perspective it provides.

Remote Control

In several situations, it is useful to control a camera remotely. For example, when you are using slow shutter speeds, holding the shutter open with the BULB setting, doing closeup photography, or taking pictures through a telescope, any camera motion during the exposure is likely to blur the image. If you can control the camera remotely, you can avoid the danger of moving the camera as you press the shutter button.

As I discussed in Chapter 9, the RX10 has a built-in Wi-Fi capability that lets you connect a computer, smartphone, or tablet to the camera wirelessly. Besides using that feature to transfer images from the camera to the other device, you can use a smartphone or tablet as a wireless remote control. However, as I noted earlier, you can control the camera only in limited ways with that option, and the camera will ignore most advanced settings while being controlled by a smartphone. Therefore, the Wi-Fi remote control option, although useful for some purposes, does not give you the functionality of a traditional remote control.

Fortunately, with the RX10 you can connect a Sony wired remote, model number RM-VPR1, to the Multi port on the left side of the camera. With this device, you can turn the camera on and off, use the autofocus system, zoom the lens, take a still image, lock the shutter for a long exposure, and start and stop video recording.

This remote control comes with two cables—one for cameras with a Remote terminal and one for cameras like the RX10, which has the Multi terminal. Take the cable that has identical connectors at each end and plug the end with the smaller plastic housing into the camera, as shown in Figure A-8.

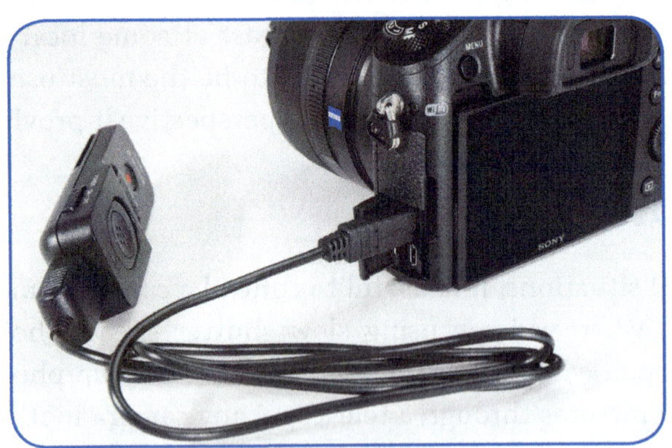

Figure A-8. Sony Remote RM-VPR1 Connected to RX10

Plug the other end of the cable, which has a larger housing, into the remote. You also can attach the included clip to the underside of the remote if you want to clip the remote to a tripod or other support.

Now, you can control the camera using the buttons on the remote control, as shown in FIGURE A-9.

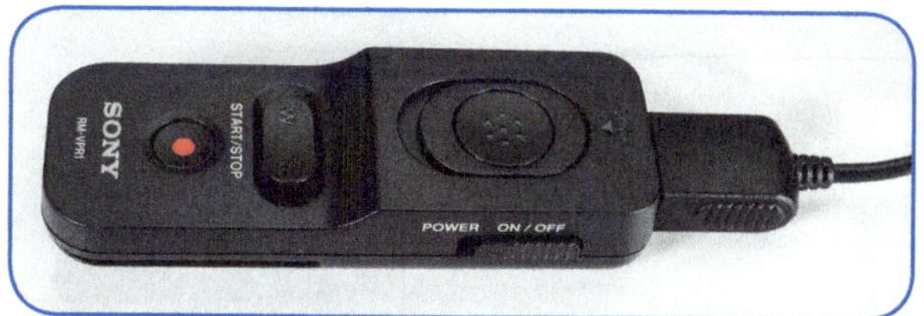

Figure A-9. Sony Remote RM-VPR1

You can half-press the shutter button to cause the autofocus system to operate (if the camera is in an autofocus mode), and press the button fully to take a still picture. You can press the shutter button down and then slide it back toward the other controls to lock it in place. This locking is useful when you are taking continuous shots using the Drive Mode settings, or to hold the shutter open using the BULB setting in Manual exposure mode. Press the button back in its original direction to release it.

The red button labeled Start/Stop is similar to the Movie button on the RX10 camera. Press it once to start recording a movie and press it once more to stop the recording.

The power switch on the side of the remote control can be used to turn the camera on and off, and to wake it up from power-saving mode. Press the switch back toward yourself as you hold the control to power the camera either on or off. You need to give this switch a very quick press to get it to work.

Cable Release

There is one more type of external control to discuss—the traditional, mechanical cable release. Although, as noted above, you can operate the RX10 using Sony's wired remote control or a smartphone, Sony also has designed this camera with a shutter button that is threaded to accept an old-fashioned cable release.

This inexpensive device, an example of which is shown in FIGURE A-10, screws into the shutter button.

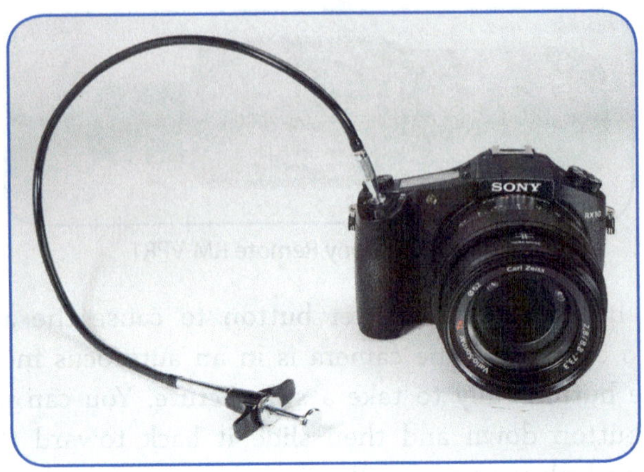

Figure A-10. Cable Release Attached to RX10

You can press the plunger at the other end of the cable to trigger the shutter, and you can lock the cable to keep the shutter pressed until you unlock it. This device is useful for general shooting when you don't want to risk causing motion blur by pressing the shutter button with your hand. It is especially useful for exposures using the Bulb setting, when you have to hold the shutter closed for many seconds.

External Flash

The RX10 is equipped with Sony's special Multi Interface shoe, where you can attach an external flash unit, among other items.

The most obvious choice for using external flash is to use one of the units offered by Sony. The smallest Sony flash for use with the RX10 is model number HVL-F20M, shown in FIGURE A-11. This unit is very small and fits with the camera nicely. It has a guide number of up to 20 at f/2.8 and ISO 800, meaning it can reach up to 20 meters (66 feet) with those settings; it has a shorter range at higher apertures and with lower ISO values. It has a Bounce switch, which rotates the flash head upward by 75 degrees to let you bounce the flash off a ceiling or high wall.

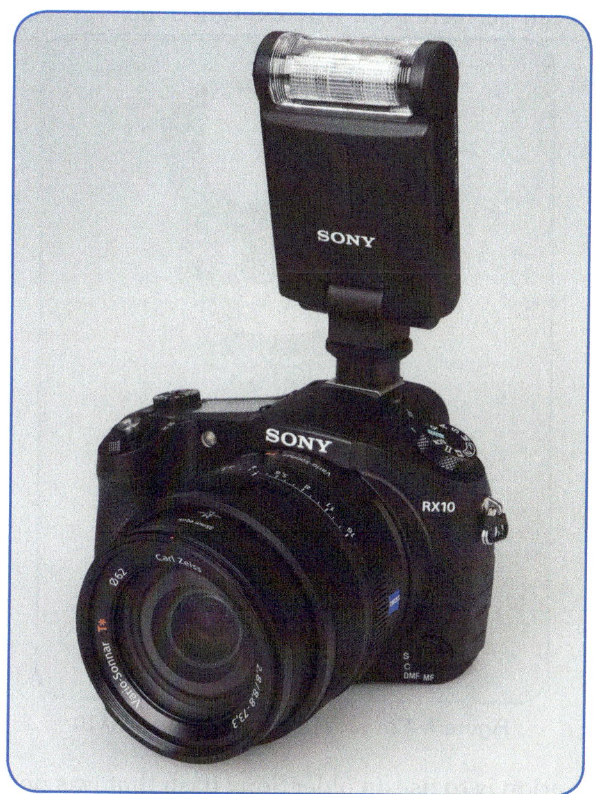

Figure A-11. Sony HVL-F20M Flash on RX10

The F20M is capable of acting as the trigger unit for Sony's wireless flash control system. As discussed in Chapter 4, the RX10's built-in flash unit does not provide that function. So, if you want to fire other flash units remotely using Sony's system, the F20M is the least expensive option for that purpose. Note, though, that the F20M cannot be fired remotely using that system; it can act as the master unit, but not as a slave unit.

The next step up with Sony's external flash options is a considerably larger unit, the HVL-F43M, shown in Figure A-12. This powerful flash, which has a built-in video light, can act as either the trigger unit or a remote unit with Sony's wireless flash system. Or, you can opt for the largest unit, the Sony HVL-F60M, which also can perform both wireless functions.

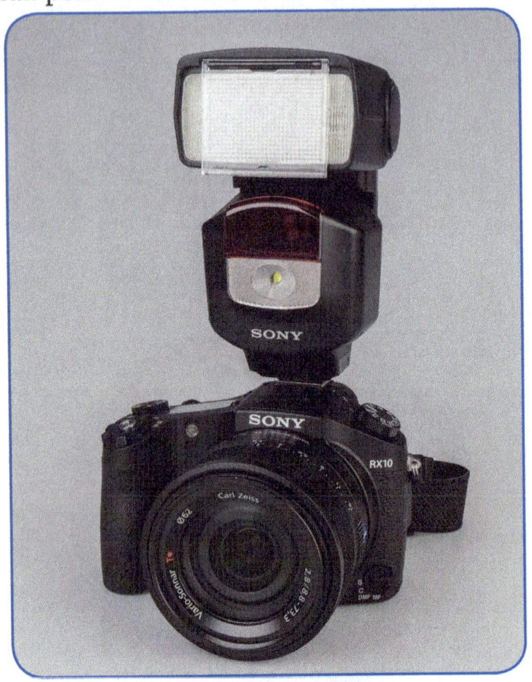

Figure A-12. Sony HVL-F43M Flash on RX10

Another option is to use an older Sony flash that was not designed for the Multi Interface shoe. In that case, you need to get Sony's shoe adapter, model number ADP-MAA, so the flash will work automatically with the RX10.

There also are several non-Sony flash units that will work with the hot shoe of the DSC-RX10 and will fire whenever the camera's shutter button is pressed. However, with these units, there is no communication with the flash unit through the camera's accessory shoe. Therefore, you have to set both the camera and the flash to their manual modes and determine the exposure through trial and error or by measuring the light with a meter.

I have tested several non-Sony units that fire reliably from the accessory shoe of the RX10, including the Canon 430EX II; the Yongnuo YN560 III, a versatile and quite inexpensive unit; the Fujifilm EF-20; and the Zeikos Digital Slave Flash.

If you are not using the built-in flash or a Sony external flash, you probably will want to set White Balance to its Flash setting, because the Auto White Balance setting will not take account of the use of flash unless the flash communicates with the camera.

Here is one other issue you need to be aware of when using a non-Sony external flash unit. When you set the camera to Manual exposure mode, the camera's display screen is likely to be black or very dark because the Manual exposure settings would result in a dark image if you were not using flash, and the camera will not "know" about the effects of the non-Sony flash. Therefore, it may be difficult to compose the shot.

Sony has provided a menu option to deal with this type of situation—the Live View Display option on screen 2 of the Custom menu. If you select the Setting Effect Off option for that menu item, then, when you use Manual exposure mode, the camera's display will not show the dark image that would result from the shot without flash; instead, the display will show the image with normal exposure, so you can compose the shot with a clear view of the scene in front of the camera.

Another way to deal with external flash is to use a radio flash trigger system, such as model number NPT-04, by CowboyStudio. As seen in FIGURE A-13, I mounted the transmitter in the camera's accessory shoe and attached the receiver to the Yongnuo YN560 III, an external flash unit discussed above, which I placed on a tripod. I made sure the transmitter and receiver were set to the same channel, and I turned on the power of the receiver. (The transmitter does not have a power switch, but it has a battery that needs replacement about once a year.) Then, with the camera set to Manual exposure mode and the camera's flash mode set to Off, when I pressed the Shutter button, the external flash fired.

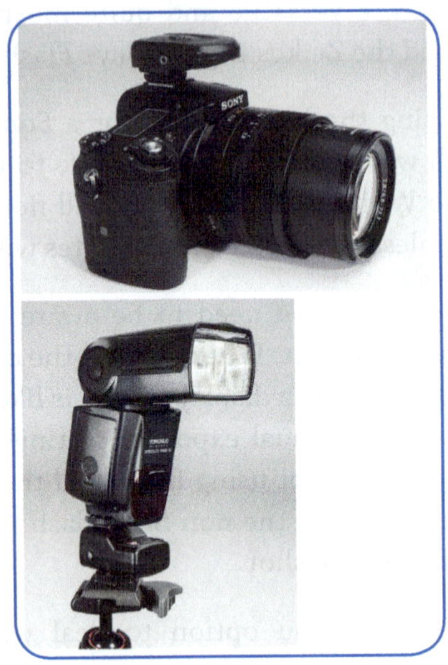

Figure A-13. CowboyStudio Flash Transmitter and Receiver

With this system, you can use any flash unit that is compatible with the receiver. I have found that you need to use a flash that has a manual mode, like the Yongnuo unit. External flash units that have only automatic (TTL) exposure systems do not work, in my experience.

I also tested another radio transmitter, the Hensel Strobe Wizard Plus, which I use for triggering monolight flash units for photography with a DSLR. It worked well in the accessory shoe of the RX10, triggering the monolights perfectly.

You may want to consider one other accessory for use with any external flash unit—a softbox, like the one shown in Figure A-14. A softbox is an enclosure that surrounds a flash unit and diffuses the light through a white, translucent surface, enlarging the area that lights up the subject. The effect of using a softbox is to soften the light because the larger the light source, the less harsh the light will be, with softer shadows. This softbox is a Photoflex LiteDome XS, whose enclosure is about 12 by 16 inches (30 by 40 cm).

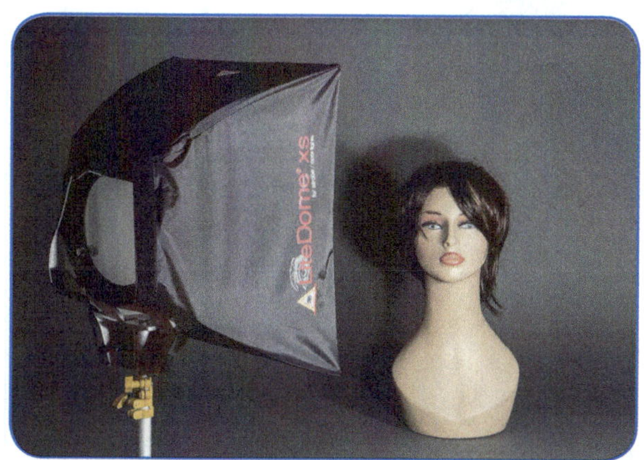

Figure A-14. Softbox with Sony HVL-F43M Flash

As shown in Figure A-14, I placed the softbox on a light stand over the Sony HVL-F43M flash Unit. I attached the Sony HVL-F20M flash to the RX10, with both the flash and camera set to Wireless mode. I then took the image seen in Figure A-15.

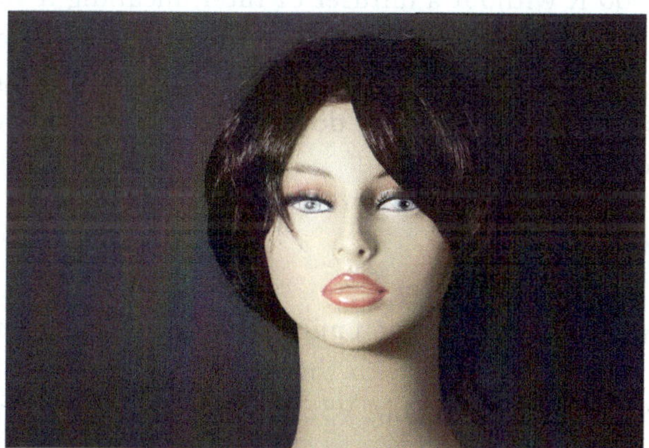

Figure A-15. Image Taken Using Softbox and Sony Flash in Wireless Mode

One other item that is not a flash unit can be useful for supplemental lighting, especially for taking video—a continuous lighting unit like the Sony HVL-LE1, shown in Figure A-16.

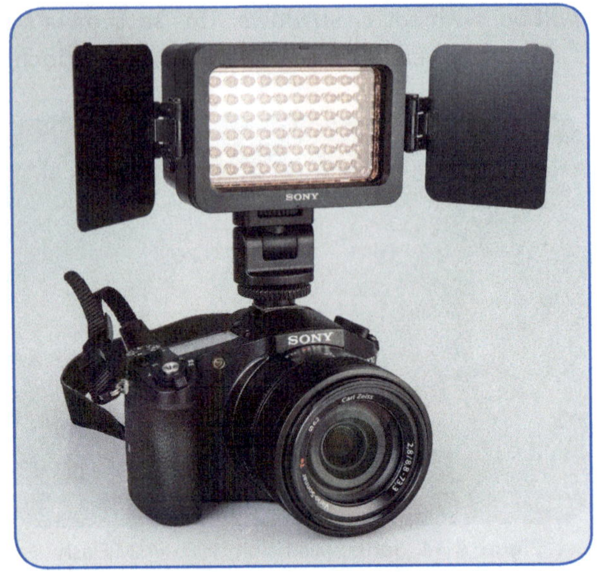

Figure A-16. Sony HVL-LE1 Video Light on RX10

This battery-powered light, which fits nicely in the camera's accessory shoe, has 60 LEDs that can be continuously dimmed or brightened using a rotary control on the side. The light is rated at about 5,500 K without a diffuser or filter, meaning it works well with a Daylight setting for White Balance. It comes with a diffuser and one color conversion filter rated at 3,200 K (Incandescent), and it is equipped with "barn doors" on the sides that can limit and direct the light it casts.

LCD Monitor

There is another accessory you might want to consider for viewing live and recorded images with the RX10. The Sony Clip-On LCD Monitor, model number CLM-V55, is an add-on unit with a 5-inch (12-cm) screen. This small monitor, shown in Figure A-17, comes with a foot that attaches securely to the accessory shoe of the RX10. The unit includes a short HDMI cable, but the connector at the camera end of that cable is the wrong size for the RX10; you will need to get either an adapter or a different cable that ends in a micro-HDMI plug at the camera end.

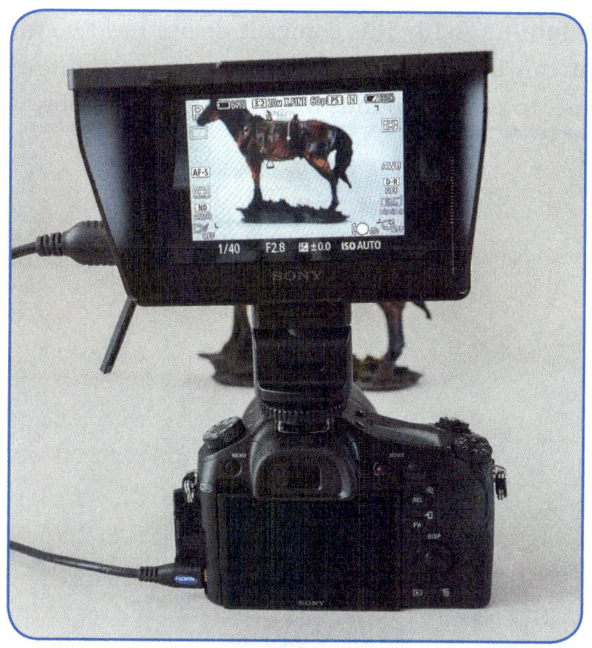

Figure A-17. Sony CLM-V55 LCD Monitor on RX10

The Sony LCD monitor works well with the RX10. It adds a good deal of visibility, both for viewing the live shooting screen and for playing back recorded images and videos. You also can install it backward, so you can view the live scene from the front of the camera for taking self-portraits. This unit costs about $400 at the time of this writing, but if you need the extra screen size or versatility, it is worth looking into. (As a bonus, if you plug it into a Blu-ray player or other source of HD video and audio, it can function as a small HDTV screen.)

External Microphones

With the inclusion of the Multi Interface accessory shoe, the DSC-RX10 can use a Sony microphone that gets its power from that shoe. As of this writing, the only relatively inexpensive microphone I'm aware of that connects through the camera's special interface shoe is Sony's model number ECM-XYST1M, shown in FIGURE A-18. This compact device has two microphone units that can be kept together or separated by 120 degrees, as shown here, to pick up sounds from different directions.

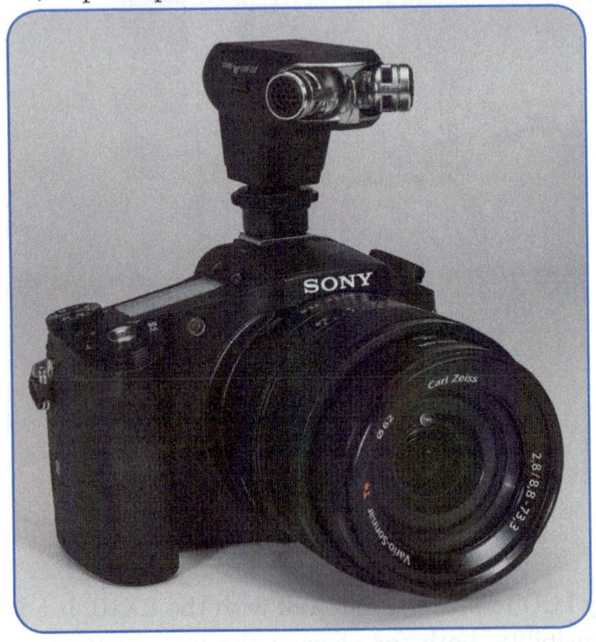

Figure A-18. Sony ECM-XYST1M Microphone with Modules Separated

I did some informal testing to see if I could hear a difference in sound quality with this microphone installed as opposed to using the built-in microphone. I noticed an increased amount of lower frequency sound and some added sensitivity. If you are recording a concert or other musical event, the external microphone might enhance the quality of the audio, but for everyday use, I find the sound quality with the built-in microphone to be fine.

Sony also offers another, much more expensive and sophisticated option for using external microphones—the XLR-K1M adapter kit, shown in FIGURE A-19 and FIGURE A-20, which connects to the camera's Multi Interface shoe and provides inputs for two professional-quality XLR microphones. That type of microphone provides balanced input, which results in lower noise and cleaner sound.

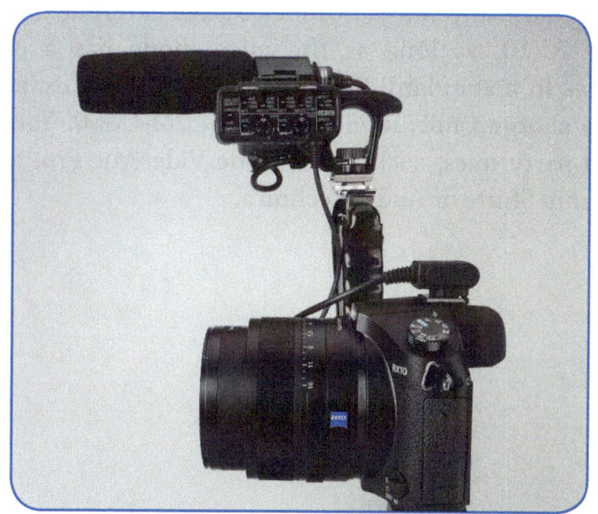

Figure A-19. Sony XLR-K1M Microphone Accessory on RX10

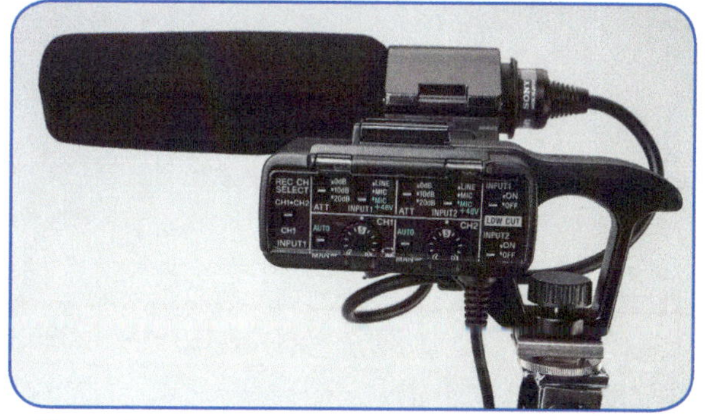

Figure A-20. Closer View of Sony XLR-K1M Accessory

The kit includes a single Sony shotgun microphone with an XLR connection, as well as a connector for another microphone and controls for both inputs. You need to use a standard flash bracket to attach the kit to the camera using the tripod socket; that bracket is not included with the kit. I used a generic bracket.

You may not want to spend $800.00 to add this capability to a compact camera, but, given the RX10's excellent video features, it could be a worthwhile expense if you use the camera heavily for video production.

You also can use any of a multitude of other external microphones with the RX10, as long as the microphone has a cable that terminates in a standard 3.5mm stereo plug. One example from Sony is a shotgun mic, model number ECM-CG50. You also can use third-party mics, such as the Rode VideoMic Pro, or various models from Shure or Audio-Technica.

Appendix B: Quick Tips

This section includes tips and facts that might be useful as reminders. My goal is to give you small bits of information that might help you in certain situations or that might not be obvious to everyone. I have tried to include points you might not remember from day to day, especially if you don't use the RX10 constantly.

Use continuous shooting. Consider turning continuous shooting on as a matter of routine, unless you are running out of storage space or battery power, or have a reason not to use it. Even with portraits, you may get the perfect expression on your subject's face with the fourth or fifth shot. Call up Drive Mode, scroll to Continuous Shooting, and select it. Continuous shooting is not available when the camera is set to the Sweep Panorama mode or any Scene mode setting other than Sports Action. You can shoot more rapidly if you use the Speed Priority setting, but the camera will not adjust its focus after the first shot.

Use shortcuts. You can speed up access to many settings by placing them on the Function menu for recall with a press of the Function button. You can assign your most-used settings to the Control wheel or a control button using the Custom Key Settings option on screen 4 of the Custom menu. Speed through the Shooting menu by using the Control wheel to move rapidly through the items on each screen, and use the Right and Left buttons to move through the menu system a full screen at a time.

Use the Memory Recall shooting mode. The two numbered positions on the mode dial give you a powerful way to customize the RX10 by setting up your two most important groups of settings. You also can use it for more specific purposes. One thing I like to do is have one slot set up to remove all "special" settings, such as Creative Style, Picture Effect, and Drive Mode, so I can quickly set up the camera to take a shot with no surprises.

Use the extra settings for White Balance and Creative Style. When you set White Balance, even with the Auto White Balance setting, you can press the Right button to use the amber-blue and green-magenta axes to further adjust the color of your shots. This setting is not obvious on the menu screen, but it gives you a useful tool to alter color settings. Just remember to undo any color shift when you no longer need it. Also, you can press the Right button after selecting a Creative Style option and then adjust the contrast, saturation, and sharpness settings. (Saturation is not adjustable for the Black and White or Sepia setting.)

Play your movies in iTunes, and on iPods, iPhones, and iPads. If you set the RX10 to record movies using the MP4 format (as opposed to AVCHD), the files are compatible with Apple's QuickTime and iTunes software. You can use iTunes to copy your MP4 files to a device such as an iPad. Open a window on your computer to display the icon for a movie file (using Windows Explorer or Macintosh Finder), then open iTunes on the same computer and drag the .mp4 file from the Explorer or Finder window to the panel for the Library in iTunes. You can then play the movie from iTunes. To play it on an iPod, iPhone, or iPad, select the video in iTunes, then select File on the iTunes menu, then from that menu item select Create New Version, and then choose Create iPod or iPhone version, or iPad or AppleTV version, as appropriate. After you sync iTunes with your device, the converted movie will play on that device. (If you have trouble locating the .mp4 files on your computer, see the last part of Chapter 8.)

Use the lens hood. Sony includes a lens hood with the RX10. It's a good idea to attach it to the lens when shooting outdoors, especially when the sun is bright, to protect against glare.

Diffuse your flash. If the built-in flash produces light that's too harsh for macro or other shots, use translucent plastic pieces from milk jugs or broken ping-pong balls as homemade diffusers. Position the plastic between the flash and the subject. When using Fill-flash outdoors, use the Flash Compensation setting on the Shooting menu to reduce the intensity of the flash by -2/3 EV.

Use the self-timer to avoid camera shake. The self-timer is not just for group portraits; you can use the 2-second self-timer whenever you use a slow shutter speed and need to avoid camera shake. It also is useful for macro photography. Don't forget that you can set the self-timer to take multiple shots, which can increase your chances of getting more great images.

Be aware of conflicting settings. There are times when a feature will not operate because a conflicting setting is in place. One excellent feature of the RX10 is that it often will explain the conflict when you try to select the feature. For example, if you have Picture Effect turned on and then try to select Creative Style, when you press the Center button to select it, the RX10 will display an error message about the conflict. There are many such conflicts; one important one to remember is that you cannot take still images when the mode dial is set to Movie mode.

Use Flexible Spot for the Focus Area setting. With this option, you can move the focus frame around the display and change its size. To use the feature most efficiently, make sure the Center button is set to Standard in the Custom Key Settings menu option. Then, just press the Center button to make the focus frame movable.

Be aware of functions available only by assigning a button. The RX10 has several features that do not appear on any menu and that can be used only if you use the Custom Key Settings menu option on screen 4 of the Custom menu to assign them to a button. These include autoexposure lock; AF/MF Control Hold or Toggle; Lock-on AF; Eye AF; Smart Teleconverter; and Deactivate Monitor.

Take advantage of two shooting modes that are hidden in menus. The Superior Auto shooting mode is not on the mode dial; to set it you have to set the mode dial to Intelligent Auto mode, then use the Auto Mode menu option to select Superior Auto, which adds the capability of taking bursts of shots to create composite images with improved quality. To get to the Multi Frame Noise Reduction setting, which involves bursts of shots to reduce noise, you have to use the ISO menu option. With MFNR, you normally would want to set the ISO level to a high value or Auto, but you also can use that option with a low ISO value to get higher image quality from the composite image.

Use DMF for focusing. Set the focus switch to DMF for direct manual focus. Then you can use autofocus, but still turn the focus ring for further adjustments with manual focus. If you have MF Assist turned on to enlarge the manual focus image, you have to half-press the shutter button to get the enlargement when DMF is in effect. I originally viewed DMF as an exotic option for difficult focusing situations when I needed to alternate between manual focus and autofocus. But I have found this process helpful for fine-tuning focus, and you can check focus using the Peaking feature.

Use Auto ISO in Manual exposure mode. Not all cameras allow this. With this setting, you can set aperture and shutter speed as you want for a particular effect, and let the camera adjust the exposure by setting the ISO automatically.

APPENDIX C: Resources for Further Information

Books

There are many excellent books about general subjects in photography. I will list a few especially useful books that I consulted while writing this guide.

C. George, *Mastering Digital Flash Photography* (Lark Books, 2008)

C. Harnischmacher, *Closeup Shooting* (Rocky Nook, 2007)

H. Horenstein, *Digital Photography: A Basic Manual* (Little, Brown, 2011)

H. Kamps, *The Rules of Photography and When to Break Them* (Focal Press, 2012)

J. Paduano, *The Art of Infrared Photography* (4th ed., Amherst Media, 1998)

S. Seip, *Digital Astrophotography* (Rocky Nook, 2008)

Websites and Videos

Since websites come and go and change their addresses, it's impossible to compile a list of sites that discuss the RX10 that will be accurate far into the future. One way to find the latest sites is to use a good search engine, such as Google or Bing, and type in

"DSC-RX10." I just did so in Google and got more than 1 million results.

I will include below a list of some of the sites or links I have found useful, with the caveat that some of them may not be accessible by the time you read this.

Digital Photography Review

Listed below is the current web address for the "Sony Cyber-shot Talk" forum within the dpreview.com site. Dpreview.com is one of the most established and authoritative sites for reviews, discussion forums, technical information, and other resources concerning digital cameras.

http://www.dpreview.com/forums/1009

Reviews and Demonstrations of the RX10

The links below lead to reviews or previews of the RX10 by dpreview.com, photographyblog.com, and others, as well as some YouTube videos with useful demonstrations.

http://www.dpreview.com/reviews/sony-cybershot-dsc-rx10/11

http://www.photographyblog.com/reviews/sony_cybershot_dsc_rx10_review/

http://gizmodo.com/sony-rx10-review-a-first-rate-camera-with-a-do-it-all-1486437613

http://www.pcmag.com/article2/0,2817,2429566,00.asp

http://www.pocket-lint.com/news/124410-hands-on-sony-cyber-shot-rx10-review

http://www.imaging-resource.com/camera-reviews/sony/rx10/

http://www.cameralabs.com/reviews/Sony_Cyber-shot_RX10/

http://www.ephotozine.com/article/sony-cyber-shot-rx10-review-23331

http://www.amateurphotographer.co.uk/reviews/compacts/129455/1/sony-cyber-shot-dsc-rx10-review

http://www.whatdigitalcamera.com/equipment/reviews/compactcameras/129713/1/sony-cyber-shot-rx10-review.html

The link below is to a video demonstration of the RX10 by Steve Huff.

http://youtu.be/wAPhAS35IhQ

The link below is to another detailed video demonstration of the RX10.

http://youtu.be/S4AoejbgW9Q

The link below is to a short YouTube video made by a member of the dpreview.com forum on Sony Cyber-shot cameras, giving an excellent demonstration of how to use the Focus Peaking feature on the RX100 camera. The same technique applies to the Peaking Level feature on the RX10.

http://www.youtube.com/watch?v=jmalmqev7kw

White Knight Press

My own site, White Knight Press, provides updates about this book and other books, offers support for download of PDFs and eBooks, and provides a way for readers or potential readers to contact me with questions or comments.

http://www.whiteknightpress.com

The Official Sony Site

The United States arm of Sony provides resources on its website, including the downloadable version of the user's manual for the RX10 and other technical information.

http://esupport.sony.com

https://docs.sony.com/release/DSCRX10_guide_EN.pdf

https://docs.sony.com/release/DSCRX10_connection.pdf

Equipment Suppliers

Eye-Fi is a company that makes the series of Eye-Fi cards, which are SD memory cards containing tiny transmitters. With these cards, your images can be uploaded wirelessly to your computer or other device over a Wi-Fi network.

http://www.eyefi.com/

Telescopeadapters.com is a site that sells adapters that let you connect the RX10 (as well as other cameras) to the eyepiece of a telescope, provided that you have a filter adapter.

http://www.telescopeadapters.com/

Pole Pixie Camera Accessories is a site that sells adapters for attaching cameras to poles for pole aerial photography, as discussed in CHAPTER 9.

http://www.polepixie.com

Index

Symbols

A

B

C

E

F

G

H

I

J

L

M

N

O

P

Q

R

S

T

U

V

W

Z

CPSIA information can be obtained at www.ICGtesting.com
Printed in the USA
LVOW01s2304011114

411023LV00009B/32/P